Through
Survivors'
Eyes

THROUGH SURVIVORS' EYES

*From the Sixties
to the Greensboro Massacre*

Sally Avery Bermanzohn

Vanderbilt University Press

NASHVILLE

This book is printed on acid-free paper.
Manufactured in the United States of America

Library of Congress Cataloging-in-Publication Data

Bermanzohn, Sally A., 1947–
Through survivors' eyes : from the sixties
to the Greensboro Massacre / Sally Avery Bermanzohn.—
1st ed.   p. cm.
    Includes bibliographical references and index.
ISBN 0-8265-1438-3 (cloth : alk. paper)
ISBN 0-8265-1439-1 (pbk. : alk. paper)
    1. Civil rights workers—North Carolina—Greensboro—
Interviews. 2. Political activists—North Carolina—Greens-
boro—Interviews. 3. Greensboro (N.C.)—Biography.
4. Greensboro (N.C.)—Race relations. 5. Greensboro
(N.C.)—History—20th century. 6. Massacres—North
Carolina—Greensboro—History—20th century. 7. Riots—
North Carolina—Greensboro—History—20th century.
8. Ku Klux Klan (1915–)—North Carolina—Greensboro—
History—20th century.
I. Title.
    F264.G8B468 2003
    323'.092'275662—dc21   2003012401

To the memory of
César Cauce,
Mike Nathan,
Bill Sampson,
Sandi Smith, and
Jim Waller,
> *who died on November 3, 1979,*
> *fighting for equality and justice,*
> *and to all those who carry out*
> *their legacy.*

CONTENTS

PART IV

Keep on Walking Forward

ILLUSTRATIONS

ACKNOWLEDGMENTS

Many people made this book possible. I especially acknowledge Michael Ames for a decade of guidance that enabled me to transform a traumatic, bitter experience into a book. My other mentors for this project include Stanley Renshon, Philippa Strum, Martha Garvey Jr., and Emily Mann. I thank Sydney Nathans, Ted Striggles, Sally Alvarez, Lynn Karow, Gary Kenton, Brenda Blom, Andrew Zuckerberg, Marcus Green, Joyce Johnson, Yonni Chapman, Lucy Lewis, Henry Sholar, Joe Frierson Jr., Bev Grant, Pat Humphries, Yuko Uchikawa, and James Bernard for their help. The team at Vanderbilt University Press—Anne Bower, Lisa Dellwo, Gary Gore, Dariel Mayer, Bobbe Needham, and Polly Rembert— were wonderful.

Without financial support and course release time, I would never have finished. A fellowship from the Ethel Wolfe Institute for Humanities at Brooklyn College enabled me to write full time for a year. Brooklyn College also supported me with two New Faculty Research Awards. My union, the Professional Staff Congress, gave me a summer research grant.

Above all, it was those closest to me who made this project possible. My dear friends Willena Cannon, Nelson Johnson, Marty Nathan, Kwame Cannon, and Paul Bermanzohn were patient and encouraging through endless hours of interviews spanning two decades. My father, Roy Avery, has given me unwavering support and encouragement, as did my mother, Elfie Greene Avery, until her death several years ago. I thank my husband, Paul, and my daughters, Leola and Sandy, for their love, understanding, and critical reading of countless drafts.

INTRODUCTION:

The Greensboro Massacre

November 3, 1979, 11:23 A.M. ■ At the corner of Carver and Everitt Streets, black and white demonstrators gather to march through Greensboro, North Carolina, a legal demonstration against the Ku Klux Klan. A caravan of Klansmen and Nazis pull up to the protesters and open fire.

Eighty-eight seconds later, five demonstrators lie dead and ten others wounded from the gunfire, recorded on camera by four TV stations. Four women have lost their husbands; three children have lost their fathers.

After two criminal trials, not a single gunman has spent a day in prison, although a civil trial won an unprecedented victory for the victims: For one of the only times in U.S. history, a jury held local police liable for cooperating with the Ku Klux Klan in a wrongful death.

I was on that Greensboro corner. My husband, Paul Bermanzohn, was shot in the head and arm, critically wounded. After five hours of brain surgery, Paul survived, partly paralyzed. Those killed were close friends of mine; one had been my first husband. Paul and I narrate this book along with four others who had gathered to march against the Klan that day. It is the story of the massacre through the eyes of survivors.

Our story begins in the 1940s and 1950s, the last decades of the Jim Crow South. Most of the victims of the Greensboro massacre were born during these decades, members of the post–World War II baby boom. In the 1960s, we were known collectively as the protest generation. African American college students challenged segregation in a sit-in movement that swept the South and energized the civil rights movement. Antiwar protesters by the millions helped end the Vietnam War. Young women broke the barriers of gender discrimination and forever altered the U.S. labor force and family structure. Our generation fought on many fronts: black power, Latino power, Native American rights, Asian American equality, gay rights, unionization, environmental protection. We roused the nation from its slumber in the 1950s, and this experience transformed us; it changed the direction of our lives.

Protesters who challenge the status quo need a rationale and strategy for action. Martin Luther King Jr. galvanized the civil rights movement with active nonviolent resistance. King's strategy embraced the American principles of free-dom and equality and battled the hypocrisy of racism; his leadership dominated the social movements until the mid 1960s. We who survived the Greensboro massacre had joined other sixties activists who explored Marxism in the seven-ties. Karl Marx's century-old call, "Workers of the world unite," inspired many in search of ways to organize people across barriers of race, religion, and gender. We were awed by the Russian Revolution of 1917, the Chinese Revolution of 1949, and the Vietnamese Communist Party's defeat of the U.S. military in 1975. Closer to home, we were impressed by the U.S. Communists who were the backbone of the great union drives of the 1930s and 1940s.

We read about the repression of people's movements. African Americans who strove for basic rights had faced Klan terror, lynch mobs, and riot police. Work-ers who built unions had been beaten, jailed, and shot. The Palmer raids led by J. Edgar Hoover in the early 1920s had rounded up, imprisoned, and deported thousands of leftists, immigrants, and labor unionists. McCarthyism in the 1950s had targeted the Communist Party USA and routed a powerful labor move-ment. In the late 1960s, police murdered Black Panthers in their beds.[1]

We never dreamed it would happen to us. The massacre that killed my friends in 1979 helped usher in the triumph of conservatism in the 1980s.

November 3 tore my life apart. Never will I fully recover from the loss of my five friends and the crippling of my husband. Writing this book has been a major way I have coped and healed. A few months after the murders, I interviewed the demonstrators who had witnessed the attack; I knew early on that we needed to tell our own story. A decade later, as a graduate student, I sought out every person who had participated in the anti-Klan protest that day. Black and white, male and female, poor and middle class, they came from widely diverse back-grounds. I found their life stories compelling—how they became activists, how their political beliefs evolved, how they had coped with the massacre and its after-math. These fifty-three interviews became my doctoral research.[2] But my disserta-tion was scholarly, removed, and inaccessible to a broad audience. I wanted to write for the U.S. public, and I wanted to include feelings as well as information.

For this book, I had to choose the main characters from among the many people hurt—physically, emotionally, economically. I wanted to include every-one, but ultimately I chose to tell the life stories of only six survivors, and in their own words. Besides myself, they are Nelson Johnson, Willena Cannon, Kwame Cannon, Marty Nathan, and Paul Bermanzohn. They represent varied backgrounds and were each profoundly affected by the massacre; I have a strong personal connection to all of them.

Nelson Johnson grew up on a farm in the segregated South, where he learned of the struggle for black freedom at his parents' knees. He served in the air force in the early 1960s and attended college in Greensboro on the GI Bill. Articulate and charismatic, he rose as a leader in the city's black liberation movement in the 1960s and 1970s.[3] He organized our demonstration on November 3, 1979. During the massacre, a Klansman stabbed him in the arm. When the police arrived after the murders, they attacked Nelson with clubs, arrested him, and threw him in jail. A decade later, he became a minister and founded the Faith Community Church in Greensboro, where he continues to lead the fight for human rights.

Willena Cannon grew up in a sharecropper's family in South Carolina, haunted by racist violence. She fled her hometown for Greensboro and college in 1961, jumped full force into the student sit-ins, and has been part of the justice movement ever since. On November 3, police arrested Willena as she tried to protect Nelson Johnson from their attack. Today, Willena still lives in Greensboro, where she is a community activist.

Kwame Cannon, Willena's son, was ten years old when he witnessed the Klan/Nazi attack in 1979. In this book, he describes that experience and its devastating impact on his life.

Four women were widowed on November 3, and each has a poignant story of personal loss and rebuilding worthy of its own book; Signe Waller, the widow of Jim Waller, has written her account, *Love and Revolution*.[4] For this book, I chose Marty Nathan, the widow of Michael Nathan, my first husband. Marty and Mike grew up in white families of modest means; their fathers worked blue-collar jobs and died young. Marty and Mike became medical doctors who served poor people, and their first child was born shortly before Mike was killed. Marty turned her sorrow and anger into creative activism, pushing for justice in the courts through public education and organization, and built the Greensboro Justice Fund, which she still directs.

Paul Bermanzohn, my husband, is still paralyzed on his left side as a result of the November 3 massacre. The son of Jewish survivors of the Nazi Holocaust, Paul left the Bronx for North Carolina to study medicine. Today, he is a psychiatrist and political activist.

I grew up in a white, middle-class family that was part of the postwar suburban expansion on Long Island. I went South to college, joined the social movements, and stayed in North Carolina for fifteen years. Today, I am a college professor at the City University of New York.

Through Survivors' Eyes proceeds chronologically. Part I follows the five older narrators from childhood to young adulthood on both sides of the racial divide in the days of segregation. In the 1960s, as social activism swept the country, we all went to college. Fighting for civil rights, black power, peace, and women's liberation inspired each of us to believe that society could be fundamentally changed.

Part II covers the 1970s, when our paths crossed. Unlike the vast majority of sixties activists who returned to conventional lives, we continued to organize, taking blue-collar jobs in factories and hospitals. We got to know each other as we studied Marxism and revolutions in Russia, China, Africa, Asia, and Latin America. We became more and more involved in day-to-day organizing in North Carolina, where industrial wages were among the lowest in the nation. We built unions, pushed for better health care and quality public education, and fought police brutality and the unjust imprisonment of activists. We decided to merge our collectives (one black, the other white) and to join a national group that eventually became the Communist Workers Party. Kwame Cannon, born in 1968, begins his narrative in these chapters, describing his memories of childhood and his mother's activism.

Part III opens in 1979, when the Ku Klux Klan reemerged in North Carolina after a decade-long hibernation. The KKK vowed to "take back the South for white people," to overturn black political rights, and to stop the unionization of black and white workers. In the Carolinas, the Klan organized paramilitary training camps, passed out racist literature on the streets, and held recruitment meetings at public libraries and community centers. In the textile town of China Grove, we confronted the Klan in July 1979 as it showed *Birth of a Nation*, its recruitment movie. The Klan, Nazis, and Greensboro police organized a death squad that attacked our anti-Klan march on November 3. The six narrators share their memories of that massacre.

Part IV includes the immediate aftermath of the murders and the trials that dealt with them. In the first two trials, all-white juries found the Klan and Nazi gunmen not guilty. In the third, a civil trial, a jury with one black juror held the Greensboro police, the Klan, and the Nazis liable for wrongful death. The Greensboro Police Department paid a $350,000 judgment; the Klan and Nazis got off scot-free. As we struggled through the trials and afterward to rebuild our lives, Kwame Cannon had perhaps the hardest time. When he was sixteen, police caught him breaking and entering and charged him with six counts of burglary. His punishment—two life sentences, a minimum of twenty years in prison—represented three times the average for multiple burglaries. Thirteen years later, a vigorous campaign led by Kwame's mother, Willena, set Kwame free.

Our continuing efforts to learn the full truth of the attack against us and to achieve justice today focus on the Greensboro Truth and Community Reconciliation Project, intended to reassess the massacre. Greensboro survivors hope the Greensboro Truth and Community Reconciliation Project can become a model for such communities who, like us, want to address human rights abuses.

PART I

Black Is Black and White Is White, and Never the Twain Shall Meet

1
Growing Up

Willena Cannon and Nelson Johnson were born to African American families in the rural South in the early 1940s. In Europe, the United States waged war against the Nazis and their theory of Aryan supremacy. On this side of the Atlantic, the United States maintained segregation—politically, economically, socially—based on a theory of racial superiority and inferiority. "Black is black and white is white," the folk saying went, "and never the twain shall meet." In the South, especially in the rural areas, any black person's alleged offense against the social order could bring brutal punishment. Ku Klux Klansmen and other white murderers or rapists were rarely tried and never punished.[1]

Sally Avery, Paul Bermanzohn, and Marty Arthur were born to white families in the late 1940s and early 1950s, part of the postwar baby boom. Across the country, economic good times led to a growing white middle class and expanding suburbs. Government programs made it easy for white families to get mortgages to buy homes, while explicitly closing such opportunities to minorities. TV's Leave It to Beaver, *and* Life *and* Look *magazines, portrayed the United States as a happy, stable, and white middle-class country; poor people, whatever their color, remained outside the frame in America's official portrait. Calm on the surface, the country simmered with tension underneath.*

Willena Reaves (Cannon),
born March 1, 1940, Mullins, South Carolina

I will never forget the night the Klan burned a man alive. It was 1949, and I was nine years old when I saw it with my own eyes, about a quarter mile from my house. I was out with my cousin Tina. The weather was hot, and often it felt too hot to breathe. But that night was nice; the air felt good. We heard commotions, saw people running. Tina and I ended up in a clump of people behind some trees. I saw a white woman crying; she was bleeding. The white men had hit her with rocks and bricks or boards. But then the focus switched to the man, and they grabbed him and threw him to the ground and put him in this barn.

The man was black, the woman white. They had been going together. They both consented to the relationship, and black people in Mullins knew that. The men chasing them were from Orry County, known to be Ku Klux Klan country. Orry was the next county over, and we were all scared of Orry County. Black people from Mullins would work over there picking tobacco, and sometimes people would never return. Their families would never know what had happened to them. They were afraid to ask too many questions because they might disappear too.

When the Klan found the couple, the girl didn't cry rape. In those days, many times white girls in that situation would say, "He raped me," to save their own lives. And then the whites would lynch the black man. But this girl did not do that—and she got beat bad.

I didn't know the man, but I knew of his family. The Klan threw him in a barn, an old abandoned tobacco barn. They locked him in.

And then the sheriff came. I knew because of his uniform. He should have stopped that murder, but he didn't. He probably heard something was happening and came out to see what it was. The Klan and the sheriff talked. The sheriff saw that it was the whites doing the brutality, so he said it was "the people's business," not his. (He would have acted very differently if it had been black folk hurting whites.) So the sheriff left. It was the most blatant thing. I was only nine years old, and I thought the sheriff should have saved that man's life. Instead he acted like he knew the Klansmen and agreed with what they were doing.

After the sheriff left, the Klan threw kerosene on the barn with the man in it and set it on fire. The barn was old and burned real fast. The man hollered and hollered; his scream got deeper and deeper. And then silence. Nothing. Tina pulled me away back to our house. That man was dead. The barn burned down to nothing. I would wake up hearing that man's scream. His hollering went on in my nightmares for a long time. There was no newspaper, no report. That man just disappeared. And nobody was supposed to talk about it.

That was a traumatic experience. And my memory of it went on and on. Sometimes I would wake up hollering. I was not supposed to talk about it. My mother wanted to keep everything quiet. She was afraid, and with good reason. She thought the safest thing was not to talk about it at all. If you talked, people would see you as a troublemaker. If white people found out, it was not a good thing.

And that put something in me that I couldn't get rid of. I couldn't do anything about it. It was this hard thing on my life that stacked up, kept stacking up. I didn't get rid of it until I left Mullins and joined the civil rights movement.

I was born and raised on a farm just outside Mullins, South Carolina. I'm one of ten children, six girls and four boys. Mullins is small. The population when I was growing up was about seven thousand, counting the dogs. It is about forty miles from Myrtle Beach on the Atlantic Ocean. This area has rich black land, where farmers grow tobacco, cotton, corn, and soybeans. I stayed in Mullins until I left home after high school.

We were sharecroppers. Bill Goss owned the land, and we farmed it. Bill Goss was white and powerful. He owned the radio station and lots of land. Sharecroppers got to keep only a percent of the crop we farmed, less than half of it. My father got a bigger percent from Bill Goss than most folks did, although I did not know why for a long time. So we did better than most other sharecroppers, but still we just barely survived.

Our house was an old house, no modern conveniences. We had wooden floors, bare boards, which we washed with lye water. We didn't have closets or any sheetrock on the walls. Instead there were bare beams. We hung our clothes on nails between the beams. The toilet was outside. We had an old-fashioned bathtub on the porch. In the winter, you washed in your room with a tub.

We heated the house with three woodstoves, which were in the kitchen and living room. We made fires at night and in the morning. Living on a farm was rough, constant work. Every morning, I had to make the fires, which was one of the chores. We alternated chores. When my sisters made the fire, I took my turn milking the cow, milking three of the teats and leaving one for the calf. Then I got dressed and took the cow out to the field so she could graze—all before I went to school. That night I would bring the cow back up to the barn. My older sister Annette learned how to cook from my mother. (She is a good cook!) My brothers had different chores like plowing in the afternoons. We got a tractor from Bill Goss when I was eleven years old. Only the boys were supposed to use it, but I learned how to drive it too.

We worked hard and didn't have anything to show for it. But we did eat good. We raised guinea hens, turkeys, chickens, pigs, cows. We couldn't afford to buy bologna and weenies, but my father hunted wild pigs. I would take a country ham biscuit to school and would be ashamed of it. People called it "poor people meat" because we made it. Then I got older and found out the opposite was true—that our food was better than the store-bought food.

There was a time before my parents moved to the farm that they were very poor. My mother told how she would open the last jar of peaches and not know how she would feed her kids the next day. She would make the peaches with biscuits or dumplings and pray for food. There were five kids ahead of me. By the time I came along, we were on the farm, and we ate good.

My father would go fishing and sometimes bring three hundred fish back. We would scale and clean all these fish, and we would freeze them in pans of water in our big old freezer. Then we stored the frozen blocks of ice with all these fish in them. Good eating for later.

We always wore hand-me-downs. I wore clothes that were handed down from my older sisters, which were hand-me-downs from white people. My mother would trade for clothes. She would trade our green beans or ham or whatever, and get the clothes and shoes. I could never wear the white people's shoes, cause my feet were fat. My sisters had slim feet, but one of my sisters got bunions because of the real narrow shoes she had to wear. It was degrading not to have your own shoes.

It was special like Christmas when my mother made us a new dress that no one had never been in. She made our new clothes from feedsacks that had these flowers printed on them. She would put lace around them.

There was a store for sharecroppers where you could get things for credit. We did better than a lot of families and were able to pay off the bill and have a little left.

We lived on that land for two decades. Sometimes it felt like our land, but other times, you would work the land and would be tired, and then the owners would drive by and look. Bill Goss hardly ever did that, but his wife did. His wife was from Texas and poor, and she married into his money. She was bossy, and she would drive up, stop, and watch us work. Suddenly, reality would strike me. The land was hers, not ours. She would just stop and watch to see if we were working. It was degrading. We were expected to wave like we were thankful. I hated that role of saying "I'm subservient to you." I would never wave.

Those times I would hate white people, and it showed when I went to school. After Mrs. Goss would come by, the next day I would be uglier to white students when they would cross our path on the way to their school. We would get in fights with them. After the man burned in the barn, I would fight the white kids every day. Not me alone, but with other black kids too. These fights became an issue in Mullins. The town changed the school hours, made us get out fifteen minutes later to give the white kids a chance to get out of our way.

There was a poor white family who lived nearby. They were poor farmers, like us in many ways. We had helped them dig ditches so the water would run off when their crops were being flooded. And they would do the same with us. They had a little girl named Carolyn who was my age. We had played together in her yard and my yard, and our friendship was genuine. I had actually stayed at their house, in her room. But they were still white, and there was still that race thing. Even if you tried to get past it, there still were ways that you got put back in your place. On Saturday when I would go into Mullins with my family, I would see her on the street and she would see me. And she would pretend she didn't know me. Neither of us would speak. It wasn't acceptable in Mullins for us to be friends.

Mostly I played with my brothers and sisters. It was fun to have all those sisters and brothers. We had to learn to share. We had one bicycle for all of us. Those were good times. Except the contact with white people, who always looked down on us. We felt like we couldn't do anything about it.

Even talking about white people was dangerous. If you expressed how you felt about the Klan, your family would quiet you down. It was dangerous to talk.

Something could happen to you or your family. You had to be quiet. So there was lots of whispering. That was what the world was like: We were there to be used by white people.

Our family was light skinned. You can tell by looking at us that we have African, Indian, and white in us. My father's side has Indian in it that you can see in me. My mother's side was very fair-skinned black people. Most black folks in Mullins were dark. There were only three other families that were light skinned.

In school, I was privileged in the teachers' eyes because I was light skinned. The color thing had the teachers deal with me differently than the others. Most of the teachers were dark skinned, but they had been indoctrinated that light is better. That is why they automatically treated me better. At first I didn't understand, because I was as poor as the rest of the students. But the other students in my class saw the favoritism toward me, and it made them mad. They dealt with me after school, calling me "half-breed." That hurt a lot, because I was not accepted by the whites and then my black peers called me names.

Sometimes kids beat me up. In third grade, one guy named Smokey Joe fought me all the time because he said I was a half-breed. His big loud mouth scared me. My big sister Annette (two years older than me) told me, "Why you let Smokey Joe fight you? You beat up half of those guys on the farm, why you gonna let him whup you?" She was serious. She told me if I let him beat me again, *she* would whup me. The next time he came out and jumped on me, I started fighting him back. I almost killed him. Annette and them had to pull me off. Smokey Joe never bothered me no more.

As I got older, the girls started bothering me. The guys called me "red bone." I hate that 'til today. If you're a red bone, you're special.

I hated whites because I knew where the light skin came from—from white men raping black women. Rape was on both sides of my family—all these white people were my ancestors.

When I was fifteen, my mother sent me with some rolls to take to my grandparents' house for a guest that they had. So I went to my grandmother's house, and this white man came out of her guest bedroom with pajamas on! And my grandmother looked at me like, "Don't ask me no questions." You know that look.

So I went home. I asked my mother, "Who was that white man?" He had blue-green eyes, blond hair. There are some light-skinned blacks that look white but have some black features, but this man had none. My mother told me that was my grandmother's brother. They had the same mother and father. The guy was a white man! He lived in Georgia, had a family, and they knew nothing about us. He came to my grandmother's once a year, stayed one or two nights. He came by night and left by night. That time I brought the biscuits was the only time I ever saw him.

Years later, I saw my grandmother moaning. Somebody had told her that her white brother had died. My grandmother didn't even know how to get in touch with that family, so she couldn't go to the funeral. My mama told me why Grandmama was moaning. Grandmama never talked about it.

Everything was so secretive. Nobody ever talked about things. To my grandmother and my mother, the safest way was not to talk at all, not to pass stories on to the children. Sometimes my grandfather would try to talk to us, and my grandmother would say, "Papa, you need to stop that. You're going to get these kids in trouble." After my grandmother died, my grandfather told us a lot about my family that I didn't know, like we are related to Mary McLeod Bethune! Mary and my grandfather were first cousins; their mothers were sisters. I didn't learn about the great things Mary McLeod Bethune had done until I went to college. She became high up in Washington, D.C., in the government, one of the first black people to do that.

My mother thought that being proud like Mary McLeod Bethune put you at risk. My mother and her mother looked at Mary as a troublemaker who was "going to mess up things for people." My mother was in a photo with Mary, and she told me, "Mary McLeod Bethune is so determined, she wouldn't let nothing stop her. She even tried to pull a plow with a mule slip" [harness]. She was stubborn and people would tell her to stop, and she wouldn't. She maneuvered her way all the way up to talk to the president at the White House.

When I got involved in the civil rights movement, Mama said, "Oh, Lord, I have ten children, and Mary had to get in one of them." She saw Mary's spirit in me. None of my brothers and sisters got involved in the movement. Even now, my sisters (except Annette) tell me, "You're going to get in trouble." But my mother, at the end of her life, admitted to me that the civil rights movement did make things better.

My father did stand up for himself, at least with Bill Goss, the white man who owned the land we lived on. They would sit out in our yard or on the porch and have a drink and argue. My father would say to Bill Goss, "I don't want to hear that shit!" You didn't say that to a white man! But Daddy was firm with Bill Goss, and I didn't know how he got away with it. Mama was always afraid my Daddy was going too far.

My father was strict with us kids. What he said, you did. There was no discussion or explanation why. You could not ask questions or say what you wanted to do. He was especially strict with us girls. There was to be no dating, no boys hanging around, no makeup, no fancy hairstyles. When we went to the beach, he would take us straight to the water, past the places where they played records and danced. He was too strict.

In high school, I was a majorette for four years. We marched with the band and twirled our batons during the football games. My mother and I kept it a secret from my dad. My mother sewed uniforms for me and all the rest of the majorettes. But then in my third year, Daddy found out. The parade came through when he was downtown in Mullins. He happened to be at the intersection where everybody was watching the majorettes. I was a lead majorette with a whistle to lead the different moves. My father saw me, and he did his finger like, "Come here." It was the most embarrassing thing. Everybody in Mullins knew him and how strict he was. But even so, it was so embarrassing. I had to stop, put my whistle down. Another majorette just picked it up, 'cause they knew I was out of there.

My Daddy didn't say nothing all the way home. When we got home, he said, "Go in the house and get some clothes on. I don't want to ever see you half-naked in the street again."

He was afraid that doing those kind of things would attract the guys. He didn't allow lipstick and fingernail polish. One of my sisters had all her makeup at a friend's house. And she would go to that house in the morning, put it all on, fix her hair, and go to school. After school she would come back, take it off, and plait her hair up again. I just didn't bother.

My mother knew he was too much. She played a role between what Daddy was trying to do but, at the same time, trying to give us some help.

As sharecroppers, my family did not make enough to pay for college educations. But all of us went to college. How could poor sharecroppers send all those children to school? I found out how when I was sixteen years old: moonshine. My father made and sold moonshine. He would make it in the woods and keep it there. He never had it in the house. He sold it in half-gallon jars, not liquor by the drink the way a lot of folks did. We knew people came up to our house and stayed in their cars or trucks, and my father talked to them, and soon they left. We were told never to go to the door; children did not answer the door. What was happening was people came and bought half-gallon jars of moonshine. Money was exchanged, and they drove off.

When I found out my father sold moonshine, I was ashamed. But later on, I thought about it. My father had three kids in college at one time. In Mullins, that wasn't heard of for any black person or for many white people either. Most girls got married at fifteen, sixteen, or seventeen. To finish school was considered a waste of time for women. My father had in mind that we would do more than just get married. So my father sent us to college, and there were so many of us. We could pick whatever we wanted to study, but it was understood that we would go to college. My father dropped out of school in fourth or fifth grade to help out with his family, so he was determined to get an education for us. And selling alcohol was a way to do that.

Making and selling liquor was illegal, and the feds were always looking for the moonshine operations. But Bill Goss would let my father know when the feds was coming in. The federal agents would come in and wouldn't find anything, 'cause my daddy was prepared for them. Black people or poor white people who made that stuff had no way of being warned. Bill Goss was very powerful in Mullins, and my father never got caught.

After he started selling the liquor, that is where most of our money came from. Growing tobacco was just a cover. We still lived the same way, dressed in hand-me-downs, shared the one bicycle. Daddy was saving money, and he didn't even tell us. When he died in 1959, he had money left for me and the younger kids to go to college. We had two years to decide if we were going to school. And if we decided we weren't going, the money went back to my mother's estate.

Years later, when I was forty years old, I learned a big secret: My Aunt Lena was really my grandmother, and Bill Goss and my father were half brothers!

Until 1980, I always thought Aunt Lena was my aunt. But when she was a teenager, she was raped by old man Goss, the white man she worked for. Nine months later, she had my father. She was only fifteen or sixteen years old at the time, and her family raised her baby as her brother. But actually, my father was Aunt Lena's son.

Old man Goss was married to a white woman and had another son by his wife, named Bill. Bill Goss was my father's half brother, and I didn't even know it through my whole childhood.

That was why my father would talk to Bill Goss almost like they were equals, not like a black man would talk to a white man. That was why Bill Goss would warn my father about the feds. So Bill Goss was decent, but most white people weren't.

Bill Goss told my father that when he died, he was going to leave my father some land, maybe about thirty acres. Bill Goss died before my father did, and his wife told my father that he had left him land. Then all of a sudden, that land disappeared from the will. The lawyers made it disappear. It was like white people said, "They're colored, don't give them no land."

My father got sick when I was in the eleventh grade. His muscles started deteriorating. They said he had muscular dystrophy, but honestly, they didn't know what it was. Over three years, his muscles from his feet up to his throat collapsed on him and actually strangled him. After he got sick, we modernized the house to help take care of him. We got electric lights for the first time, and water in the kitchen, and a bathroom with indoor plumbing.

It was in my mind to get away from Mullins. I went to Palmetto High School, which was for blacks. (Mullins High School was for whites.) My eighth-grade class had sixty-six students, and by twelfth grade half of them had gotten married and left school. Only two of us went to college. In my senior year, I was the homecoming queen and voted "Miss Dependability."

I needed to get away from the farm, the woods, the dirt roads, swimming in the river holes, riding on mulebacks—the whole thing. We got a TV in 1957 or

'58, and I began to watch some television and see a whole world out there beyond Mullins.

My father was sick, and I wanted to be a doctor to help people, cure them. My older brother thought I had lost my mind. He said that I would be wasting money and that nobody would go to a woman doctor. He thought there was something wrong with a woman who wanted to be a doctor. This chauvinist stuff with my brother is so deep. His thing is, a woman is put here to be a wife, to raise children. To talk about wanting to be a doctor was way out in left field. "No sister of mine is going to be a doctor," he said. "Mama, you need to talk to her. This is crazy."

My mother was indoctrinated with the idea that women could only raise children too. She told me, "Listen to your brother. You got him all stirred up."

So I was like, "Okay, okay, forget the doctor thing. I'll go in the service."

I didn't even think about the military service in terms of war. I didn't deal with what it really meant. To me it was a way to get off the farm, to get away from these white people, this oppression. It was a way to see the world.

To my big brother, my aspirations meant something was wrong with me. He said, "Only dykes go into the service, or girls who are so ugly they can't get a husband." I wasn't ugly, and therefore my brother thought people would think I was "funny."

I rebelled much more than my brothers and sisters. I wanted something better for my life. It started happening when I was fourteen. I was always with my sister, and she tried to act like white people. That was her standard: White was right. And I hated that. I hated being called "half-breed" and "red bone" by kids at school. And our light color was based on white men raping black women! I hated white people for it. I reacted against the view that white is better.

I wanted to get away from Mullins and all that oppression. When I finished high school, I got married. My brother was pleased! And my father was not; he could see through it.

Getting married was a big mistake. I really liked Louie as a friend. And he was in the service, which meant I could get out of Mullins. I didn't know anything about the physical stuff of what marriage meant. So we got married in July and separated in October. We lived in Annapolis, Maryland, for a while. Most of the time we were having problems 'cause there was no basis for getting married.

My father got worse after I married and moved out of Mullins. So I came back to help him. My father's sickness was wearing down my mother, about to kill her. He had to be turned over every fifteen to twenty minutes. To relieve Mama, I started sleeping in the bed with my father so I could turn him. I stayed a month.

My father and I talked like we had never talked before. It was strange, because before that I had never felt any love for my father. During my whole childhood, he had told me what to do. There was no discussion; he wouldn't allow questions. So I didn't know his motives. To me, he just added on more oppression to the oppression of the white world.

But when he was sick, I learned what motivated him. He was coming from a good place. He was afraid of what sex and marriage would mean for us, so he was real strict. He wanted us to have more life than he had. He asked me, "What other ways could I have done it?"

I stayed a month with him, and my father saw that I wasn't anxious to get back to my husband. He said, "You made a mistake in getting married, and I wondered when you were going to see that. You've been here a month, and you don't even miss your husband." He hit the nail on the head. When Louie would call, I would say, "My father is so sick," and Louie couldn't question that.

Then I went back to Annapolis. On October 12, 1959, my father died. I was so sorry I wasn't there with him at the very end. Soon after that, I called it quits in the marriage. My father left money for the four of us who still needed to go to college. In August 1961, I left to go to A&T [North Carolina Agricultural and Technical State University], a college in Greensboro, North Carolina.

Nelson Napoleon Johnson, born April 25, 1943, Arlie, North Carolina

I am the great-grandchild of slaves. I grew up two miles away from a white family who had owned my great grandparents. My family's small farm was contiguous to the master's land. I was born in 1943, eighty years after the Emancipation Proclamation. My whole understanding of reality was shaped by race.

My mother's family name is Thorne, the same name as the slave master's family. When I was growing up, Will Thorne, who was about the same age as my grandparents, owned the Bank of Littleton. William Thorne Jr. was my age. When we were teenagers, we both got jobs driving school buses. We both grew up in the Arlie area, but in two different worlds.

The discussion about race in my family was unending. Early on, I learned that the power of color altered your whole notion of who you are and what you represent.

My ancestors had been slaves on the Thorne plantation in Louisiana. At the end of the Civil War, the Northern army destroyed the Thornes' place, blew up their mill, and seized their property. The Thornes had relatives in North Carolina who still owned land after the Civil War. North Carolina got into the war late and was half-hearted in the Confederate effort, so the Union troops did not scar North Carolina as much as many places in the South. In Louisiana, the Thornes lost everything, so they decided to join their people in Arlie, North Carolina. And some of their former slaves—my grandfather's family—came with them.

My grandfather, Nelson Thorne, and his family walked practically the entire way. My grandfather and his little brother, Dee, were small boys at the time. I never knew my grandfather, because he died in the early 1930s. But I knew his brother, who was my great-uncle Dee Thorne. We called him Uncle Dee, and he lived in a house across the pasture from us. As I was growing up, he was revered as a respected elder. He told us stories that I still cherish.

Uncle Dee always had a bulldog. We were all afraid of the bulldog, and properly so, because he was known to bite. Uncle Dee kept him on a stake in front of his house, and the bulldog walked around with him wherever he went. Uncle Dee told us that he came to love bulldogs when he walked from Louisiana. He and my grandfather were very small, and a bulldog walked all the way to North Carolina with him. Since that day, he'd kept a bulldog.

Although I never knew my grandfather, I learned about him through stories that my mother and Uncle Dee told. My mother conveyed our family's history, showed me his picture. We lived in his house, and I felt like I knew him, even though he died eleven years before I was born. My sense is he was a strange mixture of house Negro and field Negro. In the language of the black community, a "house Negro" is someone who is dependent and often subservient to his white owners. A "field Negro" is more likely to express his anger. My grandfather was enough of a house Negro to stay with the plantation owner, come to Arlie, work, save money, and end up with a good piece of land. A lot of black folks bought land in those days, good rich farming land. But my grandfather was enough of a field Negro that a number of fairly strong stories grew up around him.

My great-uncle Dee told us about my grandfather taking a stand at the cotton gin. Cotton was a big cash crop in our area, along with tobacco and peanuts. Both black and white farmers grew cotton and then brought it to the cotton gin in Arlie. Arlie was just a crossroads, with two stores and a cotton gin. Around the crossroads are some antebellum plantation houses that people still live in today. And beyond that are the smaller homes of black and white farmers, some of them log cabins or unpainted frame houses. We lived about a mile and a half away from the Arlie crossroads, and I grew up hearing that cotton gin compacting the cotton—boom! (pause) boom!

When the farmers brought in their cotton to the gin, folks would get in line in their mule-pulled wagons loaded with cotton. It took a while to get a load of cotton to get ginned, so if there was a line, it could take the better part of a day. It was the habit of the white folk to just pull around any black person there and get in front of them. People did it all the time. Not every white person did it, but if they were in a hurry, they didn't ask your permission, they just did it. Black folk were scared to do anything about it.

One time my grandfather Nelson Thorne challenged the white person who pulled in front of him. He said was not going to put up with it and pulled his mule up. These two sets of mules were jostling for position in front of the cotton gin. When a black person stood up in those days, some kind of violence was likely to happen. It could be the reason given for a lynching, or a late-night visit by the Ku Klux Klan.

In a situation like this, two tendencies come out in the onlookers. Either black folk gather around and put up a united front of support, or everybody clears out. In this case, everybody cleared out. But my grandfather stood his ground. Then Will Thorne interceded. Will Thorne was my grandfather's contemporary, the leading white man in the area, who owned the bank in Arlie. He stopped what could have been an unhealthy ending. My grandfather held his place. When he came home, all the brothers, cousins, and friends came over to the house to congratulate him.

My favorite part of the story was when Uncle Dee mimicked one man named Wiggins Lee. Wiggins Lee told my grandfather, "I's wid you at the gin. I was right wid you. Here's where I was, all the way up to the top of the gin, where the little door was. If he'd a laid his hand on you, I'd go sail out of that door and jump down on him."

Now, we all knew that anyone who'd jump from the top of the cotton mill would've killed himself. Wiggins was hiding; he was scared to death.

There was constant talk in my household about the white man—the white man this, and the white man that. It was like the white man was omnipotent. It was almost a love-hate relationship. "You can't trust the white man, he will cheat you, beat you, kill you." Yet, on the other hand, there was this whole thing about "we need to learn to act decent like white folk." It went on and on. As a child, I distinctly remember that I could not figure out why black people didn't just get these white people back. I resolved at a very young age that I wasn't going to take this from white people. I remember thinking, When I grow up, I'm going to do something about this.

I grew up in my grandfather's house. My mother was the youngest child, and her father gave her the homestead and a good piece of land, the barn, horses, cows, chickens.

It was a big house for a small farmer. It almost looked like the master's house, except it was built on only one level, and with cheap wood and material and a tin roof. But it was clear that my grandfather tried to build a big house, and he painted it white. In that neighborhood it was considered to be a good house. During my childhood the house became rundown. When I was in about the sixth grade, my older brothers painted it. It really looked good. I stayed in that house until I graduated high school and left home for the air force.

Across the pasture Uncle Dee had a big house. Then there were smaller houses, some log cabins, wood-frame houses that weren't painted, where Dee's children lived. Across the branch, which is what people called a stream, was where the Price family lived. They lived on Mr. Thorne's land and were his sharecroppers. I could never figure out if they were our relatives or just friends. We called them "cousin," which people pronounced "cuttin'." (People ground up words, like "nearly about" is "n'bout.") That's how we related to just about everybody, we called them "cuttin'."

Interestingly enough, the white people who sought to befriend black people would never call them "Mr." or "Mrs." They would call them "cousin" too— "How Cuttin' Molly doin'?" Mr. Harris, a white man, was like that. He set up a little store near the Thorne's crossroads store in Arlie. He supplied mule collars and plows and different farm implements. And on Saturday night, people would sit around at Harris's little crossroads store, sitting on sacks of wheat and little benches and talking. That would be the most intimate relationship between blacks and whites that I saw as a child. Sitting around at the crossroads store with Mr. and Mrs. Harris, who knew everybody, there would be jokes and talk.

Life was lived within a racial framework. White women of the better-off families were invisible. I cannot remember what any of them looked like. They stayed in these big houses, back off the road, and we never saw them.

Within that racial framework, there was no ongoing fear at Arlie except for one incident, when I was small. There was a white Thorne, George Thorne, who was a rogue, who cursed, drank, and acted crazy. He stole cars and went to prison. The white Thornes presented themselves as genteel, and George Thorne embarrassed them. George sometimes befriended black people, maybe just to piss off his father. But sometimes when George drank a lot, he would curse black people.

Once, George was drinking liquor with my cousin Jack and his friends, and George got drunk and denounced them. My cousins denounced him back. Then George threatened Jack and left to get all his brothers—the most powerful white family in the area. And my cousin Jack got his relatives, who were big powerful black men. And they all got their guns.

I was little, and I still feel that sense of fear and excitement. Black folk, the former slaves of the Thorne family, were going to fight! All of my cousins, ranging from age twenty to thirty-five, everyone young enough to feel their juices, was going to fight. It was the first time I saw a group of black men prepared to fight white folk with guns.

The dispute between George and my cousins got started on Saturday evening, and by eight or nine o'clock it was building to a head. It had been kicked up by George Thorne, and everyone, even white people, knew George did everything, including stealing from white people. And that is why old man Will Thorne got involved. Because he knew that even if the sheriff and deputies came, somebody was going to get seriously hurt—and not only on the black side. So old man Thorne stepped in and settled the whole thing down. It never did explode. I don't know if my uncle Dee was involved, but generally the way things got settled was that old man Will Thorne would call Uncle Dee, and these old men would apologize to each other and then tell everyone, "We settled it."

Other than that, I did not grow up with a sense of fear. My family owned enough land to farm. We didn't have to work for white people. And there was some measure of civility in Arlie, if you lived within the racial framework. But if you stepped outside certain expectations, then there could be trouble.

In Littleton, it was a different story. Littleton was nine miles away, the "big" town in the area, with a population of about fifteen hundred. It had two stop lights on Main Street, and it was the place to go on Saturday night. People paraded up and down those streets like they do at a shopping mall today. On Saturday night, 99 percent of the people on the streets of Littleton were black. Most of them didn't own any land but lived and worked on land owned by somebody white. They would come into town on Saturday and get them a little drink. And some, in the course of having a good time, would get into a little fight or something. The police, who were white (I never saw a black cop until I was an adult), would put them in jail. In the process, the police would humiliate people, slap them across the face with an open hand.

I saw a policeman slap a black man across the face, this way and that way. That man was bigger than the cop, but he knew that if you even acted like you were going to resist, they would kill you. Everyone knew they would kill you.

Routinely, every Saturday night, a bunch of black folk would get beat up and put in jail. Then on Monday morning, Mr. Bernis West, the biggest landowner in Littleton, would come to the jail and get all his folks out, thirty to forty people out of jail. He would pay off the sheriff; it was part of the way the town financed itself. And everybody would go back to the field.

If you didn't work for a white man, anything could happen to you. In the jailhouse the police would ask you, "Who your boss?"

"Mr. Bernis West," the lucky ones would say.

"Get on in there," said the police, pushing them toward the jail.

The next one, the police would ask, "Who your boss? You ain't got no boss?" You might get a stick upside the head right then. You might end up in jail for months if you didn't have someone to bail you out. But mainly, they wanted to get you back working in the fields.

It is hard to imagine the fear of being black in small southern towns. There really were no rights. You couldn't bring a charge against a white man. If you did, white people would get mad, and they would make sure you got punished. So no one brought those charges. The court was used only if you wanted to bring another black man in. And in the court they played games with you, and whoever they liked won. I was in court one time when there was an alimony case. A black couple was in there and the lawyers made fun of them. "When did you go out? Where did you go? Who were you with? Ha, ha, ha!" It was entertainment. And they'd humiliate the guy, and he'd have to sit there and take it.

It took courage to stand up in those days. In the 1950s, I grew up with older people who were right on the edge of slavery, some born in it. If you were eighty years old, you were born in it. And some of the worst experiences came after slavery. I think it is hard for people to imagine the lack of democracy and rights, and the fear that came along with it.

I grew up in a highly color-diversified community. There were black people who were as white as any white person; you couldn't tell the difference. There were black people who were darker hued than I am. There was a lot of color consciousness. I was never free from the stigma of color. It operated within my family and my neighborhood. Race and color shaped how I saw everything.

My mother was dark, maybe a little bit darker than I am. My father is from a fair-skinned family. My parents were married sixty-two years, until my mother passed in 1992. I was one of nine children, and we range in color from dark like me to tan to light skinned. A bunch of colors in one family.

Light-skinned people were considered axiomatically more beautiful and more acceptable. The word "black"—"you black so and so"—was used commonly among us children in the neighborhood as a put-down. Children imitate what the dominant culture tells them, and do it in some hurtful ways. Such talk was not allowed in my family, but it was common outside my home.

I didn't realize how much I was a victim of this color thing, growing up. My brother Ivan, who is only fourteen months my senior, is light skinned. As a teenager, he was much more socially outgoing than I was. I grew up with an inferiority complex and didn't know what it was. I was nervous around girls; he would always have the pretty girls. He seemed to be like flowing water, talked that talk and told jokes that everybody laughed at. Meanwhile, I would be computing what to say.

I grew up aware of the power of color, and how it altered your whole notion of who you are and what you represent. It was right in my family, always around me. I was never aware of my mother or father making any distinctions among us. But once I was an adult, I could look back and see some. It was never anything cruel or vicious, but it was there.

As a child, I also learned about class differences among black folk, which were based on land ownership rather than shades of blackness. We didn't call it "class" back then. Within the black community, some people owned land, while most people had to live on a white man's land. My mother exalted her parents and our immediate family because we had land. She presented us as better than others. She would speak negatively of the white man, but at the same time, she aspired to white standards of the landed aristocracy.

An ongoing argument between my mother and father was that my father didn't have anything when he married my mother. My mother had a farm. As a child, I got so tired of hearing her say, "When you married me there was mules in the barn, wheat in the field." I appreciated my mother's pride in our history, but I didn't like her view that we were better than other people just because we owned some land.

I have much less sense of my father's background than my mother's. I know my father came from Tabron, a community that is linked up with Hollister, a Native American village about four miles from Arlie. Hollister had a series of crossroads, eight stores, a post office, and a sawmill where people brought their lumber to be cut up. I know that lineagewise, a portion of my father is Native American.

My father has been a tower of respect to me. I've grown up admiring him. He's not a great speaker or singer or preacher. But he is a good thinker and a heck of a hard worker. He had the inheritance that came with my mother, but he further developed it by buying more land. He bought what we called the lower farm, which was much better land than my grandfather's land. My father bought the lower farm from the white Thornes. The lower farm was about four miles away from where we lived. It had two good fields in it, and that was what you were looking for.

If my father had been white, he would have been a very successful man. To us he was a success. As a small farmer in the 1930s, '40s, and '50s, even with all your energy, you could just make ends meet. As we grew up, my brothers and I did a lot of the farm work. After my father could count on us to do most of the farm work, he bought a truck, a 1942 Chevy, a big investment for us. He learned to estimate the amount of pulpwood timber in a tract of land. When it came to walking through a set of woods and estimating how much pulpwood was there, he was as good as they come. He got his first jobs in connection with William Thorne, my father's contemporary. The white Thornes owned the bank. His brother hauled for the Halifax Paper Company in Roanoke Rapids. That was a huge paper plant. My father would estimate the amount of timber, do the contract, and then he would haul the wood. He bought two trucks and started to do it for himself. He effectively became a small contractor.

Black people owned a good bit of land with timber on it. My father would estimate the timber on a parcel of land and cut it up. He got a good little bit of business from white farmers too. He developed a relationship with a white man in a little town called Arcola, a rich man who ran that town and had a big house and horses. That man got rich working with people like my father. My father couldn't deal directly with the mill, because the mill wouldn't buy from a black man. He had to sell through an agent, a white man. So although my father did the work, this go-between white person became a millionaire. It was a version of the Perdue chicken farms today: You raised the chickens, and they tell you you're in business for yourself, and Perdue gets rich. You make some money, just enough to survive. (My older brother ran into that problem in the 1980s with the Perdue chicken farms.)

While I was in high school, my father had eight or ten men working for him in the pulpwood business. He had a good relationship, a peer relationship, with those men who worked for him. I commend him for it. Those men are old men now, in their sixties and seventies. When we have our family reunion nowadays, all of them come. Their relationship with my father has endured over the years.

He always wanted to go in business for himself; it was his dream. But he never got beyond the pulpwood. And in the late 1950s, he was driven out of pulpwood. The pulpwood business became more mechanized; heavy equipment was needed to make a profit. Before then, all you needed was two men, a crosswood saw, and a truck. You went out and sawed, worked hard, loaded the truck, and sold the wood. But in the sixties, increasingly you couldn't make it that way. Poor people like my father couldn't get the heavy equipment. Even though he was one of the best estimators of timber, the bank wouldn't lend him money for equipment. The mill wouldn't cooperate with any black folks. So, effectively, black contractors like my father were driven out of the pulpwood business. So he got into long-distance hauling of tobacco and crops from Florida to points north, like Baltimore and New York.

There was no shortage of race talk in the family. My mother shared a lot about our history. My father subscribed to the *Raleigh News and Observer* and read it every day, and he would talk about what black folks ought to do. He was civic minded and talked about registering to vote well before the sixties. And he did register. There were so few black people voting that it really didn't matter. White folks controlled everything politically, but we still registered and voted.

In the early 1950s, as the civil rights movement began, my father and other black landowners got together and formed the Enfield chapter of the NAACP. Enfield was the other large town, along with Littleton. And there were more black landowners in Enfield, including a black family who owned a funeral home—still own it. These men got together in the early fifties and formed a branch of the NAACP, and my father served as president for a good many years.

I didn't go to those meetings, because children didn't go to them. I know they would talk and make plans. The exceptional NAACP chapters, in moments that history presented, did certain extraordinary things. My father's branch was more typical. It promoted a certain dignity and propagated a sense of self-esteem, of brotherhood, sisterhood. And all of them registered people to vote. Most people wouldn't register; they were afraid.

Church and Sunday school played a big role in my family. That is where a lot of discussion took place. My dad always spoke up in churches and other places and was always advocating for the right thing. In a sense of speaking, he was a local leader of the civil rights movement, but there wasn't much of a movement in that area. He was a great encouragement to me.

I remember talking with my father about the Supreme Court's 1954 *Brown v. Board of Education* decision. One of my cousins said, "If whites don't want to be with me, I don't want to be with them." I disagreed with her. I saw integration as a step towards equality. At the time, I was going to a one-room schoolhouse in Tarapin. My class was a mixture of many colors, from dark to tan to high yellow. But no whites were there. I never went to an integrated school.

Instead, after 1954, North Carolina found a way to become even more segregated. There were many Native Americans in my childhood, although the term "Native American" was not used then. Indian people were called "issues," and I've never heard that word used anywhere else. It was a derogatory word, comparable to "spics" or "nigger." (There is a way "nigger" is used among black people that is not derogatory but familial. I think it was the same way for "issue." If I used it, it would be negative.) I later determined what the word means from my understanding of history: It's "issued," something issued from the white race to Native Americans. An Indian person who was "issued" something from the whites became, in popular terminology, an "issue."

Anyway, after the 1954 Supreme Court decision, part of Hollister village became Native American, and the other part of the population protested against it. Hollister was mainly a community of mulattos, fair-skinned people who were a mix of white and black. The whites did not acknowledge their mulatto children. There were some Indians, but more mulattos. So after 1954, the State of North Carolina chartered them as Native Americans to give them some rights, calling them the Holiwarran Indian tribe. And the tribe is still recognized by the State of North Carolina.

I remember my friend Raz, who lived across the branch from me in a house on my father's land. Raz was very fair skinned. We were in the same grade. Raz told me he wasn't going to come to my school anymore.

I said, "Why?"

He said, "I'm an Indian."

I said, "When did you get to be an Indian?" We were in second or third grade. Raz and a group of people just left and set up a separate school for Indians. Later I realized that North Carolina was doing this to indicate that the state would continue to be segregated. They turned the Native Americans/mulattos into pawns and created a division within the village of Hollister. Some families refused to leave the black race, even as another part of the same family registered as Native American.

I was growing up right at the point where change was coming. But it hadn't come yet. So I periodically experienced the old southern-style attitude. Getting my driver's license was the most humiliating experience. I grew up driving things—tractors, trucks—I drove everything on the farm. I knew how to drive up and down the fields and on the county roads. I took the written driver's test, where a lot of people had problems, and passed it the first time.

Then came the road test. I knew this should be easy because I had so much experience driving. But at the driver's bureau in Littleton, there was this big, burly, white Marine guy. He told me to sit down, and then he took care of every white person that came in. I sat there from noon until the office closed, when he told me to come back the next day. I came back the next day, and he said, "You were here yesterday. Go sit in your car, and I'll come out there." And I sat in my car until the office closed that day. I got so humiliated.

I had my driver's permit, which meant I could drive with a licensed driver in the car. My cousin, who was much older than I was, came with me because my father was away working pulp work. Because nothing was happening in Littleton, my cousin and I decided that we would go to Hollister to start the whole process over. So we drove from Littleton to Hollister. I drove, and it was legal because he was with me. I went into the Hollister station and tried to act like I didn't have a driver's permit. I wanted to start over again, including taking the written test. The problem was, the Hollister man said something that indicated that he saw me drive up. Which meant that I violated the law, and he could call the police and put me in jail. So I had to tell him that I already had a permit.

He said, "Where did you get that?"

I said, "Littleton."

And, boy, did he chew me out: "Do you think you can come down here and run around?" And that whole thing.

So I ended up going back to Littleton. The Marine guy finally took me out for the driving test. When we were coming back, he didn't ask me to parallel park, which they usually did. Instead he said that I didn't stop at a Stop sign.

I said, "How could I be taking a driving test and not stop at a Stop sign?"

And he just got up and left me.

Finally I got my license. I think at some point that guy just decided to give me a license. It had nothing to do with any kind of test.

Most black people grew up taking this kind of stuff all their lives. To the extent that you interact with white people, basically you take it all. Or you think of some supersmart way to get back at people so they don't know you are getting back at them. There's a whole culture there that adjusted to that.

Where people got their nurturing was in our own community, in the family, school, and the church. One of the powerful things about the black church that is both misunderstood and gradually being lost is how much a community of faith was needed to nurture people in those situations. When I was a little boy and I came out to give my speech on Sunday on children's day, there was no such thing as doing it wrong. People clapped. That's how we got shaped; that was powerful affirmation. And in that sense, segregation came to be a shelter in the storm. Our community was a place where you could be formed, your core could be formed sufficiently. Even if you got beat up by the hostility of racism, you still knew your fundamental identity. You are somebody. You will survive.

In 1958, two friends and I tried to hold a sit-in. This was two years before the famous Woolworth sit-in. My classmates George Pitchford, James Eaton, and I were three close buddies, fifteen years old, in the tenth grade. There was a drug-store named Three Fountains on Main Street in Littleton. It had two tables with marble tops and wicker-wire chairs. George and I decided that we were going to buy a soda and sit down at one of those tables.

It was Saturday, and everybody had come into town from all the fields and farms. This whole throng of people was parading up and down the street, laughing and talking. We had no plan other than to go into the store, buy a soda, and sit down. We were just as nervous as we could be. The white guy came from behind the counter, yelling, "Get out! You niggers get out!" He scared us, took the starch out of us. We got up and got out. We were seeking for a way to stand up against this thing. So we stood up—and got crushed.

What would have happened if we didn't get up and leave? We instinctively knew the police would come in and beat us. If we resisted, the cops would have killed us, and that would have been that. They would have beaten us in front of all those black people in Littleton. Two or three drunk people would have come to our defense, and they would have been beaten worse than us. And everybody else would clear out. Half the people would be talking about how crazy we were, and how we should know how white folk are, and how we were making it worse for everybody. The other half would have been moaning, wishing they had some way to support us.

George Pitchford recently said to me, "Ever since that day we got thrown out that drugstore, I have always thought ahead about a backup plan. That time we had no backup plan."

But what could have been a backup plan? We just plodded into the drug-store, scared as hell, and we carried out the first part of our plan: We sat down. We knew the guy behind the counter was going to do something. When you did something like that, you were like a sacrificial lamb. We could have held our ground, hoping that circumstances and history would bail us out, like at Woolworth's in Greensboro two years later. But it wouldn't have happened in Littleton, it's too small a place. If we had held our ground, we would have been hurt. There are so many people who did lifetime jail sentences because they tried to have a little bit of dignity.

In 1959, I was beaten on a bus for trying to sit in the front. I was in high school and active in student government and went to the state student-government convention in Gastonia. On the bus.

I took the trip with my buddy James Eaton. I was small, but he was smaller than I was. As soon as we left Littleton on the bus, we had been thinking about sitting on the front seat. We knew about Rosa Parks in Montgomery, Alabama. But buses were still segregated in North Carolina.

It was the longest trip I've ever taken on a bus. We were sitting in the back, getting up our nerve to move up front. Through all these towns—Raleigh, Durham, Greensboro, Winston-Salem—hour after hour on the bus, we were working on it. When the bus got to Charlotte, it stopped at the bus station. There were a lot of empty seats up front. We made up our mind to make our move.

We got up, walked down the aisle, and sat down in the front section in the second row of seats. The bus was just sitting there in the Charlotte bus station, the driver in the driver's seat. White people started to ball up paper and throw it at us, and there was a murmuring about "niggers getting out of their place." We were afraid to look at anybody; we were hearing them but trying not to hear it. But it is hard to ignore balls of paper falling on you. The bus driver just sat there. Tension built up; the whole bus was aware of what was going on. A white man got up from a seat behind us and walked to the front of the bus. He turned around and glared at us. He was wearing a brown trench coat, and he held up the coat with one hand, to shield his other hand. He turned and hit me with his fist, poom! against my head.

It stunned me, and I fell over in the lap of Eaton. I took the blow because I was sitting on the aisle seat. I was scared. Eaton was scared.

"What we going to do?" he said.

I said, "I'm moving back."

We both got up and meekly made our way to the back and sat down. As I stood up, half of the white people were looking as if nothing had happened. Some were looking out the window; a few glared at us. The bus driver did nothing. We sat down in the back, and the bus took off. We sat back there, mum, for twenty-one miles to Gastonia. The man who hit me sat there up front.

And we got off the bus in Gastonia and went to the student-government convention. I told some kids, and there was some discussion among us teenagers. There was bravado about what to do. But actually, nothing came of it. We weren't at the level of organizing a significant protest. On the trip back to Littleton, we didn't try to sit on the front of the bus.

I told my dad about it, and he told me I definitely should put it in my report on the trip. He said when all the students come together for chapel, I should tell about me and Eaton and our trip. The most significant thing that had happened to me on that trip was I got beat up for sitting on the front of the bus.

I told my principal, Mr. Finch, that I wanted to put it in my report. The principal said, "Johnson, you can't tell that. That would get me in trouble and the school in trouble. And you don't want to do that. Wipe that out of your mind, and go on." So the principal ordered me to act against my father's wishes and not to say anything about it.

I did basically what my principal said. There was no discussion. I knew the principal was telling the truth. My father was a member of the NAACP, but teachers got fired if they joined NAACP. My father could be in it because of his relative independence; he worked his own land and own business.

So I did what my principal said. I put it aside, and that was it. Those kind of humiliating things happened, and you just take it in. A lot of times, when a black person seems to explode out of nowhere, it is really the straw that broke the camel's back. You can't take any more of this crap, and so you feel like, "Go on and kill me, and be done with this." I can see how that happens to people.

As I was growing up, farming was becoming a harder and harder way to make a living. Many black farmers lost their land. The farms that were making it were the huge farms owned by whites. The only way to make a small family farm work was to have your whole family farming it with mules and horses. Black farmers couldn't get bank loans to get good tractors and other equipment, so you did your best with your old piece of tractor. But increasingly that wasn't really working, and most of the young people wanted to leave the farm for better luck in the city. People from my hometown either went to Baltimore, New York, or D.C. Ninety percent of the young people left. There were streets in Baltimore you could go to and say "I'm from Littleton," and half the people on the street would know you.

I was sick of farm work. My brothers and I used to ride through the woods across two or three other farms to get to our lower farm, where we would plow and work in the fields. We would get up early in the morning; we would ride there and work. We would come back at noon for lunch and then go back to the field and then come back at night. The horseflies would tear you up going through those woods. Particularly in the evening, when you were sweaty and sticky, the flies would get you. They would all get on the mule's ear, and the ear would be bleeding, and the mule would be flopping his ears. Farming was no future I wanted.

And as I was growing up, crop allotments came into being. This meant county agents came out and everybody was allotted a certain amount of land for cash crops. It was based on tillable land, meaning cleared fields. The more land you had, the bigger allotment you got. If you had a small farm, you could only grow so much tobacco, cotton, and peanuts. If you planted more cash crops, they would require you to plow it up. If you sold your allotment to the government, your allotment went into the soil bank. The fields would become overgrown in weeds and bushes, and then they were no longer tillable and you would lose your allotment. Which means that you had some land, but no right to plant a cash crop on it. If you lost your allotment and your right to grow cash crops, you still had to pay tax on the land even though you had no crop. People end up losing their land, being forced to sell the land. A huge number of small farmers lost their land this way.

We still have our allotment, our tobacco allotment. When my father went into pulpwood, we children kept up the farm. When he went into long-distance hauling, we were expected to run the whole farm. I was sick of the farm; I needed to get away.

As I was coming to the end of high school, I faced a big decision. Tradition has it that, as the elder son at home, you do what you need to do to ensure the family's survival. My father's pulpwood business had collapsed, and as a hauler, he was away most of the time, coming home on the weekend. The farm was not making much money, but it was making some money if someone would work it.

The general thinking was I would stay home and work the farm. But I wanted to go to the air force.

My brother Ivan, who had graduated a year earlier, had gone to New York to stay with my oldest brother and my aunt. I called Ivan, and he came home so we could discuss which one of us would work the farm. I was pleading with him to let me go to the air force. He was planning to go to college, but he could go to college and still farm in the summer. I was the fourth of five boys. The ones before me had gone into the army, and they always sent back a portion of their earnings to our family, to our mother. She had agreed to use it for Ivan to go to college. I thought Ivan and I had a basic agreement that he would do the farm. I wanted the agreement so bad, I may have added to it in my own mind.

My two good high school friends, Charles Williams and George Pitchford, and I had all decided to go to the air force. We had already met with the recruiter; we had all passed the test and had been put in various areas based on our scores. We all wanted to go to basic training together. The day after I finished high school, we hitchhiked up Route 158 to Jackson, North Carolina, to meet with our air force recruiter. To our total astonishment, he told us he had filled his quota for that month. And we were just totally undone, but all we could do was hitchhike back to Littleton. We were hanging around Littleton when the recruiter shows up. He drove all the way from Jackson to Littleton to tell us that new spaces had opened up and he could take us right away. "Get in the car," he said.

So we got in the car. He bought us tickets to Raleigh, and we took the medical examination and the oath in our civilian clothes. At the point you take the oath, you are officially in. You get your uniform, and your superior officers have license to curse you out. The three of us got on an airplane and flew off to Texas for basic training. I hadn't even said goodbye to my family. I had never gone out of state overnight and not told anyone.

I called my mother from Texas. My family didn't know where I was. My brother thought that we were still discussing who would do the farm! I thought we had an agreement. He felt stuck, but in the family ethics of that situation, he had to stay.

I upheld my end of the bargain. I immediately took a substantial portion of my pay, and for four years, I subsidized my brother. He went to A&T, and for all four years, he came back home during the summer. He and I pretty much got over it.

I was ready to get up out of there. I just couldn't envision myself working on that farm. It was like no life to me. I needed to go somewhere, to see the world, to experience something new. I didn't have a clear view of what I was going to do. I was very clear on what I didn't want to do. I didn't want to follow the path of my brothers and go to New York. I didn't want to farm. The recruiter made the air force sound so exciting. All these pictures, going to different countries, and getting training and money. I never thought of the ethics of war.

Sally Avery (Bermanzohn), born June 6, 1947, Wilmington, Delaware

My parents both worked in the war effort for Dupont Chemical Company in Wilmington, Delaware. My mother was one of the Rosie the Riveters, a large number of women hired to work during the war and then pushed back into the home to have babies. Mom said she left Dupont happily because she wanted to have children. She bore three baby-boom babies; I was her first.

We moved to New York in 1950, after my father got laid off from Dupont and got a new job in New York City as a science writer for the American Chemical Society. My parents bought a little house on Long Island for $15,000 through the Federal Home Mortgage Program. My family became part of the expansion of the Long Island suburbs for white people. (It was decades later that I learned how people of color were denied the federal mortgages). We lived in Port Washington for seventeen years, my entire childhood. Port Washington is on the end of the Long Island Railroad line. My father, along with most of the fathers in the neighborhood, got up every morning, walked three blocks to get on the LIRR to New York City, and then came back at night. We knew Dad would be on the 6 p.m. train. Sometimes we ran up the block to meet him.

My parents were from lower-middle-class families that got wiped out by the Great Depression in the 1930s. Both worked to put themselves through college so that they could become part of what my father called the "great middle class." I grew up with a sense of American progress, of things getting better. Times had been tough in the Depression and during the war years, but in the fifties everything was growing. We weren't called the baby boom yet, but I certainly saw the population explode in my town. People were building new houses on every empty lot. New public schools opened, and babies were everywhere. The slogan of the American Chemical Society where Dad worked was "Better living through chemistry." That motto pervaded our home. Things were on the way up. We were part of the suburban explosion.

My mother tried hard to live in that optimistic framework as the happy homemaker. With three kids and only my father's paycheck, she had to stretch the dollars. So she cooked our meals according to the three-major-food-group advice of the times, and she cut corners on taste but not nutrients. She bought cheap margarine that was white, like lard, and put yellow food coloring in it so it would look like butter. She bought boxes of dried milk, mixed it with water, and told us to drink it because it was as nutritious as regular milk. But it tasted awful, so she compromised by mixing it with regular milk. We had cats, and canned cat food was pricey, so she would cook cat food out of all sorts of awful things like horsemeat and mackerel. She sewed our clothes and was a good seamstress.

My favorite picture from those days is a snapshot my father took of us kids on bicycles in 1955 [see photo in Gallery I]. As the oldest, age eight, I am on a big bicycle. Sam, my brother, age six, is on a smaller bicycle, and Martha, my three-year-old sister, on a tricycle. My father bought all those cycles secondhand, repaired and painted them. In the photo, we all have on plaid flannel shirts and corduroy pants that my mother had sewed for us. It was a happy childhood.

But conflicts brewed. By the mid-1950s, my mother was sick of being a happy homemaker. This was before the women's movement, before Betty Friedan's book *The Feminine Mystique*. Women were not supposed to want to be more than homemakers, and I am sure my mother felt alone with her frustration. But she had a master's degree in chemistry and had worked as a teacher, as well as a Dupont lab chemist. She was sick of refinishing furniture and scrubbing the kitchen floor. A big debate developed between my parents. Mom told Dad that she wanted to get a teaching job after my sister started kindergarten. She argued that we needed the money, especially to send three kids to college. My father resisted because he saw himself as the provider. In line with the norms of the day, he wanted his wife and kids at home, living off his wage.

I remember the tension between my parents, even though I never heard them raise their voices. My father was such a nice guy, and he did not like arguments. My mother found it hard to get anywhere with him and much easier to yell at us. She was frustrated, and she took it out on us. If she had to be the perfect housewife, then we had to be the perfect kids. I didn't realize the connection at the time. I just remember that she insisted that we keep our room real tidy. And like most kids, we were slobs at heart.

I tried to accommodate my mom. When she announced an inspection, I quickly cleaned the room I shared with my sister by cramming stuff in my dresser drawers and closet. But that wasn't good enough for my mother. She opened the closet and my drawers, yelled at me for the mess, and then she dumped the contents of all the drawers in the middle of the floor. A huge pile of junk now made the whole room a disaster area. It really got to me, but I was not allowed to express my feelings.

Very quickly, I learned to keep my drawers semi-neat, enough to pass inspection. But my sister, five years my junior, could not or would not. And several more times, Mom emptied Martha's drawers in the middle of the floor. At the time, I did not realize it was connected to her frustration as a housewife, but it was.

In 1956 or '57, when I was nine or ten, my father relented on the job issue. He said it was for economic reasons. Mom convinced him that we needed the income, so he let her get a job teaching high school biology. Before she started working, I remember that my father believed—and therefore we believed—that her job would be bad for the family. But we kids found it a big relief to get her out of the house. It just gave her someplace to focus her energy. She had homework to do, lessons to plan. She was a meticulous teacher, the kind who gave lots of quizzes. She needed something to obsess over, and she was a good science teacher.

After she got a job, Mom stopped looking into our drawers. But her rules continued. At six o'clock every night, she would stand just outside the back door and ring a cowbell. We had to drop whatever we were doing to run home. Whoever was not in the house at 6:01 p.m. would have to stand in the corner for twice as many minutes as he or she was late. Following Mom's rules was a challenge. For example, you had to anticipate that Mom was going to ring the cowbell so you could be close enough to home to get into the house on time.

My younger siblings, Sam and Martha, tended to break the rules and get punished over and over. I tried to follow the rules because I found that easier than rebelling. Fighting with Mom took too much energy. So I became the "good girl." But that did not mean I got affection from Mom, just less punishment. She was not an affectionate person, except to our cats. I remember coming home in the late afternoon, seeing my mother sitting in the living room in the dark, petting a cat, drinking sherry. It seemed that our cats were the only beings that she got along with. Everybody else aggravated her.

My grandmother (Mom's mother) and Mom would bicker with each other all the time over stupid stuff, like what to cook or whether the living room was vacuumed. I would look forward to my father coming home, because as soon as he walked through the door, all the fussing would stop. He would bring peace into the household. Nobody could argue with him. He had a sense of how he wanted things to go, and what he said was what happened. End of discussion. And that was a relief to me. When he went away on business trips, I sometimes tried to mediate between my brother and my mother. Once I even tried to get my mother and grandmother to calm down. I gave up on that quick!

Dad in the house meant the restoration of peace and quiet, but it did not solve whatever was bothering Mom. Sometimes she would just take off in the car. She would leave dinner cooking on the stove and get in the car and drive around for hours and hours and hours. I wouldn't see her until the next day. No one ever asked her where she went, and she never told us anything. We all acted like it hadn't happened.

Even after she started teaching, my mother was still determined to have the tidiest house on the block. We were her workforce, and she established a weekly regimen. We had to clean bathrooms, vacuum, grocery shop, weed the gardens, and so on. On Saturday morning, I could not go out to play 'til I had washed the bathroom and vacuumed the living room and passed Mom's inspection. Sam was supposed to mop the kitchen floor. Sam resisted, of course, and my parents had a big argument. My father didn't think a boy should have to mop the floor. My brother loved that! He got relieved from doing "women's work." I thought it was unfair. I wanted Dad to get me out of my chores too.

I coped by doing my chores real fast. I can clean a bathroom in record time. That's how I became an efficient person. Why waste time cleaning or arguing with Mom? I'll just do it real quick, just good enough to pass inspection. And then I got out of the house. It was good training for life.

I idolized my father. He was physically affectionate, always hugging us, wrestling with us. Dad didn't obsess over details the way my mother did. He figured out what was important and focused on that. But I disagreed with him on what was important. Because what he thought was important was *my brother*! He loved my sister and me; we were nice to have around. But his priority was his son; he was thrilled to have a son.

Sam was born twenty-two months after I was. As a toddler, I became aware that this baby brother of mine was a bigger deal than I was. This little creature had something that I could never have: a little penis. And my father favored him, spent time with just him.

When I was seven or eight, I confronted my father. I told him I wanted him to do something just with me, the way he did things just with Sam. Dad said, "This is a house full of women. Your mother, your grandmother, you, your sister. I have to spend time with Sam because we are both men."

That was the first time I saw the world could be categorized by gender. Before then, I saw our household split between kids and adults. Dividing it by gender put me in the same category as my mother and grouchy old grandmother. And it elevated Sam to be with Dad. On Saturdays, Dad would take Sam to go do guy things, like playing war in the woods with Dad's friend who was a World War II vet.

I saw Sam as my equal; we were close in age and played together all the time. When we were very small, we made up a game called beaver. I was the father beaver, and Sam was the mother beaver. It all had to do with size—at age five I was bigger than my three-year-old brother, and weren't fathers bigger? When push came to shove, I saw myself as superior to Sam because I was two years older. I could beat him up until I turned eleven and he turned nine, and suddenly he was stronger than me. I remember the moment it happened, our last wrestling match.

I was constantly competing for my father's affection and my mother's attention. One successful approach was being a good student. By the time I was nine or ten, I developed a fantasy about what I would do when I grew up. Both my parents were chemists, and scientific developments were a big topic at dinner table discussions. We got *Time* and *Life* magazines, and my dream was that I would grow up to be so important and such a famous scientist that my picture would be on the cover of *Time* magazine. I'd get married and my husband would be a famous scientist too, and he would be on the *Time* cover too, but a little behind me.

With that fantasy in mind, I went to my father. I thought that he must recognize what a jewel he had in me, so I asked him what he thought I should do when I grew up. I expected him to say, "Oh, be a famous scientist. Get your picture on the cover of *Time* magazine." I expected him to push me into science; after all, both he and my mother were chemists. Instead, he kind of scratched his head and said, "Well, you could be an executive secretary. Or since you're so energetic, maybe a gym teacher."

A secretary? I guess that was the model woman for him. He wanted me to use all my energy to make some man important and effective. I was crushed.

Then I asked my mother the same question. She told me that girls were as smart as boys, and that I could be whatever I wanted to be. I could have a career. But if I wanted to have children, I would have to take time off, like she did. Most important now, she said, was to do well in school. So I learned to get parental attention by being a good student. It spurred me to go out there in the world and do things, because that's how I got recognized at home.

When I was in first grade, I got in wrestling matches all the time in school. I behaved properly in class, but I was hell on the playground during recess. My classmates and I had wrestling matches to establish the pecking order of who was toughest. I earned second place. First place for toughness went to a boy named Glenn, and third place to a boy named Ricky. I don't remember any other girls being involved. It was just Sally and the boys wrestling it out. Being second toughest was a pretty good achievement, especially since I was not only a girl, but small. I was always the second-smallest kid in the class.

One time on the way home from school, I got in a fight with the boy who lived in the house behind us. He was small like me, so it was an even match. I can't remember what we were fighting about, probably who was toughest. It was a knockdown, drag-out fight, right on the sidewalk a few blocks from home. Kids gathered around, cheering for him. Why didn't they cheer for me? I won the fight, but nobody rooted for me. I went home and with tears in my eyes told my mother this story. My mother was sitting in a rocking chair, breast-feeding my baby sister. She looked up at me and, in an off-handed way, said, "Well, they were rooting for him because he was a boy." And I thought, Oh, that's why.

My mother was a feminist, although she never used the word. She just thought women should be treated equally. She never told me that girls weren't supposed to be wrestling boys. (My teachers let me know I wasn't being ladylike, and by second grade I had stopped wrestling during recess.) My mother explained to me that it was an unfair world. Boys and men get the best stuff, even if girls or women are better.

In the 1950s, Port Washington was a middle-class town with some very wealthy areas and a few poor areas. Our house was on a tree-lined street that was the border between a middle-class and a poor neighborhood. There was a hodge-podge of houses on our street, including big old rundown houses with over-grown yards (some were inhabited by old women who we kids were sure were witches), small houses with meticulously planted gardens (like ours), newly built houses, and a few apartment buildings.

My family's friends in the neighborhood were people who belonged to our church, Saint Stephen Episcopal Church. It was a low Episcopal church, my mother explained, not "high falutin'" like some Episcopalians. Most families on the street were white with two or three kids.

But there were lots of different kinds of people on the block. A few houses down from us, three or four Italian families lived in one old house. A big Irish Catholic family lived behind us, and every year Mrs. Malley had another baby. My mother talked about poor Mrs. Malley as an ongoing lesson in the virtues of birth control. She pointed out how harried Mrs. Malley looked, and how she started losing her hair at a young age.

Across the street and down a bunch of steps, there was an apartment build-ing that black families always lived in. The building faced our street, but it was part of the poor neighborhood that adjoined ours. There, little ramshackle houses filled with Polish and Italian immigrants lined narrow streets. Mary Intintoli lived there, and once when she and I were in first grade, I went over to play with her. Her house was narrow and dark, and nothing was painted inside or outside the house. The floor slanted to one side. This strong strange smell pervaded everything—garlic! I had never smelled garlic before and didn't even know what it was. Years later, my classmates would call Mary and her brothers the "ten-ton Tolies" because they were overweight. Kids were mean to those who were dif-ferent.

As long as we lived in Port Washington, several black families always lived across the street from us. One of the children was my age. Willie Barrett and I went to the same schools from first through twelfth grade and graduated from high school together. Looking back, it is amazing to me how little I knew Willie Barrett. It was as if we lived in parallel universes. Sometimes there were ball games in the street that we both played in. And when it snowed, and they closed the street to cars, we all played with our sleds. But those were rare occasions. Mostly my siblings and I played in our backyard with white Protestant kids.

Even in our integrated, ethnically diverse neighborhood, old southern cus-toms persisted. Only once do I remember Willie Barrett coming up my driveway. I was sitting in the yard, and when I saw him, we both suddenly stopped and looked at each other. We were both around ten, and I remember thinking, What is he doing in my backyard? Poor guy. His mother probably told him he wasn't allowed to ring the front doorbell, so he was trying to get to the back door. He had come to tell me that my pet rabbit had been killed by a car.

My awareness of segregation came in 1958, when our family took a trip down south. My mother grew up in the South, and the summer I turned eleven, we went on vacation to the Smoky Mountains in North Carolina. We camped, which was the way we could afford to take a vacation. For several days, we stayed at a campground in Boone, North Carolina, where there is an outdoor theater that performs "Unto These Hills." It is the story of the Trail of Tears, when Cherokee Indians were forcibly removed from North Carolina in the 1830s and marched to Oklahoma.

We kids were thrilled; it was the first time we'd been to an outdoor theater. Before the show started, we were sitting in the audience. My mother said, "This is a show about discrimination against Indians over a hundred years ago. But right here in this theater, colored people are being discriminated against right now." And she turned around and pointed out the "colored section" in the balcony. I looked and saw that the balcony was filled with black people. It was a shock to me, because I had never heard of segregation. Mom told us that segregation was wrong, morally wrong. It wasn't just something in the past; it was happening right there.

But my mother was not about to step out of line and be an activist for integration. Being socially proper hemmed her in. For example, she could have encouraged us to befriend Willie Barrett and other black kids living across the street, but she never did. Instead, she talked about how the world was unjust. She said, "If you are colored, that's a strike against you. If you're a woman, that's a strike against you. If you're a colored woman, that's two strikes against you. And if you're a crippled colored woman, then that's three strikes against you." She saw that discrimination was wrong, but she had no conception that she could do anything about it.

As the 1950s ended, I was a twelve-year-old scrawny girl. I never saw myself as pretty. I had buckteeth, so I wore braces. I was nearsighted, so I got glasses. As I became an adolescent, I got oily skin and pimples and continued to be flat chested. These were the days when Marilyn Monroe was the model for American womanhood. I hated Marilyn Monroe. Not only was I her physical opposite, but I also despised the way she was so vulnerable and subservient to men.

Paul Carl Bermanzohn,
born April 8, 1949, Munich, Germany

Both my parents are Jewish survivors of the Nazi Holocaust. The Nazis killed my grandparents, uncles, aunts, and cousins. One of my father's brothers survived because he went to Brazil in the 1930s, before World War II. He was the only one besides my father. When I was growing up, all the kids in the neighborhood visited their extended families on Sunday. We couldn't have big family dinners, because the Nazis had killed everyone off. I remember being alone in the schoolyard on Sundays. Sundays still spook me out.

My mother, Tema Rosemarin, is the sole survivor of her family. She was seventeen years old in 1939 when the Nazis invaded Poland. She lived in Biala Podlaska, a Polish town near the Russian border. The Nazis killed her parents, three brothers, and one sister. She still grieves for them every day. It is amazing that my mother made it. The Nazis put her in Majdanek, a concentration camp. She escaped twice by jumping off trains to Treblinka, an extermination camp. The Gestapo called her "the Bird" because she would always fly away, out of impossible situations. After she first escaped, she hid out with friends in the woods for weeks. After her second escape, a Christian family sheltered her for nine months, risking their lives. She didn't look stereotypically Jewish—she was blond, blue-eyed, and fluent in Polish, as well as Yiddish, and knew a good deal of Russian as well. She helped the Christian family take care of the children. They taught her the Catholic catechism, which she later used to pretend she was Catholic. The family lived deep in the forest, but after nine months, the Nazis became suspicious and she had to leave.

My father, Leib Bermanzohn, was a slave laborer for the Nazis during World War II. He was twenty-nine years old when the war started, living in the Polish town of Krasnik, also near the Russian border. He was a well-respected tailor in his town, as were his father and his grandfather before him. He had begun working as a tailor when he was twelve. He joined the Jewish Socialist Bund and went on strike with the Bund when he was fourteen. The Bund was an organization of radical Jews in Poland. They formed unions of workers and craftsmen and fought for decent wages and working conditions. My father only told me about this late in his life, because he didn't want to encourage me to become politically active.

When the Nazis invaded Poland in 1939, they enslaved or killed almost all the Jews. The head Nazi warlord in Krasnik forced my father to make a suit for him. The Nazis then forced my father to make Nazi uniforms during the war. In 1944, when the Russians drove the Nazis back and took over Poland, the local Russian boss forced my father to make him a suit. You could tell who was in charge by seeing who wore one of my father's suits.

Krasnik was unusual because the Jewish population was not completely destroyed. About 10 percent, or five hundred out of five thousand, of the Jews survived. The vast majority died. My father has one photograph of his family that he gave me. He told me about everyone in the picture—his grandmother, father, mother, four boys, and three girls. He told me about how each of them died. I don't remember all their stories, but I do remember one. The Nazis drove a lot of Jews, including his brother and youngest sister, into a synagogue and then burned it down, killing everyone in it.

Before the war, my father had his own place, his own store, and a fair amount of money. During the war, he used his money to bribe guards and help improve the conditions for family and friends who were in concentration camps. He got a great reputation for being a dedicated and selfless guy, because he risked himself repeatedly.

My mother, after her second escape and capture, was taken to Majdanek concentration camp. In 1944, the Russians invaded Poland and drove the Nazis back toward Germany. My mother's last escape was during this Russian advance. She was on a forced march from Majdanek to Auschwitz, in front of the Russian advance. The Nazi apparatus was falling apart, but she and the other Jewish prisoners were still wearing striped prison clothes, which identified them as Jews, and which Nazis dogs were trained to attack. She pretended she needed to pee and sneaked away from the guards. She managed to get a civilian skirt and sweater and escaped.

She made her way into Krasnik, my father's town, and met some Jews. She was introduced to this guy who was twelve years older than her. The war ended, and they got married very quickly. They wanted to leave Poland, because after the war there was still an enormous amount of anti-Semitism. Some Poles continued to see Jews as the source of all evil. Roaming gangs of Polish fascists were still killing Jews. My parents fled from Poland to Germany, which was safer for Jews because it was occupied by Allied soldiers. It was also a point of departure to come to the United States. There was tremendous chaos in Europe right after the war. Millions and millions of people had been dislocated and were trying to find some way back to something like a normal life.

My parents lived in Munich for four years, 1945–49, before they were able to get a plane ticket to the United States. It typically took four or five years to get the necessary papers from the United States. "The Americans were in no hurry to have us come," my mother says. Meanwhile, my mother got pregnant, and I was born in Germany on April 8, 1949. Finally they got a plane to the United States in September 1949, when I was six months old.

By the time they landed in New York City, my parents had only two hundred dollars to their name. My father's savings were gone; he had used up all his money during the war and in coming to the United States.

My father had great hopes for the good life in America. He thought he could get a good job, since he was skilled and had a great reputation as a tailor in his hometown. He brought his sewing machine and patterns with him from Poland. But for all his skills, he had a hard time finding work. There was a large immigration of Jewish and Italian tailors at that time, so there was a lot of competition.

My father spoke no English at all, but he immediately set out looking for work. Someone gave him directions about which train and which bus to take to a place where they thought some people might give him work. Of course, he got completely lost in Manhattan. He was all confused, and he didn't know what to do. So he walked up to a cop and pointed to his directions and with his hands asked the guy how to get to this place. And the cop spoke Yiddish, one of the few cops in New York who did.

My father never learned English, even after he had lived here thirty years. Even though he was fluent in Yiddish and Polish and knew some Russian and Hebrew, he could hardly speak English. I got the feeling from him that he had really been defeated very badly in the United States. The war devastated him; he lost his whole family. But he still had his status and reputation in Krasnik after the war. In the United States, he had neither. He was an anonymous, faceless worker, lost in the big city. He slumped. He never said much; he kept everything bottled up inside.

We lived a rough immigrants' life. My father got a job as a custom tailor in a fancy men's clothes shop. They paid him only forty bucks a week. No one could survive on that, and my father was supporting a wife and me, a little baby. We lived in a rundown, raggedy apartment in the Bronx for a year. One day the ceiling collapsed into my crib. I was not in the crib at the time, but it scared my parents. It convinced them that they had to find someplace else to live.

Many Jewish tailors went to work in factories as cutters, working on the assembly line, making suits at high speed for Hart, Shaffner & Marks–type companies, making suits for the racks. My father did not want to work in a factory. He had a very strong thing about not being a worker in any kind of industrial proletarian sense. He always talked about it. A friend of his, an older guy who deserved a lot of respect because of his age and his skills, had been badly mistreated in a factory. His supervisor, some young jerk, yelled at him, and this guy could do nothing 'cause his livelihood depended on it. Despite repeated offers, my father refused to work in a factory.

He was a member of the ILGWU, the International Ladies Garment Workers' Union, which was the big union of the garment district in those days. When he was without a job for four months, he got a few dollars a week in unemployment benefits. But he felt that the union should have gotten him a job.

Finally in the early 1950s, he found a job at Grossman's Department Store on 103rd Street and Lexington Avenue, in Spanish Harlem. He worked there for thirty years, his whole work life. He was the alterations guy, a tremendous diminishment compared to the kind of work that he had done. He could make suits from scratch, fitting people, using patterns. Armies had invaded his town for a Bermanzohn suit! I know firsthand how good he was, because he made suits for me.

He took me to work a few times. That was great fun. Grossman's sold some appliances and clothes, and they did alterations, lots of alterations. My father had a room in the back, a dirty, dingy room with an oily window. I would watch him sew and iron. I was five or six years old, and I got bored. So my father figured out that the best thing I could do was make boxes. They had these cardboard boxes that were flat, and you would fold up the sides, and they had these little cutout sections and hooks that would go through, and you fold them together and you would have a three-dimensional box. So I made boxes and got a penny a box. I made a couple of hundred in a day and would come home with a buck or two. It was great.

My father told me one thing over and over again when I was growing up: "Whatever you do, don't be a worker. A worker's life is a slave's life." He knew, because he really had this miserable job. The Grossmans were decent folks, and they spoke Yiddish. But his conditions were miserable, working in the dingy, dirty back room for low wages.

He had to work six days a week, including Saturday. He and my mother came from Orthodox Jewish families, and we went to an Orthodox synagogue. When they came to this country, my father was determined to remain religious. But he couldn't keep the Sabbath because he was obligated to work on Saturdays. His job pulled him away from what was important to him, going to synagogue every Saturday. He wanted me to become Orthodox, and I'm sure I disappointed him very badly.

Every day he would get up real early, while I was still asleep. He took the No. 5 subway from the Bronx to Manhattan and at the end of the day took the subway back home. My main memory of him when I was a kid was him coming home and sitting down in the living room on this chair, an ugly old chair with thick, scratchy, blue upholstery. It was his chair. He would pull out the *Jewish Daily Forward*, which he read every day in Yiddish. He would read the paper and fall asleep in his chair. That was his existence.

He had little formal education, only third or fourth grade in school in Poland. But he was an intellectual. He had a huge number of books, hundreds of books in Yiddish. He loved to read.

My father was the provider; my mother was the homemaker. At least in that respect, we were a typical 1950s family. My mother saw her work as raising me and my little sister. And she was—and is—intensely proud of the fact that she never had a job outside the home. To her, it was proof that she was fulfilling her role as a woman and a mother. Leaving kids alone or under someone else's care meant that they would grow up rotten kids, prey to all kinds of evil. She was determined that I and my sister were going to grow up to be fine people, modeled after her, no doubt. And that's a pretty good model.

After the ceiling collapsed into my crib, my parents moved to another apartment in the Bronx. I was two or three years old, and that is where my memories begin. Our apartment was in a big, comfortable building on 175th Street off Prospect Avenue, filled with families and lots of kids. We had three and a half rooms—one bedroom, living room, kitchen, half a dining room, bathroom. Every room had windows.

I was given my own room. Ha! My room was the dining room. Everyone had to go through the dining room to get to the kitchen. I had no door, and everybody had to pass through. We ate all our meals in the kitchen. So my room had no privacy at all. Ever. And I lived in there until I finished junior high school—junior high school with no privacy.

When I was five, we got our first telephone. That was very exciting. And around that time we also got a TV, which, of course, made us truly American. We watched *The Ed Sullivan Show* and *The Honeymooners*, with Jackie Gleason as Ralph Kramden the bus driver, the great working-class hero, who I always loved for that.

More than anything else, I grew up with my mother's stories about the Holocaust. She talked constantly about being pursued by Nazis and hiding, her intense fear of being caught. Her parents were taken away, and she didn't know what happened to them. She told me she was in a hiding place, and she saw dogs dragging corpses. She looked out to see if it was her parents that they were dragging. She was a teenager when the war started. It was an immense trauma. She's never gotten over it. You can never overcome something like that. And she still can't stop telling the stories. It's a constant movie in her head that she can never turn off.

One of my earliest memories is being in the park near the house. We lived one block from Crotona Park, a big, beautiful park. The park was our backyard. My mother took me every day to the park when I was little. I remember sitting in the park, and she was trying to force-feed me some juice. She was always trying to feed me something. She was spooning me orange juice from a cup. I was only three or four, and I'm looking around, and she was trying to get my attention. She let a spoonful of juice drop back into the cup, which would form little bubbles. And she would describe the bubbles as if they were a bunch of Jews being pursued by Nazis. She tried to focus my attention on the juice that way.

She couldn't think or talk about anything besides her experiences during the war. She would tell me stories about her family being killed. Her brilliant older brother, the pharmacist, who always helped their parents and looked out for her and her little sister. Her beautiful little sister, with blond curly hair and a lisp. When our daughters were babies, they reminded her of her little sister.

She would tell me these stories and start to cry. I would feel enraged and helpless, wanting to do something to protect her, to make things right somehow. I admired her as a hero and felt an overwhelming need to protect and defend her.

Her stories have haunted me. Whenever I'm on a train or a bus, I always have the thought of whether I could jump off a moving train like she did. Her memories became my memories, even though I never lived them.

The constant theme in my childhood was the danger in the world from the Nazis and the need to be on constant guard. That was the only conclusion from my mother's unending stories. You had to be careful. You had to be prepared. You always had to be ready to get out of town. And, I decided later in life, you had to fight them.

But the Bronx when I was growing up was idyllic. It was a safe and happy time. The neighborhood was filled with Jewish immigrants. Yiddish was commonly spoken. We spoke Yiddish at home. Yiddish was my first language, and I still speak it fluently. To keep secrets, my parents spoke in Polish. When I was five, I started to learn Polish, so they stopped. Had they kept up talking in Polish, I might have learned Polish too.

And across the street from our building was the school that I spent most of my young years in. I went to kindergarten, first, and second grade there, and later to junior high in the same building. School was a very big deal. My parents saw education as the most important thing you can do. They always told me, "Whatever happens, they can't take your education away from you." That was an important value—they had had everything taken away from them.

When I started kindergarten, I didn't know much English. While I was learning English in kindergarten, my mother was going to night school to learn English. I was the first kid in my first-grade class to get a library card of my own. My parents were thrilled, and I was thrilled because they were so proud of me. Having a library card meant I was on my way to being a wonderful student, which was the biggest thing that I could do. Throughout my life, education has been important. I always took school very seriously, and when I didn't, I was relentlessly pursued by my mother. My mother saw to it that no friends interfered with my schoolwork. Homework was the biggest priority, and nothing, nobody, could get in the way of that.

My mother was a very clever and resourceful person. She would never buy stuff for herself. We had a family ritual of shopping at Alexanders, this huge department store at the corner of Fordham Road and the Grand Concourse, at the center of the Bronx. The whole family would go to Alexanders and buy clothes—tons of clothes—and they were always huge on me. My father was the expert on the quality of the material and the quality of the sewing. He was a maven about clothes. And my parents always bought clothes for me real big, so I could grow into them. We would spend the better part of an afternoon or evening at Alexanders. It was two buses to get there and two buses to come back. And when we got back, there would be this fashion show, where I would put on every article of clothing and then my father would feel the material again and we would discuss all this stuff. So he was very involved with dressing me. You know how in some families, food is a way to express love? And in some families there are other ways to express love. In my family it was clothes.

From the time I was a little kid, I was my parents' eyes and ears, their interpreter and guide. Even though I was little. I was the one who spoke English. I knew the society and supposedly what was happening. Sometimes it got us into some pretty funny fixes. Like everybody else, we got junk mail. If you send the return slip back, they are going to send you this and that. So when I was six or seven years old, not reading that well, I was convinced that we were going to get a free Ford Thunderbird. I was sure of it. I filled out the slip and sent it back to them. For months, I would rush home from school thinking that we were going to have a new car. My father was not interested in driving, and neither was my mother. But I thought we were going to get a car, and I was going to make them want to drive. I wanted them to be like normal parents. They were strange; they hardly spoke English; they were immigrants. When my father spoke English, it was almost always to denounce the United States.

When my parents saw something that was innovative and obviously a form of thievery, a way to get your money, they would say, "Amerikeh goniff!" which literally means "America the thief!" But they also had a certain admiration at how innovatively the United States conspired to take your money.

I was their guide in a lot of respects. I was always expected to help them sort through mail and figure out what things meant, and what to do about this and that. To this day, my mother often has me fill out forms for her to be sure everything is right. I probably developed some of my self-confidence in response to being put in this position from the time I was a little kid. I was making decisions that were clearly over my head, but what are you going to do? It was a constant thing. I've heard from other kids in the same kind of Jewish immigrant families that they were put in the same position. You just had to look out for Mom and Dad and take care of them.

I was always treated as a prince, with exaggerated respect. The first-born son, Jewish immigrant family, I was at the head of the table all the time for Passover seder and all the ceremonies. I was the main attraction.

My sister, Fran, was born when I was about eight and a half years old. Status was based on sex in my house, and my sister was the unlucky one in that respect. She was younger and female, and so she was treated as a second-class citizen. She rebelled and became a feminist and a super-high-achieving Wall Street lawyer.

My mother is a very intense person. She doesn't talk so much as she harangues, and she is not even aware of it. She gets upset when people feel that she is attacking them, because she just talks like that. She is a very high-pressure, driven person, not someone who relaxes very much.

My father, on the other hand, was a very quiet, even passive, kind of guy. "Laid back" is not exactly right, because he was a worrier. He was a quiet, withdrawn man. My mother could not stop talking about the Holocaust, ever. My father never talked about it, and I had to pressure him to get any information about his experience during the war. They were real opposites, and since opposites attract, they must have been extremely attracted to one another. Actually, I think my father would withdraw into reading because my mother was always talking, and he just liked it low key and quiet.

When I was a kid, I always thought that my mother was the strong one, whose strength led her to be able to talk about the Holocaust. I was about fifteen or sixteen when I mentioned to my father that I felt my mother was strong. He looked at me sadly and a little surprised and said, "She is so nervous." It was a whole different spin on my mother. But later in life, I began to realize that my father wanted to protect us from what was just too horrible for words. And now that I am a parent, I understand my father better. When our kids were growing up, I didn't talk to them much about the Greensboro massacre at all. Why lay it on these little kids?

My dad was a man who really loved beauty. A few years before he died, I started taking him to concerts. He was totally into music, especially Mozart. My mother wouldn't go with us; she didn't want to leave the house. At my father's funeral, my sister said that she always went to my father when she wanted something beautiful that might cost some money. My mother was real tightfisted.

My best friend, Donny Grenadier, who lived up the block, had what looked to me like a normal family. When Donny turned thirteen, he had a bar mitzvah, a big fancy celebration of coming of age in the Jewish community. I wanted a bar mitzvah like that. Now, his father was an accountant and his mother's father had a clothing store that they owned, so they were in much better financial shape than we were. My father asked me if I wouldn't prefer a family car rather than a bar mitzvah. I said, "No, I want a bar mitzvah," because it was a big social event. So my mother was determined to get me a bar mitzvah just like Donny's. My father was dragged along in this. At my bar mitzvah, my father was really nervous, because it was costing him several thousand dollars for this party. His hand was shaking, and he drank at the bar mitzvah—and he was not a drinker. He was trying to steady himself with some alcohol. And only later I realized, Wow, this was not his idea. It was my idea and my mother's idea. I think my mother and I were often aligned.

The neighborhood had many of the qualities of a shtetl, a little Jewish town, right in the middle of New York City. There were five or six huge apartment buildings on the block on 175th Street filled with Jewish immigrants. Anywhere

I went, particularly in the warm weather, there was a line of women sitting in chairs along the block, chattering away in Yiddish or broken English. They knew all the kids, and as you passed by they would make comments on whether your shirt was hanging out of your pants, or whether you were clean. "Where are you going? Does your mother know where you are?" As I got older, that got to be a huge pain in the ass. But looking back on it now, with the kind of society we live in today where things are so atomized and fragmented, it was very safe. It was a very nice place to be.

My mother was really extremely protective—overprotective, I would say. And she didn't want me to do anything. I was not allowed to cross the street myself until I was ten years old. It was only when school required it that I was able to cross the street.

I remember one particular night, when I was five years old, being brought to the park late at night. These days you don't go in Crotona Park after dark. But I distinctly remember being dragged along by the hand by my parents into the park at night, and it was filled with people. About a block into the park was Indian Rock, which was covered with people with instruments. All these people had gotten together for this improvisational little concert, and they were all jabbering away in Yiddish and playing music. It was boring to me at the time, but it is really pretty amazing in retrospect.

But suddenly, in the late 1950s, Jews rapidly moved out of the East Bronx and people of color moved in. The people moving in were poorer, and the neighborhood became rundown. Eventually landlords began burning down their own buildings so they could get insurance money. Many people blamed the deterioration of the neighborhood on black and Puerto Rican people. But the truth is that they were the biggest victims of big economic and social forces at work.

A big factor that weakened the old neighborhood Bronx was the construction of the Cross-Bronx Expressway. To go to school, we crossed through the construction site, through the debris. One day, my shoe got sucked off in the mud.

Robert Caro, in his book *The Power Broker*, on Robert Moses, describes how the highway construction wrecked the area, destroying hundreds of huge apartment buildings and displacing thousands of people. This construction stimulated the migration. School friends of mine disappeared as their families moved out.

The neighborhood had become racially mixed gradually over the years, and there was a lot of racism against blacks. One of my closest friends in grade school was Clark Jones, a black kid. And some of our neighbors frowned on me hanging around with Clark and complained to my mother. My mother said, "This is a kid, and my son's friend. His color is not important. He's welcome here whenever he wants to be here." Often Clark would come with me when I went home for lunch or after school. Clark liked to come over because my mother always gave us cookies.

During the highway construction, the neighborhood became less desirable. Gang activity picked up as the neighborhood became poorer. Many people blamed the gang activity on people of color, but white street gangs preceded the black gangs. I was attacked twice in grade school by white gangs. Once I was stuck with a handful of pins; another time, a group of white thugs surrounded two friends and me and spat at us.

When I was in junior high school, there started to be more gang violence in the neighborhood. The main gangs were the Kings and the Crowns, and they contended for territory in our neighborhood. Several times, I saw these absolutely horrifying gang fights where people got hurt badly. One time from my window, I saw a guy smash another guy over the head with a gumball machine. Another time, I was playing with a bunch of kids in a basketball court right next to the school. Suddenly the area was surrounded by a gang, and everybody got quiet. The gang told everybody to get out of the basketball court, because they were looking for somebody who had done something and they wanted revenge. This was right when the movie *West Side Story* came out, so gangs were becoming a recognized explanation for New York's problems. Like in *West Side Story,* problems were seen racially.

Very quickly, it seemed, many people moved out of the neighborhood. The people who stayed were the ones who couldn't move out for economic reasons, like my family. For years when I was in junior high school, I wanted us to move. I had friends who had moved to Pelham Parkway, which was further north in the Bronx and which had a large Jewish population. A girl I liked lived there, and I wanted to chase after her. Eventually, we did move there.

In the following decade, burned buildings made the South and East Bronx a national symbol of urban decay. As poor people moved into the Bronx, rents became harder to collect. Landlords torched their buildings, and much of the South Bronx in the sixties looked like Europe after World War II. Strong old buildings were reduced to charred rubble. A few buildings on my block went that route.

But we had moved to Pelham Parkway the summer before I started high school. My parents planned our move so it wouldn't interfere with my schooling. By this time, I was really aware of my father's working-class status. He worked hard; he was paid lousy; he really didn't have much of a life. Moving was a shocking experience because everything that my family owned, absolutely everything, fit into this little truck. And the truck drove to our new apartment in Pelham Parkway, which was too small. Somehow my mother worked out a way to get into the public housing projects in Pelham Parkway. That was a very big deal, because they were really hard to get into. For the first time, I got my own room, a room that had a door on it! Fabulous. High school was a time I actually had privacy for the first time in my life. I went through high school and college living in the projects with my parents and my sister.

Marty Arthur (Nathan), born January 17, 1951, Westerville, Ohio

My earliest memory? I was two or three years old, dressed only in my underpants, running around the neighborhood with a gang of kids. I loved being outdoors, and in the summer I was always outdoors. We kids played all the time, making mud pies, making piles of leaves and jumping in them. When we got bigger, we made forts we climbed into. We roamed through the backyards, and in and out of each other's houses.

We were always getting into things. I was the younger daughter and I got into trouble a lot. I broke my big sister's dollhouse—that's what I was told over and over.

But there was a pall over my happiness. My mother was emotionally ill, and my parents argued a lot. Mary Ann, my sister eight years older than me, worried whether this family was going to stay together. Soon I worried too. I knew something horrible could happen.

When I was five or six, many nights after I was supposed to be asleep I would hear my parents yelling at each other. I would go to the top of the stairs just to check to make sure that my parents were okay. I was afraid they might hurt each other. I just wanted to hear their voices. "Are you okay?" I would say in a little voice. "Everything is okay," my mother or father would say. I would feel better but would still worry.

We lived in Westerville, a very small town in Ohio, a Republican farm town. When I was growing up, there were less than a thousand people living there. We lived in a "double," a double-occupancy house, which we rented from an old man. It was a low-rent house built at the turn of the century, on a nice old street where everybody knew everybody and no doors were locked. We shared a big backyard with the other side of the double. My mother grew a flower garden, and I played with the neighborhood kids.

It was nice. We didn't have a lot of money, but we did okay. I think we paid fifty dollars a month rent. That's what I remember my dad saying.

My parents' marriage was conflicted from the beginning. My dad, Bill Arthur, was the town rebel. He was smart, good-looking, and poor. He was a poor kid who grew up to be a union organizer and who fell in love with the daughter of the richest man in town.

My mother, Marian Jones, was a beauty and college-educated. Her father, Hanby Jones, was outraged that she fell for the town rebel, this lower-class socialist labor organizer. Hanby Jones's family had lived around Westerville for generations, and he became rich as a lawyer and then a landowner. He sold off much of the land around Westerville, and I imagine that there were scandals involved, but I never knew them. He was not a very nice man to me. I never liked him; I was afraid of him. He was elderly and infirm by the time I knew him.

In the 1930s, Hanby Jones sent my mother to New York City to get her away from Bill Arthur. Marian worked for two years in New York City as a secretary during the Depression. There are wonderful pictures of her walking down the streets of New York. She was a very beautiful lady, and she looked very free during those years. My grandparents' plan for their daughter didn't work. Marian had a good time in New York and then came back to marry my father.

My father had conflicts in his own family. His father, Lew Arthur, was an abusive alcoholic. My mom told me he was in the Ku Klux Klan, although the family denies that now. Lew neglected his family and may have beat his wife and kids. He couldn't hold down a job, and his family of five sometimes lived on the dole. I remember my father being angry at his father.

So as a child, I learned who the bad guys were. They were racists, they were greedy, they abused women, and they were right there in my family.

I also learned that there were good guys. My father was my working-class hero. He was strong willed, independent, honest, controversial, and hard talking. Sometimes he was harsh, but overall I developed deep respect for him.

I learned very early about class, about the difference between rich and poor. Conflicts could be complicated, and often class issues—exploitation, injustice—were in there. My father went to work at fifteen to support his family. As a teenager, my dad learned firsthand about workers getting exploited. Later he found the labor movement to be an answer to his struggles. Building unions consumed his life.

When he married, he found more class conflict, because his in-laws scorned him for being poor and radical. He was a socialist, he told me once in the early 1960s. He added, "I know this is a dirty word for some people." He let me know that this was something I shouldn't go around and talk about.

In 1943, my sister was born. When she was only a few months old, my father was drafted into the army and sent to England as a supply sergeant. He should never have been drafted—he was thirty-seven and had two hernias, poor vision, and an infant child.

He was drafted for political reasons, because he was one of two organizers for Eastern Greyhound for what later became the Amalgamated Transit Union. Everyone who knew him believed that Greyhound got him drafted to break up the union work. He was a leader who came back from the war and eventually was elected president of two or three bus-driver locals. He also held a position as an elected official in the national union.

My mother had to move back in with her parents while my father was away in the war. She had this brand-new baby and was worried about my father. She got severely depressed and developed obsessive-compulsive disorder, which plagued her for the rest of her life.

That was the family into which I was born.

Growing up, I got strong messages from my parents—mainly positive from my father and mainly negative from my mother. First, my father said that the most important thing for people to do was "work for the working man." (Of course I later transmuted that to "work for working men *and women*.") Second, he taught me, "You be honest and fair." Third was "get an education." Those were what I was to do in my life. And that was radical in small-town Ohio, where folks were very conservative. Good folks, kind folks, can be generous folks—but not generous the way my father meant generosity. He thought that people should share the product of their labor! That was not something that sat well with Hanby Jones's Westerville!

My mom felt caught in the middle, between her husband and father. She was also struggling for her own issues, like, "Why am I being left alone all the time?" because my dad was never around. He had two jobs, as a bus driver and as president of his union, and they kept him on the road.

His absence was the source of my parents' arguments. He did virtually nothing to take care of us kids. But we loved him; especially I loved him. My sister didn't know him very well. Maybe it was because she was born while he was away in the war. The conflict he raised for me early on, which flowered in my own life, was the contradiction between the political and the personal.

When I was five or six, my mom got worse and threatened suicide. She was hospitalized for eight weeks. She went through electric shock therapy and was on medication.

While my mother was in the hospital, my father was home. I liked having him around, even though he was a gruff son of a gun. I learned every swear word I know from him and from my mother, who also used to use them constantly. I remember curse words fondly because that was the language of work. That was the language of unions. You don't let a sentence go by without using it as a chance to swear! My father was hard but he was fun too. I understood that my dad was doing important work and I liked that.

I learned about victims from my mother. I watched people treat my mom badly because she was emotionally ill. I got the feeling she was not considered acceptable in polite society. She talked about her fears and problems and didn't hide her illness. That made her completely uncool. I loved my mother deeply and I felt for her. At the same time, I saw how society could shun people who were not acceptable. I wanted to protect her but felt inadequate.

So in the late 1950s, as a young child, I'm trying to figure my place in the world. I was on the nine-year-old's quest: What do I want to be when I grow up? I have a mother who is emotionally ill but who loves me very much. And a father who is giving me this strong message about fighting for the working man, but who is absent a lot. It was confusing, to say the least.

But I knew what I wanted—to grow up and get the hell out of there! That was what my father did. He got the hell out of there. He was gone. And he stayed away most of the time. My mother's depression was sad—to be in a house with depression is a sad thing. You bear the burden of your parent's sadness, and you want to make it better all the time for that parent who loves you. She was a very loving mother. But I felt, I've got to get out of here. I got to run away from this. This is too much for me.

Children don't think of themselves as children, they think of themselves as somebody who should take care of everything. I didn't feel like I could take care of my mother and I didn't want to be unhappy like her. It was clear to me that to get any happiness and respect, I had to leave my family, get an education, and get a job. That was where my drive to become a professional came from, to be an actor in the world like my father. That is where my obsession with work comes from. If you stay at home, you lie in bed all day crying like my mom.

Gallery I.
Growing Up
and the Sixties

Willena Reaves, farm girl
with piglet, late 1950s.

Willena Reaves in high
school, 1959.

Sally Avery, *right,* with brother and sister, 1956.
(Photo by Roy Avery)

Sally and Mike Nathan at Duke graduation,
1969, two months after they married.

Marty Arthur with her father, big sister, and
mother, 1950s.

Paul Bermanzohn with his parents, Munich,
Germany, 1949.

Paul Bermanzohn at
City College, 1968.

Nelson Johnson,
March 1968.
(Courtesy of *News &
Record*, Greensboro,
N.C.)

2

The Sixties: Joining the Movement

In the mid–twentieth century, the United States portrayed itself as the leader of the free world at the same time it segregated its own citizens. In the 1950s, a grassroots civil rights movement led by Martin Luther King Jr. challenged the social order. In 1960, four black Greensboro college students sat down and asked for service at a Woolworth's lunch counter. They were denied service and returned the next day with hundreds more students. The sit-in movement caught fire in cities throughout the South and other parts of the nation. Young African Americans overcame the fear that had paralyzed generations of blacks and gave new energy to the civil rights movement. Meanwhile, halfway around the world, the war in Vietnam escalated. As the nightly news reported the rising death toll of American GIs and the destruction of Vietnam, an antiwar movement mushroomed on college campuses.

During the exuberant early sixties, new national leaders emerged: John Kennedy, Martin Luther King Jr., Malcolm X, Robert Kennedy. But hope and enthusiasm turned to anger as assassins took the lives of these national figures and the war ground on.

Nelson ■ The sixties was a decade of great hope, high expectations, and energy. A huge number of people got involved in the process of change, and that was revolutionary in itself.

Paul ■ We fought against the U.S. military's war in Vietnam and for civil rights. Martin Luther King Jr. was my hero.

Willena ■ The sixties was a brand-new world opening up for me. We didn't have to take all that stuff from white people anymore. We made changes; everyone was involved, young and old. It was a blossoming time, a learning time about what was really happening in the world.

Kwame ■ And in 1968, I was born!

Marty ■ The sixties for me was a time of sadness, the deaths of my father and my sister. At the same time, a wonderful movement for social change grew.

Sally ■ I joined the civil rights movement in the sixties, and by the end of the decade, I was fighting for women's liberation as well.

Before 1960, Willena, Nelson, Paul, Marty, and I were leading our separate lives. But in the 1960s, we all were affected by the same big events—the Greensboro sit-ins, Kennedy's election and assassination, the war in Vietnam. We began the journeys that would ultimately bring our lives together.

Greensboro Sit-ins, February 1, 1960

Nelson ■ On February 1, 1960, four young men from North Carolina A&T College walked into Woolworth's in downtown Greensboro. They bought a tube of toothpaste and then sat down at the lunch counter and ordered coffee. The waitress told them, "We do not serve Negroes." So they sat in until closing time that day.

I was a junior in high school and watched it on the TV with my family. It reminded me of my sit-in with my friend George at the ice cream store in Littleton. But in Greensboro, the A&T students made the news and stayed in the news.

The next day, and the day after, the A&T students came back with more students who demanded to be seated. Woolworth's shut down the lunch counter rather than serve blacks. White owners waffled on giving in, but the new sit-in tactic took hold. Within two months, the sit-in movement spread to fifty-four cities in nine states. Within a year, more than one hundred cities had had student-led demonstrations against segregated public facilities. Some scholars have compared the Greensboro sit-in with the Boston Tea Party in terms of its impact on history.

Many young people today think the four students sat down at Woolworth's and then restaurants throughout the South desegregated. In truth, the struggle to desegregate that one lunch counter in downtown Greensboro went on for six months. Even after Woolworth's started serving blacks, all the other businesses continued their racist practices.

A&T has a strong tradition of activism. The full name of the school is North Carolina Agricultural and Technical State University. It was formed during Reconstruction and has been a center of African American culture and resistance. Going to college at A&T is a strong tradition in my family. My father went to high school at A&T. Five of us kids ended up going to college at A&T.[1]

Willena ■ When the A&T students sat down at Woolworth's, they made the news all over the country. But I was in Mullins, and people didn't talk about nothing in Mullins. I didn't hear about the sit-ins until I came to A&T as a freshman a year and a half later.

Kennedy versus Nixon, the 1960 Presidential Election

Nelson ■ In 1960, I was the mock-campaign manager for Nixon in my high school. The presidential contest between John F. Kennedy and Richard Nixon generated a powerful discussion in my high school, leading up to a straw vote.

Why was I for Nixon? Because of Jackie Robinson, the baseball great, the first African American player in the national league. Robinson was everybody's hero, and I heard Robinson speak in 1959, just a few years after he had retired from baseball. Greensboro had just built a brand-new coliseum, and I went with my father to hear Jackie Robinson speak there. A lot of black people from all over the state came to hear him. And Robinson was a spokesperson for Nixon. That did it for me: I went and campaigned for Nixon. And in the straw election, the majority of kids in my high school voted for Kennedy. I lost.

Forty years later, my Nixon history caught up with me. Last year, I was invited to be on a panel in Winston-Salem for the fortieth anniversary of the sit-in movement. I did my speech, trying to put the sit-ins in context. During the question period, a guy got up and said, "I'm from Littleton, North Carolina, and I have been following you, and I'm proud of you. But one thing I've never been able to figure out. When I was in the fourth grade, I remember you campaigned for Nixon."

Here I am in this auditorium full of people, forty years later, and I said, "Oh—there's a long story. The short version is, blame it on Jackie Robinson."

Sally ■ My parents supported Nixon in 1960. My mother usually voted Republican, because she was from the South and hated the Dixiecrats, who were pro-segregation Democrats. My father voted Republican because he was from the Midwest, and most people were Republicans out there.

I was in eighth grade, and my social studies class had a debate over the election. I was part of the pro-Nixon team. My mother told me that it would be bad for Kennedy to be elected because then the pope in Rome would be telling the president what to do. I felt obligated to repeat that to my class, many of whom were Roman Catholics. After the debate, the teacher asked the class to raise their hands to show who they supported. To my surprise, Kennedy won!

Paul ■ My family and my whole neighborhood were for JFK. I remember one of my friends saying, "They'll never let Kennedy win, because he is Catholic."

Willena ■ I remember my father talking about John Fitzgerald Kennedy as the great white hope. He thought Kennedy was decent and would do the right thing about civil rights.

Marty ▪ I was nine years old and living in a Republican area. I was one of two kids in my fourth grade class who supported Kennedy. I wore a Kennedy hat, Kennedy dress, Kennedy everything, just covered from head to toe with Kennedy paraphernalia. I went to class and gave a speech in a mock debate on the election. My father wrote the speech—I don't think I understood a word of it.

To be pro-Kennedy in our town was to be a left-winger. That was my first experience of being a political minority. I noticed that all the people who were comfortable were voting for Nixon. And all of us who rented were voting for Kennedy. I thought, Okay, that's how you divide the world—the people who own houses and those who rent.

Westerville was all white, all Protestant. There was one African American family in the whole town. I never met any Jews until I moved out of Westerville. The only minority person in my class was one Irish Catholic.

My father was pro–civil rights; he talked about it a lot. He respected Martin Luther King. Although he rarely talked about being in World War II, he did tell me that he was in a group with South Carolina whites. Something happened, something involving race. Every time he talked about it, he got bitterly angry and said he never again wanted to put up with "crackers." In his union work, he supported getting the baggage men, who were black, into the union with the drivers, who were white. He was known for pushing for equal rights.

In 1961 we traveled south to Florida, and I remember just being appalled by what I saw—the combination of race and poverty, black people living in shacks in the South. And I thought, Something has to be done about this. That is my main memory of the trip. I don't remember the beaches in Florida; I just remember the shacks on Route 301.

Growing Social Unrest, 1961–63

Willena ▪ I came to A&T to college in September 1961 and got involved with the student movement. The Woolworth sit-ins had just happened the year before, and people were talking about doing more. All that struggle in '60 meant only that we could go and eat at Woolworth's and sit on those uncomfortable little stools. But we could not get served at other places, like the K&W Cafeteria, which had good food and nice tables. If we wanted to eat K&W food, we had to go to a window and buy the food and then walk down the street to eat it. We couldn't go inside.

That kind of stuff causes a lot of pain inside you. I felt like I already had experienced a lot of damage. I had a big burden from growing up in South Carolina and seeing the Klan murder a man when I was just a young child. I wanted to get rid of that baggage. Through joining the protests, I got rid of that burden completely.

There was lots of discussion among the students. My boyfriend, John Cannon, who I later married, was from Springfield, Massachusetts. He said that they didn't have segregation there, and that he wasn't going to get involved. I told him he was a nigger no matter where he came from, that he faced restraints, and that it was a fight everywhere. He decided to join in. Of course, I'm not sure if I convinced him or if he joined in because we were dating.

We focused our sit-in on K&W Cafeteria and Carolina Theater, where blacks could only sit in the balcony. People at A&T told the juniors and seniors not to protest, because it could hurt them graduating and getting jobs. "Let the freshmen and sophomores do it," they said. But the juniors and seniors said, "Why should we graduate and go out there in this mess? Let's fight it right here, right now."

We went to K&W and tried to go in. The police were there and said, "Move! You cannot go in. If you don't move, you will be arrested."

The whole school came out in protest—four thousand of us! We were sitting on the street at a major intersection downtown, the corner of Elm and Market Streets. We filled the road, making a huge cross, blocking downtown Greensboro. Then came the paddy wagons. I was afraid—These people are going to run over us; I know what they are capable of. But after a while, even if they treat us like dogs, we've got to stand up and fight. Even if you have to die. A paddy wagon fender pushed us enough to try to make us run, but we didn't move. They arrested so many of us, we filled up the Greensboro jail. They had to convert buildings to jails and put people in jails in High Point and Graham.

Nelson ■ My brother Ivan was a student at A&T with Willena, and he also was arrested in that protest. He told me how the students clogged up the jail. The students wanted to stay in jail until the K&W owners decided to serve black people at their restaurant. Finally the A&T president told the students that Martin Luther King was coming to speak at A&T, and that they needed to get out of jail to hear him. So they left the jail. But there was no Martin Luther King. It was only a trick to get them out of jail.

Willena ■ The things I did as a student—the sit-ins—felt so good. It was a taste of freedom. Any time we won, it did something to me. I was getting even, even though it wasn't directly for me. I was getting back at the system. We started protesting any injustice. When the sheriff was trying to put a woman with eight children out of her house, we surrounded the house and made such a big deal that the sheriff had to leave.

We began to discuss which way to freedom. How do you really get rid of this whole racism and secondary citizenship? That led me to look at and study all kinds of things.

Paul ■ The trial of Adolf Eichmann made a big impression on me. Eichmann was a Nazi, Hitler's Jewish expert, who had engineered the mass extermination of the Jews during World War II. In early 1961, Israeli Secret Service agents located Eichmann in Argentina and kidnapped him. They flew him in a special plane from Argentina to Israel and put him on trial for crimes against humanity. Dozens of Jewish Holocaust survivors were brought to Israel to testify in court.

The Eichmann trial was riveting. I vividly remember the images on TV of Eichmann being humiliated. There was such hatred of this guy, which I shared fully, that they were afraid someone would kill him. In the courtroom they put him in a little glass cage with bulletproof glass. I was so glad that they got that bastard.

Suddenly, all the stories that my mother had told me were being trumpeted by the media all over the world. For the first time, my mother was able to talk about things in a more coherent way, rather than just frothing over. I think it was very helpful to a lot of survivors for that trial to go on. I learned a lot about what happened. I collected every article I could find in the *Daily News* and the *Post*.

I also remember seeing civil rights demonstrations. In Selma, the march across the bridge. In Birmingham, the police using water hoses and dogs against demonstrators.

I started high school in September 1961. For the first time I could travel on the subways by myself to get to school. This was a big deal in my struggle to get away from my mother's clutches. I went to the Bronx High School of Science with all these kids who were the smartest kids in their junior high schools. We were all brought together into this super–pressure cooker of a high school. I hated it because it was so intense, the expectations so high. There were lots of Jewish kids and a large number of African American kids. The racial tensions were intense. I remember a couple of white guys making nasty racist jokes about niggers getting killed that they thought were very funny. And these black girls gave them outraged looks. I began to become aware just how bad this sort of "humor" was.

Sally ■ I loved to debate. It was one way I could get my aggression out. In high school, I was in a debate titled "Labor Unions: Good or Bad?" I volunteered as a debater before they decided which side I would be on. Then they put me on the pro-union side. I was upset, because my main motivation was to *win* the debate. I thought it would be easier to win the anti-union side.

To argue pro-union, I had to learn something about them, and nobody in my family knew anything. But my grandmother worked as a typist for a man who was a consumer advocate. He was an atheist, which my grandmother strongly disapproved of. But he was also pro-union, and he was a great source of information. He gave me a graph showing that workers' wages had gone up, but not near as much as corporate profits. So I went into that debate armed with information, and my side won! I was extremely proud of myself. And in the process, I became genuinely pro-union.

My mother was becoming pro-union at the same time that I was. She had gotten a job at Plainview High School and joined one of the early teachers' unions. Soon after she joined, the teachers went out on strike. Teachers' unions were very controversial in the early 1960s, and the press portrayed the teachers as selfish, shirking their responsibilities to their students and the public. But my mother resolutely honored the strike and refused to cross the picket line. I encouraged her to walk on the picket line, but that she would not do.

I was proud of her for supporting her union and felt I had played a role in winning my family to unionism. This made me feel powerful and influential in my family. For the rest of her life, my mother was pro-labor. She also became resolutely pro–civil rights, switching her party allegiance to the Democrats in 1964. My father followed suit a few elections later.

The civil rights movement became real to me in 1963 when I met two Freedom Riders, two young, white college students who spoke at a meeting of the Honor Society at my high school. They talked to us about their bus ride through the South to protest segregation. There were blacks and whites on the bus, and they had been attacked by racist whites. The young woman kept her hat on because her hair had been burned off, and she was embarrassed about how she looked. These Freedom Riders had a huge impact on me. They were only a few years older than I; they were doing something to right what was wrong.

A lot of grownups in my town supported the civil rights movement. They brought speakers to our high school, like Jesse Gray, a tenant organizer leading a rent strike in Harlem. Many of those supporting civil rights were Jews, and I learned about the Holocaust in Europe and racial discrimination in the United States at the same time.

The Diary of Anne Frank was the most important book to me growing up. Anne Frank died in 1945, less than two years before I was born. I loved her diary and started keeping my own. She had all these conflicts with her sister and with her family, and their life was so hard, hiding out from the Nazis in secret rooms, year after year. I felt that she knew that she was special, that her diary was special. She was trying to survive the war so that she could be discovered. I identified with her; I wanted to be discovered.

I decided to go South to college and join the civil rights movement. I wanted to be part of what was happening down there. I took a trip during the summer before my last year in high school and fell in love with Duke's beautiful campus (and a cute admissions officer). No one else in my high school class wanted to go south for college. One friend told me he didn't think there was such a thing as a smart southerner.

My mother obsessed over the civil rights movement. She was against segregation, but also against the Freedom Riders. She thought they were like the carpetbaggers, who during Reconstruction came from the North to the South and supported black political rights. She said that in the South if somebody didn't like you and you were from out of town, they labeled you a carpetbagger. You were an outsider messing in the South's business. Her logic made no sense to me. Segregation is wrong, but you can't do anything about it? I felt obligated to do something for equal rights.

As I decided to apply to Duke, my mother strongly encouraged me. She didn't like the way many northern liberals wrote off the whole South. So I headed off to North Carolina with a sense of mission—to work for civil rights and to see what was really happening, not just what my friends thought was happening from a distance. I listened to Bob Dylan sing "The Times, They Are A-Changin'," and I wanted to be part of it. The South pulled me like a magnet.

Nelson ■ I volunteered for Vietnam. It was before the Gulf of Tonkin, before the massive buildup of American forces. I wanted to go, so I volunteered.

Then I went to New York City on my pass, to stay with my aunt for a couple of days. I told her I had volunteered for Vietnam. She was stunned and said, "I had no idea that my sister raised this big a fool."

That hurt, and I couldn't understand why she would say that. She asked me, "Why do you want to go to Vietnam?"

I told her, "Because I want combat pay." I was sending money home to my brother, and it was a chance to make eighty dollars more a month for combat pay.

My aunt looked me in the eye and said, "Do you know that is a war that is killing folk? What have those folks done to you?"

I couldn't answer her question. I didn't know what they were fighting about. All I could say was, "I'm going to defend the country."

"Defend the country? Just how do the Vietnamese threaten the U.S.? What have they done to you?" It planted a question that I never could answer. My aunt was not a politico. She was concerned about my life.

As it turns out, I didn't go to Vietnam, because I was considered too young and too inexperienced. At the time they were looking for older, more seasoned men. I was still a teenager, was just turning twenty. I got sent to Europe.

My aunt's questions made me begin to grapple with the deep dual allegiance that I had. I was loyal to black folks and to America. For a long time, I didn't see the contradictions. In my mind, the America I was loyal to was almost empty of people. It was the high ideals—democracy, freedom, justice, "the American way." I didn't connect it to the white people that were so offensive to me.

The Assassination of John F. Kennedy, November 22, 1963

Nelson ■ I was stationed at Westover Field in Springfield, Massachusetts. I was an air policeman in a restricted zone that had to do with Strategic Air Command. While I was on patrol on November 22, 1963, word came out that we were immediately dropping to a DEF CON Two—Defense Condition Two. That was one level above Defense Condition One, which meant war is imminent. We had just been in Defense Condition One around the Cuban missile crisis.

Word flashed that the president had been assassinated, and we were all frozen: All leaves, all passes, everything was killed. We took on all these tasks to secure the base. It meant staying on the base, out there in the cold weather, guarding these planes. It was a deeply mournful time, affecting everyone across the board. I grieved along with everybody else. We were stuck on duty and stuck on base, and we all grieved there together.

Marty ■ I was in seventh grade, and at the end of the school day, there was an announcement over the public address system that President Kennedy had been shot. Some kid yelled out, "Yeah! Kennedy's been shot!" Kennedy was hated in my town because not only was he a Democrat and a Catholic, but also pro–civil rights and pro-union. For us in the workers' movement, Kennedy was our man. My family was in mourning, and we just sat and watched the TV for three days. We watched Lee Harvey Oswald, the man accused of killing Kennedy, get murdered right there live on TV. It was amazing that such things could happen.

Sally ■ When JFK was assassinated, I was in gym class in high school, playing volleyball. Suddenly, the loudspeaker came on and a radio voice said that President Kennedy had been shot. Everything stopped. A girl ran shrieking across the room; the rest of us just sat on the floor, stunned. A short time later, the loudspeaker came on again, announcing that Kennedy was dead. They closed school early, and I remember walking down Main Street with other kids, a quiet, sad little procession, to various churches in the town. Even though my parents had not voted for Kennedy, he was our president. And my father had heard him speak at a conference and was impressed.

Willena ■ I was at A&T when Kennedy was killed. I actually felt two ways. On the one hand, Kennedy represented hope; I wanted to believe that he was going to do something for black people. On the other hand, I knew that he was getting the CIA to fight national liberation struggles in Africa and Latin America.[2]

Paul ■   I was walking down the hall in high school, and suddenly people were turning on radios, which was not allowed. An announcement came on that the president had been shot. There were gasps and demands to know what was going on—what's happening? They let us out of school, and a bunch of us walked to the subway station, talking about what was going on. The big comment was, "I hope they got Lyndon Johnson too." People hated LBJ because he was a southern redneck, and the civil rights movement had made rednecks the worst possible thing that you could be.

The Assassination of Malcolm X, February 21, 1965

Willena ■   When Malcolm X was assassinated, it was a really bad time for black people. I loved the man, everything about him. I felt he spoke the truth about the problem of this country and black people. There was nothing wrong with him. But there were blacks who said he was trouble, that he was leading people down the wrong road, that he taught hate. I felt like the government was behind killing him. And later I learned that Malcolm was getting ready to bring the black problem to the world stage. He represented a most sensible way of gaining freedom. The day of his assassination was truly a bleak day.

Sally ■   When Malcolm X was killed, I was a senior in high school on Long Island. My town was fifteen miles from Harlem, but I had never heard of Malcolm X, not even that he had been killed. It was like Harlem was a different country. My main source of news was magazines like *Time* and *Life*, and they only portrayed white people.

Several years later, I read *The Autobiography of Malcolm X*, and that was where I learned what an amazing person Malcolm was, and how outrageous it was that he was assassinated.

Nelson ■   When Malcolm got killed, I was stationed in Europe. All the press— *Life* and *Colliers* magazines, and *Stars and Stripes,* the official military paper— printed negative articles on Malcolm, using all the language about him being in a hate group. These articles polarized the discussions in the barracks. At the time, I was a deep believer in Martin King, drawn to his integrity. I felt King was a powerful speaker and a persuasive person, true to himself and to his beliefs. I had heard very little about Malcolm X except the news articles that presented him as a crazy man, a demon.

The discussions after Malcolm X's death were intense. My experience in the air force was a maturing one, socially and politically. Socially, I guess I could be called square. Didn't smoke, didn't drink, and I was in the air force! Went all the way through high school and never had a drink. When you are in the military, you've got to do one of those. When I got to Europe, I had some beer. More significant was my political growth. In Europe, I met black GIs who were militant. They were from urban areas, and older than me. I was just getting old enough to interact with them as men, to see someone not just as a sergeant ordering me around, but as a person I could sit down and talk to. Gene Hill, who had gone to Tennessee State University, who was a quarterback over there, took a liking to me, and we worked a little bit on football. He gave me a whole different picture of America.

Every day we would sit and talk in the barracks—on the black side at the end of the barracks, where all the black airmen would meet. There was always a political discussion. About the March on Washington in 1963, the murders of civil rights workers in Philadelphia, Mississippi, in 1964, and Goldwater's bid for the presidency. I was fairly outspoken, and people thought I was fairly smart. But they thought that I didn't know what was going down when it came to the struggles of black folks, because I was for Dr. King. And one day, two good brothers from Norfolk, Virginia, argued with me, pushed me on the nonviolent thing. What if somebody just walked up and slapped you in the face, and all you could do is turn the other cheek and stand there until you're swimming in the head? They told me that was absolute nonsense, crazy. And I didn't have an answer. But it became clear to me that turning the other cheek, trying to convince the enemy through moral persuasion, didn't really accord with what the enemy was all about. After Malcolm X was assassinated, I changed my views because I realized I could not support nonviolence with integrity. I reassessed Malcolm, and he emerged in my mind as a powerful force. I became open to strategy not just limited to nonviolence.

The most powerful point, we never discussed. We're all sitting in the military. With guns. We were military police. I wore a .45 on my hip every day. If I was into nonviolence, what was I doing with this gun? My very role and occupation was a contradiction to nonviolence.

The whole discussion about Vietnam became very intense. The U.S. bombed the Gulf of Tonkin, a seaport in North Vietnam, based on a false report, an invention used to escalate the war. After the Gulf of Tonkin, the U.S. spread the bombing to North Vietnam. I had gone through the Cuban missile crisis gung-ho to defend America out there in the cold Massachusetts weather, guarding these planes. But this time, I saw it different. For the first time, I questioned not just the behavior of some racists, but more fundamentally what was up with this country. It was my aunt's question: What have these folk done to us?

The Gulf of Tonkin happened just before it was time for me to make a decision to re-enlist, what they call a "re-up." I was entertaining the idea of re-enlisting, because I actually enjoyed my tour in Europe. I'd been TDY [temporary duty] to the gym for three or four months, where I trained as a boxer. I went to Germany, where we were in the mountains for a while. We went to Paris as part of the boxing team. I technically wasn't part of the team. I was a trainer, which I got to be because my best friend, Ken Wilson from Jacksonville, Florida, who was quite militant, was the welterweight champion. We were on a Canadian base, so there was not a U.S. boxing team there. So they were going to transfer him, until he convinced them he had a good boxer there to train with at the Canadian base. I had never boxed in my life, so he had to train me to be his sparring partner. And I had to be good enough to spar with the champ.

I really enjoyed it. I learned to box. Ken pulled his punches on me most of the time. One of the great joys of my life was, he allowed me to use everything I had. When you are sparring, when you are hurt, you put your hand up. I had never been able to hurt him. One day I was able to get in to the side and back to the head, and he put his hand up. I must be getting good, I thought, I hurt the champ.

Our team had twelve people—ten were black—and we fought around Europe. I did mainly sparring, and I got a fight here and there. When you are TDY, you have your training—it's like football in college—you are released from duty. So we hung around Fountainebleu, trained hard, but only for four or five hours a day.

But the war in Vietnam stopped me. I kept thinking about my aunt. Everybody who re-enlisted was almost guaranteed to go to Vietnam. And that helped me make a decision to leave the military.

Willena ▪ In the sixties, I felt that we were changing some things in Greensboro. But there were places like Mullins, my hometown, that were the last places in the world to change. I went back to Mullins on holidays and for visits to my family. When I went there, I refused to revert back into the old ways of behaving, and I got into some serious trouble.

Once I had just gotten back into town—it must have been the summer of 1964 or '65—and I forgot the way things were there. There was a Dairy Queen, which was mainly a hangout for white teenagers. There was a DJ playing music from the roof of the Dairy Queen, and a big parking lot. Inside there was a small area with tables for people—white people—to sit down. Blacks were supposed to drive up outside in their cars. A black person would bring you your stuff, and you were to drive off immediately.

But that day, I was in a hurry. I forgot that blacks weren't allowed inside. I was with my brother and his girlfriend, and we were on our way to a club. I went inside to get a milkshake. Inside the Dairy Queen everyone stopped what they were doing and stared at me as if a Martian had landed. Oh, I'm in Mullins, I thought to myself. I had been so involved in the struggle in Greensboro, I forgot about the way things were in Mullins. But I decided I could not walk back out with my tail between my legs.

So I sat down and said, "Are you going to serve me?" They said nothing. It was something they had never seen before. So I sat awhile.

Then I decided I would get bold. I called the police. The police told me that what was going on at Dairy Queen was not the business of the law. It was the business of the man who owned Dairy Queen. The police chief suggested I just leave. So I hung up. I pulled a notepad out of my bag and started to write a letter to my sister. It gave me something to do. I was in for the long haul.

Finally, the Dairy Queen people called the police. The two police and two highway patrolmen came in. They walked past me into the back of the Dairy Queen. I heard them mumbling, "We can't do that," and "We think she may be planted here by that Martin Luther King."

Then they came back past me and right out the door. While the police were in the back, the white kids started driving around the parking lot, like covered wagons circling around. Anything could have happened. I wasn't thinking about any of that; I was holding my ground. After the police left, the DJ came down from the top of the building, and everybody left. No one was there but the workers inside the Dairy Queen.

My brother had been parked two blocks away while this whole mess was going on. He drove up. I came to the front of the Dairy Queen to talk to him but kept my foot in the door.

"I'll be back tomorrow," I said. The next day, the Dairy Queen was shut down. My friends talked about going back there the day after that. But my mother brought a black preacher out to our house to talk to me that day. He was old and telling me about how bad Martin Luther King was and I was. I was taught to respect the church, so I sat and listened to him. That's how my mother kept me closed up at home. Meanwhile, all my friends are at the Dairy Queen, *inside* the Dairy Queen, getting served ice cream. That was how the civil rights movement came to Mullins.

My mother was so scared about me being in the movement. She thought I was going to disappear and never come back. She would often ask me if anyone in the movement was missing. But I decided that everywhere I went, I would try to change things.

1965

Nelson ■ After I came home from the air force, I got this scar on my neck when I was almost killed. I had gone to this little club outside Littleton, about seven miles from my family's house. I was twenty-two, it was Saturday night, and everyone was out having a good time.

I saw this young lady with light-brown skin who had grown up not far from me. Boy, was she looking good! So I went over and asked her for a dance. I had matured a little bit from being as socially square as I was before the air force. This was great—dancing to the music.

Somebody walked up and called my name. When I turned around, he open-hand slapped me—pow! I was in the best shape of my life. When you are in good shape like that, you really do think you can beat just about anybody. I had been training as a boxer, I'd been playing football, so I hit him, and I hit him right. If you know how to hit, how to put your weight into it, put the flick into it, like when Ali knocked out Sonny Liston—he hit him right. The guy went down and I jumped on him, 'cause I was outraged, getting slapped like that.

Then four people jumped on me with knives and cut my neck, back, under my arms. I jumped up. I was dressed in a sports jacket (at that time you always dressed up). I jumped up; I didn't know how bad I was cut. The guy was holding my coat, so I slipped out of it. I was trying to get out of the building. As I jumped into my car, I saw people coming after me with shotguns. I hunched over, gunned the car, spun out, and drove the seven miles home.

I was bleeding like a stabbed pig. My sister opened the front door and screamed. I was totally wet with blood coming out of my neck and back. My dad wrapped me in a quilt and put me in the back of the car. Halfway to the doctor in Weldon, I passed out; I could feel myself drifting away. The doctor stitched me up and did all he could do. I regained my consciousness and composure. I really was in good shape, so my body came back fast.

The owners of the club knew me and liked me. I was a young man just out of the air force and enrolled at A&T as a freshman. The owners knew the people who stabbed me, and they called the police, who made arrests. The parents of these boys came to our house, where I was bandaged up, recovering. I couldn't quite place who they were, but my father knew them.

Two of the attackers were my classmates in the first grade. And the girl I was dancing with wasn't even their girlfriend. They had been caught up in this color thing. She was a fair-skinned girl, and I was a dark-skinned man dancing with her. I hadn't done anything to them or said anything to them. Their mothers asked my father to ask me to drop the charges. I refused to drop the charges. My father got me a lawyer, a white man named Julian Alsbrook, who was a state senator from Roanoke Rapids.

At this time, Herbert Aptheker was supposed to speak at the University of North Carolina. Aptheker was a member of the Communist Party who had written a Ph.D. dissertation about slave rebellions. There was a whole discussion in the press about Aptheker speaking—pro and con, and whether the state legislature should pass a speaker ban. So I go meet with my lawyer, Julian Alsbrook, to talk about my case. He was an older, southern, genteel-nobility type. He engaged me in this conversation about how he was glad to see somebody at A&T, and how much he thought of A&T. Then he asked me if I knew about the speaker ban.

I told my lawyer, yes, I knew about the speaker ban and I was against it. Alsbrook told me he was *for* the ban. Here was my lawyer, preparing to represent me in this case, and he said, "If you had a church, would you invite the devil to give the sermon?" He jammed me up. He said, "We pay the light bills, we pay the tax bill, why should we have somebody like Aptheker speak here?" I said that it seemed to me that freedom of speech was important, people don't have to agree with everything Aptheker says. We didn't resolve our difference. I wasn't even savvy enough to think that this guy might not even do my case right.

We went to court. It was the first time I saw these guys who had stabbed me. Their attorney was named Branch. He was from Enfield, the leading racist in Enfield, who was probably going to figure out some way to get those guys off. Their families were all hooked up to his farms. And Alsbrook, my attorney, was the leading racist in my county, and he's arguing with me about the speaker ban. Both Branch and Alsbrook were making money off this case.

So I talked to my attackers in the back of the courtroom. They said, "We're sorry. We didn't know it was you." I said, "What difference does that make? What was that all about?"

They said, "We were drunk, we just saw you dancing with the girl." They were light skinned. These guys were cutting on me over some bull about dark skin. So we had a discussion.

I said, "I was in my best suit. Pay me for the cost of my suit and my shirt, and the cost of court, and my medical bills, and we'll shake hands on it." And we did. I think I made the right decision. Why try to send these guys to jail? Let's cut bait. And these guys have been my friends since then.

The whole incident shows how the color thing operated in that area. I went back to A&T looking like I just got off the battlefield.

Marty ■ The 1960s were hard for me. My father died in 1965, my sister in 1968. In the early sixties, my dad had several heart attacks, high blood pressure, and emphysema. But he kept working as a bus driver and union leader. Finally, he gave it up for a desk job because he just couldn't breathe from his health problems. Greyhound had been pressuring him to take a job in management, because they wanted to weaken the union. He finally chose a position as a union advocate in management. He became the pension administrator for the workers' health and welfare at the Greyhound headquarters in Chicago.

So in 1964, we moved to a fairly upscale Chicago suburb called Homewood. It was an area that cost more than we could afford, so we bought a house on the poorer side of the tracks. We lived in the poorest part of this wealthy suburb.

I was thirteen, in the throes of puberty. I wanted to fit in and be like everybody else. But we didn't have the money. I remember being ashamed of my father (my beloved father) because he was a belching, coarse-mouthed, working-class man among these very rich folks. I just wanted to be what everybody else was. I used to stay up at nights hemming up my sister's hand-me-down skirts, so I too could have a different outfit every day. I remember one young boy was given a Corvette for his sixteenth birthday, and another one who had his own railroad car. And this was a conflict for me, because I was steeped in my father's belief that the only way people can get along is if there's not this big distance of wealth and poverty. Here I was struggling to look rich!

I started having arguments with my dad. Some of them were adolescent stuff, some were political. He was a strong LBJ supporter, pro–civil rights and Great Society. But also pro–Vietnam War. In 1964–65, I started arguing with him about the Vietnam War.

My father died after an adolescent fight. I still remember with sadness and regret that night. I wanted to go to the fair with my boyfriend. My father wanted me home; he just wanted to see me. He was a man of the 1950s, and he had a hard time saying those sorts of things. We had a big argument, and I went to the fair. I never saw him again. He went to work the next day and he died at work. Sudden death. It was horrible.

My mother was completely torn up. My sister was her favorite, but Mary Ann had left home to go to college and to build her own life. Leaving home was a big deal in my family. My mother's demand was, "Don't leave." It's the struggle of living with a mentally disabled mother: Can you leave? Mary Ann had moved out of the house; she led the way for me. My mother needed my sister, but Mary Ann left even though she loved my mother very much. She needed to build her own life, which was very important.

For my father, especially, education was an absolute. It was to be savored. It was the only way to get out of a dead-end job. It was the only way to get an understanding of the world. My father had saved every cent he could to give us a college education. He would have preferred to have sons rather than daughters, but he had two daughters, and he lived vicariously through us. We were told that we would go to college—or else! My sister was the valedictorian of Westerville High School, and she went to college at the University of Cincinnati. She came home from college one time and told my father she wanted to be a nurse. My dad hit the roof. "What are you talking about?" he said. "You're going to be a doctor! You aren't going to be cleaning out anybody's bedpans!"

Sally ■ Duke University accepted me, in part because I told them that I was for civil rights. In 1965, they needed at least a few white students who didn't mind rooming with the few black students they had admitted. Duke's women's college was all white until 1963, when they admitted three black women. By the time I got there two years later, there were perhaps six black women out of fifteen hundred. One of them was Joyce Hobson, who later married Nelson Johnson.

Duke administrators must have been worried about racist displays. They hand-picked white students who they knew were pro–civil rights (and whose families were pro–civil rights) to room with black students. I was assigned to a freshman advisor who was black. All the girls on my hall were carefully selected to help desegregate the school.

I came south to join the marches, but by 1965 the wave of sit-ins had passed, Congress had passed some legislation, and the civil rights movement was in a lull. All that people were doing was talking, and I loved my American history class because we discussed racism. As I looked around Duke and Durham, North Carolina, continuing segregation was far more apparent than civil rights. Duke was rich and 99 percent white; Durham was 40 percent black, almost all of them poor.

For two years, not much changed, and I fell into the campus social life. In high school I had been categorized as a nerd; at Duke I studied hard during the week and partied hard during the weekend. But after two years, I grew tired of the superficial campus lifestyle and frustrated with sweet southern hospitality. I thought about transferring back up north but instead applied to take part in a "living and learning" project where Duke students, male and female, lived in a poor community on the other side of Durham.

Paul ▪ I entered City College, part of the City University of New York, in September 1965. A lot of people from my high school went to City, so I had lots of friends. And I made new friends fast. College was great. CUNY was tuition free in those years. I lived at home and rode the subway to Harlem to go to school. City College was located in the middle of Harlem, but in the sixties there were not many black students there, particularly considering it was located in the middle of probably the largest black community in the country.

There were beginning to be anti–Vietnam War demonstrations on campus. The idea of opposing the war seemed impossible to me. Soon after I got to City, I remember walking across campus with Peter Vogel, an upperclassman who was Mr. Preppy; he always wore a blue blazer. He was president of the Inter-Fraternity Council, and he was trying to recruit me to his fraternity. We walked by these students who were expressing overt public opposition to the war. I told Peter I thought they were outrageous. How could people be against the war? Against government policy? And Peter, Mr. Preppy, looked me straight in the eye and said, "We'll see how you feel about the Vietnam War in a few years."

It shook me up. I thought things were very stable in my life, and then there is the assassination of Kennedy, and now people were opposing the government on the war in Vietnam. It was like all these stable, seemingly immutable structures were starting to look shaky all of a sudden. It gave me the feeling that anything was possible.

Willena ■ In the early sixties I fell in love. At first I didn't like John Cannon—he was so light skinned. I thought of him as that "yellow nigger," and when he came by my dorm, I would tell my friends, "Tell that half-white nigger to leave my window." I didn't want to have nothing to do with him. But he was so persistent. He would wait for me; he would corner me in classes. He had a great sense of humor—he would make jokes and have me cracking up. So finally I pushed the color thing back.

We got married in 1965 in New York City and lived in Harlem for a year. I worked in a department store. New York was so big and different. It wasn't just that there was no open space and we had to lock the door. There weren't the neighborhood connections where you would find out what was happening in this mill or that project. I couldn't see the movement. I kept in touch with people in Greensboro and longed to go back there.

John and I had left A&T in '65. I needed only one semester to graduate.

A Radical Turn in the Movement, 1965–68

Nelson ■ North Carolina A&T was the center of the movement. I didn't realize that until I got there. I had no idea who Jesse Jackson was. He had graduated in '65, just before I got there in September. People were protesting everywhere. Right away, I met people at A&T who were more militant than the folks I was with in the air force. They were powerful, militant, quoting Frederick Douglass and Nat Turner. I got in with them. I agreed with them, based on what I had gone through; I remembered the white guy knocking me around in the bus. I could see that was part of a pattern that was endorsed by the whole nation. My new friends would trash Abraham Lincoln. Was he really for ending slavery? Or only saving the union? Abraham Lincoln had been my hero, but I had to drop him too.

That year I came of age politically, and the consummation of it was a demonstration against ROTC and the war in Vietnam. So we went to the Bowl, which is the gathering place at the A&T campus, where people hang out and play informal games of football. We are holding our protest, and an army major came over and raised hell with us. He said we were "ungrateful niggers." He was black; everyone there was black. He said we didn't have any respect for our country. I was shocked. I thought that whether we agreed with him or not, this was our freedom. He got up in our face like he was going to go to war. It made me more determined. For a black man to do this to us was stunning to me. That got me on my path. It ended my journey out of the military and placed me where I was looking at America in a whole different way.

I was not disloyal. I developed a more honest understanding of the great flaws in our social system. That led me into the life of activism in Greensboro ever since.

Paul ■ In college, I learned that we have to think for ourselves. In the mid-1960s, the demonstrations against the Vietnam War grew in size and ferocity. The antiwar movement grew in tandem with civil rights. Some of the best people from the northern campuses went down south to the Mississippi Freedom Summer and voter registration drives in various areas.

For a political science research paper, I wrote on the political trends on the campus. I interviewed the leaders of sixteen different groups, from the furthest left, SDS [Students for a Democratic Society], to the furthest right, Radicals for Capitalism. It began a process of clarifying my own thinking. I remember interviewing one guy who was in SDS and had been on the Freedom Rides. I asked Bill, the Freedom Rider, "What do you see as your social role?" He said, "I see my social role as being dysfunctional, to fuck things up." I know many people had a great experience in SDS, but I could never go for it, because at City College it had this negative, throw-a-monkey-wrench-into-the-works perspective.

The opposition to the war grew on campus. There was a state of constant ferment. New ideas came up, and people were challenged to think things through for themselves. The strongest defense for the government's actions was that the people in government know more than we do about the situation, so that's why they're the ones making the decisions. I held onto that view: Our political leaders know more than we do, so we just have to do what they say. But then I read this book that described how Vietnam was fighting for its independence for hundreds of years. The book thoroughly critiqued the U.S. role in Vietnam, and before them the French. I realized that I should not just rely on what the government says is happening. It was a political awakening. In the ongoing conversations on campus, I became increasingly against the war, along with everybody else. The breakthrough in the movement came when people realized that we have to think for ourselves.

The movement at City College was fabulous. It was so easy to hold a demonstration. If you put out a leaflet twenty minutes before lunch hour, you could have four hundred to five hundred people gathered in front of the library for a rally. If you talked loud, people would gather around expecting a rally. I started getting active in student government, speaking out against the war. I got elected president of the sophomore class.

Black and Puerto Rican students were organizing for open admissions. Not everybody got along, and there were lots of arguments and even some physical fights between black and white kids. Some of the white radicals were devoted to supporting the black students, but a lot of whites were not. It was not a unified struggle, but divided along racial lines: the whites against the war, the blacks for open admissions.

Martin Luther King Jr. began to speak publicly against the war. He planned to lead a big demonstration in the spring of 1967 that was both pro–civil rights and against the war. The march would go from Central Park to the United Nations. I wanted to go.

My parents argued with me about going to the demonstration. I was still living at home. My mother kept saying, "Be a grueh mensch," which in Yiddish means a "gray person." "Don't stand out. Don't do anything to draw attention to yourself, because the FBI will kill you," she said. She was horrified that I was going to publicly oppose the government, because governments kill people. That was her experience with life. She offered to take my place at the demonstration.

But of course, I went with my friends to the demonstration. To our surprise, it was gigantic. There were half a million people there! There were senior citizens, people from unions, loads of students. People were handing out daffodils. The march started moving, and it was extraordinary to move with so many people. It seemed like we would never get out of Central Park. It was so exciting, I felt a great rush of enthusiasm. It marked my entrance into activism.

Sally ■ I fell in love with Mike Nathan when I was twenty years old. It was September 1967, and I was a junior in college. I had joined a student "living and learning" program off campus and moved into a dilapidated house in a slum called Edgemont. Michael Nathan was one of the handful of Duke undergraduates living there. He was tall, with narrow shoulders on a thin, straight body. He had dark curly hair, hazel eyes, olive skin, and a mustache like a Latin revolutionary. My first impression was that he was cute, but too quiet for me.

One Saturday night, a group of us piled into Mike's old Plymouth and went to a documentary-style movie about nuclear destruction. We all felt depressed afterwards. I thought we were heading back to the house, but Mike drove us to a small Italian restaurant. The dining room was full, so the waiter led us downstairs to an empty, darkly lit room with a few tables and a jukebox. "It's safe here," Mike announced. "It's a bomb shelter."

We laughed and ordered a pizza and several bottles of Chianti. Mike put some quarters in the jukebox and suddenly the pop hit "My Girl" filled the room. Mike started asking the girls to dance. I sat there watching him dancing around the floor with my roommate, a sly smile on his face. I wanted him to ask me to dance, and finally he did. We rock-and-rolled, jitter-bugged, cha-chaed, and tangoed. He tried to teach me some fancy maneuver that involved him throwing me over his shoulder. I landed on my butt. We laughed and laughed. And I fell in love.

Mike and I became inseparable. We went to school together, studied together. I loved his long, lean body. Dressed in a blue workshirt and jeans, he could care less about appearances. But he always looked cool, a nonchalant casualness. Mike was a radical activist, and he helped me to become one.

In 1967, Lyndon Baines Johnson was president. I had been a fan of LBJ because he championed the cause of the poor with his Great Society programs. One of those programs was called the Community Action Program, which had offices in cities across the country. The Durham CAP, called Operation Breakthrough, was located just a few blocks from where we lived in Edgemont. Mike worked there as a community organizer. But Mike criticized Lyndon Johnson because he did not keep his campaign promise to end the war in Vietnam. Instead, Johnson kept sending more American troops.

Mike took me to my first peace demonstration: the 1967 March on the Pentagon, the war headquarters. We were among a hundred thousand demonstrators chanting "Hey, hey, LBJ! How many kids did you kill today?" We marched under a bridge as a lone black man stood over us with a sign stating, "No Viet Cong ever called me nigger."

By the time we got to the Pentagon, the front ranks of the demonstration had broken through the barbed-wire barriers surrounding the building. "This is scary," I whispered to Mike as I followed him, carefully stepping over the horizontal remnants of the barbed-wire fence as we walked up to the Pentagon.

"You think those old geezers might get you?" Mike grinned at me gently.

I laughed. Why should I feel afraid, surrounded by a hundred thousand determined demonstrators? Mike made me feel safe, even as we stood on the steps of the Pentagon, staring in the eyes of the heavily armed soldiers. A newspaper photographer caught the image of a protester putting a flower in the barrel of a soldier's rifle. That photo became a symbol of the antiwar movement.

My little sister, a high school student, had never demonstrated before. She hesitated to march with us that day because she did not know any of my college friends. But Mike made her feel welcome in our group, asking her about herself and teasing her as we marched along. That was Mike; he always connected with the odd person out. My sister loved him for it.

Back in Durham, Mike and I divided our time between Duke's elegant campus and Edgemont, where we lived. Edgemont was on the other side of town, over the railroad tracks, down a hill, a bleak landscape of rickety shacks. The houses were only a few feet apart on narrow dirt alleys with deep ruts. In stormy weather, the wind blew inside the houses and the water rushed down the alleys, making the ruts even deeper. Just a few years earlier, poor whites lived in those houses, but increasingly blacks moved in and whites moved elsewhere.

That year was my first experience living in a poor neighborhood. But not for Mike. His family had been poor as far back as he could remember. Mike's father worked as a government printer. But he was sick off and on throughout Mike's childhood, from a disease he got when he was a GI in the Korean War. He died when Mike was only fifteen. Mike's mom, a housewife, never recovered from her husband's death. The government pension did not cover the rent on their modest apartment, so she reluctantly went to work as a department-store sales-girl. As a teenager, Mike decided to become a doctor.

There was a sad, withdrawn side of Mike. It was part of him I never could reach. At that point in my life, I had faced no personal tragedies greater than the death of my family cat. But when I spent time with Mike, I felt connected to him, and he seemed happier.

I got hired as a youth organizer at the Edgemont Community Center. I had no idea how to organize teenagers. Mike had six months of experience as orga-nizer by then, so he trained me. He took me with him as he made his rounds of the neighborhood. "How 'ya doin'?" he would ask in his friendly, straightfor-ward manner. "Did the landlord fix that leaky faucet? What about the crack in the kitchen wall?"

Landlords were the biggest problem for many people; they demanded rent on time but failed to keep the houses in good repair. I remember the Barrett family, one of many Mike worked with. For months, Mike tried to help Mrs. Barrett get the landlord to repair the steps leading to her front porch. The house was a square, one-story, four-roomed wooden structure that looked like it was barely standing. We carefully climbed up to the porch, because the steps were loose and one was missing.

I could hear a scratchy record playing Aretha Franklin's "I Say a Little Prayer for You." Through the open front door, I saw kids bouncing as Aretha sang: "At work I just take time/And all through my coffee-break time/I say a little prayer for you." The room was full of children, more than a dozen of them, from full-grown teenagers to toddlers, all bopping happily. The smallest was dressed only in diapers. Someone saw us, the music stopped abruptly, and the kids stared at us. Mike asked for Mrs. Barrett, and Tressa Barrett, one of the big kids, disap-peared into the back room. She returned quickly to tell Mike that her mother was sick and couldn't talk to him. The scratchy record began again. The kids returned to dancing, laughing. Aretha's music seemed to make life possible.

My job was to organize a teen council for the community center. Mike and I knocked on every door in the neighborhood; he seemed to know every teenager by name. I invited each of them to a meeting at the community center, includ-ing the three Barretts who were teens. At the meeting, we talked about what a teen council could do. I suggested protesting for civil rights. Tressa Barrett suggested holding dances at the Edgemont Center. The other teenagers liked Tressa's idea best. So we did both. We joined protests as they happened, but we spent a lot more time socializing.

Every Saturday night, youth packed the community center as Marvin Gaye and Aretha Franklin blared from the record player. My favorite was "Heard It

Through the Grapevine"—seven solid minutes of dance music. People formed two lines facing each other and stretching the length of the center. We bobbed and sang to the music, and each of us took a turn to boogie down the middle. That was how Mike and I spent Saturday nights for the next two years.
We made good friends in Edgemont. Twelve years later, many of them came to Mike's memorial service.

Nelson   ■   I grew up in the spirit of the civil rights movement, but in the midsixties, I became a black nationalist. There was always a sense in our home and among my friends that you had to stand for what was right and against what was wrong. In 1954 after the Supreme Court's *Brown v. Board of Education* decision, I remember one of my cousins saying, "If whites don't want to be with me, I don't want to be with them."[3] I disagreed with her position because at the time it was accommodating the status quo. I thought the barriers of segregation needed to be torn down.

Discussions had gone on in my family, then in the air force, and then at A&T. It was natural for me to end up actively involved. When I first got to A&T, I started tutoring at the Ray Warren Homes housing project. A very nice lady, Dr. Ann Graves, directed the program that included tutors from Guilford College and Greensboro College, white colleges, as well as A&T and Bennett. Racially, the tutors were a fully mixed group. That summer I got a job with the Youth Educational Services [YES], which was another statewide tutorial and community-organizing group. It was a Terry Sanford–built program. Terry Sanford was the "education governor" of North Carolina at the time.

A lot of the children I worked with asked for white tutors, which bothered me at a time when social consciousness of our own history as African American people was rapidly on the rise. Several other black tutors were also having problems. They felt that the program was integrated in a way that greatly belittled racism. It almost celebrated the presence of white people doing good and pious things in the black community. That just didn't set right. Increasingly, I got into discussions with the other black tutors. The question of why we had to tutor in the first place was linked to what the school wasn't doing and what the society wasn't doing—like, how could a kid read if the lighting in the house is not proper, and how can the light get proper if his father isn't making enough money. The questions went into the social root of things. And the more you raise those questions, the more the hypocrisy of the society starts to come out. Our discussions led me to challenge the view that tutoring was the primary way to fight poverty.

Increasingly I was drawn to the Student Nonviolent Coordinating Committee, which was the militant part of the movement then. In 1965–66, SNCC leader Stokely Carmichael was all over the newspaper, talking about black power.[4]

In YES, tensions developed in the group over integration versus black power. Unfortunately, the whites in the group didn't understand what we were raising. They thought we didn't appreciate them. And the more they said that, the more I didn't appreciate them. I gradually pulled away from YES, making a respectful break with the people in YES. I told them I was convinced that black folk working with black folk was what I needed to be doing. I told them I respected them even though I disagreed with them.

Sally ■ The black power movement hit Durham only a month or two after I started organizing black teenagers in Edgemont. One day, Mike and I went to a citywide mass meeting to discuss plans to hold a boycott of selected white-owned business. There were hundreds of people gathered there in a big church in the middle of the black community. The meeting was chaired by a man named Howard Fuller, who is one of the most charismatic people I have ever met. He was well over six feet tall, lean, and articulate. I had met him the previous spring at Duke and (in my typical fashion) had a secret crush on him. Mike had met him too, because Fuller had been Mike's boss as the head of Durham's antipoverty program.

But on that day in late 1967, Howard Fuller told the audience that he would no longer use his "slave name" of Howard Fuller; he was now to be called Owusu Sadaukai. He was talking black power, which he said meant "No whites allowed." Then he expelled Mike and me from the meeting. That hurt. I felt humiliated as we left the church. Then we got outside and everything seemed the same, at least on the surface.

Suddenly, there were lots of discussions about black power. A citywide black teenage council was organized, but I wasn't allowed to attend because I was white. Black power advocates said that whites should organize poor whites. That made sense to me, since there certainly were a lot of poor whites in Durham and no one seemed to be working with them. But I didn't like the idea that no whites and blacks should work together. Plus, I had an immediate problem. I was the staff person for a newly formed teen council. Should I quit? Mike suggested that I talk to the teen council about it. The Edgemont youth thought I had lost my mind. "You better not quit!" Tressa Barrett yelled at me. And for the next two years, we had a dynamite teen council.

To me, black power was sometimes excessive; I certainly didn't like getting kicked out of that meeting. But I also understood it in a broader perspective. There was need for black leadership, and whites (especially white men) could be overbearing. I felt it was a generational thing. Our generation, black and white, male and female, saw the need for bold new leadership. We were in our twenties then, and we had grown up in the civil rights movement. We saw it as just the beginning of a much longer struggle. Youth energized the movement in 1960 with the sit-ins. In 1967, the energy of the young was needed again to break down deeper, more entrenched barriers. Mike and I saw ourselves as part of the tradition of the young upstarts. Much more needed to be done.

Paul ■ I become a student government leader at City College. In spring 1968, left-wing students at City College took over the Student Center to provide sanctuary for two AWOL soldiers. AWOL stands for "absent without leave," and it basically means running away from the military. Many soldiers were going AWOL because they didn't want to go to Vietnam. If they got caught, they faced serious punishment—often they headed for Canada, where they would be safe once they were out of the country. At City College, students protected the AWOL soldiers from capture by surrounding them and taking over the Student Center. They dared the FBI and police to come get them.

I felt like the movement was bad news. I was scared to death when I gave my first speech at a demonstration. [Gallery I includes a photo of Paul taken just before he spoke.] There were a couple hundred people standing there and no amplification equipment. All I had was my loud voice. I denounced the antiwar movement, saying, "I'm opposed to the war in Vietnam, but the movement is just missing the boat because it's not reaching out to working-class people."

My political development all the way through really rested on a single basic principle, and that was that it had to reach people like my parents. They represented the working class to me. They didn't support the war in Vietnam. They thought no wars make sense because it's always poor boys who go get their asses blown off. The poor boys get killed, and the rich guys make more money—that was their view. And they are right. So my speech criticized the antiwar movement for failing to reach out to working-class people. I was very angry at the elitist attitudes that a lot of the movement people had. I was amazed at the reception I got from that crowd. They cheered and clapped and carried on. It was exhilarating.

It was my first taste of being a political leader, really. I ran for student government president against a conservative, pro-war candidate. I was antiwar and for student power, and I won the election. As the student government president, I was a kind of a Kennedyesque figure on campus. I was a liberal, a progressive guy, still pro-Kennedy at that point. (I did not learn until later that JFK played a central role in escalating the war in Vietnam.) People wanted me as a middle-of-the-road type. They also wanted me as the student government president to support the vigil for the AWOL soldiers.

I supported the sanctuary of the soldiers, but I did not participate in the building takeover. I thought some of the protesters' tactics were stupid. For example, to prevent any eavesdropping by the government authorities, the people who had taken over the Student Center tore out every telephone in the entire building. Tore them out of the wall! I felt conflicted about participating in the takeover. I felt that I really should play a role, but I also felt that the protest was so far out that I couldn't participate. It just wasn't me. I was a pretty mainstream kind of guy. Also, I was trying to stay clean so that I could get into medical school.

One night, the word came that the police were massing a few blocks up from the campus and that they were going to bust up the takeover. As student government president, I figured maybe I could intervene and alleviate some of this. I went to the university president's house, which was on campus. But the president wouldn't talk to me. The students were increasingly calling on me to try to mediate with the police, and I went outside and tried to do that. But by this time, hundreds of police had been bussed in, all wearing riot gear and massing in military formation. There were searchlights on the campus, and the police were trotting in formation to assume positions on campus. They busted 167 people that night.

I was unable to do anything helpful, and I felt immensely guilty that I hadn't participated more. It was stupid to pull out the phone wires, but right to take a stand against the war in Vietnam. This was just before Martin Luther King was assassinated.

Nelson ■ The period of black power, from '67 through the end of the sixties, was intense. For years, we organized the black community against redevelopment programs that tore down neighborhoods and destroyed housing. The official policy was urban renewal, but Negro removal is what people called it. I started to work with the black parents I had met while I was tutoring. We built the first neighborhood/tenants organization in Greensboro, which was the forerunner of the Greensboro Association of Poor People [GAPP], which became a federation of six different neighborhood groups.

GAPP grew out of our recognition of the need to help people figure out how to deal with these bigger problems. It was founded in 1968 to deal with a wide range of issues: housing, redevelopment, welfare issues, protesting against intimidation or harassment. We had good relations with the NAACP and we worked on their voter registration drives, and the NAACP gave us free office space, which we called the Poor People's Office or GAPP House.

The GAPP House was in an excellent location, in the middle of a poor black neighborhood and near A&T and Bennett College. It became a hangout for community people and students. Dot Johnson was a seasoned fighter on housing and other issues, and the GAPP House became her base of operations. She had children and grandchildren and cooked food for them and anyone else around the GAPP House. There was always good smells coming out of there—blackeyed peas, collard greens, pigs' feet, fried chicken.

Our organizing focused in the neighborhoods and also was deeply connected to the college campus. Student interns became the foundation of GAPP. We could bring out a hundred students to stand with a mother threatened to be evicted from slum housing. We would surround her house and prevent her eviction.

Once we brought twenty or thirty people from A&T to a meeting of the Housing Authority Board. In this case, all the students were men. At the time, Afro hairstyles were in vogue, and there were some fantastic and huge Afros. The Housing Authority Board routinely would not let any housing residents into their meetings. But this time, we pushed the door in at the Housing Authority and went in, saying, "We're here with our sisters, and they have things they need to talk about."

That Housing Board was petrified, and the next day there was an article in the newspaper about what we did. The press covered other actions we took. We built a relationship between students and community the likeness of which I had not seen before. The basic principle of the group was, "Don't go anywhere by yourself." When we went to the Welfare Department, we always took twenty to thirty people, and we took care of people's business that way. We supported the cafeteria workers' strike at A&T and at the University of North Carolina at Greensboro [UNCG]. We organized the blind workers and the garbage workers.

We became part of a statewide movement. Howard Fuller had directed the Community Action Program in Durham for its first years. He left that job to form the Foundation for Community Development in 1967, which promoted community organizing around the state. I met Howard in 1966 and was quite taken by his tremendous gifts of analysis, his power of articulation, and his capacity to organize. I became a disciple of his. He talked a strong black power line. There was a lot of interracial dating among activists at that time, and he challenged us to stop it. He whipped on any black man dating white girls so hard that it was no longer in vogue. With Owusu [Howard Fuller], I got into the movement for black community control and then into pan-Africanism. Owusu was my connector to the broad black power movement.

Many black people at A&T were drawn to us. We could bring out crowds of people. We could call a mass meeting at 1:00 a.m., and people would show up. There is a picture in the A&T *Register* newspaper that shows the clock in our meeting room at 3:00 a.m.—and we were in full session. That says something of that time period and the people who were active and organizing.

Police in Orangeburg, South Carolina, killed three South Carolina State students as the students attempted to desegregate a bowling alley. The Orangeburg massacre went through the emergent black power movement like a bolt of lightning. Owusu Sadaukai called a meeting in Durham, and black students came from sixteen different colleges around the state. Many of us had been part of a summer internship Owusu had organized, so there was a network in place. At the Durham meeting, we decided to hold creative demonstrations all at the same time on our different campuses. People on each campus had to figure out what to do.

The demonstration we organized in Greensboro is what first thrust me into a public leadership role. When we came back from Durham, we were not clear on what we would do at our demonstration. I was mulling it over. I often mull things over and don't come quickly to new decisions. When I say something, it's because I've been thinking about it. In this case, I found myself putting together a plan based on people throwing around different ideas. Should we hang the governor of South Carolina in effigy? Or should we carry a casket? Sometimes people got into arguments. The basic thing I was able to do was to listen to people and reconcile the differences. Why couldn't we do all of them?

I was not the most militant person at A&T. Bill Chafe, in *Civilities and Civil Rights,* which describes Greensboro in those years, points out that there were several campus groups more radical than I.[5] But I was the one who could communicate with the range of people both on campus and in the black community. I didn't summarily dismiss anybody. I tried to hear what somebody was saying, even if I strongly disagreed with them. I was usually able to get things done.

My situation growing up prepared me to become a leader. I was the middle child in the family, child number five out of nine. I was a dark-skinned person in a family of many colors, and in a society where light meant right. This meant I was negotiating all the time. I was insecure and didn't assume that I understood. I was always trying to figure out what was going on. So I listened carefully to what people were saying.

In any event, in planning for our protest against the Orangeburg massacre, I listened to everyone. And we came up with our plan. We made an effigy of the South Carolina governor and went to a cemetery and got flowers. I went to the undertaker, where I had never been. I spoke to Mr. Hargett, making a case for him lending us a casket. I promised that we would safely return it after the protest. And the undertaker agreed. I got some guys to go over there and get the casket and put it on a pickup truck with the flowers. So we had an effigy and a casket. (I can't remember where the heck we got the pickup truck to put it on.) I realized that all these things—caskets, trucks, flowers—were present within the people, and the key was to think how to bring it together. And bringing them together was the role that I played.

We went to A&T with our casket and flowers. Several of the young men hoisted the casket on their shoulders, and we started to walk across the campus. Most people didn't know what was happening. We didn't have any flyers that told them. So we talked to people as we walked through the campus. We said that our brothers in South Carolina had been killed, cut down by police. We said we were standing against that massacre and marching downtown to protest it. And by the time we got halfway down Market Street, I looked back and I saw one of the largest marches in Greensboro that I ever participated in.

When we got downtown, we strung the governor's effigy up in a big tree in front of the courthouse. Someone, unbeknown to me, lit it on fire. There was no broadly recognized leadership; there were just people singing and chanting. I was submerged in the crowd, and I remember the police looking so surprised. The police didn't try to turn back the crowd. It was too big. And they couldn't find the leader, because there wasn't exactly a leader. I had done the principal work in organizing it, but only the fifteen to twenty people working with me knew that. No one was acting like a leader, just lots of folks chanting. Once the effigy burned, the fire department came and rushed in with all the sirens. That really threw everything into a panic. The people started to run away.

We got back to campus and gathered in the student union's new building. I went up on the balcony that overlooks the open space filled with students. I said something to the effect that this was a good thing that we did, and everybody cheered. And it reminded me almost of a movie. I felt connected to people in a way that I had never experienced before. I said a few more things and people responded. I sensed what people were feeling, and it corresponded to my own feelings, and I was able to echo that back to people.

The police only found out that I had organized the protest because of the casket. When the fire trucks came, we left the casket as we ran away. So the police got the casket. I had promised Mr. Hargett I would return his casket, and I felt a duty to him. I went to see him, and then I called the police to try to arrange for Mr. Hargett to pick up his casket. The police said first I had to come down to the police station. That's how I first got face-to-face with the police, as a step in getting that casket back.

At the police station, Captain Jackson told me how the police did things. They weren't against us, he said, but they didn't like surprises. The leader of a demonstration always called them ahead of time so they could work out things in advance. He gave me this whole speech about what I should do if I was going to be leading demonstrations.

So it was the protest against the Orangeburg massacre where I got my first sense of being a black activist leader. A friend who was a reporter called me and said, "You know you are the leader of the youth of this town, don't you?" I had never thought of it that way.

Marty ■ In 1968, my sister died; she was only twenty-five years old. She was my role model. I had watched my sister become an intellectual in college and graduate from the University of Cincinnati, and then get her master's in sociology. She introduced me to the music of Joan Baez, Pete Seeger, and Bob Dylan, which I have loved ever since.

But she became sick the year after my father died. She had Ewing's sarcoma, and they operated. It was horrible. She was sick for two years. I watched her struggle against death. Part of her statement of life was education, becoming a professional. She applied to graduate school in sociology and started classes for her Ph.D. a week before she died.

Even as my sister became very sick, she was so strong, so determined. She refused to marry this guy who wanted to marry her. She said, "I'm sick. I can't do that. And I don't love him anyway." She refused to say she believed in things she didn't. My mother had gotten into religion, an active member of the Evangelical United Brethren Church. She kept hounding Mary Ann about being saved so that she could go to heaven. My sister said, "I don't believe in God. Give me a break." In Westerville, Ohio, you don't say those things (unless you're my father, who had said the same thing). But in spite of their argument, Mary Ann did let my mother take care of her, which was good.

Mary Ann and my father were my heroes. It wasn't until later that my mother became my hero too for her struggle against her mental illness.

As for me, during this time, I was this adolescent doofus with life and death swirling around me. I was a teenager who wanted a boyfriend and to go to parties. Worried about not being invited to parties, not being accepted, I joined a sorority. I was completely blown away by the deaths of my dad and Mary Ann. I was suicidally depressed, and yet I kept going on. I worked like hell at my studies and then drank like a fish on weekends. And I tried to figure out how to deal with all this stuff.

Mary Ann's death hit my mother very hard. What she communicated to me was that the wrong daughter had died. Now, as an adult, I know that my mother loved me but was devastated by the deaths, as well as her own mental illness. But at the time I needed her to help me with the grief. Instead, I felt rejection. I developed this incredible hatred of my mother. She wanted somebody to take care of her. Once she said to a group of people, "After Mary Ann died, there was nobody left to take care of me." (This was later, after she was becoming demented.) That is what she felt, and it hurt. Here I was, seventeen; who was supposed to be taking care of who? Who is supposed to explain this thing about death? And about forgiveness and salvation in human terms? I'm not talking about pie-in-the-sky salvation, I'm talking about living on after the people you love most have died. There was nobody for me.

My religious beliefs died with my sister. Church played a big role in my life, growing up. We were members of the Evangelical United Brethren Church, the main church in town. The Evangelicals believed in the virgin birth and fundamental truth of the Bible and all those things, although they weren't as extreme as the Pentecostals. My mom and sister and I went to church every Sunday, and we all sang in the choir.

My father was not religious. He said, "I'm not sure I'm an atheist, but I am an agnostic. If I were any religion, I would probably be a Buddhist." In Middle America in the 1950s, he could have been thrown in jail for less.

After my father died and my sister got sick, I joined this group called Young

Life, a fundamentalist high school youth group. They were real pure Pentecostals who spoke in tongues. I wanted to find something that was away from the grief and the guilt. I wanted to be saved. I remember trying hard to find my state of grace.

Then my sister died. And I thought, There is no God; there can't be a good God that would allow this to happen to my family. It was hard to drop my beliefs. When you're raised in that kind of religion, it's very deep-seated. I said my prayers every night for God knows how many years. But it just didn't make any sense anymore to me.

I became a Marxist a few years later, and that made a hell of a lot more sense to me. I believe we're out here alone and have to create our own best world that we can put together as a human family.

When my sister died in 1968, I was a senior in high school. It was a time of rebellion, and there was a left wing in my high school, and I was on the fringes of it. My friends and I went into Jesse Jackson's Operation Breadbasket in Chicago. The Weathermen's Days of Rage happened.[6] Martin Luther King was assassinated. I knew there were momentous things happening, and I had friends who demonstrated against the Vietnam War. I supported them, but I did not participate. For me, rebelling was mainly on the weekends: smoking dope, thinking and talking, and what we call today "risk-taking behavior."

When my sister died, I wanted to be a doctor. That seemed like the right thing to do, because the doctors had missed her diagnosis for a year, and she might have lived if they had diagnosed her right. Like many children in families where people die, I wanted to be a doctor. My dad wanted us to be doctors or lawyers. But in my senior year, my physics teacher, Mr. Lang, told us, "Girls can't understand science." I was getting A's in his physics class, but he is telling us, "Girls can't understand science." Mr. Lang told that to girls over and over, every year. I still hate him. He made more than one bright, inquisitive girl emotionally ill in those years.

I got into Brown University. I faced leaving home, knowing that my mother didn't want me to go. It was only one year after Mary Ann's death, and Mom was still in shock, unable to cope. Before she died, my sister sent me a message through her friends. Mary Ann told them to tell me, "Marty, leave home! Get out, whatever you do!"—which I needed, because otherwise I might not have been able to leave my mother.

Both my sister and my father showed me the way: Work hard, get educated, get a job, become independent. As an eighteen-year-old, I needed to get away from home. I needed to be an actor in this world. It was the sixties, the social-movement years. I was able to take my own very personal struggle of love and death and cast it into the bigger world. I knew rejection; I understood prejudice based on class, race, and gender, and the struggle for dignity. For me, those deaths in Vietnam that I saw on nighttime TV were real. I had had my own personal Holocaust, and I knew what death meant. When I saw that famous newspaper photo of the little Vietnamese girl running, on fire from napalm, and the mother carrying her infant child, I knew what that was. I personalized the antiwar movement as my own and gave it a passion that maybe some other folks didn't quite understand.

The Assassination of Martin Luther King, April 4, 1968

Nelson ■ The day King was killed, he was scheduled to speak in Greensboro. He was originally scheduled to speak at Trinity AME Church on April 4, 1968. Dr. George Simkins, president of the Greensboro NAACP, had asked me to organize an A&T student delegation to go to the airport and greet King when he landed. He asked us to cheer Martin Luther King Jr. into the city. I was not particularly a King fan at that point, but I always respected King and loved his capacity to orate. I agreed to organize the delegation because King was coming to support the campaign of Dr. Reginald Hawkins, the first black gubernatorial candidate in North Carolina since Reconstruction.[7] I was campaigning for Hawkins, so I agreed to meet Martin Luther King at the airport.

Word came one or two days beforehand that King's visit would be delayed because he was going to stay in Memphis for a few days. The Memphis sanitation workers were on strike, and the FBI had disrupted the strikers' first march. So King decided to postpone his Greensboro trip for a few days.

So on the day that King was killed, April 4, I was headed to my family's house in Littleton. I was en route in my old Volkswagen when the news came on that King had been shot. Hubert Humphrey announced it, and it hit me like a ton of bricks. I was close to my home, and when I got there my oldest sister was just crying ferociously. I wasn't used to seeing her that angry. She said she wished people would burn down everything. I spent about half an hour at home and then immediately turned around and drove back to Greensboro. I really felt a need to be in my own community.

When I got into Greensboro, I saw some smoke near the campus. When I neared the Poor People's Office, gunshots were being fired in that area. I drove to campus and there was a whole group of people gathered there. Willie Drake, one of the organizers on campus, came to me and briefed me on what was going on. I gave some kind of little talk.

One thing led to another, and the next day the mayor put a curfew on the city. We didn't have a police permit, and we didn't ask for one. It was raining, and we were going to march no matter what. It was a period in which the relationship between the student activists and the black clergy was further developed. The whole black community was in a state of grief, and everybody, including the clergy, wanted to hold a march. But the clergy didn't want to break the law, and the mayor refused to allow a march. We students decided we were going to march no matter what. We just marched from A&T to Bennett College in the rain, and then from Bennett downtown. The police hesitated to arrest us, so we just denounced the system and came back to the black community. Then the mayor called the National Guard and shut the city down. Then the clergy and the NAACP asked to meet with us, because they respected what we did. It was one of the most meaningful periods of discussion and relationship building that went on within the entire black community.

Several months later, Bobby Kennedy was killed. I kept thinking, What the heck is this country coming to?

Sally ■ Mike Nathan and I were just leaving Duke when we heard the news that Martin Luther King had been shot. We drove to our house in Edgemont in silence. When we got there, people were walking around in shock. An old black man wailed as if the world was ending; Tressa Barrett asked if King's death meant the end of the civil rights movement.

My shock quickly became anger. The movement couldn't die; so much more needed to be done. Mike paced around mumbling, "We've got to do something." He picked up the phone and called up some friends on campus. He found out that a candlelight march to the Duke president's house was planned for the next evening. Mike also heard that some students planned to stay after the march to meet with the president to talk to him about how Duke should recognize the campus workers' union and raise their wages. That sounded like a good idea to me.

Duke was paying its housekeeping and grounds workers only eighty-five cents an hour. People called it "the plantation." The campus workers had formed a union, Local 77 of the American Federation of State, County, and Municipal Employees, but Duke refused to bargain with them. Over the previous year, Local 77 periodically organized a picket line in the center of Duke's campus. I had marched in that picket line, holding a sign that said "Recognize Local 77!"

The night after King's assassination, Mike and I joined a candlelight march to the home of Duke's president, Douglas Knight. The university had just built the president's house at great expense and controversy. Mike told me that he planned to stay after the march to talk to President Knight personally about the need for Duke to acknowledge this union. I decided I wanted to do that with him.

When we arrived at the house, Douglas Knight stood outside his front door, talking to the candle-holding students. I had met Knight only once before, at my freshman reception the day I arrived at Duke, when I shook his hand and noted his horn-rimmed glasses and concerned expression. I followed Mike as he made his way through the crowd to where Knight was standing. The front door was ten feet behind Knight, and it was wide open. "Are you coming with me?" Mike asked me, as he headed for the door.

That was the moment I became a radical. Part of me thought, Shouldn't we ask Knight if we can go in his house? But another part of me acted. I followed Mike through the open door and into a huge living room. I had never seen a living room so big—brand-new, very modern, with almost no furniture on the expanse of the plush beige carpeting. "It looks like a Howard Johnson's Motor Lodge," said Mike. He was right. The living room stretched out the full width of the back of the house, with a glass wall rising two stories high looking out into the woods behind. It was a jarring contrast to the rickety houses in Edgemont. We sat down, surrounded by other students.

By the time Knight turned and came through his front door, he found two hundred students sitting quietly in his living room. Knight was speechless. A young woman stood up. "President Knight," she began in a calm clear voice, "in memory of Martin Luther King Jr., we call on the university to recognize the Duke workers' union, Local 77, and to raise their wages."

"Yeah," another student called out from the back of the room. "Now."

Knight sighed. "I can't talk to two hundred people at once."

We quickly elected three spokespeople. One was the outspoken young woman who had just addressed Knight. She was Bunny Small, someone I had never met before, but many others seemed to know and respect her. I felt thrilled—I had never seen a woman assume leadership. She and two other representatives huddled with Doug Knight in his kitchen.

Our representatives met with Knight late into the night. The rest of us sat around and talked quietly about how our cause was just. We assumed that Duke's liberal president would agree with us. But at midnight, our representatives emerged from the kitchen, and Bunny reported that Knight had not yielded to our demands. Knight insisted that only the board of trustees could make these decisions.

Mike and some of the others were clear on what we should do: "Call in the board of trustees. Meanwhile, we can sleep here on the rug." So all two hundred of us stretched out wall-to-wall on the plush carpet. Mike lay down and quickly fell asleep. He seemed so sure of what we were doing. Not me. I lay there staring at the ceiling, still surprised that Knight didn't understand the need for the union, and wondering what would happen. Hours later, I watched the president, on his way to his bedroom, carefully stepping over the sleeping bodies, followed by his basset hound.

The next day the campus workers walked off their jobs, declaring they were on strike until Duke recognized their union. Mike and I actually left Knight's house to go to our jobs in Edgemont. Then after work, we came back to Knight's house. We turned on Knight's huge TV to watch the six o'clock news, expecting to see ourselves. Instead they reported on rioters burning down city neighborhoods in Detroit, in Pittsburgh, other cities. In Durham, a few angry youth set several cars on fire. To my surprise, there was nothing on the news about us.

Union organizer Peter Brandon came and met with us that night at Knight's house. "Focus the demands on union recognition," he said. "If Local 77 gets recognized, we can bargain for higher wages not only now, but for years to come."

We agreed. People once again bedded down on the rug, but I lingered to talk with Peter Brandon. We sat on the carpeted steps joining the upper and lower sections of the living room.

"Have you ever heard of college students taking over their president's house?" I asked him, wondering if there was any precedent for what we were doing. (This was before the building occupations at Columbia, Cornell, the University of Chicago, and others.)

"No," he replied with a laugh.

"What should we do?" I asked him.

"I have no idea," he responded, shaking his head. "That's your problem. I have to figure out how to organize the strike."

The next day, Knight got sick and went to the hospital, diagnosed with hepatitis. Suddenly we were no longer in a discussion but only a building takeover. We heard that many students and professors were appalled that we were occupying Knight's home. I realized I wouldn't want students camped out in my house.

I called my mother, collect, from a guestroom right off the living room. I expected my ever-so-polite mother to chastise me for invading someone's house. But still in shock from King's death, she said, "I know they need that union at Duke." Clearly justice was on our side, I thought. Even my mother supports us.

Cooped up in Knight's house, we heard rumors that the Ku Klux Klan planned to surround the house and attack us through the plate-glass windows. We hotly debated what to do. I remember still being confused. But Mike spoke out, sitting on the railing of the second level of the living room, overlooking the mass of students. I stood on the level directly below him, watching him gesture as he urged us to stay in Knight's house and "negotiate with Duke from a position of power."

I disagreed with Mike. With Knight in the hospital, I felt our support would slip. I watched as other students voiced my sentiments. We voted. Along with the majority, I raised my hand to march back to campus. Mike and only a few others voted to stay in the house. Mike took his defeat with a shrug and a smile.

We cleaned up after ourselves and left a small crew behind to vacuum the living-room rug. Chanting "Recognize Local 77!" we walked back to the campus, stopping at the center of the campus in front of the Duke Chapel, where the striking Local 77 members marched. We would not move, we said, until our demands were met.

Our silent vigil began to grow. Other students joined us until the core of two hundred grew to fifteen hundred. We sat on the campus on the grass, in orderly rows, day after day, refusing to attend classes. The routine of the college ground to a halt. We had shut Duke down.

We were orderly and quiet. We sat by day and slept on the same spot by night. I was glad I could lie in Mike's arms to keep me warm in the chilly April nights. One night it rained, and we ran into Duke Chapel, sleeping on the wooden pews. The next day the sun came out, and we reassembled in our rows.

Eating became a problem because the cafeteria workers were on strike. The soda and candy machines quickly ran out. To feed us, the union organized supporters in Durham to bring us food—enough for fifteen hundred of us! They were mainly black businesspeople who owned restaurants or grocery stores. We set up long tables next to our vigil, and they provided us with drinks and sandwiches. Our favorite donations were from the Chicken Box, thousands of boxes of fried chicken and biscuits.

The staff of Durham's Operation Breakthrough visited us. That was great fun for Mike because they were his co-workers. Howard Fuller led the group and applauded our "worker/student alliance." (It was the first time I had seen him since he had kicked me and Mike out of a mass meeting several months earlier.) But this day he was glad to see all those white students supporting Duke's union. He led his group through the rows of students, giving us all celebratory high fives. Mike's co-workers gave Mike and me bear hugs.

Folksinger Joan Baez came and sang, and antiwar activist Tom Hayden told us we were doing the right thing.

After a few days, the Duke Board of Trustees flew in for an emergency meeting. I guess they were worried. Their campus was shut down, the president still in the hospital. People were rioting in cities across the country. Student representatives met with the trustees. After a few hours, Bunny Small walked out. "They are not going to even talk about recognizing the union," she said.

More moderate representatives emerged from the meeting the next day. They told us the trustees' proposal: to almost double the wages of the campus workers, up to $1.60 an hour!

Along with most students, I was impressed. That seemed like a big raise.

"Wait a minute," said Bunny. "Didn't Congress just pass legislation raising minimum wage to $1.60 an hour?"

The majority of students voted to end the protest. The trustees came out on the campus and joined the throng of fifteen hundred, arm in arm, singing "We Shall Overcome."

"Overcome what?" muttered Mike, shaking his head, as we stood with Bunny on the outskirts. The protest ended. But Duke's union movement was on its way. Three years later, Local 77 won recognition through a National Labor Relations Board election.[8]

This was how I became a radical. In 1968, the United States and the world seemed in turmoil. That winter, the war in Vietnam escalated as the Communists in the North carried out the Tet offensive. That spring, President Johnson shocked the nation by announcing that he would "neither seek nor accept" his party's renomination for president. I was shocked at his withdrawal from politics; we had no idea that our antiwar protests were so powerful.

In June, as we were adjusting to King's death, Robert Kennedy was assassinated. Meanwhile a youth movement flourished throughout the world: In France, students and workers held a general strike; in Czechoslovakia, "Prague Spring" loosened the Soviet Union's grip on the country until Soviet tanks rolled in to crush the movement.[9]

The forces of repression were strong, but the energy and exuberance of the movement seemed irrepressible. We were part of a worldwide movement. Fundamental social change seemed more possible than ever if we organized, took risks, and stuck together. I had found the direction for my life.

Paul ■ Martin Luther King was assassinated while I was running for student government president. I was feeling guilty about the sanctuary vigil, that I hadn't participated in the occupation of the building.

The night before he was killed, King gave a speech—his last speech. He said: "I've been to the mountaintop and I've seen the promised land. I may not get there with you, but we as a people, we are sure to get there." Such a heroic speech. He had been warned that some "sick white brothers" might kill him, and then the next day he was killed by one of them. In that speech, he foresaw his own death, and yet he still went ahead and did what he had to do. He stood for what was right, even though he knew he might be killed. To me, that speech was the highest expression of what morality should be. Is there any higher humanity to aspire to? He gave his life for the movement.

I felt that I was too worried about acceptability, too into the mainstream. I clipped King's speech from the *New York Times* and carried it around in my wallet for years. I swore that I would stop being a coward.

That was a seed of my willingness to become a communist. I was determined from that point on to do what I felt was right. I would no longer be swayed by superficial considerations like acceptability. Physical fear was not going to stand in my way. King was my model for that.

Willena ■ Nineteen sixty-eight was a big year for the movement, and for me. By the late 1960s, I thought King was a good man at heart but he was a little bit crazy. This business of getting spit on and not fighting back was something I could not subscribe to. He was working with whites in the movement, and I thought there was a little Uncle Tom in him, that he was giving in to some whites to get a little bit ahead. At that time, I didn't see him resolving the black problem. His plan would take too long; we needed to start a revolution and get things turned around soon. Later, I gained a lot of respect for King. He was scared of white violence and was trying something that he saw Gandhi do. There was a lot of spirituality in him.

When they killed King, it was because he was bringing together the civil rights movement and the antiwar movement. That was really dangerous for the United States, and they had to stop him.

Nineteen sixty-eight was even a bigger year for me personally. John and I wanted to have children right away, but it took a long time for me to get pregnant. Then in 1968, I had a good pregnancy with Kwame. I could feel him growing inside me. When it was his time, he came really quick—I was in labor for fifty minutes. Kwame came out while the orderly was pushing us through the door of the delivery room. Kwame was hollering and so was I!

It was like I had created the world. Every day was a new day. I loved holding him, looking at him. His shade was light and he had African features. I worried he would go through the pain that I had gone through. That brought me back to the harsh world I was bringing him into. I resolved to make this a better place. It was like a big responsibility that I owed this little person.

3

Movement Peak

After Martin Luther King's assassination, the energy of the growing movement continued to take a more radical direction. In 1969, students took over campus buildings in both North and South. Black nationalism, the belief that African Americans had to build their own movement for empowerment, grew from coast to coast, leading to massive demonstrations in support of African liberation struggles. The women's liberation movement took off nationwide and included hundreds of small consciousness-raising groups, as well as national organizations and caucuses for women's rights. Antiwar sentiment expanded, pressuring the United States to withdraw its troops from Vietnam. And the repression of activists increased: The police upped their violence against demonstrators, and the FBI further infiltrated and harassed activist groups under its Counterintelligence Program (COINTELPRO).

Black-Student Takeover at Duke, February 1969

Sally ■ In 1969 in Greensboro and Durham, students took over buildings at A&T and Duke. At both campuses, police responded with violence. An A&T student, Willie Grimes, lost his life, and many believed it was from a police bullet. Repression increased around the nation, including the assassination of Martin Luther King Jr. and the murder of numerous Black Panthers. But into the early seventies, there still was a lot of energy in the movement and powerful mobilizations around many issues.

In 1969, Duke University had only one black professor. Students pushed to get more black professors and a black studies program. The black student leaders were good friends of Mike's and mine, part of the radical community that sprang up after King's assassination and our Duke vigil.

Negotiations with Duke's administration were going nowhere as the spring 1969 semester began. We woke up one February morning to the news that black students were occupying Duke's administration building. So we dressed warmly and went over to Allen building with water bottles and rags, in case there was tear gas. By this time, we had learned how to prepare for confrontations with police from years of antiwar demonstrations. We stood in the three entrances to Allen building, determined to prevent cops from storming the building. There must have been fifty or sixty of us white students, standing in solidarity with our brothers and sisters inside the building.

Nelson ■ I was in Greensboro at Bennett College with Owusu Sadaukai, who was giving a speech, when we got the word that black Duke students had taken over Duke's administration building. So Owusu and I drove fifty miles to Durham and joined the students in Allen building. That was where Malcolm X Liberation University was born, as an alternative to the institutionalized racism of Duke and other universities.

A large contingent of police arrived on Duke's campus while we were inside the administration building. We marched out of the administration building onto the quadrangle. A large crowd had gathered there. The police started teargassing everyone.

Sally ■ It had been a long day, standing in that Allen building entranceway. It was getting dark when suddenly the black students emerged. With their fists in the air, they marched out the front door of Allen building onto the main quadrangle, holding a banner that said "Malcolm X Liberation University." The quad was full of white students, many of them curious onlookers. I assumed the protest was basically over except for some chanting. I hoped there would be a few speeches, because I wanted to hear about Malcolm X Liberation University.

Suddenly, the police started teargassing everyone. From what I could see, the police provoked the riot, clubbing students who came too close to them. They chased people all over the quad with the tear gas. A bunch of students ran into the Duke Chapel to get away from the tear gas. To my shock, police ran after them, opened the door, and sprayed tear gas inside the chapel!

Paul ■ I heard about the protest at Duke and the police attacking them on the news. I was trying to decide where to go to medical school—both Johns Hopkins and Duke had accepted me. That day, I decided to go to Duke. Things were happening there and I wanted to be part of them. Little did I know that my future wife and good friends were in the middle of it.

The Dudley High School Protest and the A&T Revolt, May 1969

Nelson ■ Confrontations between activists and police increased through the winter of 1969. In February, students occupied the A&T administration building. GAPP [Greensboro Association of Poor People] held a memorial on Malcolm

X's birthday, and the police came and harassed us, surrounding us, firing tear gas at us. (Afterwards, the police claimed that some tear-gas canisters "opened by mistake.") In March, cafeteria workers at A&T went on strike, and twenty-five hundred students marched to President Dowling's in support of the strikers. Once again, police harassed students, who threw rocks at them.

That spring, I ran for vice president of A&T's student government. It never was my intention to run for office, but the students drafted me. The city campaigned against me, including the Chamber of Commerce. All that opposition meant we had become an effective force for change.

Meanwhile, tensions grew at Dudley High School, a black high school located near A&T. Traditionally, Dudley's principals exercised tight control over the students, and in 1968 and 1969, any sign of black power was seen as opposing the rules. They suspended several female students for wearing Afro hairstyles.

In the spring of 1969, Claude Barnes decided he wanted to run for student government president at Dudley. He was a perfect candidate—an honor student, junior-class president. Perfect, except that he was an activist in the black-power movement, and he had worked with GAPP and with me. A Dudley faculty-student election committee decided that he "lacked qualifications" to run but gave no reasons. When they held the election for student government that spring, six hundred students wrote in Claude Barnes's name on the ballot. But the election committee determined that the election was "won" by the other candidate, who received only some two hundred votes. Claude Barnes and five others walked out of the school in protest.

We organized a meeting in the black community, including pastors of the biggest churches, black politicians, and poor folk whose children went to Dudley. And the Board of Elections would not allow the principal of Dudley to attend. It felt like colonialism. We, the colonial subjects, were not even allowed a voice in matters that directly affected us. The white power structure, dominated by supremacist ideology, would not allow a meaningful conversation. And the Greensboro newspapers, willing servants of the power structure's view, spewed these invectives against us, against the students, against the movement. There was nowhere for that anger to go. People had gotten beyond the point of simply backing down. So it exploded.

On May 21, the police teargassed a Dudley student protest. Students were marching in a picket line that demanded Claude Barnes be seated as student government president. The police attack on the high school students was the straw that broke the camel's back. A hundred Dudley students marched to A&T. With red, watery eyes and torn clothing, the Dudley students appealed to us to help them. We rallied A&T students and joined the Dudley students, marching back to the high school four hundred strong. It felt like a liberation army.

That night, a carload of young whites drove down East Market Street and fired guns into the A&T campus. The campus reacted; basically, people were defending themselves. It was the beginning of a three-day revolt. Vehicles were turned over, and fires burned, and streets were blocked. Without consulting A&T's president, the mayor called out the National Guard to patrol the campus. Gunfire was exchanged.

And the Chamber of Commerce convened a meeting and called me to it. They asked me to negotiate a cease-fire; they assumed that I was more in charge than I was. I told them I didn't have any authority to stop A&T students, and I couldn't do it if I wanted to. They were outraged.

During the night, a bullet in the back of his head killed Willie Grimes, an A&T student. He was a mild-mannered young man, an A&T student and member of the ROTC. He was with a group of students who saw police take out their guns and fire. The students ran, and that was when Grimes was killed.

The students who were eyewitnesses to the attack were never questioned by law enforcement. We held a press conference to share information with the press. A reporter wrote an article, including a diagram of where the cops and where the students were. But that reporter was fired; the police ignored our information. The cops said simply that Grimes must have been caught in the crossfire between students. But we knew the bullet of police killed him.

Who killed Willie Grimes was never officially determined. The city's white leadership blamed *me*. The police chief and mayor described me as "the most militant and dangerous person ever in Greensboro." I was arrested for "disrupting a public school" and "inciting to riot," charges that carried a prison term.

I fought back every way I could. A series of court cases took several years to resolve. More immediately, I wrote "Open Letter to the Black Community," which was published in the *Peacemaker*, Greensboro's black newspaper. I stated: "In our efforts to promote changes, unimaginable obstacles have been place in our way. Whenever we took action, only those things that could be made to appear bad were reported. . . . We have been made to seem stupid, hateful, and violent." The powers that be always talked about "outsiders" to explain why protests happened, rather than look at the issues we raised. I wrote: "It has never been a case of outsider versus insider; instead it has been right versus wrong."[1]

My response to the city leaders' attacks was to work very hard to bring together the leadership of the black community, including the clergy of the major churches, the student leaders at Dudley and A&T, and the leaders of GAPP. I was the principal link in connecting all of these people. That, the city noticed.

I worked very hard with others to get the U.S. Civil Rights Commission to carry out an investigation of Willie Grimes's murder. The black community had to demonstrate support for the commission to investigate. So I met with the president of a new black bank, Mr. Webb, and he asked me tough questions and ultimately signed the letter calling for a federal investigation. After I got Webb's signature, I went from church to organization, place after place after place. So we got an investigation by the North Carolina Civil Rights Commission, and they issued a report that found great fault with the police and the City of Greensboro. But Greensboro's political elite trashed the report.

All that work put me into a good relationship with the black middle class, but Greensboro officialdom continued to try to break my ties with the black community. They made accusations and overtures to me to abandon the struggle. Of course, they never said, "Abandon the struggle"; they were showing a more excellent way to struggle, which was precisely to abandon it. At one point, I was offered a good amount of money to go study economics at the University of Chicago. I wasn't interested. But at that time, the attacks on me actually led to further bonding between the black community and myself.

Through this, I gradually became aware of the evil nature of the system— that people in power would lie, twist what you said, and conspire against you.

Willena ■ In spring 1969, when all that happened at Dudley and A&T, I was in South Carolina with my husband and my new baby, Kwame, just a few months old. I kept up with the news from Greensboro, and once again I was longing to be back there in the movement. That was the first I heard about a man named Nelson Johnson. He was in the news a lot. I thought, Right on, Nelson Johnson.

The Battle for Open Admissions at CUNY, Spring 1969

Paul ■ Black and Puerto Rican students took over the campus at City College, demanding that the City University of New York open its doors to all high school graduates in New York City. Even though City College is located in the middle of Harlem, the largest black community in the United States, there were very few students of color on campus. Black and Puerto Rican students boldly took over South Campus, which was surrounded by a fence, and they shut down the campus—all seventeen buildings. All the classes had to be canceled. It was way more disruptive than the takeover of the student union a year earlier, when the college continued to function.

And the administration was stymied, because the sentiment at the time was strongly pro–civil rights. The takeover became a major issue in the mayor's race between [Abraham] Beame and [John] Lindsey that year. For weeks the students maintained control of the grounds. There was the constant threat that the police were coming in to bust it up. A number of white students started making billy clubs in a woodshop, getting ready to fight with the cops. People were bringing in food, and it really became a whole siege. As president of the student government, I wanted to support the takeover. But the student leader, Serge

Mullery, would always call me "Richard Nixon." I was not a Nixonite at all, but as far as he was concerned I might as well have been. (He did give me some respect a few months later when we staged a walkout at graduation.) Finally, Mayor John Lindsey got the CUNY Board of Trustees to adopt an open-admissions policy. It was this takeover that forced CUNY to open its doors to New York's poor and working-class youth of all races.[2]

Love and Activism in 1969

Nelson ■ In the middle of all the intensity of 1968, I met Joyce Hobson. And a few months later, during the A&T revolt, we got married.

My social life was one of the areas in which I'd always felt inferior. As an adolescent, I was not cool. I didn't dance well; everybody in my neighborhood and school seemed to dance better than I did. I didn't have things to say and would always think afterwards of what I should have said. My rap wasn't on tap when I needed it. I think this sense of inferiority grew from my childhood, from that color structure in my neighborhood.

My first year in Greensboro was lonely. I had just gotten out of the air force and was hanging around with my three friends who I went to high school and the air force with. We saved a little money in the air force and spent it in Greensboro. My relationships with the young ladies were based on spending a little money that other students didn't have.

I got into the movement, and as I became recognized as a leader, girls started wanting my attention. It was a surprise to me. I wasn't used to it. All of a sudden there were fleeting glances and someone would say, "Let's go out and have coffee." I thought, Wow, this is not too bad.

So in 1966 and 1967, I began to develop social relationships where I was relaxed and at home. I was in my twenties, rather late in life, and I was overcoming some of the insecurities of my childhood. I was finding a niche where I had more respect for myself, and that engendered respect from others. So I had girlfriends—and then I had too many girlfriends. This is never a problem that I had before. I didn't know what to do, because it actually started to interfere with my capacity to do work.

The driving force of my life was the work that we were doing in the community. I wasn't a "player"—I had no experience in it, and I didn't want to be one. I had been speaking out against players, yet I was in a position to go that way. I lived in a house with two friends from the air force, and it was always an open house.

That was when I met Joyce Hobson. It was during the time that I had quite a few relationships, and I wasn't particularly looking for any new one. I was really attracted to Joyce and wanted to get to know her. She had just graduated from Duke and was going to graduate school at University of North Carolina at Chapel Hill and was involved in campus activism there. We talked a good deal about the work that was going on in Greensboro and in Chapel Hill. That's where much of our political discourse started. We discussed the problems we were each having in the work. I enjoyed being with her.

At that time, I was traveling around the state a good deal. I stopped in Chapel Hill to see Joyce. That was the first time we hugged and kissed. This is exciting, I thought. What attracted me to Joyce was her sensitivity to the things that I was struggling with, and her scope and openness—she genuinely was into this struggle. And the relationship grew from there. We started spending a lot of time together. I looked forward to those wonderful after-work meals and discussions with Joyce.

Joyce and I committed to each other during some of the thickest politics in North Carolina in the spring of '69. After the students took over Duke's administration building in February, that night we went back over to Duke, and I ended up getting arrested. I was in jail overnight. I was not happy about that. When I got out the next day, I went on to Chapel Hill, and Joyce and I had a deep talk. Joyce and I decided that we were going to be together.

I felt that I had discovered a very special person in my life. Joyce and I were together all the time for the next month. Then the A&T revolt happened, and we made a commitment to be married. Things got so ferocious, and Joyce and I decided that we would get married that next day.

So we found this senior minister and went to his house with two good friends for our best men, and that was it. We decided to spend the rest of our lives together. And since then we've pretty much done everything together. I'm not the greatest conversationalist about anything, but we do share significantly and deeply.

Sally ■   In 1969, I "lived in sin" for months and then married Mike Nathan.

After the Duke vigil in 1968, we formed a radical community of Duke students, based on the group of people who found each other when we took over President Knight's house. I was a junior, living off campus in Edgemont. For my senior year, I was expected to move back to the dormitory, because in those days, all unmarried undergraduate women lived on campus. But I could not imagine living again in a dorm. So my parents wrote a letter to the dean stating that they gave their permission for me to move into an apartment several blocks from the campus and share it with Bunny Small (the leader of the Duke vigil) and Day Piercy; both had just graduated from Duke. The dean granted my request.

So Bunny, Day, and I moved into a cheap duplex apartment at 629 Green Street near the campus, with three bedrooms and a kitchen–living room combination. The next day, our boyfriends moved in with us. (I left that part out of my discussions with my parents and the dean.) Other radicals moved into the duplexes next door. Our houses on Green Street became a hub of activism. Meanwhile, Mike and I continued to work in Edgemont. The Edgemont Teen Council continued to have dances at the community center every Saturday night.

Early in the fall, while the weather was still warm, we held a huge party on Green Street. Activist professors joined scores of radical students that Saturday night at our duplex apartments. The Edgemont Teen Council decided to shift their weekly dance to Green Street. To the consternation of some of our neighbors, the beat-up Edgemont Community Center bus arrived packed with teens from the ghetto. We partied to Aretha Franklin and other soul favorites. Blasting "Heard It Through the Grapevine," the Edgemont teens lined up between the duplex apartments and taught students and even some professors how to boogie, Edgemont style.

That fall, the women's liberation movement hit Durham. A feminist from New York arrived at Duke, and a women-only meeting was quickly organized. There must have been fifty to sixty young women jammed into the parlor of a Duke dorm, mainly activists in antiwar and civil rights protests. The feminist argued that we should fight for our own rights. It was thrilling. It was the first time I had been in a meeting that was closed to men, and it made such a welcome difference. It was neat to hear *women* talk, rather than just listening to men, who dominated meetings. (It also made me appreciate why many African Americans felt the need to kick whites out of their meetings.)

Very quickly, my women friends and I became conscious of the inequality of "women's work" and "men's work." On Green Street, we began arguing with our boyfriends over who did the cooking and cleaning. Bunny, Day, and I insisted that the guys do half the housework. We had little luck on getting the guys to clean the place (it was Bunny, Day, and myself who got rid of cockroaches). But we did successfully divide the cooking. Each person had a day that they cooked for everyone and cleaned up after the meal. Bunny specialized in Rice-a-Roni; my meal was beef, macaroni, and tomatoes. The guys resisted, but sisterhood was powerful. Mike moaned that he couldn't cook. "You can scramble eggs," I pointed out. So on Mike's day, we ate scrambled eggs and bacon for dinner.

Bunny Small taught me a lot about politics. The child of an army officer, Bunny became a radical as a teenager, when her father was stationed in the Philippines. "Look what the U.S. is doing around the world," Bunny told me. "It's not just in Vietnam, but all over. It's not just one war, but a whole system of imperialism."

Every night, our household gathered around our beat-up black-and-white TV set, with a coat hanger sticking out from the ends of the broken rabbit-ear antenna. We watched the Vietnam War and the 1968 presidential election campaign. We watched the cops beat protesters outside the 1968 Democratic Convention. We argued over how to vote. Day and her boyfriend reluctantly supported Hubert Humphrey because he was more liberal than Richard Nixon. Bunny and her boyfriend argued for voting for Richard Nixon because his election would make things worse, and that would make the revolution come sooner. Mike and I decided not to vote at all. We thought real change would only come from organizing at the grass roots.

That winter, our senior year, Mike agonized over what to do when he graduated. Should he serve the people as a community organizer or as a doctor? I lobbied for community organization, but Mike chose medicine, his childhood dream.

I wanted to get married. I saw myself as a radical activist but had no idea what that meant after graduation. Marriage to Mike seemed like a safe anchor. We set a wedding date for March 23, 1969, during our spring vacation.

During the Christmas break, Mike and I told our families of our wedding plans. My sister was thrilled, and my mother gave me a half-hearted "Jews are different" talk. I told my mother to give me a break, that I really loved Mike. Then my parents helped us organize the wedding. Where do you hold a Jewish-Protestant wedding? My father got us the reception hall of the American Chemical Society in Washington, D.C., where he worked. We got both a minister and a rabbi (one of the few rabbis in the country at that time who would marry a Christian and a Jew). We wrote our own ceremony.

We had a big hippie wedding, with two hundred friends and a jazz guitarist playing "Here Comes the Bride." Everyone got what they wanted. My mother threw a bridal shower, and her friends gave me silver tea sets and Salton heating trays. My father walked me down the aisle. Mike and I exchanged vows and smashed a glass while standing under a big flowered *chuppa*. Mike's relatives wrote us checks (our favorite gifts). And a bunch of our friends came up from Durham to celebrate with us. Twice as many people packed the hall as we expected, and the food ran out before Mike and I got any. We all had a ball.

Paul ■ In 1969, I finally moved away from my family's home. I had lived with them in the projects for all four years of college. Leaving home was very traumatic for my whole family, because I was the apple of my parents' eye, and I had violated their wishes. By being an activist, I was taking a course that they thought was suicidal.

I wanted to get away from them, to be on my own. In June 1969, I graduated from City College, and I was going to start medical school in August. My girlfriend, Erica, and I were in the middle of an intense romance. I had also gotten a perfect job working for Erica's father. He was a renowned scientist, and he hired me as a research assistant in his laboratory, where he was studying lipid chemistry of the brain. I got the job because he liked me and I was his daughter's boyfriend. It looked like Erica and I might even get married.

Erica and I sublet an apartment, and I moved out of my parents' house. My mother argued with me, fought me, hit me. She did everything she could to stop me, just carrying on. I had to push her off me more than once; it was so ridiculous. She said we were "living in sin," that is, cohabiting without the benefit of a blessing by a religious figure in the form of a marriage. She said it was the worst thing we could do. I realized that any woman that I was going to get involved with was going to be unacceptable to my mother. But she could not stop me, so I moved out.

Erica and I moved into a nice little apartment, and every day, I took the train up to Columbia Medical Center to work in the lab for Erica's dad. I had almost nothing to do with my parents, which I really wanted. I had finally gotten out of the house!

But my mother is a very determined person. Somehow she got hold of Erica's parents' phone number. She called Erica's parents the day after Erica's mother had gotten back from being hospitalized for an operation, but that did not stop my mother from giving the poor woman an earful. Of course, Erica's parents told her about my mother, and Erica's dad was my boss. When I heard about it, I felt terrible. My mother had no business calling them up like that. The next day at work, I apologized to Erica's dad for my mother's behavior. He said not to worry—his mother was the same way! I was so relieved, and for a long time I thought that he was going to be my father-in-law.

Willena ■ I gave birth to Kwame on November 23, 1968, in Greensboro. Right after the birth, my husband left to go to this new job in Charleston, South Carolina, with Manpower Development. They were holding a job for me as well, but I stayed in Greensboro for a few months to get my strength back.

I joined Johnny in Charleston when Kwame was a few months old. Charleston is right on the coast of South Carolina, and it was the biggest port for slave ships for hundreds of years in this country. I will never forget the first time I saw the slave market. The whole thing is intact, with pictures of the white slave masters looking the slaves over and checking in their mouths like people do to a horse. My imagination went wild—I could see people crowded in there and hear their anguished voices. I realized I was standing there crying. I wanted to burn the place down, as if I could burn that whole history. But then I realized it should stay there to be part of Charleston now.

I traveled out to the islands off the coast—John's Island, James Island. These islands, the Spanish moss hanging from the trees, are like something you would see in a movie. I met old women, one of them 98 years old, another 104. One of them spoke with an African language; her daughter translated. The other talked about her parents being freed and leaving Charleston to come to the islands. They never went back to Charleston; it was like a horrible dream. I felt like I was reaching back in history.

That spring, 1969, the hospital nurses went on strike to bring in 1199 as their union. Jesse Jackson came down to support the drive and to join the Mother's Day march. The mayor put a curfew on the city, but we held a meeting at church and broke the curfew. I got arrested with a bunch of folks, and the NAACP got us out. Then we were marching again and got arrested again.

My husband said, "I don't have all the anger coming out of me like it's coming out of you. Somebody's got to work and take care of our son. So I'll go to work, I'll take care of our son. You go to jail."

My mother got really worried about what was happening. She came to Charleston to see if she could get me out. But the NAACP had already made the arrangements to get me out. It felt good, struggling again. And the nurses won some concessions.

That was the good part of being in Charleston. The bad part was finding out that Johnny was an alcoholic. When I got to Charleston, I learned that John's boss was an alcoholic. He had been on the wagon but then started drinking again. He got Johnny to drink with him. At first, Johnny didn't want to drink, then he got to where he didn't mind it, and then he got to want it. Then I realized that my husband really was an alcoholic, but I didn't know what to do. Johnny got fired, but I was still working. Johnny left to go to D.C. to find a job, and he was supposed to get work and send for me, but he never did.

Eventually I came back to Greensboro and started working at P. Lorillard Tobacco Company, the best-paying job around. Later I found out that Johnny had found a job in D.C.—at a liquor store. Johnny was drinking so much that he would fall out in the street. His high school buddy called his parents, and they came to get Johnny. Then his mom came to Greensboro to talk to me. She said they wanted to work with Johnny, and he had a better chance if he had me and our baby with him.

So we moved to Springfield, Massachusetts, to live in this apartment building with Johnny's parents and grandmother. Alcoholics Anonymous and social workers—none of that worked. Johnny seemed to try even less to quit now that we were living with his family. After six months, I couldn't deal with him and his alcoholism. I hated to even see a beer can. Johnny was not a mean drunk. He was a talented person who could have done anything he wanted to do. Watching somebody I loved just waste away, that was just killing me, and I couldn't do nothing. My hair was falling out. I couldn't take it anymore.

I made a plan to make some extra money and get out of there. I wanted to get back to Greensboro, back to my family, back to the movement. First I had to make extra money so I could leave. I got a job at the Springfield Post Office. People laughed at me because I was the only woman there, and they were sure I couldn't pass the physical test. What they didn't know was that I was strong and had training in physical education. I knew how to lift seventy pounds. I passed all the tests, and that post office was the easiest job I ever had. I was supposed to be loading trucks, and those men would not let me lift anything more than five pounds! I had a good time and made good money. I got a second job and worked sixty days. Then I had enough money for my escape.

Kwame turned two on November 23, 1970. On the morning of December 4, I got Kwame up and ready to leave. Johnny was upstairs drunk, and his mother had just gone to work. I had already packed the car, a big, dark-colored old Dodge. The backseat was just for Kwame, with a lot of toys and balloons and some fruit for him to eat. I got in, ready to get out of there—and the car wouldn't start! I took a butter knife and put it in the carburetor and started the car that way.

We left Springfield, Massachusetts, and headed south. Kwame was having a good time in the backseat, eating and playing with balloons. But that trip, it was like biblical. We got to Connecticut and hail came beating down on the car. I had never seen hail in my life, and I thought it was going to break the windows. I pulled over to the side. Kwame's still playing and I'm praying. He didn't know I was scared to death. The hail ended and we got started again. I drove all the way to Springfield, Virginia. We stopped, and I went shopping for all my family's Christmas stuff. I felt a great relief.

But the next morning, I had a flat tire! And I'm trying to save this money I got, 'cause I don't know how soon I'll get a job, and I've got a child now. So I spent four dollars on a tire and paid for it to be put on. The man told me that it should take the car to Greensboro. I drove on that tire for three months.

And that's how we got back to Greensboro. I wanted to be independent. I stayed with my sister, and Kwame and I slept on a couch in the living room. I paid my sister's rent, although she said I didn't have to. I got a night-manager's job from five to eleven, which gave me time to look for a good job during the day.

Kwame ■ My earliest memories were in Springfield, Massachusetts, where I would stay with my father, my grandmother, and my great-grandmother. After Mom and Dad got divorced, I got shuttled back and forth between Greensboro and Massachusetts. I spent summers with my dad. My great-grandmother was my savior. Anytime I would do something bad, and my father would get on me, I could go downstairs to Great-grandma. My great-grandma would put me right behind her and her walker. She would fend Daddy off, telling my daddy, "Leave John-John alone!" I was John-John then; I became Kwame later.

When I think back to Springfield, Massachusetts, I think about little things. On Saturday morning, my favorite thing was to sit and watch the cartoons and go in the freezer and get popsicles. I knew my nana didn't like me having sweets that early in the morning. But I would get up before she would and eat me a sack full of popsicles. Then when breakfast time came around, I wouldn't be hungry and Nana would get on me for eating the sweets.

I always thought my mom and dad would get back together. I wanted them to so bad. They talked nice to each other, and I was sure they loved each other. I would always bring it up to my dad, and he would say, "Time will tell." That would almost give me a little hope—Dad was not against them getting back together.

Anticipating an Ever-growing Movement, 1970

Marty ■ I spent the early seventies in Rhode Island at Brown University. The movement was in full swing, and I did not expect it to ever calm down. In those days we didn't know about ebbs and flows of a movement. We had only seen a flow.

It was incredibly stimulating to be at Brown. There was a wonderful movement there against the Vietnam War, and I got involved in the moratoriums and the student strike of 1970. I developed passionate anger against our government for the destruction in Vietnam. There were terrific folks at Brown that made life livable for me, a depressed, conflicted young woman who was trying to learn how to survive.

I had lost everything. I had left home but carried my depression with me. My mother would call me up every week and cry, and I felt guilty because I wasn't there with her. I had rejected my mother and lost the rest of my family. I kept on, studying incredibly hard, participating in the antiwar movement, and partying on the weekends.

Nelson ■ When the decade of the 1970s opened, I had very little historical perspective. I thought the sixties were normal, and that we would continue to build ever-bigger mass movements for social change. For several years, there was a lot of energy in the movement around new issues and institutions, among poor and middle class, working people and students. The Greensboro Poor People's Organization [GAPP] was leading grassroots organizing in a number of different neighborhoods. Malcolm X Liberation University, which black students founded during the Duke building takeover, moved to Greensboro. It was an alternative education institution, teaching skills, promoting African pride and dialogue between Africans and African Americans.

A nationwide group of black student government leaders defected from the National Association of Students [NAS], because they felt that organization did not represent African Americans. There was increasing evidence that the NAS had been infiltrated by the CIA. So these dissident students built a national organization called Students Organized for Black Unity [SOBU]. (A year or so later, we changed the word "students" to "youth," so SOBU became YOBU.)[3]

In the regional and national meetings where SOBU emerged, I was a secondary leader. There were others who were more charismatic and better speakers. But I ended up being drafted into leadership of SOBU because we had a real base in Greensboro. People decided to hold the founding meeting of SOBU in Greensboro at A&T in the fall of 1969. And they were impressed with everything that was going on—at Dudley High School, A&T, Bennett, GAPP, the whole thing. I welcomed people and started to chair meetings, and folks just elected me president of SOBU. There was lots of enthusiasm at that meeting. One of the energetic young students was a freshman from Bennett College, Sandi Neely, who later died in the Greensboro massacre.

I faced some personal challenges in 1970. I faced a prison sentence, growing out of the A&T revolt. I was charged with disrupting a public school and inciting to riot. The law only permitted a six-month sentence for these charges. But right after the A&T revolt, the state legislature convened and passed a law making those charges a felony with a prison term of two years. The judge applied the *new* law to me, a law made after "the crimes" were committed.[4] A&T students and Greensboro's black community made a powerful petition to the governor and the Supreme Court of North Carolina that ultimately got my prison term reduced to six months. And because of the pressure from the citizens of Greensboro, I only served two months.

During all the trials, Joyce and I established a home. We both wanted children, but I had prison hanging over me. The trial and the appeal to the North Carolina Supreme Court went on for a year and a half. Joyce was concerned that she couldn't have children, but our baby, Akua, was born in February 1971, and then I went to prison.

Joyce came out to visit me in prison with our little baby and my father. That was a difficult moment. My dad wanted me to be a lawyer or a doctor, and I wanted to please him—and here I am in the can. My wife and my little child, I wanted to be with them more than anything—and here I am out there on the road gang, busting rock, cutting trees. There was a lot of pressure on our relationship, but Joyce and I didn't falter. Really, our relationship got stronger. There was a community that took care of us, took care of Joyce, so she wasn't isolated. But it was tough.

I was released from prison on Good Friday. While I was serving time, Joyce found a house on Alamance Church Road. So when I got released, I didn't know where I lived. The corrections officer brought me into Greensboro, and the procedure was to bring a released prisoner to his house, but I didn't know where to tell him to go. So I got off on English Street, and I walked over to a friend's house and tried to find out where I lived. Finally, somebody took me to this big old house that needed a lot of work—my new home. My farming years came in handy. I rented a bush hog (a big old tractor), and I just mowed down all the overgrown bushes. Joyce and I started to build a permanent life together, and we lived in that old house for eighteen years.

Sally ■ The early seventies brought confusion about what I wanted to do with my life, and my marriage was on the rocks. I had fallen in love with Mike Nathan when we were both students, both working part-time, both sharing a lot of interests. We graduated, and Mike started Duke Medical School. Medicine consumed all of his waking hours. During the little time we spent together, Mike seemed tired, distracted. He became increasingly morose, sliding back into that sad place where he still mourned his father. I didn't know how to reach him.

I became angry because I was no longer the object of his attention. As students we were always together; now I hardly saw him. I had to support us and got a part-time job at the Edgemont Community Center directing a preschool program. I brought home fifty-five dollars a week to feed and shelter us. We rented a rickety wooden shack for nine dollars a week. When the wind picked up, it blew the papers off the desk in our bedroom. Poverty can be fun when you are in love (and you know you are not stuck in it). But I was alone most of the time, and it became depressing.

I joined a women's liberation conscious-raising group. I realized that in terms of status, Mike and I had gone from an equal relationship to an unequal one, so I decided to raise my status by going to law school. I figured that lawyers were as cool as doctors, and there was certainly a lot that movement lawyers were doing.

So I went through the long application process and entered Duke Law School in September 1970. The problem was, once I got there, I hated it. Richard Nixon's portrait was on the wall of the moot courtroom. Duke had discriminated against women and was just beginning to admit them in any significant numbers. We made up 10 percent of my class—tripling the number of women the year before. But many of our all-white male professors disagreed with women being admitted to law school, and they picked on us in class and ridiculed us when we made mistakes. I lasted two months in law school. In November 1970 I became a law school dropout. I felt alone and depressed and had to figure out how to support Mike and me.

Paul ■ At Duke Medical School, my political evolution accelerated. As a med student, I had much less time to talk about politics and much more experience observing real life. Duke was horrible when it came to treating poor people. There was a joke about how every patient that came to Duke got the "green test," and the green test consisted of measuring the circumference of the patient's wallet. I despised the way the medical school treated working people, especially black people.

I witnessed how this great institution of higher learning that prides itself on being the "Harvard of the South" was a grubby, social-climbing institution that was interested in money and not interested in people. One of the first people I met was Mike Nathan, who was a kindred spirit. We were both working-class Jewish kids who hated Duke.

There were other activists in my medical school class. As busy as we were, a bunch of us made time to organize against the war in Vietnam. Our little group succeeded in organizing a day of protest against the invasion of Cambodia, and we closed down the medical school. So many students were going to boycott class that we got the professors to cancel all the classes.

We constantly had discussions exploring what is the social responsibility of a doctor. Che Guevara, who was a physician, used to talk about a doctor who is in his office and patients come in with broken legs, one after another. The doctor kept doing a beautiful, perfect medical job of wrapping up and bandaging and putting a cast on the legs, and lo and behold, the patients would heal and get better. And they would come back a short time later with a broken leg again. And he would keep healing them, and they would keep coming back. Until finally the doctor got up, went out of his office, and filled up the hole that the people were falling into. And that became like a guiding spirit to our group of radical doctors at Duke in those days. The fact that it had come from Che Guevara made it much more powerful, because Che had just been hunted down in the jungles of Bolivia, trying to make revolution throughout Latin America. God bless him.

Our political group became more and more political. We joined the Medical Committee for Human Rights, a national organization that had formed in the early 1960s to provide medical assistance during civil rights demonstrations. We began to do educational campaigns to expose the greedy ways of the pharmaceutical companies. The drug companies had (and still have) many methods to push doctors to prescribe their expensive drugs and to prevent doctors from promoting cheaper generic alternatives. MCHR's slogan was "Healthcare is a human right." We studied how Duke Medical Center was more interested in profits than providing decent health care to poor and working people.[5]

In medical school, I became more directed towards a life of political activism. As things went on, it became clearer and clearer to me that I wanted to fight for change in society. I discovered that there were a lot of things a doctor could do to help the movement. A doctor had helped the United Mine Workers organize the Black Lung Association in the coalfields in West Virginia, and that became a model for us to organize a Brown Lung Association in North Carolina. Brown lung, or byssinosis, is a disease of textile workers, afflicting tens of thousands of workers in the Carolinas. I spent my last two years in medical school focusing on pulmonary medicine, becoming a pulmonologist and a researcher in brown lung. I went out to the factories and met with workers, a fabulous experience.

After I graduated from medical school, I started a residency program at UNC in Chapel Hill in psychiatry, because it was the field I was most interested in. But while I was there, a man named Mike Szpach got a grant from the Ford Foundation to organize a Brown Lung Association, and he was looking for a doctor. So here I was, a brand-new doctor who was an expert in brown lung, so I helped Mike Szpach organize the Brown Lung Association. I was traveling a great deal, and it was incompatible with continuing as a resident in psychiatry. So after my first year, I dropped out of my residency program to do the brown-lung work.

Meanwhile, Jim Waller, who would die in the massacre, joined our effort. He was another Jewish doctor dedicated to using medicine to make social change. We both participated in the founding of the Carolina Brown Lung Association, and there is a picture of us there with some retired mill workers. We began to work throughout North and South Carolina, setting up clinics and screening workers for brown lung.

Willena ■   I moved back to Greensboro in December 1970, and as soon as I got my feet on the ground, I began to check out the movement. I went to the Greensboro Association of Poor People and finally met Nelson Johnson, who I had heard so much about. There was a story hour every Saturday morning for children at Malcolm X Liberation University; people would dress up in African clothes and talk about our African heritage. Doing that with Kwame, age two, was a good thing. And I got involved in meetings about different issues and started going to demonstrations. I felt good again; I was doing something to change things.

I got a job as a counselor at Neighborhood Youth Corps, part of the federal poverty program. I had to dress a certain way so I could deal with a lot of agencies. There were times when I would go to work in my good clothes, and then come home to change into my jeans to go to the GAPP House, and then change again to go back to work.

My family was afraid I was going to lose my job. I didn't pay any attention to that, but then I came to see the pressure on people to stop fighting for change. My boss had been a community leader when she got hired by the poverty program. In her big-time director job, she had to watch what she was doing or she could lose her job. After a while, I saw that that was where the whole civil rights movement was going. A lot of the leaders got jobs and didn't want to lose them, and so they stopped trying to change things. My boss told me, "Listen Willena, you can go to meetings after work, but you can't be seen out in the street." Which meant that in meetings, I could plan to do things, but then I couldn't carry them through in the street. My bosses were afraid of being "responsible" for me (and Nelson and a bunch of other folks) and, at the same time, afraid of us because we might demonstrate against them.

So I left the poverty program and got a good job with the Drug Action Council in 1972, and for the next seven years, I made good money.

African Liberation Support Movement

Nelson ■ The black power movement led to supporting revolutionary movements in Africa. People were fighting for independence and liberation in Angola, Mozambique, Guinea Bissau, Zimbabwe, and South Africa. We organized the first African Liberation Day in May 1972 in Washington, D.C., a demonstration of over sixty thousand black people.

Pan-Africanism was the dominant political view within SOBU aand YOBU. It holds that the liberation of blacks in America is impossible without first liberating Africa, black people are a world community without national or class differences, and the enemy is white people—all white people. I have changed my politics since then, but there were positive aspects of pan-Africanism. We learned about our African heritage and about the heroic liberation struggles in Africa.

Willena ■ We had heard about armed struggle in Africa and sent Owusu Sadaukai over there to find out how we could best support their struggles. Owusu went to the front lines and almost got shot. The African leaders said: "No, no, we don't need you on the front lines. You're in America, the belly of the beast. Go back and build up public support for this struggle."

The black community had just moved from calling ourselves "Negro" and "colored" to calling ourselves "black." That was a big step. There was still a lot of anti-African sentiment in the community about "monkeys" and "jungle bunnies" and all that stuff. A lot of people said, "Why do you talk about being from Africa?" We said, "Everybody got a place they're from, and we're African people." And they said, "Wait a minute, you've gone too far with this." We named our children with African names, and people said, "You must be getting ready to go back to Africa." We said: "We're not going back, we are staying here in America. But our people over there are being killed, and we need to support their struggle."

When we went to Washington the first African Liberation Day in 1972, we met people from around the country. There were all these different African dishes and dresses, jewelry, earrings—the whole gamut. People gave speeches in their dashikis and their bush hairstyles. It was a wonderful sight to see.

Nelson ■ Joyce and I have two daughters, born in 1971 and 1972. We chose their names from Africa. "Akua" means "girl born on Wednesday." Our second daughter was also born on Wednesday, so we named her Ayo, which means "happy girl born on Wednesday." Both have the same middle name, Samari, which means "leopard," a beautiful, graceful animal of Africa.

Kwame ■ My legal birth name is John Cannon Jr. When I went to the Malcolm X School, which was part of Malcolm X Liberation University, everyone had an African name. So we changed my name to Kwame—a school name, a play name.

I liked it. When people called me John, it sounded odd. So I told them my name was Kwame. I'd say: "I got an African name. John, that's a European name, and I'm African."

Willena ■ I liked that Malcolm X School. Kwame learned so much at that school. They were teaching the kids math and science, things they were interested in. Kwame would come home and say, "Momma, stand still," and he would go around me and explain the sun and the moon and the earth. He was only four years old.

Kwame ■ At the Malcolm X School, they was really strict. Kids knew exactly what they were supposed to do. There was a lot of discipline in that school. We were afraid to say something bad, because then they said they would put hot sauce in your mouth.

Willena ■ Then when Kwame was five, he started going to a public school near our house called the Charles Moore School. It was a white school that was just beginning to become racially mixed.

Kwame ■ At the Charles Moore School, I remember, my teacher's name was Miss Zero. She was something else. We first got into it about my name. She called me John, and I told her that wasn't my name.

Willena ■ The school called me and told me to come up to the school with my son's birth certificate. So I did. And the teacher said: "He will not answer to his name. He wants to be called Kwame. He says he is not no John Cannon, that's a European name."

So I told the teacher his name was Kwame. He was five years old and already had his African pride.

Kwame ■ It was hard for me to keep my attention on what Miss Zero was teaching. She was always going over and over something that we had already learned. I wanted to learn something new. So I would grab a toy, and the teacher would yell at me. On Fridays, Miss Zero would give out these cookies. She would have us line up, and I remember I would turn my knees away from her, thinking she couldn't see me. I wanted my cookie, but I didn't want her to see it was me. If she saw who it was, I thought, she might not give me a cookie. We went at it all year.

My next run-in was at Brooks School, when I was in third grade. We were supposed to stand up every morning and say the "I pledge allegiance." I was really sharp then. I had learned at the Malcolm X School about my heritage, my history. I learned that nobody's free yet. So why should I repeat all about "freedom and justice for all" when I knew these things weren't true?

I came home and asked Mom, "Do I have to pledge allegiance when they say to?" And Mama said no.

So I went to school the next day, knowing I was legal! Every morning, the principal would lead the pledge on the school intercom. That morning, everybody in class was standing up and pledging allegiance. But Mama had given me the green light, so I sat down. The teacher came over and took me outside the room to talk to me. But it was one of those situations where I couldn't lose— Mama said I *didn't have to pledge*. So I said to the teacher, "I don't have to pledge allegiance because I don't believe in that."

I had to go to the principal. But I knew, when they called Mama in, she would argue for me, 'cause she had told me.

Willena ■ The teacher would send him outside the class when they said the allegiance. I said to the teacher, "You're punishing him for what he believes."

Kwame ■ So every morning, they'd stand and pledge, and I'd sit there. The kids would look at me like, "How can he do that? The teacher didn't say nothing to him!"

Willena ■ Then the next year, Kwame was in another school because I had moved. That teacher was white and fifty-five years old, and she had never taught blacks. She would put Kwame in the front because he was throwing rubberband spitballs. She said he always would finish his work. So I told her she should give him extra work to do; I was trying to suggest things to keep him busy.

The teacher said, "I don't have time to give him extra work." She didn't want any of my suggestions. She just wanted to punish him.

Kwame ■ I didn't know which way I was going to go with that one. I didn't know if I had Mama's back on that one or not. I remember the teacher and Mama going back and forth on that one.

Willena ■ I wanted to help solve the problem, but she didn't want to take none of my ideas. Then I went to the principal, and I said: "I want my kid outa there. She doesn't have the interest to deal with him."

The principal said he didn't want to "send a message." I said that the teacher was already sending a message. She had all the whites sitting on one side of the classroom, and all the blacks sitting by the window except one.

"What gives with this segregation in her class? Doesn't she know that was passed?" I said to the principal.

The principal said: "Mrs. Cannon, we're going to deal with this. Please don't get mad."

'Cause I was getting loud. That teacher pissed me off when she didn't want to use my suggestions. I knew if she gave Kwame extra work that Kwame would do the work, and that would solve the problem. Kwame wanted to stay in that class because his friends were there. So I started to come to the class. I didn't want to come just when they scheduled me, when they were ready. I wanted to come in unexpected to see what's going on. So I went in and there was Kwame, still up in the front row, still trying to get the other kids' attention.

Kwame ■ Mama got on me for the spitballs. She started coming to the class a lot. One time, Mama said to me, "Pretend I'm a fly on the wall,"

I said "What?"

She said, "Pretend I ain't there."

One time, when Mama wasn't there, I started to mess up again and the teacher made me stand up there at the blackboard. All the students were finishing with their tests, and I'm thinking to myself, I should just run out of this classroom. And before I could even finish that thought, I was running down the hallway. I ran out of the school. And I'm thinking, Where ya' going?

And then I got to this tree, and the principal was standing there."

I thought, Which way is Mama going to go with this one?

Women's Liberation

Marty ■ The women's liberation movement grew in importance to me in the early 1970s. There were two things pulling on me. One was becoming a woman and going full barrel into the sexual revolution. The other was the elusive quest for women's equality as a scientist.

At first I decided to major in sociology, because that was what my sister did. But when I took a required biology class, my biology professor took me aside and told me that I should go into medicine. He said I had a great mind, which I needed to hear after my high school teacher, Mr. Lang, had said that women "couldn't understand science."

But then this biology professor started chasing me around the office, trying to fondle me and kiss me. He hired me as a lab assistant. I was poor, was on scholarship, and I needed a job. My story is the same one as millions of women. This man gave me a job and he gave me A in his classes, and he expected me to sleep with him! And I wouldn't. When it was clear that I wasn't going to sleep with him, he tried to retaliate. Although his retaliation was ineffective, he succeeded in making me feel as if the whole thing was my problem. He told me that the only reason I had gotten A's was because he gave them to me, not that I deserved them. He acted like it was normal for him to expect me to sleep with him.

I never talked to anyone about it; it was just par for the course in those days. And when Anita Hill spoke out a decade later, I thought, I know this one! That professor is still teaching at Brown. I was not his only victim. There is a whole dynamic between class and sexism. You can be sure that man never harassed any woman who was his class equal. It was only women who were financially and academically dependent on him. He hired all these women students for his lab who depended on him for their livelihoods, and then he would try to seduce them. He was just disgusting. Nice introduction to the scientific profession at the age of nineteen.

In addition to the sexual harassment, we women science majors were treated as nobodies at Brown; we were not taken seriously. So I formed a group called Women in Science, which was ineffectual, but it was a beginning. It was the early 1970s, a time when the women's movement was getting clear that we really could become doctors, lawyers, and scientists. And I was part of the new wave of women who were going to do that. Although the medical schools and law schools were opening up for women, and to a lesser extent for African Americans, they were giving us mixed messages. The professors would tell us (1) you can come, and (2) you really aren't as good as the boys are, and (3) we're going to act like you aren't really here. We're going to show pictures in physiology class of women with naked breasts. And we're going to tell dirty jokes in anatomy about women, and we're going to do all these things that are going to make you uncomfortable, that make you feel just like a body instead of a mind.

Willena ■ At first, when I heard women complain that the men were in charge, I disagreed. I felt like we were all in the black liberation movement, all struggling together, so who cares who leads it? But after a while, I began to notice the domination of the men. To me it was unfair and unnecessary, and an extra burden on us black women. I remembered how my brother opposed me trying to be a doctor. A lot of times, women had good ideas and could lead just as good, in some cases better than the men. But when we raised those things, the men got irritated. They really like their power over women.

For a long time, I couldn't understand the white women's movement. I thought, Where's that coming from? They're not oppressed; white women are free. They just had this fuzzy little problem with their men. I thought white women couldn't see what I knew. Later, I began to realize that white men ruled the whole world, and the women's movement was fighting against this domination–and it was a good fight.

But we used different methods in our movement. We thought the white women's movement was too open, too public. We struggled with our black men but didn't put it out in the street. We were fighting our men to get free from their yoke, but we also wanted to have them by our side in the fight against racism.

Before I met Nelson, I heard a rumor that he thought women should just be having babies for the cause of black power, that we were going to become strong by having lots of babies, that we shouldn't use birth control so we could populate this country. That was so against what I believed, because I was from a poor area where women had babies because they didn't have any birth control to use. So I wanted to ask some questions to this Nelson Johnson.

I was sitting on the steps outside the GAPP House, feeling discouraged. I had just gone to a public housing complex and passed out leaflets about a meeting. But people didn't come, so the meeting didn't happen. I thought organizing in the community would be like organizing on campus. You put out a leaflet and people would come without you having to remind them.

So I was sitting there, and this guy comes up and says, "What's the problem?"

I said, "People don't want to get involved."

He said, "You have to look at what you're doing."

I thought, Who do he think he is? I said, "Look, I'm Willena Cannon, and since you know so much, who are you?"

So he said he was Nelson Johnson. And I said, "Oh, yeah, you're the guy that's talking about us having all those babies."

It turned out it wasn't true about Nelson, it was just a rumor. But some black power leaders, like Stokely Carmichael, did believe women just should serve men and have babies.

So in the black liberation movement, we women had to struggle with the men. Sandi Neely (before she became Sandi Smith) was an excellent example of someone who fought for black and women's rights. I met Sandi when she was in her last year in college. She graduated and stayed around. Sandi struggled with people to be serious and not treat the movement like some game. When we were struggling with somebody, criticizing something he did or trying to get him to change his view, Sandi was someone you would want to be involved. We used that good cop–bad cop approach, and Sandi could be the one to soften somebody up, but she also would bring it on down the line every time. Sandi was a good speaker in a street demonstration, and good with children too. A warm person. I remember her doing a lot of speaking and singing. She definitely took on a leadership role in the movement, and she struggled with men.

Nelson ■ Yes, indeed. In those days, women were expected to be quiet. Loudness was unpopular, considered hard and cold. But Joyce, my wife, and Sandi spoke out anyway. For young men and young women, the movement became a way to meet. Juices were running. We energized the movement by way of talking. A little charisma would carry the day. And it was mainly men talking and expecting women to listen. But Sandi would ask questions: Why do you do it this way? Why do you think this? Why not that? That was how I got to know Sandi.

During her freshman year at Bennett, the North Carolina governor came up with a plan to "recognize" black colleges. We knew the essence of this plan was to destroy black schools, which are among the most important cultural and resistance centers black people have. I traveled down to Fayetteville State, another black college in North Carolina, with a group of young women from Bennett. I didn't know any of them, but I took notice of Sandi because she spoke up. "Y'all got to come out and fight this plan," she told the Fayetteville students. Women were generally quiet back in those days, but Sandi was a ball of fire.

Sandi was raised to be pretty and soft-spoken. She liked to dress well and have a good time. She was glad when the movement recognized "black is beautiful," appreciating the beauty of darker-skinned sisters like herself and Joyce. But she could not do the soft-spoken part. She was a lot like Joyce in that regard, and she and Joyce became best friends. They led the struggle against women's oppression, against the feudal traditions of pan-Africanism, and against male chauvinism. They fought against the political belittlement of women, criticized those men who ran around on their wives or girlfriends, and pushed for women to be promoted into leadership positions.

Sandi became very involved in the Student Organization for Black Unity and organized a chapter of SOBU at Bennett. She worked in the national office, the SOBU House, on *African World*, our newspaper.

Sandi and Joyce teamed up to even challenge me on this male stuff. I thought that it was unfair, because I was cool on this issue. I had integrity with women because I was married and my wife and I worked together. But there were no women on the SOBU governing council, and a good deal of hell was raised about that until it got changed. I was so proud when Sandi ran for student government president at Bennett. She ran on a SOBU platform, and I remember when she came to the SOBU House and told us she won. She served as president for two years.

Sandi graduated from Bennett in 1973, and she came to live with Joyce and me and our two babies. I remember Sandi's mother coming to meet us at our house. I remember standing in our driveway, and Mrs. Neely telling us that she was happy to leave her daughter with us. She saw us as a respectful family and me as a respectful man, not some guy who had a wife and was looking to seduce her daughter. And we were happy to have Sandi live with us, and Sandi became part of our household. And we would talk about things, sometimes late at night after the kids were asleep.

Sandi was like my own sister; she looked out for me and I for her. She was not adverse to criticize me, and I felt the sting of it. I was doing a good bit of traveling to conferences, and often Sandi would come to those conferences. Joyce wouldn't come because with two babies and a full-time job at A&T (which supported us), Joyce had her hands full. So one time, there was a conference in Arkansas, and this young lady came after me. She was rapping to me, and I was flattered and rapping back to her. And Sandi—Sandi came and dressed me down: "What the hell is this?" And then came back from the conference and raised a big discussion in my house with Joyce! And I don't think I was up to anything. But you never know what goes on in your mind. You're young, women are beautiful . . . So Sandi, she was acting like a sister, keeping an eye on me.

Sally ■   I got deeply involved in the women's liberation movement. I was part of a consciousness-raising group that met weekly for years. After I dropped out of law school, I worked in the poverty program as a welfare rights organizer in poor white neighborhoods. We built a chapter of the National Welfare Rights Organization, and I learned a lot firsthand about the interconnections of race, class, and gender. I found I could not be just a feminist; sexism was certainly deep, but only part of a complex of problems. I decided I was a socialist feminist, against imperialism, racism, class oppression, as well as male chauvinism. My women's group organized a women's chapter of the New American Movement, a new nationwide democratic socialist group. I went to the founding convention of NAM in 1970, and the group decided they needed half the national leadership to be women. So I ended up on the national board. Back in North Carolina, our women's NAM chapter organized a socialist-feminist conference, the first in the nation.[6]

Meanwhile, on the home front, it seemed like the more I got involved in the women's movement, the more Mike's and my relationship fell apart. I tried to talk to Mike and tell him how I felt, but I would get so angry. The more mad I got, the more he withdrew. One day, I stood in our kitchen yelling at him. He said nothing, as if he weren't there. He was like a shadow. I felt that if I had tried to hit him, my arm would have gone right through him.

Our marriage slowly crumbled. It hit bottom when Mike told me that he had been having affairs with other women. I had assumed that he was faithful; we had never even discussed it. The trust between us—so necessary for a good relationship—evaporated. I retaliated by having several affairs, which was a drag. Sex motivated by revenge is not fun. This whole experience made me decide that "free love" made no sense within the context of a serious relationship. It was just another ploy for men to avoid commitment and oppress women.

I got a marriage counselor for Mike and me, but Mike refused to come. In Mike's last year of medical school, I left him. We had no property to divide; he took the dog, I took the cat. I got my own apartment, my own used car. It was the first and only time I ever lived alone, the only time I've ever had a bedroom to myself.

After Mike got his M.D. from Duke, he left town to do an internship in Texas. I felt relief. He was out of sight, out of mind, and I went on with my life.

Paul ■ My longtime girlfriend, Erica, moved to North Carolina with me in fall 1969. She went to social-work school at UNC while I was at Duke Medical School. I assumed Erica and I would get married; it just seemed like it was in the cards.

Fidelity wasn't a concept that I was acquainted with. I didn't think through my attitudes towards women. I didn't have a conscious, deliberate set of goals or precepts. I just knew that I loved Erica and wanted to be with her, and we would get married after we'd been together for awhile. We talked about having kids.

Meanwhile, I was into the sexual revolution. I loved sex, and I was eager to do it as often as I could. At first I believed that nobody would be interested in me, but then I found they were, so I became involved with a number of different women over the course of a number of years.

Erica was involved in the women's movement, part of a group of women who talked about relationships, and apparently I was an item of some interest. As they dissected male behavior, I became an object of study because I was an all-too-typical unfaithful male.

I thought that I didn't need Erica, that she needed me. I believed I was the independent, strong one. It is this whole *Playboy* philosophy, that the macho guy can do anything, can screw around as much as he wants, and women should just accept it. If the guy wants to screw around, then the guy should be able to. It's a philosophy of extreme individualism and self-centeredness.

Then Erica left me. We had been going together for five years, basically like we were married, then suddenly the whole relationship was over. Only then did I realize how very, very dependent I was on her. I was devastated.

This free-love thing just doesn't work. We had a relationship for five years that was destroyed by my pursuit of other women. I totally miscalculated—I thought I could do all these things and she would still stay with me. This painful experience taught me that you really have to be faithful if you want a good long-term relationship. I owe Erica a great debt. She stood up to my bluster and my desperation and taught me an important lesson about relationships.

It is a lesson, a very good lesson, and it stuck. Several years later, Sally and I became involved and then we married. And I have been a very faithful husband these last twenty-five years.

Sally ■ It's true. Paul learned that lesson well.

Our radical community was like a soap opera. When Paul was running around on Erica, he was the subject of many discussions in our women's consciousness-raising group. He was a perfect example of a male-chauvinist pig. Erica's misery dealing with Paul was why we needed a strong, independent women's liberation movement.

Erica was my friend. She found another man, someone who promised love and fidelity, and had an affair with him behind Paul's back. Erica gave Paul a taste of his own medicine, and then Erica dumped Paul.

At that time, I was Paul's friend too; we both had jobs at the same place. I remember, one lunch break, taking a long walk with Paul. Erica had just ditched him, and he was distraught, grappling with the end of a relationship that he had assumed would last a lifetime. He talked and talked and agonized. I felt sorry for the guy, but I also tried to explain to him how Erica had felt. I also told him about my pain with Mike. (I knew Mike talked to Paul, since they were close friends, so I wanted Paul to hear my side.)

I wasn't interested in Paul as a boyfriend then, and he wasn't interested in me. We were both caught up in our own breakups. But I did notice that he was a good person to talk to. He expressed his feelings openly, something many men seemed unable to do. And he seemed to have learned a hard lesson about the importance of monogamy.

Decline of the Movement

Nelson ■ The movement of the sixties and early seventies was such a powerful one. At its center was a bunch of grandchildren of slaves who were moving the whole structure of the country. We were breaking loose things that got codified after Reconstruction, the Black Codes, segregation, and everything built around them. The movement pressed for full democracy, for reordering of the social structure to be consistent with full democracy. The movement had a whole lot of parts because it drew to it those who were suffering from lack of democracy—the women's movement, the youth movement, the antiwar movement, all of these.

I marvel at the power of that whole movement, all these forces pushing at the very foundation of the nation. The movement had a powerful spokesperson in Martin King, grassroots organization, and the development of some multiracial entities. The movement effectively helped end the war in Vietnam, opened legal doors for oppressed groups. It was a powerful thing. If you were part of the palace guard, defending the old establishment, I bet the movement looked threatening. The FBI developed COINTELPRO, and the establishment started organizing the political forces for a backlash.

Martin Luther King, at the end of his life, had astonishing clarity on the absolute necessity for structural changes. His view accorded with much of what Malcolm had said years before. Malcolm said it in blatant ways, and the country pumped it back at him. In the late sixties, King had come to the same realization. I often read King's last speech at the Southern Christian Leadership Conference, just before he was killed. King's presentation called into question the whole social structure, saying that if the U.S. could not accommodate all the people as it was structured, then people had to change the whole thing. The movement was turning in that direction from many different quarters. King was recognized by many as a spokesperson for the more mainstream part of the movement. And then he was killed.

Three things happened to undermine the movement. First was killing leaders—Martin, Malcolm, Fred Hampton and other Black Panthers, Medgar Evers, and many others.

Second was straight-out terrorism. The killing of people scared the masses away from the movement. The fear that once had been associated with the Klan became associated with the government. The FBI unleashed COINTELPRO to undermine the movement, to organize disinformation campaigns, to manipulate groups.[7] Many people went to prison, and some are still there. This was all part of setting up the movement to be co-opted.

Third was the promotion of more "acceptable" leadership. Nixon's black capitalism was an attempt to promote a limited, conservative strata of blacks. The slang at the time was "black faces in high places," and it was disorienting to the black masses. Our struggle was built around racial oppression, that black people can't get into positions of power. Well, what happens when a black person is the mayor, but black people at the bottom are still catching hell? The analysis needed to be deeper so people wouldn't settle for tokenism.

The electoral process could have been a powerful component in the movement for fundamental change. But in the seventies, it became unhooked from the grassroots organizing. It became increasingly characterized by pandering to media and making deals with establishment politicians. More and more, the African American role in electoral politics—the very product of our massive struggle—was used against the movement. That's how the co-optation took place. It was co-optation with coercion, with terrorism.

Kill some, frighten some, pay some. That's the trinity that went on, and then they began to redefine what the movement itself was. Martin Luther King was reinvented. People took his statement "It's not the color of your skin but the content of your character" and remade that man and twisted his words out of historical context. That led to the Supreme Court's *Bakke* decision about "racism in reverse." It was an intellectual U-turn.

The seventies became a decade of backlash. It was made possible because some of the best leadership of the African American community at the grassroots level had been co-opted into the Great Society social programs. The government restricted the political action of those programs, in stark contrast to the creative energy of the movement, of independent grassroots groups. In the seventies, everybody started trying to get foundation money and government grants, which is like having a net over you.

Those groups that struggled outside of establishment endorsement were isolated, negated, and lied about. As soon as a strong personality emerged in a city, every effort was made to co-opt that person. And if they couldn't co-opt him, they isolated him—I know the process; it happened to me in Greensboro.

That pattern took place across the nation, city after city, state after state. Coupled with other factors, the seventies was a period of bottom-up and top-down co-optation and isolation of militants, including ourselves. Our group managed to pull itself together and grow through all of the confusion of the seventies with a fair degree of clarity and a great spirit of determination.

Willena ■   In the seventies, I could see the movement declining. I saw the co-optation that Nelson talks about in the poverty programs. They took militant people from the neighborhoods and gave them jobs and then told them to cool it. Like my boss in the Neighborhood Youth Corps. She used to be so militant—middle-class and militant. Then they put her as director. And I was a counselor working under her in the community, in public housing. She started telling me: "Look, you work here, and this is the government. We can't do things that we used to. You have to do it hush-hush."

I said, "Look, I'm not doing it during my work hours." And of course I talked to people about politics, but I didn't get out there on a soapbox until after 5 p.m. And my boss was trying to tell me I couldn't do that.

I said: "Look, the time I get paid is the government's. After that, they are not going to close my mouth."

And she said: "Well, I don't know what it's going to come down to. You just need to know that what you are doing is not good, and it could cost you your job."

I said, "I'll struggle with that when it comes."

The movement got strong in the sixties, and suddenly there were all these programs: New Careers and Model Cities and Manpower Development. The powers that be picked leadership they could control and ripped off the movement. That was one big way the movement declined.

Sally ■   I experienced the co-optation in Durham's poverty program, Operation Breakthrough, where I worked for several years as a welfare rights organizer. I enjoyed that job. There were good people working at Operation Breakthrough, mainly activists from the neighborhoods. But we experienced the same process of decline.

Whenever we did a good job of mobilizing large numbers of people around an issue, our job descriptions would become more and more limited. For example, in 1972, we organized widespread opposition to the plans for building a new county hospital. Paul was working at Operation Breakthrough as a health specialist that year. We became good friends, working together on the Durham

County Hospital Campaign. The plans for this hospital located it outside town, far away from both poor whites and blacks, with limited space for outpatient clinics. We built a broad-based coalition of poor whites and blacks and health-care professionals around changing the plans. We held a big public meeting, with hundreds of people and with members of the county hospital board in the audience. People spoke their minds. There were some dynamite speeches (including Paul's flip-chart talk detailing the problems with the plans), putting a lot of public pressure on the board. But the reaction set in immediately. The next day, a young man whose speech pointed out the cowardice of the board was kicked out of Duke's hospital administration program. And our supervisors at the poverty program told us we should only advocate for individuals, not organize collective action. How can individuals make social change without coming together? I couldn't stand my job after that and soon found another.

Meanwhile, the Vietnam War was gradually ending, and that too had a big impact on the movement's decline in the seventies. It was ironic. Bringing the troops home was a huge victory. I remember being very impressed that the Vietnamese Communist Party had been able to defeat the U.S. military. But the war's end also took away the biggest issue for the white part of the movement—no more antiwar demonstrations to mobilize around.

Marty ■ I was in medical school at Duke when the war in Vietnam finally ended in 1975. I followed the peace negotiations and remember watching the evacuation of Saigon on TV. I had friends who had been soldiers in Vietnam. They told me they didn't want to talk about it. It was way too difficult for them to talk about and for me to understand their pain.

Willena ■ I lost a brother to Vietnam. He wasn't killed, but he never got over the war, and he died a young man. Macy was a lot like me; he went to A&T and studied physical education like I did. He was soft-spoken, very easygoing, and, like me, he didn't drink much. He had a beer every once in awhile. Then he got drafted and went to Vietnam.

When he came back from Vietnam, he stayed with me four months. He would not talk about the war at all. But then at three o'clock in the morning, when it's quiet, all of a sudden the whole damn war would be in my house. Macy would run hollering, screaming, and get under my table with a broom. He would yell, "Don't kill the children!" I found out everything that happened to him. The only time he wouldn't wake up and go through all that was if he sipped a drink before he went to bed. Only with alcohol would he sleep through the night. So he became an alcoholic and died drunk when he was only thirty-nine years old.

He became a different person in Vietnam. My mother said, "My son never came back." This easygoing, quiet young man became so aggressive, he would argue with a Stop sign. Macy was four years younger than me. He would still be in his fifties today.

Every time I think about Vietnam, I get mad.

Paul ■ Joe Gambino was my best friend in high school. We were born one day apart, and we competed over everything. He usually won, because he was a natural athlete (but I could do more push-ups). After we both went to college, he told me he was planning to go into the military. I tried to argue with him, but he didn't listen. That was the last time I saw him.

On April 7, 1973, his plane was shot down over Cambodia. Joe was killed on his twenty-fourth birthday. Years later, I went to the Vietnam War Memorial in Washington, D.C., and found his name on the wall of names. All those names, all those people—such a senseless loss.

Sally ■ As the war ended, we had discussions about new directions for the movement. I hoped that people would get involved in other important issues, like fighting poverty, unionization, and all kinds of economic and social issues. There still was motion around women's issues and gay rights and environmental issues, but the movement as a whole was losing steam. People started going back to conventional lives, regular jobs. I couldn't imagine doing that. My friends and I searched for ways to continue to work for fundamental change.

PART II

The Twain Meet

4
The Seventies:
Becoming Communists

Socialism developed in the nineteenth century as a vision that would offer an alternative to capitalist exploitation. Karl Marx laid out one of its most famous versions in the Communist Manifesto, *published in 1848. When V. I. Lenin led the Russian Revolution in 1917, the theory of Marxism-Leninism arose, stressing the role of a communist party as central to building socialism. Communist parties developed in many countries around the world, including the United States. Beginning in the 1930s, the Communist Party USA energized the labor movement, became the backbone of many unions, and then faced intense repression during the McCarthy era of the 1950s. In 1949, Mao Tse-tung's Communist Party began to build a socialist society in China. Inspired by the Chinese Revolution, U.S. activists strove to build a new communist movement in the 1970s. The multiracial new communist movement included activists from the black liberation, Latino, and Asian American movements, as well as whites from the antiwar, women's liberation, and student movements.*

Becoming Communists

Nelson ■ My introduction to Marxism-Leninism was by way of African students who I met through African liberation support work. We had ties with the leaders of liberation movements, including Samora Machel of Mozambique and Amilcar Cabral of Guinea Bissau. African revolutionaries welcomed support from us, but they surprised many by arguing against our politics of pan-Africanism. Amilcar Cabral visited us in the early 1970s, and he told us our main fight should *not* be the liberation of Africa but should be against U.S. imperialism. He said we needed to unite with other peoples in the U.S—like white workers—against the U.S. government. This was a real challenge to us, because we thought white people *as a whole* were the enemy. Here was our hero, an African revolutionary leader, telling us to unite with whites. On the platform where Cabral was speaking were several white progressives. After he spoke, Cabral hugged one of them. We were outraged—hugging a white person!

Community people in Greensboro also criticized pan-Africanists for doing nothing but talk. They told us that waiting for African revolution is no solution for everyday folks.

One of the early critics of pan-Africanism was Sandi Neely. She and her boyfriend, Mark Smith, organized a study group to search for alternatives. Sandi was trying to figure out how white workers could be part of a revolutionary movement. She pointed out that they worked next to blacks in the factory, also making lousy wages. Even though many white workers were racists, Sandi felt they were not the enemy. U.S. imperialism was.

But I was still a dyed-in-the-wool black nationalist. I had trained myself never to smile at white folks. I thought Mark and Sandi were being taken in by whites.

Our organization, Youth Organized for Black Unity, had fraternal relations with Pan African Student Organization in the Americas [PASOIA]. I particularly remember a Nigerian student named Jamie, who was a leader and was well studied in Marxism. With a certain tact and respect, he said that we in YOBU were somewhat infantile. A group of us called a special meeting with PASOIA to debate on Marxism-Leninism. We had brilliant people in YOBU, intellectuals from around the country who were well anchored in the nationalist idiom and politics. But Jamie and the good brothers from PASOIA dismantled our theories.

Despite the vigor of the debate, the meeting did not get bitter. Our friendship remained warm, and we ate food together. They really were trying to point out to us something that we weren't seeing, and we were too arrogant to acknowledge it in their presence. But when the PASOIA brothers left, we all looked at each other and said, "Damn, there is a lot of stuff here we've got to look at." We decided to study Marxism-Leninism.

Our African brothers made a case for having a working relationship with whites. You can't be just working in a factory and talk only to black folks. I knew that, but the idea of working with whites was hard for me because I had trained myself to believe that ultimately whites could never understand the nature of black oppression. I saw a white individual smile here and there, but within the context of a very mean, oppressive system. I believed that when push came to shove, whites would line up with other whites. That had been my empirical experience.

But I gradually became a Marxist, because I saw the need for social transformation, which required the majority of people to unite for fundamental change. Marxism described a rational basis and a method for uniting people of different ethnic and racial groups. I embraced Marxism based on struggling with my own prejudice against whites.

Sally ■ People tell me that they understand how we became activists, but not why we became communists. It was easy to become an activist in the sixties because we were the protest generation, and many of us joined the movement. In the mid-seventies, however, the movement declined, and most people returned to conventional lives and mainstream politics. To continue being a radical activist meant going against the tide.

I did not want to give up my activist lifestyle; I felt that this society needed fundamental change in priorities and allocation of resources. My friends and I believed that the lull in the movement was temporary, and that we needed to study and prepare for the next upsurge. Marxism was a guide for organizing. So we studied the works of Marx, Lenin, and Mao Tse-tung, who was still alive then. My question was, How do you make fundamental change? Communism to me at that time was an ideal, a way to build people power. Communist parties led revolutions. As we started studying in 1974, the Vietnamese Communist Party had just defeated the U.S. war machine.

Marxist politics also called for people of all races, genders, and creeds to work together against the common enemy. Black and white radical activists still traveled in parallel universes in North Carolina in the mid-1970s. Our peers in the black liberation movement refused to even talk to us. It was ridiculous. To make fundamental change, we had to find a way to work together, and there was nothing I wanted more. I heard through the grapevine that black activists were studying Marxism like we were, and that gave me hope.

Even though I majored in history in college, I had never studied Marxism or anything by or about Marx. Why didn't my professors teach us about Marxism? As our study group read about the Russian and Chinese Revolutions, I felt like we were learning the untold story of twentieth-century history. The TV and newspapers told negative stories about these revolutions, and my mistrust of the mainstream media grew. The Chinese Revolution particularly excited me, because at the very time we were studying communism, a cultural revolution was going on in China, where people were destroying entrenched power and its bureaucracy. (Not until a decade later did I recognize the excesses of the cultural revolution.)

I did have serious reservations about building a communist movement in the United States. Revolutionaries in other parts of the world called the United States "the belly of the beast," and I knew winning people to communism here would be hard. But since when did doing something hard stop us? I read *Labor's Untold Story* and other books on U.S. labor history and learned about the heroic strikes led by Wobblies in the early 1900s and the Communist Party in the 1930s and '40s. I heard about contemporary labor organizing by young communists in other regions of the country. I began to believe that Marxism could help us provide thoughtful leadership, with a long-term perspective, resolute on black-white unity and women's equality.

Paul ■ My political evolution towards socialism and communism began in college. The antiwar movement and the civil rights movement stimulated a lot of new ideas and criticism of old ways of thinking. From my own experience, I knew that this society stinks. Working-class people get screwed; my mother talked about that. My father said very little except for his admonition "Whatever you do, don't be a worker, because a worker's life is a slave's life." My father had been in the Jewish Socialist Bund, which was one of the great mass workers' organizations in Poland in the period before World War II. He had been in a tailors' strike when he was fourteen. My parents were a political touchstone for me. I knew I could only join a political group that was congruent with their aspirations, that appealed to people like them.

In college I went to a lecture by Michael Harrington, who openly advocated socialism and talked about Marxist theory. He wrote *The Other America* and became a very prominent figure who visited Kennedy in the White House. Harrington deeply impressed me, and I decided I was a socialist. I graduated from college and entered medical school seeing myself as a socialist, but I was not a member of any group because I had not yet found one whose work I respected.

At Duke, I joined the Medical Committee for Human Rights. And after several years, along with many other MCHR folks, I began to study Marxism. I became increasingly frustrated with the difficulty of providing quality healthcare to poor and working people and became an activist. I met Sally and others, and we worked on a number of health-care issues, including a poor-people's campaign to improve a new county hospital, clinics to screen textile workers for brown-lung disease and a union drive at Duke Medical Center. We joined the New American Movement, a democratic-socialist organization. There were lots of good people in it, but they were mainly on college campuses, and not many organized outside the ivory towers. It wasn't revolutionary enough, and we eventually quit.

Reading Marxism was like a light turning on in my brain. I loved Lenin, his single-minded focus on politics, his exposure of why things work as they do. I read Lenin's *Imperialism* on a four-hour bus trip to a brown-lung clinic in South Carolina. I was so into it, I don't think I looked up twice during that whole trip. I was surprised at the insight of that moldy old classic on how things worked in the U.S. seventy years later. Lenin mentioned the tobacco trust. Guess who we were organizing against every day? Duke Medical Center, built on tobacco money! We were trying to get health-care delivery that would meet the needs of poor and working people. Our enemy? The wealthy power brokers behind the scenes, who called the shots, decided what was built, all to increase their own profits. I got this sense that we were truly fighting the same enemy as Lenin was seventy years ago. Leninism was a discipline I aspired to. It called for a dedicated life, single-mindedly devoted to political struggle. Communism was a call to unity of all oppressed people. It was a practical matter.[1]

Willena ■ I was interested in how society operated, how "the system" kept control over us. I wanted to find out what they did *not* teach us in school. It would be great if things operated the way teachers said—democracy, freedom, and justice for all. But reality does not operate that way.

I met Billy Sutherland, who was very active in GAPP and the Malcolm X School. He and I got married, and we had two children, Imani and Kweli.

Billy and I joined a black study group that included Nelson and Joyce and people from GAPP and YOBU. We studied a lot of things—the Muslims, black nationalism, and eventually Marxism. We would have discussions on Sunday mornings and analyze what was happening that week in the world and in Greensboro. We talked about how black people in different economic brackets responded to things differently. That naturally led to Marxism, because we were talking about class.

Marxism really helped me understand the world, how it was divided into classes. In the seventies, there was a black bourgeois class rising from the jobs that first opened up to blacks in the sixties. These folks bought houses and cars, and they fought to protect their things. Our study group analyzed them and the role they played. Whites run everything, but there is a role that some blacks play in helping the whites keep us in place. Marxism explained who the enemy was, and who was helping the enemy, and why.

We also looked at how the class system operated among white people. Throughout my life, I was aware that there were poor whites. I had seen them—sharecroppers, factory workers, unemployed. I would tell myself that poor whites were bad off because they must not care, that they had no get-up-and-go. But when we started studying Marxism, I began to see the greed of capitalism towards them too.

But working with white people? No way! That's where I drew the line. All the pain in my life, I attributed to white people. I hated *all* white people.

Kwame ■ I was a little kid in the 1970s, so I didn't think about politics. For a while Mom and I lived in a little house on Ryan Street. It was just me and my mom. That was like the best time, because I didn't have no sister, no brother. All the attention was mine. You never realize how good you got it.

Then Mom met Billy. I told my mom I wanted a little sister, and I got Imani. Then I told her I wanted a little brother, and I got Kweli. And then I asked her for a horse, but she didn't give me a horse.

I was always reaching out for my father, John Cannon. When Billy came along, I was very young. I only wanted my own father and nobody else. And Billy sensed that, and I think he resented it. He was trying hard to get me to like him, but he just wasn't fitting the bill for me. Before he and Mom got married, Billy was all giving. But after he and Mom got married, things with Billy started to go bad, real bad. He wreaked havoc on us.

Willena ■ Billy was an alcoholic, and he became worse and worse. So I had to leave him. I became a single mother with three young children to care for on my own.

Kwame ■ I stayed with my dad during the summers, and those were some really neat times. But John Cannon just didn't know how to be a father. He just gave me anything I wanted. I'd say, "Dad, I want ———." And I got it. Anything I did wrong, Dad looks right over it. At that time I thought it meant he loves me, but now I don't.

I missed my mama; she put that structure on me. When I was bad, Mama would spank me and yell at me. There were times when, soon as I got to Massachusetts, I would be ready to get back home to Greensboro. I wanted both my parents.

I remember Christmas with Dad when I was seven or eight. Man, I would get this huge box full of wrapped-up presents. They were all mine. I told Dad, "I'm gonna start with the littlest." I pulled all the little boxes out. Dad said, "That's the most expensive, then." It was a watch, a really nice watch. And another box had a racecar set in it and all kinds of stuff. We sat on the floor for hours and played with the little racecar set.

I was the only the kid up there; I didn't have to compete with anybody. It was my world. Then I come home to Greensboro, and I'm back into sharing. Sharing my mother and sharing the attention, and the structure is right back on me. But I would be ready to come home. I can't really explain it. I didn't miss getting whuppings, but I missed being put in shape. I think kids need structure and they actually want it. But I would use Daddy against Mama. When Mama would get me for something, I would say: "I want to go back to my daddy. I want to live with him forever." That was a little threat I would throw at her every now and then.

Mama would say: "Call him. Go on up there." She would call him, and I would get scared because I didn't want to live with John Cannon. I didn't mind going to see him, but I didn't want to live with him forever.

Marty ■ When I moved to North Carolina in 1973 to start Duke Medical School, it was my first time south since a family trip in 1961. The South seemed to me to be the end of the earth. I remembered my father talking about those South Carolina rednecks. I went to Duke with visions of Faulkner, wisteria, crepe myrtle, sultry nights. I had this kind of romantic view of the South.

But the main thing I found was hard work. I wasn't from a medical family, and I didn't know the rules. Much of the medical training at Duke was to convince us that we were nobodies. It's a very abrasive and abusive teaching method, where the physician educators (or "rounders") do their best to skewer the residents and medical students. At the same time, we got very little sleep. It was terrible. I faced more emotional chaos. I think that it happens a lot for women who work very hard to get where they are—not just women, but any person who is socially at risk. The closer you get to your goal, the more you feel like you don't deserve it. That was what was happening to me. I didn't really feel like I deserved to be here. So I started acting out—lots of boyfriends. It was still this pattern of studying hard during the week and then being wild on the weekends. That was how I could avoid the issues of my life.

Then in the middle of this, I began to get involved in the world of human rights. I met Paul Bermanzohn, who was doing screening for brown lung. I got involved in a free clinic for poor people. I started going to Medical Committee for Human Rights and met people like Jim Waller, Jean Chapman, Yonni Chapman, Bill Sampson—and Mike Nathan.

I met Mike at an MCHR meeting in 1976, during my last year in medical school. A few days later, I was working at Duke, and Mike walked over and very bluntly asked me out! That was typical Mike—a little awkward but effective. We went out and had a very, very nice time.

Mike and I aggressively pursued each other. We needed what we found in each other. Both of us had fathers who died when we were young. Like my mother, Mike's mother, Esther, was a depressed older woman with a single chick in the nest who had no identity outside her child. Both our mothers needed much more than either of us could give. Mike and I had been wild teenagers, acting out sexually, running away from a tremendous sadness in our family and the overwhelming dependency of our mothers. From the start, we knew each other deeply, though we seldom talked about it. We both needed a family but hadn't known how to create one. When we found each other, we both heaved a sigh of relief. There was an acknowledged truth between us that we needed to create something solid.

Mike had had a solid marriage with Sally, and he told me he had messed it up. Then he left Durham to go to Dallas, Texas, for his internship. There he got involved with a woman who was bulimic and emotionally a mess. He really spun out of control, and he came back to Durham in 1976 burned out and lonely. That was when I met him. Basically, we said to each other, "Okay, we both have been screwing up for a long time and it's time to get down." And that was it. Within a week or so, Mike and I decided we were building a lifetime relationship!

It was time. We were maturing. I was twenty-six; Mike was thirty. I wanted to do meaningful political work and have a good relationship—both happened together for me and Michael. I was living with other students in a big old house on Hilton Avenue. Mike moved in with me, bringing Ben, his dog, and two beautiful lovebirds. Our relationship was tested immediately when my cat ate one of his lovebirds!

We did political work together. I was interested in doing overseas medical work, which Mike had done in Guatemala and Bolivia. Mike told me that working in third-world countries made him realize that the best way to help them was to change things here in the United States.

Studying Marxism and building a communist organization meant responsibility. In retrospect, I think we had an adolescent approach to responsibility: We thought we would change the whole world! In terms of human relations, getting into Marxism put some structure back to where there had been no structure. Our politics demanded honesty, fidelity, which both Mike and I really needed. We were ready for the new communist movement.

New Communist Movement

Nelson ■ The African Liberation Support Committee became the arena for a nationwide debate of pan-Africanism versus Marxism-Leninism. It was a ferocious battle over the best road forward for the black liberation movement. I overcame my reluctance and adopted Marxism. In 1973, the annual ALSC conference was titled "Which Way Forward?" I co-authored a paper with Abdul Alkalimat, a professor of political science at Fisk University, and we both spoke at the conference on the following questions:

1. Who is the enemy of African American people—all white people or a handful of monopoly capitalists?
2. What is the relationship of the black liberation movement to the multinational working class?
3. What is the best way for African Americans to support the struggles on the African continent?

I answered these questions point by point, arguing that Marxism presented the best method for us to make fundamental change. But there were devoted black nationalists in ALSC who called us "European-controlled Negroes." They said people should reject this "1860 white Marxist bull" and the "white ideology of Mao." But many others were open, particularly among the younger people. YOBU as an organization began to turn to Marxism-Leninism.

A year later, the 1974 ALSC conference held a debate on the same subject. By this time, Owusu Sadaukai had adopted Marxism-Leninism, and he presented a position paper that represented my views, as well as those of Joyce, Sandi Neely, and Mark Smith. Owusu gave a powerful speech. Stokely Carmichael argued against us, but much of the energy in ALSC turned in our direction.

We built a new organization, the Revolutionary Workers League [RWL], made up of activists from YOBU and ALSC. It was based on communist politics, and its purpose was to dialogue with other like-minded organizations with the purpose of building a new communist party. We called RWL a pre-party formation. Over the next months, RWL became established in cities across the country, including New York; Washington, D.C.; Greensboro; Durham; Houston, Texas; and San Francisco. People got jobs in factories and hospitals in order to organize unions. Sandi got a job working at a textile mill in Greensboro. Owusu got a job at Duke University in Durham as the leader of the campus service-workers' union, with the purpose of expanding the union into Duke Medical Center.

Sally ■ Owusu Sadaukai worked for Local 77 AFSCME [American Federation of State, County, and Municipal Employees]. He was so charismatic, such a powerful leader. I remembered meeting him in 1967 when he was Howard Fuller, heading up Durham's poverty program. I remembered him in 1968 when he became Owusu, decided all whites were the enemy, and kicked Mike and me out of a mass meeting. Now, six years later, in 1974, he was arguing that blacks and whites needed to work together. And in Durham, North Carolina, the best place to start was Duke, the largest employer in the city, where for more than a decade there had been a tough struggle to unionize against Duke's notorious union busting.

As soon as I heard about Owusu's new job, I got a job at Duke Medical Center so that I could be part of the drive. I got hired as a cashier in the hospital cafeteria. If you ever want to be a union organizer, get a job as a cafeteria cashier. Everybody eats; everybody comes through the cafeteria and interacts with the cashiers. You can transact all kinds of union business while you are ringing up someone's lunch. I loved it.

Lucy Lewis, who I had become friends with in the antiwar and women's movements, and other friends got jobs at Duke hospital. (Two years later, César Cauce, who died in the massacre, got a job there as a ward clerk.) We wrote and passed out a weekly leaflet called "Tell It Like It Is!" Each week there would be a new example of why Duke hospital workers should unionize. When we passed the flyers out, people would tell us about various problems in their departments, and with their permission, we publicized them, pointing out how a union would help.

Paul ■ Our "Tell It Like It Is!" leaflet led to romance for Sally and me. It was easy to write the leaflet, but time consuming to produce it. We had to type it onto a mimeograph stencil and run off five hundred copies on the mimeograph machine in our friend's basement. Then we had to be up at dawn to distribute it at Duke hospital's front door. From 6:30 to 7:30 a.m. we handed them out, so we would catch the night-shift workers as they left and the day shift as they arrived.

Sally ■ One time, Paul and I stayed up all night producing "Tell It Like It Is!" and then passed it out at dawn. I was exhausted, but something happened between the mimeograph machine and that hospital entrance. A spark ignited between Paul and me. I had known him for five years by then, but suddenly he looked awfully cute to me.

Paul ■ I had met Sally when she was married to Mike, my best friend. I didn't like Sally when I first met her. She was so competitive with Mike. She said something about him being a medical student because he wasn't creative. I avoided her.

Sally ■ And I didn't like Paul either. I thought he was just another macho medical student.

Paul ■ Then at some political conference, I saw Sally across the room, laughing and joking with others. I changed my opinion of her.

I was looking for somebody for a steady relationship. When Sally and I became involved, it was clear to both of us that this was going to be serious, not something that either of us was going to trifle with. 'Cause we had both been through very painful experiences with previous relationships.

Nelson ■ Greensboro had its share of romance. When Sandi Neely fell in love with Mark Smith, she was living with Joyce and me. I felt protective of her, like she was my little sister. Mark Smith was a Harvard graduate, articulate, and a good-looking guy. I was suspicious of him and felt I needed to defend Sandi because she was young, beautiful, committed, and the daughter of a mill worker. Guys hanging around Greensboro from Harvard like Mark Smith wanted to be in love with a working-class woman. Mark was an intellectual whiz kid, and I liked talking to him and he is still a dear friend, but I knew him too well. When Mark and Sandi started going together, I never liked it. I asked Sandi whether she really loved him—and she told me she was swept away by him. The more swept away she was, the more it upset me! But I wouldn't show it with her, because I didn't want to come off like a big brother.

So I told Mark, "Don't you mess over Sandi." Mark persuaded me that he was in love with Sandi. But it was an intellectual persuasion; I never could believe it in my soul. In 1975, Sandi Neely became Sandi Smith after she and Mark got married at her home in South Carolina. Joyce was Sandi's best woman. I made some excuse not to go, because I did not want to be Mark's best man. And ultimately, unfortunately, my assessment of Mark proved true. He started messing around on Sandi, breaking her heart. She finally left him, he moved away from Greensboro, and Sandi moved back in with Joyce and me. Sandi deserved a good, affirming relationship. She had several boyfriends after Mark, but I knew that she still hurt. And it still hurts me now to think about it.

Paul   ■   Politics was also intense in 1975. By this time, our Marxist study group, including Sally, Jim Waller, Lucy Lewis, myself, and others, had become an organizing collective and decided that we were communists. We decided to check out various communist groups to decide which one we would join, because it didn't make sense just to be local independent communists. We read journals, went to conferences, and visited several groups.

People vigorously debated how to build a revolutionary movement. Around the world, communist parties were split, some siding with the Soviet Union and others with China. In the United States, the new communist movement aligned itself with the politics of Mao Tse-tung, who we saw as more revolutionary.

The NCM group I was most impressed with was the Workers Viewpoint Organization. It was based in Chinatown, New York City, and was involved in a mass movement for Asian American equality. WVO emphasized the need to develop revolutionary theory, and to me it expressed most clearly how we should build a new party. But with the benefit of hindsight, I see that the new communist movement also got into splitting hairs, and that prevented us from building a larger organization that could have had more influence.

Sally   ■   At the time, it was exciting, although I could not make sense of all the rhetoric. To me, the important thing was that communist groups of African Americans, Puerto Ricans, Asian Americans, and whites were striving to unite with each other to build a multiracial working-class movement. In retrospect, I think there were too many people—mostly men—into macho grandstanding, with attitudes of "I'm more revolutionary than you."

Willena   ■   I was part of the Revolutionary Workers League formation in Greensboro, along with Nelson. We were studying Mao Tse-tung, trying to figure out what we could use from the Chinese struggle over here in the United States.

In Greensboro, the people involved had been active in the movement for years. But mostly it was the men who were involved in the debates, not the women. It was male-dominated, mainly Owusu-dominated. Some of the women seemed to want the men to dominate. I love black men, but they got to know that I have some sense too.

Nelson   ■   We in the Revolutionary Workers League dialogued with other communist organizations around the country with the idea of deciding to merge with one or more of them to build a new party. In 1975, we started talking to the Workers Viewpoint Organization, a New York City group with deep roots in the Asian American community.

In December 1975, RWL's national leadership voted to join the Workers Viewpoint Organization. I supported this step because WVO to me looked like the group with the clearest sense of how to build a new party. But then the top national RWL leadership balked and failed to carry out the merger. For the next six months, there was tremendous confusion and disorientation, and the Revolutionary Workers League disintegrated. It was one of the most difficult periods of my life. It pitted me against my close friend and mentor, Owusu Sadaukai.

Sally ■   There was very bad fallout from RWL's disintegration in the Duke union drive. Before then, for almost two years—from 1974 through 1976—we had worked well with Owusu. He formed a hospital organizing committee, which we joined. Lucy Lewis and I organized a grievance committee as a union-organizing strategy, and Owusu accepted our proposal. We helped people file grievances through the little-used procedure that Duke hospital had in place, and the organizing committee publicized the problems people were having and how a union could help. One of the first grievances I won was a white maintenance worker who had been unfairly fired. We won his job back, and he and his buddies called me his "lawyer." It was fun—and the grievances we worked on helped build the pro-union base among the hospital workers.

Duke fought our union drive every way they could, stalling off the union vote as long as possible. Union elections are supervised by the National Labor Relations Board. In the case of Duke Medical Center, it took a long time for the NLRB to decide what the appropriate "bargaining unit" was for the hospital. The designated bargaining unit identifies the categories of workers who get to vote for or against union representation, and who will be represented by the union if it wins. We argued that the bargaining unit at Duke should be the service workers—housekeepers, cooks and cafeteria workers, nurses' assistants, and so on. They were semi-skilled, low paid, and mostly African American women. Duke's strategy to defeat the union was to insist that the bargaining unit include secretaries, clerical workers, and lab technicians, who were better paid and mostly white. The NLRB chose Duke management's position and doubled the size of the bargaining unit. The workers added to the bargaining unit were considerably harder to persuade to sign union cards, but we redoubled our efforts and pushed forward to hold a union election.

Meanwhile, our good relations with Owusu soured in early 1976 after the RWL split over whether or not to merge with WVO. Owusu was one of the leaders who first agreed to join WVO, then pulled out of the agreement. Our collective was pro–Workers Viewpoint Organization, and suddenly the struggle over building a new communist party was right in the middle of our union drive!

We tried to keep our focus on the union drive, but then one night Lucy, César Cauce, and I went to the weekly organizing committee meeting to find ourselves locked out! Our pleas for unity on the drive and the good of Duke workers were ignored. Owusu and his RWL cronies "expelled" us. They made up excuses, claiming that I had "sided with supervisors" (a twisted interpretation of one of the few grievances that I didn't win). It was such baloney. The real reason was because we disagreed over communist politics.

We were hurt and worried about how our expulsion would upset the approaching union election. Should we pretend we hadn't been expelled? Should we do nothing while the RWL people working in the hospital spread rumors about us? This went against our grain. So we decided to go back to our leafleting and "Tell It Like It Is!" We wrote a long and complex leaflet that included what we thought was going on in the New Communist Movement, and why there needed to be a socialist revolution and a new communist party to lead it.

Over the next few weeks, we and the RWL exchanged words and leaflets back and forth at Duke. Eventually, Owusu allowed us to come back onto the organizing committee, but the damage had been done. On the union election day in the fall of 1976, some fifteen hundred Duke workers voted in the National Labor Relations Board–sponsored election. And the union lost by only thirty-five votes.

I felt terrible. Maybe if we hadn't put out those leaflets protesting our expulsion and advocating revolution, a few dozen more people would have voted pro-union. But in reality, there were many factors in the defeat, notably Duke's union-busting determination. But our leaflet and Owusu's expelling us did not help.

Paul ■   Owusu became the main spokesman opposed to the RWL joining Workers Viewpoint Organization. At a forum in July 1976 on the Duke campus, Owusu debated Jerry Tung, the WVO leader who came down from New York City, on building a new communist party. Our whole collective was there, and it was the first time I laid eyes on Nelson and Joyce Johnson. During the debate, Owusu looked glum, hesitant. We were used to his fiery speeches; instead he read a long, boring statement. Owusu, the most charismatic person I have ever known, was rendered speechless. In contrast, I thought Jerry Tung was immensely effective, and he clearly won the debate. That promoted the Workers Viewpoint Organization to everyone in our collective, and we decided to seriously consider joining WVO.

Soon after that forum, Nelson and Joyce came over to the house Sally and I lived in to visit us. We talked about politics, but the main thing I remember was social. We were feeling each other out. Are these folks we can work with? I had expected Nelson to be the militant, terrifying guy I had heard about. Instead, he was soft-spoken and couldn't have been a friendlier, warmer person.

Sally ■   I was so honored to have Joyce and Nelson come to our house. I hadn't talked to Joyce since we had both been Duke students a decade earlier. I was worried that Joyce and Nelson would think Paul and I were slobs, because we had a dog and three cats in our little house. I remember vacuuming like crazy before they arrived, trying to get rid of all the cat hair!

Nelson ■ Uniting the Greensboro and Durham collectives came at a fortunate time for me, after the bitterness of the RWL collapse. Joyce and I felt Paul and Sally Bermanzohn were serious organizers, and we also liked the Workers Viewpoint people from New York.

Most of the RWL people who were not from Greensboro left the area.

Owusu left North Carolina. He had been among my best friends, my mentor and leader. Right before he left, he and I talked one night in a parking lot. He said he felt bad about working together for ten years and then ending up on the opposite sides of this. It is one of the few conversations we ever had about this. There has never been any completion between us, even to this day.

Willena ■ Nelson told me we should start working with some whites. He said he was meeting with a white communist group in Durham that wanted to study with us.

I told him, "I'm gone." Oh, God, I couldn't imagine working with white people. I told Nelson he was being duped, that these white people would try to get control of what we were trying to do. I figured they would befriend us, act like they were for us, find out what we were doing, and then destroy what we were trying to do. I wanted no part of it.

Nelson said I shouldn't have a closed mind and should not get emotional about it.

I said: "You can say all you want to, I've lived this stuff all my life. And I'm older than you!" (Now there was a powerful argument!)

Nelson and I argued and argued. Finally I consented. He thought he had convinced me, but he hadn't. I still thought Nelson was too trusting.

I made a plan. I would meet that white group with my eyes wide open and see what was going on. When those whites moved to get control, I'd expose just how evil white people are. I'd say, "See there, Nelson, I told you so!"

I had already met Signe Goldstein. Signe was progressive, but I couldn't figure out if she was white or Jewish, or how the Jews became white. Signe would come into the Uhuru Bookstore, where I would be talking to people about the work. She would buy books, but then she would always sit there and have this long conversation about the problems. If you were showing bias against her, she just ignored it and went right on talking.

I thought, Where did that white woman come from? She is going on and on and on and on. We need to get down with our stuff, and she comes in and tries to have a conversation. She don't even know what struggle is.

Then Nelson was talking about Paul's group, this white group in Durham. I thought, What are they joining us for? How are they oppressed? What is their problem?

I lumped all white people together. The distrust for whites was so deep. On the one hand, I'm seeing the class politics, and it makes sense that white workers are oppressed. But I don't connect that to working with them. My distrust of whites had been around all my life. So I agreed to meet the Durham people, but only to show Nelson he was wrong and pull him out of there before it was too late.

5
Party Life

In 1976, the Workers Viewpoint Organization recruited communist collectives from a variety of places around the country, including Greensboro and Durham, with the goal of building a new communist party. For the next three years, the North Carolina branch of the WVO dug into union organizing and community campaigns; at the same time, we built families and raised children.

Joining Workers Viewpoint Organization

Paul ■ I was thrilled when we merged our collective with Nelson Johnson's and joined Workers Viewpoint Organization. It brought together such talented organizers into a multiracial group. We got to know each other politically and personally. Our effectiveness increased tenfold, and for the next three years, we did the best organizing I've ever been involved in.

Working day to day, side by side, for a better world—there is no better way to become friends. I was our Durham collective's liaison to the Greensboro group, and after we merged, Nelson and I were the liaisons to the Workers Viewpoint Organization. So I spent many long nights into the early morning hours over at Nelson and Joyce's house. They had two little kids, and often our meetings would last until three or four o'clock in the morning. When you meet that long and there are little ones around, a lot is going on besides the meeting. I remember Akua, who was about five at the time, waking up with a bad dream. Nelson held her in his arms for hours during this meeting. She fell asleep, and we kept talking. We became very good friends, as well as political comrades. I felt like I became part of the Johnson family.

Nelson ■ Our work in the WVO was a very meaningful period in my life. It was intellectually profound, with a great understanding of historical trends. To this very day I deeply appreciate Marxism-Leninism. I find it most useful, though limiting.

Paul Bermanzohn was an inspiring person to me. He was so energized, so excited, and so available with an explanation for stuff.

Willena ■ I met Paul Bermanzohn and it was instant love, in the political sense. He was passionate, just like a white Nelson. I didn't know white people could feel that way. I figured Paul was like that because he was Jewish and his family had been wiped out in World War II. I thought to myself, He looks white, but he got a lot of black in him. I met Sally, and I figured she must be okay because she was hooked up with Paul.

I still wasn't convinced about the rest of them. Like Marty Nathan. I remember meeting her, and afterwards I just bust out laughing. "What kind of revolutionary is this?" I said. She was just this little white girl who had this high little voice. I thought revolutionaries should be robust and loud. I was so arrogant, thinking, Somebody is going to say boo, and she's gonna run. Boy, was I wrong!

I met Jim Waller and Bill Sampson, who both would be killed in 1979, and they were so nice, not bossy or pushy the way I thought all white people were. After getting to know these people, I said to myself, Willena, you're out to lunch. Good thing I got over this hating white people thing before I passed it on to my kids.

I had to go back over history and study the Underground Railroad during slavery, where whites had risked their lives helping to free blacks. Studying Marxism, I had learned about class in the abstract. But now I was living black/white unity, and that was a wonderful thing. It gave me a glimpse of how society could be. These folks had the education to get high-paying jobs, but money was not important to them. What they wanted was a good world to live in. You can't argue with that; you can't put a color on it. These folks became my best friends.

Paul ■ Our branch of the WVO began to grow in North Carolina. Joining our group was a big commitment for a person. We recruited by organizing study groups of interested people. This way, we could get to know people, their ideas, and they could get to know us. We could plug people into the day-to-day work and see how effective and dedicated they were. It was a way of avoiding FBI or police agents who wanted to quickly worm their way into revolutionary groups and then inform on them.

Marty ■ Mike and I joined a study group that Paul Bermanzohn organized. We read Marxism and talked about social change. It was the first time that I began to think in the way my father had taught me as a child—in terms of class. Marxism helped me understand things I couldn't figure out before, like the relationship between class, race, gender, and oppression. It was really incredibly helpful.

I'm still a Marxist. I believe that the main horrors of our society are based on the control by the monopoly capitalists and the way they pit people against one another. Marxism explained to me my own experience of life. Today my views on some things are different than they were then, but Marxism still makes sense to me. It was really refreshing to me to get involved. Medicine, as it was taught at Duke, had been so self-absorptive, so narcissistic. In a lot of ways, it was so meaningless, because it dealt only with organ pathology, not human lives. As a medical student, you are not doing much for anybody. I was sick and tired of being in the ivory tower.

Sally ■ Merging with Nelson and Joyce Johnson's collective and joining WVO was like the calm in the midst of the storm. I thought we could build something good. During the long, bitter fight with RWL at Duke, I found myself defensive, constantly responding to verbal attacks. But after we became WVO, everything cooled off. I was able to think about how to get the Duke union drive back on track.

And I could focus on my personal issues. I was twenty-nine years old. My biological clock was saying, "Have a baby!" Paul and I had been living together for two years, and I told Paul I wanted to get married and have children. He was against it. He thought kids would take too much time away from organizing the revolution, and he didn't want to get married because I wasn't Jewish. He was afraid his parents would disown him. We had this discussion over and over again. I finally told Paul he had to make a choice: me or his mother. He wouldn't budge. I decided that my highest priority was to have a kid. If Paul didn't want to be the father, then I better start looking for someone else. So I moved out and got my own little apartment.

Paul ■ The first private discussion I had with Nelson Johnson was about having kids. He and Joyce have two children, and Sally and I were discussing whether or not to have babies. Sally wanted them. I thought it was too difficult a thing to have children and continue to participate in this level of political work. I was working probably eighty to a hundred hours a week, nonstop, all the time.

So Nelson and I were walking outside. It was a warm summer night, and I was trying to get into a conversation with him. I asked him, "What is it like to have kids and combine that with politics?"

He put his arm around my shoulder, which I hadn't expected, and he said, "You know how when you're real busy and you have a lot of things to do, there's a few things that you always put on the back burner?"

I said, "Yeah."

And he said, "Kids are not like that." And was he right! Merging our collectives began a process of becoming engaged in each other's families. We built a deep personal unity, as well as a political unity. Nelson was a father figure to me.

I still wasn't convinced that I should become a father. Then Sally moved out on me. Living alone again reminded me how important Sally was to me, how important our relationship was. So I reconsidered: Maybe having kids wasn't such a bad idea.

So Sally and I got married and started trying to get pregnant. One "hot" night (a time of the month when conception was possible), I had a meeting at Nelson and Joyce's that lasted 'til three or four o'clock in the morning. Joyce laughed at me because she knew what the situation was. She told me to get out of there. So I rushed home to "seize the time," as it were. But when I got home around 5:30 a.m., Sally was getting dressed to go to work!

Sally ■ Finally, I got pregnant and had an easy pregnancy. Keeping my job at Duke was a bigger challenge—management tried to fire me, alleging that I had stolen money. It smelled like a union-busting setup. Their "evidence" was that my cash register came up around ten dollars short every day for a week. I filed a grievance and pointed out that someone was probably rigging my machine, punching in a ten-dollar sale before I got there. Several other union activists were fired around the same time, so we held protests and we all got our jobs back. There were a series of leaflets; my favorite was "DWOC Wins Back Job for Pregnant Cashier!" [A photo of this leaflet appears in Gallery II.]

Leola Ann Bermanzohn came into this world on October 13, 1977. Having a baby changed how I looked at the world. Suddenly, protecting my little Leola became the most important thing in the world to me. But the political work continued, and I kept up as best I could.

Organizing

Nelson ■ We divided our political work into two parts: The first was building trade unions, and the second was working in the black liberation movement. People got jobs in factories and hospitals, and we developed work around those jobs. We also kept in touch with issues in black communities all over the state.

Justice for Charlie Lee

Paul ■ We got involved in Whitakers, a tiny place, because of a racist murder there. It was my favorite campaign, probably my best work. Whitakers is a hamlet with maybe eight hundred residents in eastern North Carolina, most of whom were African American. In the spring of 1977, a white landowner killed a black agricultural worker named Charlie Lee. Charlie bought some food at Joe Judge's store, and Joe Judge shortchanged him. Charlie counted his change and went back into the store and demanded that Joe Judge give him his right change. Joe Judge reached into a drawer, pulled out a gun, and shot Charlie Lee in the stomach, killing him.

There was outrage throughout black communities for miles around. One thousand people came to Charlie Lee's funeral. Joe Judge was a notorious racist, and his family owned a great deal of land around Whitakers. There were some meetings following the funeral, but then the resistance died down.

We heard about Whitakers through a woman named Candy who had lived in the Whitakers area and who was working with us in Durham. So Nelson Johnson, Willena Cannon, Candy, and I went down to Whitakers to talk to people about what could be done. People in town were cynical and mistrustful. There was a lot of sentiment about wanting to do something, but they looked at us as if asking: "So who are you people? What are you doing here?"

Candy knew a lot of people in Whitakers, and that eased the way a little bit. But there was still a great deal of mistrust, particularly towards me, since I was a white guy and everybody else was black. The idea of having a white guy there was not a big plus. We met with young people who were outraged and potentially militant but really had no backing from the community to go ahead and do anything. It wasn't clear what could be done.

I was the one who was assigned to do the community work in Whitakers. At first I thought this was not going to go anywhere, because black folks need to organize black folks. But I had been organizing youth in some of the predominantly black housing projects in Durham and had proved to myself that it was possible for me to be an effective community organizer in a black community. I talked to people about my own experience in a family that had been victims of the Nazi Holocaust. It made a big impact on people. I wasn't a complete stranger to their experience of discrimination or racism.

I ended up spending days and days down in Whitakers, which was maybe a hundred miles from Durham on little country roads. I was working part-time at the Emergency Room in Burlington, and the rest of the time that summer I would spend there talking to people in Whitakers, and trying to figure out how the town worked. We wanted to talk to Charlie Lee's widow, but people said she didn't want to talk to us.

Our breakthrough came when we organized a program at the Bloomer Hill Community Center. Nelson, Willena, and others came down. César Cauce, who would be killed on November 3, was there. It was a social event, a dance, with some of us making speeches about how outrageous it was for Joe Judge to kill Charlie Lee and get away with it scot-free. César thought our event was great. He spoke at the meeting and had a great time. He was excited about what was going on, because it was clear we were sinking real roots in this community.

And after that program, we got word that Leola Lee, Charlie's widow, wanted to meet with us. Nelson went to talk to her first, and Leola Lee blessed the campaign and that made all the difference in the world. After that, we were able to organize broadly throughout the black community in the hamlet of Whitakers. We built the People's Coalition for Justice.

Leola Lee became a leader in the whole struggle, out in front of everything [see her photo in Gallery II]. As the widow, she had unassailable moral authority and was a very powerful figure. And Leola Lee was so in favor of what we were doing that she ended up having me stay at her house the many nights I was in Whitakers. I remember sleeping on her living-room floor, and every morning I would wake up to this gigantic breakfast of fried chicken, eggs, bacon, grits. Leola's family, cousins, and in-laws became the core of the People's Coalition. They were the ones we could count on to participate in the various public demonstrations.

In Nashville, the county seat, we marched in front of the courthouse, protesting the fact that nothing had happened to Joe Judge. We passed out flyers about what Joe Judge had done, and how nothing had happened to him. We wanted Joe Judge to be indicted and tried for this murder. Murders like this had taken place many times in the past, and they had generally gone unremarked except privately in the black community. To make a public demonstration was a freak-out to everybody white in the area. There were ten or twenty people with picket signs passing out flyers. It was a very intimidating atmosphere with these fat and evil-looking cops behind their wrap-around aviator sunglasses and their big Smoky hats standing and looking at us.

At the urging of Joyce and Nelson, the People's Coalition for Justice decided that since the courts weren't going to act, we were going to have our own "people's trial" of Joe Judge. We put out flyers and over several weeks had many discussions encouraging people to come to it. The day before the trial, I was passing out flyers and talking to people, and the local Whitakers police car started accompanying me on my rounds. The police intimidated people from talking to me all day long. They seemed to have nothing else to do; nothing was as important to them as trying to squash our effort.

Late in that day, I was hanging around with people at this gas station, and all of a sudden there is a siren and a flashing blue light and a police car pulls up right into the middle of us. I saw one of the cops with his hand on his gun as they rushed into the gas station and grabbed Walden, a young guy who was chair of the People's Coalition for Justice. Walden was the most outspoken and persistent young person carrying out this fight. The cops yanked Walden into the police car and drove off with him a few blocks over to the police station, where they had a little jail. People were stunned that they arrested Walden and afraid the cops would beat him. So about twenty-five to thirty people made their way over to the police station, in a semi-organized manner. I was among the first group of people to get over there. We wanted Walden out. Some cops came out of the station and insisted that we disperse. They said that we were carrying on an illegal assembly.

We refused to disperse. One cop, Officer Bunn, threatened to arrest everybody for disorderly conduct. And I mouthed off to him, saying, "The only one who is being disorderly here is the police." Officer Bunn threw me up against the wall and told me I was under arrest. And I asked him why. He leaned up in my face and his lip was trembling. So I realized this guy is barely under control and he had a gun and I better just do what he says, and I got very polite all of a sudden. But nevertheless he threw me into the jail cell, and there I was in the jail, in the cell right next to Walden. Meanwhile, more people were coming over from the gas station to the police station, and we could hear the people outside yelling and chanting at the police.

The police took us out of the jail cells and put us into police cars. They took us for a harrowing ride, miles and miles through back-country roads to Nashville, the county seat, to be booked. It was the middle of the night, and Walden and I were handcuffed in the backseat with our arms behind our backs, Officer Bunn sitting there next to us telling the driver to go faster and faster. A whole caravan was following us, including several other police cars and four or five cars filled with demonstrators trying to stop any violence against us. Officer Bunn, the madman, is carrying on about "You can't be afraid to die if you want to be a police officer" and "When I was in Vietnam, I faced death many times" and "Let's just stop right here and shoot it out with them." Apparently, Bunn was very upset by the fact that there were cars of protesters in the police caravan.

Finally we got to Nashville, and they booked Walden on some trumped-up charge and me on a charge of "congregating." (When my trial came up, my lawyer said, "How can one man congregate?" They dropped the charges against both of us.)

But that night, the arrests of Walden and me had the opposite effect the police intended. Everybody in Whitakers knew what had happened. The next day there was a huge turnout at the people's trial—over a hundred people from Whitakers, a big percent of the total population. The jury was the assembled folks who were there. Joyce Johnson was the prosecuting attorney, and she did a great job presenting the evidence. Joe Judge was overwhelmingly convicted. The people's trial made it clear what the people of Whitakers thought about what was going on with the regular court system.

And it had an impact. Some time after that, Joe Judge was indicted, and the North Carolina court forced him to pay a settlement to the widow of Charlie Lee. It was a landmark case in the state. Even though Joe Judge was not put in jail, it was the first time that a white man who killed a black man was forced by a court to pay a settlement. It helped build our reputation in the state and helped us become leaders in the issues that followed. I became recognized as a leader in the black community, which was really kind of funny since I was a white kid from New York.

Nelson ■ Twenty-five years later, I was invited down to Whitakers to take part in a commemoration of that struggle against Joe Judge. Leola Lee received a plaque, because the black community of Whitakers sees our People's Justice

Campaign as the beginning of African American empowerment there. Now, Whitakers has a majority of blacks on its city council.

Paul ■ Leola Lee was such an inspiration to me and such a good friend, Sally and I named our first child after her. Sally was six and then seven months pregnant that summer, and we still hadn't decided on a name for our child. One day, I thought about girls' names as I was driving home from Whitakers. Why not name our baby—if it was a girl—after Leola Lee? I told Sally my idea, and she said, "Let's look at what it means in the baby book." And the book said that Leola means "a woman with the strength, courage, and fortitude of a lion." Wow! How could you beat that?

So we named our firstborn Leola. Leola Lee sent us a pink knitted sweater and a card that read "From Big Leola to Little Leola."

Stop the Test

Kwame ■ I grew up going to protests with my mama. I went to places all over Greensboro with my mother, and most of the times I enjoyed it. But I didn't know the issues. A lot of times, Mama said, "I gotta go here, and you gotta go too." That was basically the explanation I got [see Gallery II for a photo of Kwame in a picket line].

My favorite campaign was the Stop the Test movement. In 1977, Governor Jim Hunt decided that all North Carolina students had to pass a competency test to get a high school diploma. They ran a pretest, and more than half of the black students failed it! Lots of poor whites flunked it too. The kids who didn't pass the test were only going to get a Certificate of Attendance. That was embarrassing.

Nelson Johnson, Sandi Smith, my mom, and other WVO people started a Stop the Test movement, holding speak-outs, marches, pickets, and other demonstrations in towns around the state. Lots of people got involved—teenagers, adults, and older people. Older people from the projects, because it affected their children and grandchildren. I remember this little old lady, Miss Fannie, carrying a poster that said "Stop the Test." The whole community came together around the Stop the Test campaign. Sandi Smith was a big leader for this in Greensboro.

I was about nine years old at the time of the Stop the Test campaign. My mom was organizing the Revolutionary Youth League [RYL] for teenagers. They came up with these songs that explained things, like "We got to all get together and stop these tests." One of the lines was, "You're either stupid, unable, or disqualified/And they forget about the twelve years you tried/If you fail the test." That let you know what you were fighting for. Nobody could dog you for being out there for something like that.

There were a lot of teenagers in RYL, and they would spend time with me, explaining, so I would get a better grip on the issues. It was their fight, because they were going to have to take that test. I was too little to be in RYL. (Soon after that they came up with Junior RYL, which was my organization.)

I was proud to go and protest at the Greensboro Board of Education. We made a picket line, a circle picket, and there was about fifteen to twenty people and we all had signs. For me it was one of the more fun demonstrations; I felt like I was a part of it. The media was there. I thought I could go to my school and say: "Hey, I'm in the news. There I am." But then on the news clip they showed my little raggedy tennis shoes! What they showed on the clip was the voices saying, "We're going to all be together to stop the test." But they didn't show the faces, just the marchers' feet. When my feet came up, I knew it was me because my tennis shoes were so raggedy! So I was like, Dag!

Willena ■ We held all kinds of demonstrations in those days. Big loud ones, with lots of chants—it felt like the 1960s again. Every year in May, we held an African Liberation March in Washington, D.C. We brought busloads from North Carolina to march with people from all over the country. I remember talking and singing on the bus, and the huge amount of food people brought. There is a photograph of the North Carolina delegation, with banners flying and people chanting, that captures some of our spirit [see Gallery II].

Our biggest demonstration was to free the Wilmington Ten. The Wilmington Ten were activists, including Ben Chavis, who the state of North Carolina sentenced to thirty years in prison for firebombing a grocery store. We knew Ben and the others were innocent and that they had been jailed to thwart the movement. Ben was pushing to desegregate the Wilmington, North Carolina, public school system, as part of the United Church of Christ Commission on Racial Justice, when the government imprisoned him.[1] The campaign to free the Wilmington Ten started in 1972 and dragged on for year after year. When we joined WVO, we built a coalition with the United Church of Christ and put together a major demonstration in Raleigh that took place in April 1978. About three thousand people mobilized from around the state to march through the streets of Raleigh. People came up with the chant "Fired up—won't take it no more!"

Our Campaign to Free the Wilmington Ten March was effective. Ben Chavis and the others got out of jail not long after our demonstration. I took Kwame when a bunch of us went to welcome Ben home.

Kwame ■ I remember Mama taking me when Ben Chavis was being freed, and I got to meet him. Little did I know that some twenty years later people would march in Raleigh for me, chanting, "Free Kwame Cannon!"

Five Great Organizers

Sally ■   Every time I think about the work we did, I remember the five people who died. They were all such good leaders, and they died so young. Sadness still washes over me, but it is important to remember them. Their stories illustrate the work we did.

Sandi Neely Smith: Leading the ROC

Nelson ■   Sandi Neely Smith was only twenty-nine when she died, but she had already made her mark as a leader: as student government president, as an activist for more than a decade, and as the leader of Revolution Textile Mill's union drive.

Sandi was born on Christmas Day in 1950. She was the only child of a textile worker and a schoolteacher. Her father worked for many long years at JP Stevens, one of the nation's largest textile companies. He always had a job outside the mill, because there were no inside jobs for "the colored." Her father's experience profoundly affected Sandi.

Sandi went to high school during the desegregation era. While she went to the black high school, the media focused on the white high school where the first few blacks had been admitted. There was talk about closing the black high school to merge it with the white one. Sandi said, "Why don't they send white kids to our high school?"

In 1969, after graduating from high school, Sandi came to Greensboro to go to Bennett College.[2] She got very involved in all the movement activity and still managed to be a good student and student government president. She graduated in 1973. By then we were in the middle of the struggle to bring Marxism-Leninism to the black liberation movement. Sandi led by example: In 1974, she got a job in a textile mill. She married Mark Smith, and then unmarried him, still working at the textile mill.

Sandi's job was at Cone Mill's Revolution Plant. "Revolution" was such a misnomer, because Cone considered Revolution Mill its pet textile mill, the one that couldn't be unionized. In 1976, after our collectives merged into WVO, other activists, black and white, followed Sandi's lead and got jobs there. The workforce was black and white, so it helped to have a black and white core of organizers.

Willena ■   I remember passing out leaflets with Sandi at Revolution Mill. She laughed and talked to all the workers, including the white women. She talked to them about how rough it was to be a worker with kids and these hard jobs. She really got on with people.

Nelson ■ The union activists in the mill pulled together the Revolution Organizing Committee, better known as the ROC. At first they met secretly, because people were afraid they would get fired for talking union. Through their secret network, they got fifty workers, black and white, to join the ROC and spread the word of unionizing to over half the plant. But a union can't be organized in secret, so the ROC had to become public.

The ROC had to pick a chairperson for their union drive, someone who was not intimidated by Cone and who Cone could not easily fire. Sandi was the clear choice. She had worked in the mill for three years by then. People knew they could count on her. So on April 3, 1977, the ROC publicly opened the union drive with a mass meeting. Cone tried to scare people from coming to the meeting by red-baiting and race-baiting the union activists, saying the union was being manipulated by communists and was only interested in black workers. But 180 workers came to the mass meeting, and Sandi did a terrific job as chair, making everyone feel comfortable and pointing out the task before them.

Cone started laying off workers at Revolution. The ROC responded by demonstrating at Cone's corporate headquarters in Greensboro. Sandi, in her stylist bell-bottom jeans, stood on the sound truck and led the chanting: "Organize Revolution Mill! Jobs for all six hundred workers thrown out in the streets! Seventy-five cents an hour raise for all Cone workers!" [see photo in Gallery II]. It was the first rally ever at Cone headquarters.

Since the 1950s, workers at Revolution Mill had made four separate attempts to unionize the mill, all unsuccessful. The American Clothing and Textile Workers Union locals at two other Cone mills in Greensboro voted to support the ROC's union drive. Then the ROC contacted the regional officials of ACTWU, asking them to take up the drive. ACTWU officials heard that communists were involved in the organizing, and they told the workers they wouldn't touch the ROC with a ten-foot pole. Union leaders were using anticommunism as their rationale to do Cone's bidding. No wonder people got angry at union bureaucrats.

Then Cone came down hard. They fired five of the union activists (they wanted to fire Sandi, but she was too established). Then they laid off nearly a third of the workforce at the plant, threatening to close down entirely. [A few years later, Cone did close Revolution.] The ROC held rallies at the plant gate protesting all this. But Cone had scared most of the workers lucky enough to still have jobs. Many stopped coming to ROC meetings, and the union drive petered out.

Sally ■ Sexual harassment was common in workplaces across the country, but back then very few people discussed it. Sandi was one of the early ones to expose it. She wrote the following leaflet with other ROC members, exposing sexual harassment before the word was in our vocabulary.

Women Workers at Cone Mills

Everybody who works at Cone Mills has it tough. That's no secret. It's also no secret that *women* workers at Revolution and other Cone Mills plants face a lot of *special* problems that make things even tougher. We can begin to turn this situation around only by organizing to fight now and to struggle to build a strong union.

SUPERVISORS: KEEP YOUR HANDS TO YOURSELVES. One big headache for women workers all over the mill is supervisors making passes at them, pestering them to go out with them, etc. Some of these men have even told certain women, "don't worry about making your eight hours here if you'll just . . ." There's a *big difference* between workers doing this and men *supervisors* doing it, because the supervisors always have the threat of harassment or firing to use if women don't go along or at least keep quiet. And although this stuff is bad enough with white women, with black women the supervisors are downright *outrageous.* In fact, the same guy in the Card Room who has been calling white union supporters "nigger lovers" is well known for his roaming hands and slimy personal questions to black women!

Of course Herman Cone will claim that this doesn't go on. He'll say: "If you have a complaint, take it to your overseer and he'll straighten everything out." But we know better. In the spinning room a young woman worker reported to the overseer that one supervisor kept making passes at her. What did the overseer do? He laughed at her!

A lot of women are angry about this kind of stuff. But some women just try to play along with the supervisors, laugh them off, and hope they'll go away and leave them alone. The ones that don't give in get harassed and the company covers up for the bossmen. Here's one example:

There is one supervisor in the Card Room _____ who is notorious for this kind of stuff. He is known all over the mill for the dog that he is. He had been trying to get next to a young white woman for months, when she finally got fed up, she went to the overseer, complained about it, and asked for a transfer to another mill to get away from this creep. She did not get the transfer and she continued getting the same dirty spare help job. She finally quit work—but the supervisor is still here doing the same old dirty thing, and the company covered the whole thing up.

WOMEN WORKERS SHOULD NOT HAVE TO PUT UP WITH THIS GARBAGE TO HOLD ONTO THEIR JOBS!!

Women who are getting abused like this should know that it's happening to *lots of people*, not just them. When you get harassed like this you can stand up and fight it. Tell the ROC and the workers in your department. File a grievance against the supervisor and the ROC will help you push this and organize fighting support for you. It is by all workers uniting behind women who get harassed that we will put a stop to all this junk.

Paul ■ I got to know Sandi when she and I trained people on how to give a speech at the Wilmington Ten demonstration. Everyone rehearsed their speeches. One person made a particularly poor speech with no spirit to it. Sandi said that to make a good speech, you have to do three things: (1) Think concretely about what you are talking about, (2) combat hesitancy, and (3) organize your thoughts. This was what WVO had taught us, and Sandi really communicated that to the group. The next time around, everybody did better—and the poor speaker did great. Sandi said, "See—communism is a science."

Kwame ■ I felt close with Sandi. I met her through Nelson's daughters, Ayo and Akua, my best friends in the world. I was with my mama over at their house probably four or five times a week. Ayo, Akua, and I would play upstairs, and there was a lot of times when we would get rowdy. Sandi was the babysitter, and she would always come up there: "Y'all too loud up here." She was a babysitter, but a cool babysitter. She wasn't our age and she wasn't my mama's age, she was like a cool in-between.

There were times when Nelson and them would be in a heavy discussion and really didn't need a disturbance. Sandi would be upstairs making sure that we didn't get loud, period. She would always have us doing something—something constructive—either drawing or writing our names or getting us to do various things.

We could never be able to guess what kind of hairstyle Sandi would have. There were times when she would wear this big Afro, and next time she would have it plaited down. She had lots of different styles.

Bill Sampson: Organizing at the White Oak Textile Mill

Paul ■ Bill Sampson was a guy who seemed to be able to do anything and everything, including energizing a do-nothing union local at the White Oak Textile Mill.

Bill was born in 1948 to a family with Swedish ancestry. Bill's parents were research scientists who worked on the Manhattan Project during World War II, helping to produce the first atomic bomb. After the war, Bill's father got a job with DuPont, transferring his family from Wilmington, Delaware, to Camden, South Carolina, to Richmond, Virginia, while Bill was growing up. In Camden, Bill saw the Ku Klux Klan burn a cross on a neighbor's front yard, which angered and upset him. In high school in 1965, Bill participated in civil rights demonstrations.

Bill went to Augustana College, where he got every honor available: Phi Beta Kappa, national honors, president of the residents' council. During his junior year, he studied at the Sorbonne in Paris. Bill arrived in France during the 1968 worker and student uprising. Many French people didn't like Americans much; sentiment against the U.S. role in Vietnam was strong. Bill found that people in Europe did not like the way the American government looked as if everyone in the world should serve them. Bill was used to people liking him, and the cool reception surprised him. He took to heart the French critique of the U.S. and decided he must look beyond his own country. He read everything he could get his hands on—Marx, Lenin, Proust, Sartre.

Before he went to France, he was unsure how he felt about the war in Vietnam. When he came home to Augustana, he organized protests against the war. He became a conscientious objector. After he graduated, he headed for Boston because it was a center of antiwar activity. He enrolled in Harvard Divinity School, thinking that as a radical minister he could best serve the movement. After an antiwar demonstration in Boston, Bill was jumped on by cops. He was hospitalized, lost hearing in one ear, and almost lost his eye. Bill became disillusioned with churches because he felt many refused to take a strong stand against the Vietnam War, and he decided to do something else.

Bill studied Marxism and decided he was a communist. He met Dale Deering at Christmastime in 1975. She had never met a communist before and fell in love with him. A year later, they both moved to Greensboro because they wanted to be part of the work we were doing. They both got jobs at White Oak, Cone Mills's biggest plant in Greensboro, and soon got married.

Sally ■ After Bill Sampson died, I sought out his co-workers and close friends. Big Man was an older African American from rural South Carolina who had fought the Klan in the 1930s. Big Al was Bill's age, but he grew up in Bermuda under segregation, British-colonial style. As their names imply, Big Man and Big Al are both, well, big. I wanted to know how they befriended Bill, whose background and experience was so different than theirs. Here are excerpts from the interviews.

Big Al: The first time I saw Bill was in June 1977, at the end of a long hot day. It was 11 a.m., the beginning of our work shift. Big Man and I walked in the front door of the mill and saw this white guy coming out of the personnel office. He was tall, but thin. He wore green army pants, an old white shirt, and big boots that looked brand-new and like they didn't fit him right. He walked with these little steps, like his feet hurt. He held his head so high it looked like he was almost leaning backward.

I nudged Big Man and nodded towards the skinny white man. "Betcha five dollars he's going to the dye house," I said.

Big Man: "Naw," I told Al, "you gotta be big, black, and healthy looking to work in the dye house." But then we followed that skinny man all the way through the weave room to the dye house. He ain't gonna make it, we thought. Ain't got no ass to him.

Big Al: The dye house is the dirtiest place in the mill. And hot—a hundred degrees even in the winter. White Oak Mill is the biggest producer of denim in the world. Chances are your blue jeans were woven and dyed at White Oak. To dye the denim, they pull the cotton threads together in a rope two inches thick called a warp. The warp's gotta move through the dye at a steady speed, because delay changes the color. When the warps finish being dyed, they come through the machines into the room where me and Big Man and Bill worked. We caught the warps in a bag, let the bag fill up, and then cut the warp and loaded the wet bag—several hundred pounds—on to a hand truck. The work was hard and fast, a battle with the machines.

Big Man: Bill didn't know his job. I was to learn him. We tested all the new men. We especially tested Bill. He was the only white man in the dye house at that time. We put him through some rigid things. We had to know if he could carry his own load. I didn't think he would last.

Big Al: Bill's job was to replace the bags after the warps were cut. There are five machines, each with twenty to thirty warps passing through them. If the bags weren't replaced fast enough, the hot, sticky blue warps would pile up on the floor and it would take twice as long to bag them. I wondered what would happen if the warps in all five machines came down at the same time. It happened on Bill's second day of work.

Bill started jumping. He ran around each of those machines. By that last machine, he was dragging. He was blue from the dye, itchy, and sweaty. We watched him real close. Would he give up or get angry? Would he take out his anger on us?

Big Man: Bill got angry, but it was a cool rage, and he aimed it at the bossman. Bill was okay, I decided. He hung in there. The next day he comes strollin' back. He passed the test. We knew he was here to stay.

Every morning at 6 a.m., an hour before their shift ended, the dye-house workers would get harassed by a go-getter supervisor who would push them to work faster. By that time they had already worked seven hours and were tired, hot. Keeping pace with the machines was hard enough—they could not deal with a speedup.

Big Man: That bossman was just trying to look good. It was always one or two of us who dealt with him, man to man. "Don't do this to me!" we yelled at him. We schooled Bill in this and he would yell at the supervisor with us.

Big Al: But Bill suggested we talk it out first, not just act spontaneous. He talked about how the bossmen have the whole government to back them up. We have the whole working class. That's why we've got to organize; that's why we need a rank-and-file union. Bill said we should try to get the whole department—and the whole mill—to back us up.

So all of us in the dye room talked it over. That morning at 6 a.m., that bossman came up like always. We just stopped working. All of us in the department just glared at him. "We're tired of you hurrying us up to make you look good," we yelled at him. He left fast. He was scared that those machines would slow down and the color would be off. Then he would look *bad*. That was the last time we saw him at six in the morning.

North Carolina is a so-called right-to-work state. "Right to work" sounds like it guarantees you a job, but that is a deception. The only time the government ensures the right to work is when there is a strike. Then police protect strikebreakers who are crossing the picket lines. It really should be called the "right to scab." These antiunion laws outlaw union shops, where the workers automatically become union members. Instead, each individual decides to join or not to join. Those who join the union have to pay dues; those who don't get the same benefits but save the cost of the dues. This keeps the unions weak and the membership fluctuating.

The union at White Oak Textile Mill was typical. When Bill went to work, there was a union affiliated with the American Clothing and Textile Workers Union, but there were only thirty dues-paying members out of 2,200 workers. ACTWU had a "sweetheart contract" with the company that gave the workers few rights and low wages. People wanted higher wages and better working conditions but had no faith that the tired old ACTWU could improve anything, so why join and pay union dues? At the meetings, ACTWU officials attacked Bill and Big Al and others who were trying to strengthen the union. The threat of firings and layoffs hung heavy over people. Most departments didn't have shop stewards who would stand up against management. When problems came up on the shop floor, workers suffered the abuse or fought alone.

Bill's challenge was to demonstrate to people that they could stick together and rebuild their union local to fight for better conditions. Soon after Bill started working, Rand Manzella, a young white man, joined them in the dye house. He had worked in a factory in Buffalo, New York, until he got laid off and his marriage broke up. He came to North Carolina looking for work. Rand was shorter than the others, but strong. He soon passed Big Man and Big Al's test in the dye house and became close friends with them.

> Rand: I started working right after Bill, Big Al, and Big Man drove away the supervisor. The people in the dye house were real tight, glad they had won that battle. They loved Bill. The new supervisor was trying to split Bill from the rest of us, but he failed completely because Bill pointed out exactly what was going on.
>
> During my first few months on the job, while I was still on probation, the management was speeding us up. We decided we need to all go down to the overseer about it. We talked about how to do it, and the whole dye house went down there—everyone. People went in there strong, but scared too. Just all of us being there was significant. Bill was the main speaker, many others didn't say anything. We stood by Bill—he was our leader, our speaker.
>
> When Bill told me he was a communist, I thought he had a sick sense of humor. But I respected Bill—he chose to work in the mill, facing all the aggravation. He didn't act like a big deal, just an average worker trying to get by. He was an excellent leader.
>
> Cone tried to split me away from the others: They offered me a supervisor job. The bossman said to me, "A smart guy like you shouldn't be working in a place like this." If I had done what he said, I would have ended up snitching on my fellow workers, and proving to black workers that you couldn't trust white workers.

The solidarity of the dye house set an example for the rest of the mill. There were other WVO members working in other departments, as well as communists in other organizations. Together, the activist workers formed the White Oak Organizing Committee. The WOOC helped people take up fights on the shop floor and encouraged them to join the union. The WOOC put out leaflets about the dye house and the other departments, so workers all over the mill would know what was happening. It made the supervisors think twice about coming down on workers—when they did, they saw their name in print the next day.

Cone fired several black union activists, including Big Man. The WOOC filed lawsuits with the NLRB [National Labor Relations Board] because it is illegal to fire someone because they are a union activist. Big Man got his job back.

In 1978, Cone arrested Bill when he went with fifteen workers to the supervisor's office to file a grievance.

> Rand: Management was no match for Bill. Bill won the grievance, and it made them so angry they made fools of themselves. Bill was cool, not even

raising his voice. The bossman flipped out, pounded his fist, jumped up and down. He called the cops and arrested Bill for trespassing! They took Bill downtown to jail. But the workers started a slowdown in protest, so Cone couldn't fire Bill.

Bill kept his job, and the union began to grow. Its membership rose eight-fold, up to 250 dues-paying members.

In February 1979, one month before officers elections, ACTWU put its five union locals in administratorship. These locals included White Oak, where Bill and Big Al ran for president and vice president of the union, and Granite, where Jim Waller was president. "Administratorship" means taking the union out of the hands of the local members and placing it in the hands of the top levels of ACTWU to administer it. No shop stewards were to be recognized by Cone; no union meetings were to be held. This is a long-time tactic of companies and union bureaucrats to smash militant union locals.

Bill Sampson, Big Al, Big Man, and Rand Manzella worked side by side in the dye house and continued to organize the plant. They were hopeful that the adminstratorship would lift and they would run for union office. Then Bill was killed, deflating the union-strengthening effort. They mourned their friend. "Bill was like a brother to me," said Big Al.

"Funny part about Bill," Big Man added. "I never seen him mad. He never raised his voice. He never cursed. He was such a quiet man. But then you see him fight the enemy—he was like a knife."

Kwame ■ As a matter of fact, did Bill ever get really mad? I can only recall Bill Sampson with a smile on his face. There were times that I could see that he was serious, but it wasn't like a threatening kind of serious.

I was eight and nine years old, and one thing I noticed was people getting mad. To me Nelson is one of the greatest people in the world, but there were times when I could see his anger. Dale [Bill's wife] could get mad, and most other people weren't shy about showing they were upset. But Bill was a happy-go-lucky kind of guy.

Willena ■ I was impressed with Bill Sampson because he was a white man and he was humble. He was always asking questions or listening to people, like he was really interested. I remember watching him in the public housing projects. He was passing out union leaflets, and people wanted to sit and listen to him, and he asked questions so he could listen to them. It was such a blatant contrast with other white men, like landlords.

Jim Waller:
Wildcat Strike at Haw River

Paul ■ In 1978, at the age of thirty-five, Jim Waller led a wildcat strike at Cone's Granite Textile Mill in Haw River, North Carolina. It was a long way for a kid born to Jewish shopkeepers in Chicago who became a movement doctor for over a decade. But Jim always was remarkable. He went to the University of Michigan and then to medical school at the University of Chicago. He wrote letters and kept journals that included poetry and notes for speeches. He left a record of his life.

Jim was always a character. In medical school, he refused to shave off his beard. No medical students ever dared to wear a beard when they started working on the wards. But Jim staged a protest called SWAB—Save Waller's Beard. The administration threatened him, but he refused to put a razor to his face. His classmates rallied to his side, signing petitions, and he kept his beard. Jim staffed medical teams at protests through the sixties and seventies, including the Native American standoff at Wounded Knee in South Dakota, the Attica prison rebellion in New York State, antiwar demonstrations in Washington, D.C., and the 1968 Democratic Convention in Chicago.[3]

In the early 1970s, Jim joined the Lincoln Collective at Lincoln Hospital in the South Bronx, New York City. Lincoln Hospital was responsible for serving some of the poorest people in the U.S., and people in the neighborhood called it the butcher shop. The Lincoln Collective was a group of doctors and nurses working to pressure the health-care system to meet people's needs. For years, the Lincoln Collective fought hard, but health care at Lincoln remained wretched.

In 1974, Jim decided to move to North Carolina because he heard about the organizing we were doing. Jim took a job at Duke Medical Center, sought us out, and quickly joined our organizing collective. He was with us when we joined WVO in the fall of 1976. Jim and I attended the first meeting of the Carolina Brown Lung Association in Columbia, South Carolina, in September 1975. It was a sea of coughing gray heads—every one of the 120 retired textile workers there had a breathing problem. I spoke on how brown lung could be prevented, how the drive for profits led mill owners not to install proper ventilation. As soon as I finished, hands shot up in the air for questions. I was struck by these older workers' concern for others. Over and over they told us: "It's too late for me, but if there is anything we can do for the young workers in these mills, I'll do it. Anything." Jim and I were both moved by their attitude.

That is when Jim began thinking about leaving medicine to get a job in a textile mill. Giving up medicine was difficult for Jim, who had been a doctor for more a decade. But Duke's greedy hospital administration helped him decide to leave medicine. Jim would visit sick kids he treated after hours, and talk to their parents. He learned Duke was charging the families for these visits. He was incensed. He complained to the administration that the hospital was billing for his personal time. But the administration wouldn't budge. And Jim left his doctor job to work in a factory.

Sally ■ Jim got a job at Cone Mill's Granite Finishing Plant, which was located in tiny Haw River, North Carolina, halfway between Greensboro and Durham. Like Bill Sampson, he was placed in the dye house during the night shift. Unlike Bill, he did not hit it off right away with his co-workers, who were all men, most of them white.

Jim stood out in rural North Carolina. He wasn't black, but he also wasn't anything like a white southerner. He had thick black hair on his head and face. He talked with a northern accent. He liked weird food, like pastrami on rye, pickled herring on homemade bread, and tofu with bean sprouts. The guys gave him endless grief over his strange taste in food and his beard. They started calling him Wolfman, and one drew a cartoon about his eating habits.

His first year at Granite was hard. Every chance he could, he tried to talk to people about the need for revolution. One time, when a worker asked him why the textile union leaders were such sell-outs, Jim went on and on, tracing the social development of capitalism. "I hadn't even gotten to the history of trade unions, when I looked up and the guy was halfway out of the room," Jim told us.

He began attending union meetings. Local 1113T of the American Clothing and Textile Workers Union was in sorry shape. The membership fluctuated between twelve and thirty people. The other six hundred workers at Granite refused to join. When they had a problem on the shop floor, the workers had to fight alone. In a stronger union, if a worker has a disagreement with the company, he walks off the job and files a grievance. ACTWU in the 1970s was worse than most unions. It was a rubber stamp for the textile companies.[4]

Charles, a pro-union worker, told me how he first met Bill:

Charles: I remember the union president coming to me and telling me there was this communist working right in the mill. I said, "What is a communist?" I decided to go to the very next union meeting just to see what this communist looked like. I saw this funny-looking guy with all this jet-black hair. He said, "This ain't right and that ain't right and we need to build a strong union here at Granite." The president told him to shut up and sit down.

Jim didn't win many workers at Granite to communism. But he did convince them that he could stand up to the boss, that he could lead them in building a stronger union. He transferred to the cutting room, the heart of the plant. The cutters cut the grooves in corduroy. Corduroy was one of Cone mills' biggest products, and Cone was dependent on Granite Finishing Plant to produce it.

One day, while flipping a heavy roll of corduroy onto a hand truck, a cutter got a hernia. Jim angrily spoke out, saying that Cone was responsible, that the hand trucks were so old, the wheels so clogged with cotton dust, that they wouldn't roll. Cone was too cheap to replace or even repair them.

Jim and several other workers circulated a petition that ninety-one out of one hundred cutters signed. When they went to the union president, who was also a cutter, the man refused to sign, saying, "It won't do no good." But the president could not stop the petition's momentum, because the union was so weak. A bunch of guys went to the supervisor's office and raised Cain. The company tried to scare people, saying that they were planning another wage cut. But Cone management bought new hand trucks.

The petition was a turning point in Jim Waller's work. His new nickname became Blackbeard. Black and white workers started bypassing the do-nothing union president and going directly to Jim.

> Charles: At work, Jim kept coming to talk to me, 'cause he heard I was strong on the union. Whenever he came, I'd look around to be sure no one saw me talking to him. But then every time someone had a problem, they would go to Blackbeard. He'd take out his contract and tell him, "This ain't right." Then he would go with them to the bossman's office. And the bossman couldn't say nothing, because Jim knew his contract and how to talk them down.
>
> Finally people got to like Jim, and we elected him shop steward. Then he really took up building the union.

Every time something happened at the plant, the guys called Jim Waller. Whenever a grievance was filed, Jim and other workers would leaflet the plant so that everyone would know what was happening. About 60 percent of the Granite workforce was white, the rest black. Building unity was difficult, because people generally didn't mix and racist ideas were strong among many of the white workers. Jim took up grievances of both black and white and often talked about the need for unity. He got a following among the white workers, but many blacks were stand-offish. The union president was black, and his hatred of Jim fed the mistrust many blacks felt about whites. But Jim eventually won the confidence of many black workers.

I helped Jim pass out leaflets at the mill during the spring of 1978, when we organized the march to free the Wilmington Ten, who were black activists unjustly imprisoned. The plant was the biggest building in the tiny town, dominating the landscape. It was seven o'clock in the morning, dark and cold. As cars drove through the gate, we hoped to get people to roll down their windows enough to take a flyer. Most did take a leaflet, because they knew Jim. But when they read "Free the Wilmington Ten," some became hostile. (The protests against the incarceration of the Wilmington Ten had been in the media for years, and many whites thought the jailed activists were troublemakers and got what they deserved.) One of Jim's white co-workers, whom he had socialized with on the weekends, yelled at Jim: "You goddammed nigger lover! If you ever come to my house again, I'll kill you."

"You keep talking like that," Jim yelled after him, "and Cone keeps laughing—all the way to the bank!" Black workers respected Jim for supporting the Wilmington Ten.

After Jim got elected shop steward, guys that befriended him turned into union activists, and some of them were elected shop stewards. In June 1978, Cone management posted a wage cut—the tenth cut in three years. That night, Jim's co-workers came to him saying: "Turn off the machines. We've got to talk." All the workers in the cutting room turned off their machines, telling their bosses that if the wage cut went through they would strike. To back up their threat, the next night many called in sick and others slowed the machines down. But Cone would not budge; the wages were cut.

The men called a union meeting, where they talked about whether they were strong enough to strike. Chairing the meeting, Jim listened carefully to all the pros and cons. There were lots of decisions to make—when to begin the strike, how to spread the strike from the cutting room to the other departments in the plant, how to raise strike funds, how to deal with the ACTWU bureaucrats, who they knew would oppose the strike. One man said, "You decide, Blackbeard, you know all about these things." But Jim would not make the decision alone. The men as a whole had to decide.

When they voted to strike, more than a hundred workers jammed into the small union hall across the street from the plant. Charles said that he felt they could strike because "we finally have a man with enough backbone to lead us against Cone."

I drove to Haw River to be part of the picket line, to encourage workers to honor the strike and not go to work. The strike was scheduled to begin at 11 p.m., the end of the second shift, when most people are going to bed. As I drove into town, everybody and everything seemed to be asleep except for the mill, where the lights were blazing. About fifty picketers, most of them cutters from the plant who worked on the first shift, massed at the front gate. At 11 p.m. the whistle blew. The picketers held their breath. The plant doors burst open. "Shut her down!" roared second-shift cutters as they ran out and joined our picket line.

At the main gate, the picketers tried to stop third-shift workers from coming to work. This was the main way to spread the strike to the workers in the other departments. As each car drove up, the men surrounded it. The picketers knew the dangers. Everyone in those cars needed money. Sometimes a man's house was on the line in the next paycheck. Did some of them need a paycheck bad enough to pull a gun on you?

"They cut our wages, they can cut yours. Turn around, no work tonight," they told each car. "We're striking for you, man," another would say. "Things ain't so great in your department. Think about the guy who fell off the crane in the warehouse. Cone didn't give a damn about him. And they don't give a damn about you."

Most cars backed up and left. Some went through the gate. "Goddammed supervisor!" someone yelled after one car. "I hope you have another heart attack!" The lights in the plant still blazed, but the noise of machines pounding day and night stopped. Granite Finishing Plant was shut down.

The guys organized picket lines during the day to turn away the trucks, the huge eighteen-wheelers delivering raw corduroy and picking up the finished product. "On strike!" yelled the workers. The morning I was part of the picket line, all the big trucks backed up and pulled away. No Cone corduroy today!

People from miles around came to support the strike, rank-and-file union members from as far away as the Carolina coast, where we had supported dockworkers when they went on strike. Black-white unity was not automatic. I brought several black union activists from our Duke organizing drive. A white striker I had met earlier nodded toward my black friends and whispered mockingly in my ear, "Looks like *everybody's* out here tonight."

I tensed up and told him, "They are leaders from our union in Durham."

He backed up, paused, and changed his tone of voice. "Well, they're welcome. We need all the help we can get."

The strike electrified the sleepy little town of Haw River, where the sidewalks roll up at 7 p.m. A striker wrote to Alamance County's *Alamance News* on July 3, 1973:

We know our strike is effective, because of the way Cone schemed to use the court and the Sheriff's Department against us. Last Wednesday, they slapped an injunction on us limiting the number of pickets to two per gate and said there could be no strikers or strikers' cars within 1000 feet of the gate. This is a sign of their weakness and our strength. Likewise the Sheriff has shown his true colors. He won't give us any answers. If we ask him anything, he will go straight to Cone management's office. They arrested a striker, kept him in jail 12 hours and put him on a $500 bond for blowing a whistle, after a deputy told him to blow the whistle. At the same time when a strikebreaker drove his car at high speed into the picket line, nearly killing us, the Sheriff did nothing. And when a strikebreaker actually hit one of us with his car, the magistrate didn't want to swear out a warrant.

During the course of the strike, Local 1113T grew from twelve to two hundred members. But the strong solidarity of the first week began to fade by the end of the second. When Cone management posted the jobs of the strikers for new workers—scabs—to fill, some of the men went back to work. After a few more days, the drift back to work grew.

Jim met with Bill Sampson, Nelson Johnson, Paul, and me. We talked over the situation. Jim told us that some of the workers, including himself, were arguing that they should keep the strike going to get concessions from Cone. But he was worried that they couldn't convince everyone to stay out. Even some people thought to be solid were going back to work. The economic pressure was just too strong, and many feared losing their jobs for good. A union meeting was scheduled the next day to decide what to do.

I told Jim that I thought that the worst thing would be for the union to divide, with some going back to work, others staying out. I suggested that Jim put forward several options and try to get a union consensus for one of them. One option could be staying out. But they also should discuss the option of everyone going back to work as a group, united on keeping up the struggle even while people were working again.

At the union meeting, the guys debated all the options and decided to go back to work as a group. "It's a retreat, not a surrender. We're preparing for bigger battles in the future," they told a local newspaper reporter.

Cone fired Jim Waller. The company said the reason was not his union work, but because Jim had lied on his application—under education, he had not listed that he had an M.D.! Jim and his co-workers petitioned the National Labor Relations Board to try and get his job back. They argued that it was clearly his union work that Cone didn't like.

The union had grown more than tenfold during the strike, and the new energy continued after the workers returned to work. Even though he was no longer working inside Granite, Jim's co-workers elected him president of the union.

Nelson ■ Jim Waller had a spirit of humility and self-deprecation. He didn't mind exposing his weaknesses. It was hard for him to write a speech, to speak in public. He was so methodical, he would start way ahead of time. Because of his leadership of the Granite strike, he was asked to speak at African Liberation Day in 1979. He wrote his speech weeks before ALD. He read it to me and went around reading it to different people. I could never do that. Most of the speeches I gave, I made up right ahead of time, while we were marching.

Paul ■ Jim met Signe Goldstein during the spring of 1977, and they fell in love. They wrote poetry to each other, and in January 1978, they got married. There was a big wedding party, where I got to meet a lot of his co-workers.

Signe had two children by her previous marriage, Antonia, age thirteen, and Alex, age ten. Jim tackled being a parent with the same zeal as he did everything else.[5]

Kwame ■ I got to see a lot of Jim, because he was Alex's stepdad. Me and Alex were the same age and really close. As a child, I had some bad ways as far as picking—I used to pick on Alex a lot because he was kind of nerdy. We would go over to Alex's house, and Jim was so soft-spoken. I couldn't imagine him getting upset or really mad. We would go into Antonia's room—Antonia was Alex's big sister, a teenager. She had these huge closets, and we went in her closets and tore all her stuff out, tore her room all to pieces. She went downstairs and told Signe. I was waiting for the spanking—but the whupping never came! Jim and Signe's was a place where you could be a kid and mess up without worrying about getting a spanking. They were soft, yeah, but they were cool. I remember when Alex was in the karate classes and Signe got me to go with him.

The most memorable time that I had with Jim was one day when my mother wanted to get me extra-clean in the bathtub. My mom put some kind of detergent in my water, Fresh Start, I think it was. I was just learning how to swim, so I liked to go underwater and hold my breath. I would have my eyes open. I stayed in the bathtub about an hour, playing. So when I got out of the water, my eyes were really glossy. Everything looked glarey. Mama said it was just because I had been in the water so long, not to worry about it. I tried to lay down for bed. In the middle of the night, I woke up 'cause my eyes were burning real bad. I woke my mama, and she took me over to Jim's house. It was super late. And Jim stuck my head into his kitchen sink and kept flushing my eyes out. He kept saying, "Just do it one more time." He had the little dishwashing sprayer, and he had me open my eyes and he just sprayed them, over and over and over. Then he put some kind of medicine in my eyes, I think—greasy, Vaseline kind of stuff. He put some patches on my eyes and told my mama to call him tomorrow. And after that, I was fine.

Willena ■ One time the daycare center called me because Kweli, my three-year-old son, got sick. I was tied up at some important meeting, so I called Jim Waller about what to do. Jim said he wasn't busy, so he could go over there and see Kweli. So I said, "Cool."

Next thing I know, the daycare center calls me again. They said, "Who is this white guy who wants to see Kweli, and who says he is a doctor?"

César Cauce:
Latino Activist and Duke Union Organizer

Paul ■   César Cauce was only twenty-five years old when he was killed, but he had already proven himself to be an excellent student and a terrific organizer. He was born in pre-revolutionary Cuba, into political elite. His father was minister of education under Batista, the dictator that Castro overthrew in 1959. César was only five years old when the Cuban Revolution ran the Batista regime off the island. César's family fled to Miami, Florida, where he grew up. His family went from being top of the social structure to immigrants struggling to get food on the table.

César's father became active in the exiles' anti-Castro movement. As he became a leftist, César had bitter political arguments with his parents. César would ask his father about the literacy rates under Batista, when education was only for the elite. Literacy under the Communist Castro regime was far higher than under the supposedly democratic state of the dictator, Batista. César loved to remind his father of that.

Although divided by politics, César's family shared a love for things Cuban. His parents sent him tins of guava jelly every month wrapped in anti-Castro newspapers. César threw out the newspapers but thoroughly enjoyed the guava jelly. He shared it with friends, including me, and I agreed that it was delicious.

César was an excellent student who went to Duke University and planned to become a professor of Latin American studies. While he was at Duke, he got involved in activism, and he became very interested in what we were doing. When he graduated magna cum laude in 1976, he had to make a big decision: Should he accept the full scholarship he was offered to study history at the University of California at Berkeley, or should he stay in Durham and join the union drive at Duke hospital?

César stayed in Durham and joined WVO. He got a job at Duke hospital as a data-terminal operator, which he explained was an underpaid, high-tech ward clerk.

Sally ■   The first time I saw César Cauce, I was in a bus as it pulled up to the Duke campus. César was waiting at the bus stop, just standing there with a smile on his face. But I couldn't help noticing him. He was so big—and such hair, this big bush of brick-red hair. He looked friendly, approachable.

Then in 1976, César got a job at Duke hospital, where I was active in the union drive. How cool, I thought. But César joined the union drive just as the conflict with Owusu and the Revolutionary Workers League came to a head. César's first organizing committee meeting was the one where RWL locked us whites out! Over the next few months, we lost the union election, Owusu left town, and everything got very quiet. All seventeen hundred workers who had voted for the union, including Lucy Lewis and me, were discouraged.

Everyone was glum—except César. He was upbeat. César's energy was calm, not hyper like Paul is sometimes. He was optimistic and told us that we had to put things in perspective, that the energy would pick up again. And he was right. In early 1977, we stared talking about renewing the drive, and César was in the middle of it. We started putting out "Tell It Like It Is!" again, focusing it solely on union and hospital issues. We caught Duke management by surprise. They thought we had all shrunk into the woodwork.

Management responded by trying to fire several of the activist leaders, including me, a union-busting plot. So we got together and decided to each pursue our own grievances and to file charges with the NLRB against Duke. Then together we held a press conference/ picket line. By that time I was pregnant with Leola, which made a good headline in "Tell It Like It Is!": "Duke Tries to Fire Pregnant Cashier!" Duke failed in its effort to get rid of us.

A new union drive began, with César as one of the core leaders. I had been on pregnancy leave, and when I came back four months later I was exhausted and had an infant to care for. I was so happy to have César there. He was smart, thoughtful, and such a sweet guy who got along with everybody. He was skillful at working out differences among people.

César worked with the long-time union activists to set up a new organizing committee. This time there was more involvement of the international union, American Federation of State, County, and Municipal Employees. This had good aspects, in that there would be no rash expulsions from the organizing committee. But it also made the organizing drive duller. People were not allowed to put out "unauthorized" leaflets like "Tell It Like It Is!" Instead, the leaflets were more generic AFSCME flyers. The second NLRB election was held in early 1979, and once again it was a heartbreaker. Once again the union lost in a close vote. And once again César looked forward to the next drive.

During the spring and summer of 1978, there was a strike wave in North Carolina. Dockworkers struck in Morehead City, garbage workers struck in Asheville and Rocky Mount, Jim Waller led the Granite wildcat strike. In Durham that summer, poultry workers walked out of the Goldkist Chicken Plant, notorious for its low wages and terrible working conditions. César went down to their picket line, quickly made friends, and asked them what he could do. "We need to let the public know what is happening," the poultry workers said. So César organized a strike support rally and brought out a good number of people from different workplaces. And César gave a good talk in his low-key, upbeat way.

Willena ■ I remember seeing César Cauce at demonstrations. He was good at chanting and speaking. I was trying to figure out what he was; I knew he wasn't all white, 'cause I could see other features. I never thought about him being Cuban. First I thought he was mixed, but I wasn't quite sure. I liked him. He had a good smile and seemed to be easygoing, wanting to help. Not at all like the bossy kind of men.

Kwame ■ Since he lived in Durham and I lived in Greensboro, I just saw César at rallies. He would always remember me, and we would always speak. He was a big guy, with this big Afro, super curly.

Sally ■ César met Floris Caton at our big African liberation demonstration in 1977 in Washington, D.C. Floris was from Panama, lived in D.C., and was an activist.

> Floris: César came up with a big group from North Carolina, a bunch of buses full of people. After the demonstration, a bunch of us went to a big party that lasted until the sun came up. I talked and danced only with César. We both were from families that had immigrated from Latin America. He told me about his father being minister of education in Cuba under Batista, and about all their arguments.
> "Are you married?" I asked César.
> "No," he said.
> "Do you mind if I write you?" I asked him.
> And he said no. Then he called in sick to his job at Duke, and that night we went out to dinner to a Cuban restaurant. I brought him home to meet my parents. César spoke Spanish, and they loved him immediately.
> That was how it started. We wrote, we talked on the phone. But then I thought he was a pushover, a wimp. I guess he was being too nice, and I had mistaken kindness for stupidity. So I called him up and told him I wasn't interested. Then he wrote me a twenty-two-page letter! He rebutted my telling him I wasn't interested, point by point. He said he didn't believe me, and that I was wrong! I was impressed, but I didn't respond. A few months later, I heard he was in a car accident and in the hospital. So I called him, and we got back in touch. Then I went to Mardi Gras on vacation with my roommate, and our plane stopped over in Durham. César had us over for dinner.
> Later, I said to my roommate, "He's so nice, why did I drop him?" She told me she always thought I was crazy for that. So I called César up, and I went on from there, with letters and phone calls and visits. To this day, I treasure those letters.
> On my second visit to Durham, César asked me to marry him. I was surprised and felt special. I moved down to Durham and lived with César. I quickly grew to love him and respect his strength and ability. He was a great organizer—very smart. I liked him to keep me company. I could just bask in

his attention. He made me feel protected. People respected him where he worked and among our political friends.

In June 1979, we got married. We were just newlyweds, loving and fussing with each other, and at the same time being activists in union drives and on community issues. I wanted the American dream—to buy a house, have kids. I remember saying to César, "Stay home sometimes, lets talk, make plans for our future." He didn't want to; he wasn't ready for all that. It was not just politics. In many ways, César was still just a big kid.

Then, only six months after we got married, César was killed.

Mike Nathan:
Medical Aid for African Liberation

Paul ■ One of the most significant African liberation struggles in the late 1970s was in Rhodesia. The Zimbabwean African National Union led the effort that succeeded in turning colonial Rhodesia into independent Zimbabwe. T. J. Kangai, ZANU's chief representative to the United Nations, spoke in Durham in October 1977. We asked him, "What can we do to help?"

"Raise medical supplies," said Kangai. "Our freedom fighters are dying of malaria and other diseases."

Mike Nathan and Marty and others formed the Committee for Medical Aid to Southern Africa. Within two years, they shipped over $40,000 worth of medications to Zimbabwe.

Marty ■ Mike and I became close to Judy and Anthony Mushipe, who were revolutionaries and members of ZANU. They were in the United States to study, and Mike sponsored Anthony so that he could reside in the U.S. We worked closely with them on the medical support work and became close friends.

Mike and I left North Carolina for a year in 1977 to go to the University of Virginia in Charlottesville. We were in residency programs, working long, long hours, on call every third night, so we could not do much political work. But we did continue collecting medical supplies for ZANU. A year later, I was very happy to come back to Durham to do Marxist political work. Mike got a job as the head of pediatrics at Lincoln Community Heath Center, in the middle of Durham's black community. I wanted to quit medicine and get a job in a factory.

When we came back to North Carolina during the summer of 1978, I saw around me a lot of good work. Jim Waller was leading a strike at Granite; César Cauce was involved in a strike at Goldkist. A lot of stuff was going on. I started studying Marxism more and more and worked with Durham WVO people on a number of issues, including with a student group at North Carolina Central

University. We protested the state budgets that gave black colleges much less funding than the traditionally white colleges, a clear example of institutional racism.

In the midst of all of this, I got pregnant, but I continued to do political work up to the day before Leah was born. Mike was so excited, he was beyond happiness. It was our dream come true; we had become the family he wanted. I hadn't thought a whole lot about what it meant to have a baby, but as soon as Leah was born, I fell in love with her unlike any other love I had ever felt. It was towering, immutable, physical. It transformed my understanding of social change. I wanted to work with Mike to make the world safe just for Leah.

The summer of 1979 was busy. Mike worked with Tom Clark (a good friend and political activist) and Floris Caton Cauce in organizing at Durham County General Hospital, where Leah had been born. Laundry workers there had skin tests that showed that they had been exposed to tuberculosis on the job, and the hospital was ignoring it. Mike and the laundry workers protested at their annual staff picnic. Mike spoke out, condemning the hospital, whose whole purpose was dedicated to heath but who was ignoring the health threats to its low-paid, mainly African American laundry workers. It took guts for Mike to speak out—his boss was in the audience.

Mike headed the Department of Pediatrics at the Lincoln Community Health Center. He was totally devoted to his little ones at work and his Leah at home. He worked long hours at an underfunded health facility. He devoted his full attention to each patient, seeing up to fifty children a day. He would come home exhausted.

At home, he was an amazing father, his long, graceful, gentle fingers caring for Leah. Mike treated her with gentleness, which was his natural calling. He adored her with a passion that I tried to capture in a million pictures with my camera.

Building a New Communist Party

Sally ■ By 1979, we had energy around us—lots of dedicated people attracted to us through our work in the strike wave, the union drives, and the campaigns Free the Wilmington Ten and Stop the Test. We had study groups of teenagers, young adults, and older people, black and white. We had ups and downs in the work, but in most cases where there were setbacks, people still kept their jobs in the mills and hospitals. Jim Waller had been fired from Granite, but even there the work went on, and Jim kept close ties with the folks in the plant.

So we embarked on an ambitious expansion plan to stretch our work throughout North Carolina and into Alabama. We paid increasing attention to recruitment and to training people in all types of organizing.

In early 1979, Communist Workers' Party leader Jerry Tung asked me to head up the work in the southern region, a job called regional secretary. Jerry always decided who the leaders would be. He talked to people and picked the leaders based on his assessment of the work and what WVO needed at the time. Nelson Johnson, Paul, and I had been on the southern regional committee for a while. We were pleased when Jerry added Jim Waller and Bill Sampson to our regional leadership committee. Our regional committee discussed the work and would come to consensus about how to move it forward. My job as regional secretary was to communicate between the WVO center in New York and our region.

Our big topic of discussion as we entered 1979 was How do you build a new communist party?

Paul ■ Jerry Tung's size-up of our North Carolina work in 1978 was that we clearly could lead mass struggles. We had so much going on. He thought we should shift our focus to building a new communist party. Such a party could reap all the mass struggles we had led up to this point and further lead them in the future. I agreed with him.

Jerry criticized us for the tendency to lose ourselves in the united front, meaning that we would put lots of energy into building a broad-based coalition but then we—as WVO—would disappear. He pushed us to talk about why we needed a socialist revolution and a working-class party to lead it. Jerry criticized Nelson Johnson, who led our black liberation movement work, and Sally, who coordinated the trade union work.

Nelson ■ At the time, I grudgingly accepted Jerry's criticism, because I wanted to be loyal to the organization that I am a part of, even if I didn't fully agree. Over time, I came to agree with Jerry's view, because my framework then was building socialist revolution, so I thought that we needed to build a party to lead it. But in retrospect, I think the party-building focus led us to work in a less effective way. We became invested in showing the correctness of the party. That made it hard for us to be in coalition with other groups.

Marty ■ When we openly advocated revolution in the trade unions, it was a disaster. I know, because I did it.

We were trying to bring what we were studying to the workers' movement. I was organizing brown-lung clinics with the People's Alliance, a liberal populist organization in Durham and Chapel Hill. They had been working with rubber workers at the Kelly Springfield Company, screening them for occupational diseases. The workers had been exposed to toxins and were trying to unionize. WVO worked on the screening and the unionizing, but WVO's focus was socialism, the overthrow of capitalism. I was studying with WVO in a study group with Paul. We were trying to put out our ideas as strongly as we possibly could.

We organized an educational meeting of Kelly Springfield rubber workers, and I spoke at the meeting about what I had found out about toxins and their health hazards. At the very end of my talk, I said that the only way really to improve occupational health was through workers' control and socialism. A representative of the international union happened to be there, and he started to red-bait the union organizers based on my words. The union drive was badly hurt. People's Alliance to this day has not forgiven me or any of us for that. It was a naive mistake on the one hand but also illustrated that the union hierarchy had no inclination to support constitutionally protected free speech.

I felt terrible that my words hurt the union drive. I really liked the rubber workers and fully supported their union drive. I had grown up with union organizing, and I knew how difficult it was. I didn't agree with Paul Bermanzohn's assessment that it was okay that it happened. But I also felt a real loyalty to the WVO people and agreed with them that this system was fully stacked against workers and their health.

In actual fact, why did my words make so much difference? Why did they mean so much harm to an organizing effort? My heart—all our hearts—were with the workers to try to build the union. I felt that deeper, more fundamental change—socialism—had to take place. It could not happen without a fight. Understanding what needs to be done is important, and those ideas have to be talked about, and the place they need to be discussed most openly is among workers. But we were not sensitive to the immediate potential harm that could happen. Much of what we did went over people's heads and brought fears of repression or, in the case of the rubber workers, repression itself. It was not necessary or effective. We were naive and youthful. We had this idealism that we could make such a big difference so quickly. We wanted to change things too fast. That was a character of our youth—we were hotheads.

Willena ■ Before I found out what communism was, I was scared of it. Communism was a bogeyman because people were scared of something they didn't even know about. Then I found out that communism was good stuff that helps you see how the world works. But when WVO told us to be open communists, I thought back to when I was scared of it. I thought, God, we're going to mess things up. Why do we have to say that?

WVO people said we needed to be honest with people and open with them so they'll know what we're about. I agreed with that, but I was afraid that we wouldn't get the chance to tell people, because they weren't going to listen. And that did happen. But it was like the majority ruled, and I just hoped people would listen to us and not be too scared.

Kwame ■ In 1978 or so, a lot of my friends were starting to recognize who my mom was. A lot of them stayed in Greenfield Homes, which was right around the corner from where we lived, which was right around the corner from Ayo and Akua Johnson's house. My friends recognized Mama and Nelson Johnson.

Sometimes it was good, like around the Stop the Test campaign. But not around the concept of communism. People look bad on communism. My friends said: "You're mama's a communist? Git away from me."

And I'm like, "You don't understand." But I didn't understand either! I didn't get it either. I was like everybody else: I assumed that the word "communist" belonged beside Russia or China, that it was not American.

My friends asked, "What is a communist?"

I said, "Somebody who's fighting for you, fool!" But it was one of those points that I could not argue. I was not informed about it. I was ashamed of it.

All of us who were in Junior RYL [Revolutionary Youth League], we stuck together. Ayo would sort of argue, but we were both on the same lane, uninformed, arguing the best we could. Akua was like, "That ain't my daddy." Then there was our friend Sister, whose mom also worked with WVO. Sister was not intimidated by anyone or anything. She'd say, "Yeah, that's my mama." Whoever wanted to argue with her had to be ready to fight.

Sally ■ I was struggling to figure it all out. My life was tied up with the WVO, and there were people I truly respected, like Jim Waller, Sandi Smith, and Paul, who were enthusiastic about openly advocating communism and revolution. I was trying to learn from them, although deep in my gut I had a lot of problems with it.

Of course, it is easier in retrospect to see the problems. At the time, I couldn't connect the dots. I was keenly aware of the series of negative experiences that had come with advocating revolution—during the Duke drive, at Granite, at Revolution, at Kelly Springfield. Being open communists led to immediate problems. Others argued that it was our militant pro-unionism that led to the repression. I'm sure it was both, but we really had not figured out how to solve those problems. I thought it was something we would work out along the way.

Jerry Tung and others in WVO leadership pushed us to focus on party building, and I went along with it. I tried to carry out my role as regional secretary, to convince others that party building was the way to go.

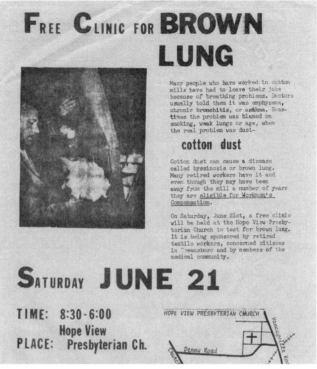

Left: Student Organization for Black Unity (SOBU) pamphlet.
Right: Flyer for a brown-lung-screening clinic organized by Paul Bermanzohn and Jim Waller.

Sandi Smith speaks against Cone Mills's firing of union activists at Revolution Mill, 1977. In background, *from right:* Nelson Johnson, Willena Cannon, her daughter Imani, another child, and Dale Sampson. (Photo © Wayne Michael Lottinville)

Sandi Smith at microphone during demonstration in front of Cone Mills corporate head-quarters, 1977. (Courtesy of Greensboro Justice Fund)

DUKE WORKERS NEWSLETTER
published by the Duke Workers Organizing Committee (DWOC), July 29, 1977

DWOC Wins Back Job for Pregnant Cashier!

In early June, Sally Bermanzohn, a hospital cafeteria cashier, was suddenly transferred off her job. Although she had worked as a cashier for two and a half years with a good record, management said that she was $10 short four days in a row. They transferred her to working behind the cafeteria serving line, although she had told management that she could not stand on her feet all day because she was pregnant. Sally has been one of the strongest fighters in the DWOC and also helps put out the "Tell It Like It Is." At the same time she was transferred, Duke management was harassing other active workers. But even though Duke tried to harass and fire us, we have fought them back even harder! We called press conferences, put out leaflets, and filed grievances. As a result--- Sally has won her job back! DWOC FIGHTS FOR ALL WORKERS!

"UNITE ALL WORKERS TO FIGHT DUKE!" demanded the people at a rally organized by DWOC. The rally was held at noon in front of the hospital on June 30, 1977. For more pictures, see page 3.

Duke Workers Organizing Committee newsletter; protest (*third from right*, Paul Bermanzohn; Sally Bermanzohn, *lower right.*) When Duke Medical Center attempted to fire union activists in 1977, DWOC pickets and protests won the jobs back.

Leola Lee in Whitakers, North Carolina, summer 1977, protests the legal system's failure to punish the murderer of her husband.

Kwame Cannon, eight, with Jim Waller and Sandi Smith, in a picket line for union recognition of Cone Mills textile workers, Greensboro, 1977. (Courtesy of *News & Record*, Greensboro, N.C.)

Paul Bermanzohn and our first daughter, named after Leola Lee, at the strike against Cone Mill's Granite Plant, Haw River, North Carolina, 1978. (Photo by Sally Bermanzohn)

Bill Sampson, *left,* plays guitar at Traders Chevrolet strike, Greensboro, 1978.

César Cauce, as organizer of a strike-support rally for Goldkist Poultry workers, Durham, North Carolina, 1978.

Bill Sampson, *right,* on picket line at Traders Chevrolet strike, Greensboro, 1978.

Mike Nathan, *left*, collects medical supplies with Dick David for Zimbabwe African National Union, 1978. The ZANU led the liberation struggle against British control of Rhodesia.

North Carolina delegation at African Liberation Day makes the cover of *All Africa Standing Up,* 1979: Sally Bermanzohn, center; Jim Wrenn with banner, *right;* Chekesha Powell, Sandi Smith, Bill Sampson, and Paul Bermanzohn among crowd.

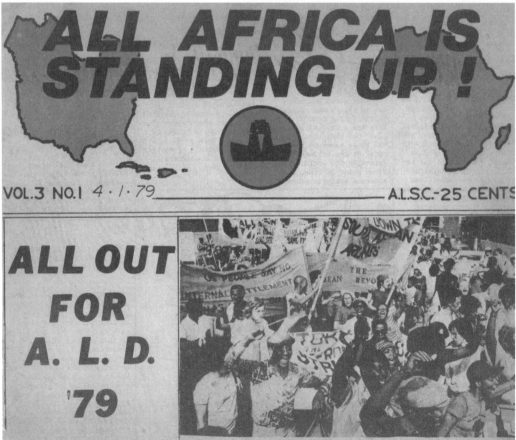

Sandi Smith, African Liberation Day, 1979.
(Courtesy of Greensboro Justice Fund)

Jim Waller, African Liberation Day, 1979.
(Courtesy of Greensboro Justice Fund)

Dale and Bill Sampson. (Courtesy of Dale Sampson)

Sandi Smith.

Jim Waller and Bill Sampson. (Courtesy of Dale Sampson)

César Cauce and Floris Caton marry, June 1979. (Courtesy of Floris Weston)

The Wallers: Signe and Jim, with Jim's stepchildren, Antonia and Alex Goldstein. (Courtesy of Signe Waller)

Michael Nathan and Marty Arthur marry, 1978. (Courtesy of Marty Nathan)

Michael Nathan and daughter Leah, 1979. (Courtesy of Marty Nathan)

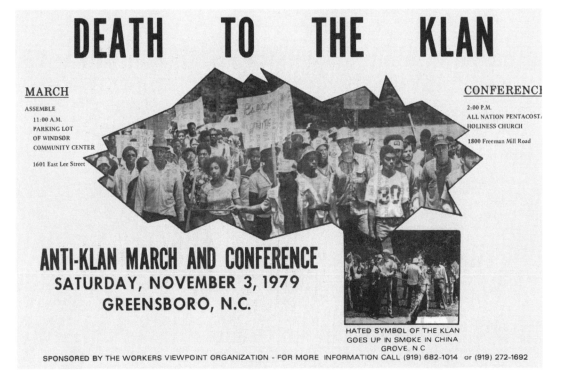

Flyer for November 3, 1979, anti-Klan rally features photographs from anti-Klan rally in China Grove, July 8, 1979.

PART III

Ku Klux Klan: "Take Back the South for White People"

6

We Back Down the KKK

The Ku Klux Klan was born just after the South surrendered in the Civil War. Made up of ex-soldiers and Confederate officers, it helped defeat Reconstruction. The KKK is best understood not as an organization, but as a terrorist social movement for white supremacy; it uses violence and the threat of violence to achieve its political goals. Not monolithic, the Klan has included disparate groups that have grown, disbanded, and reemerged with different names and forms. Over the years, the KKK seems sometimes to have disappeared, only to revive decades later. In the 1920s, Klan membership grew to 4.5 million. Between the 1930s and the 1950s, it included small clandestine bands in the South that threatened, attacked, and sometimes killed black activists, union organizers, and whites who worked for equal rights.

Key to analyzing the effectiveness of the Klan is its often shadowy relationship to government, particularly to law enforcement. Before the civil rights movement, southern governments, with the acquiescence of the federal government, allowed racist violence: Whites escaped punishment for violence against blacks; blacks were often brutalized for any infraction against the racist social order.

The KKK grew in the early 1960s as it tried to defeat the civil rights movement, but the vigor of the movement overwhelmed the Klan, and its members once again seemed to vanish. In the late 1970s, after the social movements had died down, the KKK reappeared in North Carolina, Alabama, Louisiana, Texas, and other states, marching, burning crosses—and shooting people.

Paul ■ Suddenly, in 1979, Klansmen reappeared all over western North Carolina. In April, they held a one-day "historical exhibit" at the public library in Winston-Salem, N.C., just thirty miles west of Greensboro. We read about it in the newspapers. I was outraged that a public library would allow a violent racist group to hold an exhibit. People in Winston-Salem, black and white, protested. There were more demonstrators shouting their hatred of the Klan than there were people attending the exhibit.

A month later, May 1979, in Decatur, Alabama, the Klan opened fire on civil rights demonstrators. The Southern Christian Leadership Conference led a protest against the conviction of a retarded black man, Tommie Lee Hines, blamed for a rape he could not have committed. Near the end of the march, at a bend in the road, the black marchers faced a hundred armed Klansmen chanting, "White power!" As fights broke out, a number of Klansmen ran to their cars, pulled out guns, and started shooting. Five people were wounded, three of them black marchers and two of them Klansmen. The police shot one of the Klansmen. The other Klansman was wounded when he attacked a black family in their car. In a pattern all too typical, no Klansmen were even charged for the wounding of three blacks. But the man protecting his family was indicted and convicted of shooting a member of the Klan.[1]

The actions of the Klan, the police, and the courts in Decatur infuriated people. The Southern Christian Leadership Conference called for a massive protest demonstration. But people criticized the SCLC for their tactics of unarmed passive resistance and called for armed self-defense in dealing with the Ku Klux Klan. We heard through the grapevine that people in Decatur, Alabama, and Tupelo, Mississippi, had organized armed self-defense patrols.

Nelson Johnson, Sally, and I drove down to Alabama to participate in the SCLC march. More importantly, we talked to people in the armed patrols in Decatur and in Tupelo.

Sally ■ The Decatur anti-Klan march was the first time I saw robed Klansmen. There were several dozen of them behind a solid wall of police, as thousands of us marched by and chanted against them. The KKK seemed unreal to me. I had lived in North Carolina for fourteen years and had never seen a Klansman before. Of course, I had heard about the Klan, but I thought it was a relic of the distant past, a scary story people told around a campfire.

Willena ■ The Klan was very real to me. The Klan haunted me growing up, and I still remembered them burning that man in the tobacco barn. Even all these years later, I was always on the lookout for Klannish people. By "Klannish," I mean white people who are hostile to you before you even open your mouth—the types you feel could get violent real quick, and for no reason. Klan types are dangerous, especially when the cops and courts let them get away with the violence.

In the sixties, the Klan laid low 'cause they were scared of the movement, but they were still out there. And we would talk about them in the black community, warning people if we thought someone was Klannish. Like, "You don't want to take a job at so-and-so's; the bossman over there is Klannish."

In 1979, suddenly the Klan was back in its sheets, not only in the newspapers but on TV. Sometimes the TV showed just one man in his sheet in a open field. Why would they show that? It was nothing newsworthy. In the black community, people were asking us questions. They said: "Did you see them? Why show all that Klan stuff? They must think it's slavery time."

Sally ■ That spring, I learned about Willena's childhood and how she had helplessly watched the Klan kill a man. I also found other friends whose lives had been profoundly affected by the KKK.

Jean Chapman, a white friend who grew up in southern Alabama, told us that her father had been in the Klan! Her revelation took me aback. I liked Jean, a slim vivacious young woman with thick brown hair. She was feisty, outspoken, smart. I knew she came from a rural background, but her father was a Klansman? Jean described her father as affectionate toward her and kind to other people on an individual basis. But he was a failure as a breadwinner. His small business went bankrupt, and he refused to work for somebody else.

Jean told me: "He was one of those curious Southern paradoxes, because he was a kind person one-on-one. He would pick up hitchhikers and bring people home off the street, black or white. But he was very racist in the way he dealt with his own failures: He projected his unhappiness on to black people, the typical scapegoat for a southern white man."

I asked Jean if her father was involved in any violence. She said she didn't know, it was all very secret; "I remember going with him to two Klan rallies. I have no recollection what the grownups were doing. I just remember playing with the kids and worrying about getting grass stains on my white pants."[2]

Paul ■ Big Man was the one who impressed me. He is an older black man who carries his shoulders square, his back straight, head held high. He worked with Bill Sampson at Cone Mills and told us about his experience fighting the Klan. Big Man grew up in rural South Carolina in the 1930s, one of six children born to impoverished sharecroppers. They never had enough to eat. But as the family struggled to survive, Klannish whites would not leave them alone. Big Man remembered the Ku Klux Klan going into people's houses, dragging them out, beating them, hanging them.

One of the victims was Big Man's cousin. "They drug him out, hung him from a tree, and started shooting. They shot at him 'til there was nothing left but the rope," Big Man told us. "Being a kid, I was searching myself. Is this the way it's gotta be? I resolved, it won't happen to me. Nobody will ever do me the way I don't want them to do. They will have to kill me first."

Big Man kept a proud, cool exterior. He learned to use a gun, and he made sure that everyone in the county, white and black, knew that he was an expert marksman. When the Klan marched through the town one night in 1940, Big Man and his friends attacked them from the rear with sticks, stones, and pistols. "After that," he recalled with a tiny grin, "the Klan didn't come back no more."

Armed self-defense, that was Big Man's motto. "You don't go after nobody. But if they come after you, you protect yourself."[3]

China Grove

Paul ■ In June 1979, we read a newspaper article where the KKK announced they would show their recruitment movie, *Birth of a Nation*, on July 8 in a *public* community center. Once again, government was allowing the Klan to promote itself and spread its hatred.

Birth of a Nation is one of the earliest motion pictures, considered by some to be a masterpiece. It is also a Klan recruitment tool. D. W. Griffith released his movie in 1915, which was based on Thomas Dixon Jr.'s 1905 book *The Clansman: An Historic Romance of the Ku Klux Klan*. It is blatantly racist. When the movie first came out, the NAACP and Jewish groups protested it. In New York, people threw eggs at the movie house; in Boston, the protest became a riot. But Dixon had powerful friends—like the president of the United States. Dixon gave Woodrow Wilson a private showing at the White House. The cabinet and Supreme Court justices also saw it. After watching his first motion picture, President Wilson stated: "It is like writing history with lightning. And my only regret is that it is all so terribly true." The U.S. president put his stamp of approval on *Birth of a Nation,* a justification of Klan terror. The movie played throughout the country, and in its wake the Klan began a recruitment drive.[4]

Six decades later, in 1979, the Klan was again using *Birth of a Nation* to recruit.

Sally ■ The Klan planned to hold its recruitment meeting in China Grove, North Carolina, just outside Kannapolis, the location of the largest textile plant in the nation. Cannon Mills built Kannapolis as its company town in 1906, and the wages and conditions it provided for its workers led to a series of union drives. In 1921, workers went on strike for ten weeks, but Cannon refused to negotiate. In the early 1970s, workers organized a drive and petitioned the National Labor Relations Board to hold an election. Cannon waged a vicious antiunion campaign of threats and firings, and the union lost the 1974 election. (When Cannon Mill workers in Kannapolis finally won union recognition in 1999, the *New York Times* for June 26 headlined the story "Union Victory at Plant in South Is Labor Milestone.")

In 1979, North Carolina was ripe for unions. The state was among the least unionized in the country, with among the largest number of industrial workers, and was ranked last in per capita wages paid to production workers.[5] People were restive; a strike wave had passed through the state the year before. In Roanoke Rapids, in the eastern part of the state, an ACTWU union drive was making headway at J. P. Stevens—the movie *Norma Rae* was about this drive. In the western part of the state, the Teamsters were organizing several plants. And in Kannapolis, workers at Cannon were talking about renewing their union drive. Sandi Smith had just moved from organizing Cone Mill's Revolution plant in

Greensboro to get a job at Cannon Mills in Kannapolis and become part of the union drive.

In 1979, the repression of organizing drives continued, while Klan activity increased. The Klan had helped companies defeat union drives. The KKK drives a wedge between black and white workers because it evokes different responses from each group. While the Klan provokes fear and anger in blacks, whites often think the Klan is harmless and funny in its white sheets. Moreover, it is very dangerous to deal with groups like the Klan that are so prone to violence. Building black-white unity is essential for a union drive, and dealing with the KKK makes it much harder for people to see eye to eye. Dividing workers along racial lines is a tried-and-true tactic companies use to keep out unions.

Nelson Johnson, Paul, Jim Waller, Bill Sampson, and I—our leadership committee—met in Jim and Signe's backyard. It was a beautiful summer day. We talked about the Klan and unions and what we should do. We discussed the newspaper article on the Klan's plan to show *Birth of a Nation* at a public community center in China Grove. We decided to find out what the people in China Grove thought about all this.

Nelson ■ The next day, I drove down to China Grove, which is close to an hour's drive from Greensboro, going southwest. I went to talk to people in the black community. I found Westside, China Grove's black neighborhood, and spoke to a few folks. I was directed to someone I knew from organizing we had done in the sixties.

I was invited to a private meeting where folks were arguing over how to deal with this situation. Paul Lucky, a charismatic young man from the area, had just led a delegation to the city council. Lucky asked the council to withdraw the police permit issued to the Klan permitting them to use the community center. The city council told Lucky no, they would not retract the Klan's permit. Lucky told the council the black community was planning to protest. The council told Lucky that he needed a permit to protest the Klan, and that the council might or might not issue one to him. Furious, Lucky looked the public representatives straight in the eyes, declaring that his group would march, with or without a permit.

A few days later, I had a long talk with Sandi Smith, who had just rented a house in Kannapolis hoping to get a job at Cannon Mills. She had met union activists in Kannapolis worried about Klan activity exacerbating the tension between black and white. She told me about new race-baiting tactics used by a nearby company fighting a union drive. It had sent all its employees a record they could play in their home. On the record, voices yelled out in conflict. The pro-union strikers, who sounded black, were attacking the nonstrikers, who sounded white.

Sandi urged us to get involved in the China Grove protest. She couldn't play a public role because she was applying for a job as an apprentice loom fixer. Getting a job inside a big mill like Cannon was an organizer's dream.

Paul ■ A few days later, I drove down to China Grove with Nelson Johnson and Willena Cannon. We met with people in Westside who were still trying to agree on a plan for protesting. It was a tough situation. How do you stop the Klan? How do you puncture their image of invincibility? Some activists were afraid, but others were angry and determined.

Older ministers wanted to hold a protest rally in Westside during *Birth of a Nation*. A young woman asked them, "How do you fight the Klan when you're over here in Westside, and the Klan's showing their movie on the other side of town?" The younger blacks thought the ministers were giving in to old fears. Several Vietnam vets argued for bombing the community center.

Willena ■ People at that China Grove meeting were talking about ambushing the Klan. Some of them had a real elaborate plan, with disguises and people hiding in trees and shooting tin garbage cans that would explode. I thought, Oh my God, these people are getting ready to blow this thing up. And then they would get caught and go to jail.

But I was glad they were planning to do *something*. People in my hometown of Mullins didn't do anything about the Klan. Doing nothing meant that, in a way, they were accepting it. In China Grove, people were determined to protest. And at that meeting, people seemed glad to hear our suggestions.

Paul ■ Paul Lucky, Nelson Johnson, Willena Cannon, and I strenuously opposed the plan to use explosives. Nelson suggested a middle position. He supported Lucky's ideas of a protest, suggesting a march right up to the community center. People agreed, working out the details on where and when to gather on the morning of July 8. Excitement filled the room. The Klan might show its movie, but people were not going to cower in fear.

The Klan had this reputation of invincibility. For over a century, they had terrorized blacks, Jews, and anyone else who opposed them. In 1979, the Klan could grow if everyone was afraid to oppose them. As communists, we saw ourselves as tribunes of the people. How could you be a tribune of the people in the South and not vigorously oppose the Klan? If we were serious, we had to face our fear and boldly confront the Klan.

I felt strongly that we were trying to do the right thing, and I still feel that way. My parents were the only members of their families to survive fascism in Poland in World War II. Fascists must be fought head-on.

Willena ■   So we kept going down to China Grove to work on the anti-Klan protest, traveling back and forth. The only time I was afraid was late at night when I would see these old pickup trucks that Klan-type people drive. They could have been Klan in those trucks or just regular folks, who knows? I think there was a couple of times that Nelson was wary of that too. So we started staying down there, sometimes five of us sleeping in one motel room, sleeping in our clothes.

The night before the rally, we stayed up to 3:30 in the morning trying to figure out this and this, that and that. And then we had to get up early the next morning. I remember being tired but excited.

Confrontation

Sally ■   On July 8, 1979, Nelson Johnson, Willena Cannon, and Sandi Smith were already in China Grove. The rest of us drove down there that morning— Big Man, Jim and Signe Waller, César and Floris Cauce, Mike Nathan, Paul and I, and a bunch of others from Greensboro, Durham, and other North Carolina towns.

We gathered in the community, meeting new marching friends. We hung out under the trees to get relief from the hot sun. Excitement and fear hung in the air. Even the trees seemed to hold their breath. I felt nervous but determined. I thought we were doing the right thing.

Our forces gathered, more than a hundred strong. Most were people from China Grove, reinforced by a good contingent from Workers Viewpoint Organization. We had some shotguns, but we left them in our cars. We marched unarmed. We would show them that they could not scare us. We headed toward the community center, chanting "Decease, decease, decease the ugly beast!" "Down with the Klan!" and "Death to the Klan!"

We marched a half mile down the deserted streets of China Grove. We passed the edge of the woods, and suddenly, twenty yards in front of us was the community center, a small one-story brick building surrounded by a big field and trees. On the porch were about a dozen Klansmen, brandishing their weapons. A Confederate flag flew from a pole planted in front of the center.

Nelson led the way, and we marched right up to them, chanting. They cursed back at us. We were so close, we could almost touch them. I saw a man with a Nazi swastika tattooed on his arm, another with "White Power!" on his T-shirt, and another in a blue serge suit. But it was the guns that held my gaze. The Klansmen were snarling at us, and they were all holding big guns, rifles, shotguns.

Paul ■ The Klan was heavily armed, and we were not prepared for anything but a shouting match. A hundred demonstrators stomped up to those surprised Klan and Nazis, yelling right in front of their faces. It was tense. Several policemen were standing with the KKK on the porch, and I assume they urged the Klan into the community center. At a signal from a man in a blue suit, the Klansmen disappeared into the building.

We were surprised and thrilled—the Klan had retreated! What did we do now? The Confederate flag still flew above us.

"Burn the flag!" someone yelled. Someone had a match, and the symbol of slavery went up in flames in front of the Klansmen who stared out the windows of the center. We disrupted the showing of *Birth of a Nation*.

We made our point. Nelson led the march around the community center, and then we marched back across town to the black community. We took our shotguns out of our cars for symbolic display of armed self-defense.

Willena ■ When I saw the Klans with the guns I got nervous, really nervous. But when they backed up into that community center, all my nervousness left. It was payback time! I was pushing back at those scums for all the wounds and hurts from my past. It felt good; it was jubilation to me. Afterwards back in Westside, it felt really good. I wanted to beat on my chest and everything.

Paul ■ I thought that the China Grove confrontation was a resounding success. We had humiliated the Klan. The demonstration was covered on statewide TV, and we watched ourselves that night. TV cameras recorded the whole scene.

Paul Lucky from China Grove looked straight into the lens of the TV camera and said: "We don't want any trouble. We just want the Klan to go home. If they live here, go home. If they live there, go there. We will not have it. We will not tolerate it. If we have to die here, we'll die here. But there will not be any Klan—today, tomorrow, never. Death to the Klan! Death to the Klan!"

We had punctured the Klan's invincibility, impeded their ability to recruit. It would help the unions and the community struggles.

Sally ■ The TV also showed Grand Dragon Joe Grady tell the TV cameras, "There will be revenge for this."

The demonstrators were thrilled. So was I, at first. We hung out in China Grove, celebrating. Mae Jones, an African American friend of ours from Durham, was jubilant. She found the march hard on her arthritic knees but worth it. "I wish my grandmother was here," she cried. "The Klan ran—and they had the guns!"

While we celebrated, Sandi Smith, Big Man, Paul, and several people from Westside stood at the corner of the road leading away from the neighborhood. They were armed with shotguns, anticipating that the Klan might try to retaliate.

Nelson   ▣   I stayed overnight in China Grove, monitoring the CB radio. White men railed against the black people of China Grove.

Sally   ▣   We drove back to Durham. I was exhausted, and as the adrenaline faded, another feeling grew: fear. Mike Nathan rode in the car with Paul and me. We drove to his house and got out with him to say hello to Marty and see their new baby. Paul enthusiastically described to Marty what happened in China Grove. I remember watching Mike's mother, Esther, who was sitting there eating spaghetti. As Paul talked about our "exciting victory," Esther stopped eating and looked at him, her fork in midair, her mouth hanging open.

Marty   ▣   I did not go to China Grove, because Leah was only three months old. But I was excited by the anti-Klan campaign and saw it connected to our day-to-day work. I thought that by organizing against the Klan, we would be leading the struggle against racism. It was something we could talk about to people in the mills and hospitals. With the Klan active and in the news, we were not just talking abstractly but leading opposition to them.

After Mike came back from the China Grove demonstration, and after Paul and Sally left, Mike said: "I was scared to death. We almost got ourselves killed." And I thought to myself: "What's wrong with you, Mike? Why don't you have more spirit?" That became a rift between us.

Sally   ▣   I felt the way Mike did, but I didn't know he felt that way. We didn't talk about it. That night, I still felt like we had done the right thing. But the next morning, my elation was gone. No longer was the Klan a remote phenomenon. With my own eyes, I saw the hatred in those men's eyes. I saw their guns. What if they had opened fire on us? They scared me. A feeling of dread crept over me and stayed there. I couldn't get the fear out of my mind.

But I couldn't hide; I was the regional secretary, responsible to the WVO center. I decided I needed to talk to Jerry Tung and others in leadership to tell folks that this was dangerous and to discuss seriously how to proceed. That day, I decided I needed to talk to them right away, and not by telephone.

Nelson Johnson was planning to drive up to New York City the next day, and I decided to go with him. On the ten-hour drive up the interstate, Nelson and I had a good talk. He was not freaked out like I was.

Nelson   ▣   The China Grove confrontation didn't terrify me. I saw their guns, and I remember making the decision to walk right toward them and keep walking. I did have fear, but I was guided by a view of how these sorts of confrontations work. I never thought they would shoot, because there were two policemen there.

Sally ■ Nelson's size-up made sense to me. I hadn't considered the role of the police. Nelson had experience in power relations when guns are involved. He had grown up in a rural area where people used armed self-defense, and he had been in the military. For me it was all new. I was used to power relations in union drives, where economic pressure is the main thing used, not brute force. I had read about armed revolutions in China and Russia and thought it was so heroic. And then came China Grove, and I was totally freaked out by the guns.

On the drive up to New York City, Nelson and I agreed that we should not repeat this type of demonstration. In China Grove, we had the element of surprise, but it was too dangerous to repeat the same type of march in another town.

But when we got to the WVO headquarters in New York City, it was a different story. I said my piece, and Jerry Tung immediately launched into heavy criticism of me. There was no discussion of tactics, of dangers—just of my inadequacies. Jerry said that I was timid, that I had lost my bearings and failed to assume leadership. Rather than address the issue of danger, Jerry said that the China Grove confrontation was a "shining example" of struggles that WVO should be taking up.

No one else in the room said anything. I looked around and realized that, of a dozen people, I was the only woman there. I backed off, feeling like my gender and my white middle-class background must explain why I was such a chicken.

There were lots of other things going on at the WVO headquarters. People were making plans for a founding congress, when Workers Viewpoint would become the Communist Workers Party. Jerry was stressing that party building should be the focus of all our work, that we should be taking up militant struggles like the anti-Klan campaign. The whole thing made me shut up and toe the line.

Marty ■ It makes me upset that Sally didn't tell anybody how she felt. Okay, I know what the rules were about upholding the leadership's line. But I saw Sally as firmly behind this anti-Klan campaign; I saw everybody as firmly behind this.

I didn't know what happened in China Grove because I wasn't there. I only listened to what Paul Bermanzohn said. He was my ideal; he knew everything. And Sally wasn't saying anything to contradict it. Mike and I saw Sally as this staunch revolutionary who was critical of everyone who didn't agree with the line.

Sally ■ I thought I was the only one who felt afraid. Paul, Nelson, Willena, Jim Waller, and Sandi were so enthusiastic about the demonstration, I assumed everyone else felt the same way. I didn't know how Mike Nathan felt. I thought I was the only one who was afraid.

In retrospect, I cannot justify my behavior. I remember feeling confused and trying to follow the rules of democratic centralism. We all studied democratic centralism in a book called *Basic Understanding of the Communist Party of China*. The rules were summed up in slogans: "Seek to unite"; "Unite and don't split"; and "Don't intrigue and conspire."[6]

As regional secretary, my job was to communicate the leadership's line to the base in North Carolina. This was certainly not a problem when I agreed with the leadership, but after China Grove, in my gut I did not agree with the leaders. But the rules of democratic centralism were that I should "seek to unite." I should put out the party's line even if I disagreed with it.

Maybe if I hadn't gone to New York to discuss it immediately with Jerry Tung, we would have had more discussion in our region. But once I had discussed it with the top leadership, the rules were that I could not discuss my differences with the base, because that would be "intriguing and conspiring."

What democratic centralism comes down to is: Don't cross the leadership. The way WVO practiced it, it was pure centralism, with that nice word "democracy" tacked on. There was really no room to disagree once the leadership had laid down the line. It was like a corporation, the military, or any organization where there is a hierarchical power structure. The person or people with the power give directions, and the rest carry out what they say.

After the massacre, I felt terrible that I had not argued against the anti-Klan campaign. I wish I had "intrigued and conspired" and derailed the whole thing. But at the time, I was not confident of my feelings. I was very confused. I thought I felt the way I did because of my privileged background and female weakness. I believed I needed to "remold my class outlook," but I couldn't shake off the fear. Marty Nathan remembers me as a staunch revolutionary, but I remember being disoriented and depressed. I did as little political work as I could. I got pregnant and had morning sickness. Only after the massacre did I learn that other people also had similar fears about what we were doing.

Paul ■ November 3 happened because we were doing good work. We were shot to stop our growing movement. The government supported and organized the Klan against us.

Nelson ■ We need to critically look at what we did. At the very same time, our mistakes are not an explanation or a justification for the actions of a North American death squad on November 3, 1979. It was organized, conscious, malicious, and took advantage of our weaknesses.

Planning for November 3

Nelson ■ My main concern at the time was continuing our anti-Klan campaign. I thought the capitalist class was promoting the Klan to split the working class. I wanted to continue our campaign to expose why the KKK was rising, and who its secret supporters were. To do this, we needed a conference where union activists and community leaders could speak, and we could share experiences and unite people on a deeper understanding of the Klan as a tool of the ruling class. And I proposed that the conference should be preceded by a spirited march through the streets of Greensboro.

I understood Sally Bermanzohn's concerns. We would not be chasing the Klan all over the state. We would hold our march and conference in our home base, in Greensboro.

At the end of the march, there was going to be a conference with speeches from different trade unionists. I was going to give the Communist Workers Party speech and talk about how the decay of capitalism was leading to the emergence of Klan and Nazis.

Willena ■ I thought having a conference was a good idea. It was a way we could analyze Klan activity to teach people how the Klan was tied into the whole economic system and the class system. We could explain how the government was for the capitalists and how they used the Klan. People—especially black people—were really interested in it.

And I thought having a march through the neighborhoods was a great way to rally people to the conference. We passed out leaflets in the neighborhoods ahead of time. Then on November 3, we would march through there. People would say, "Oh yeah, that's the anti-Klan protest." We would get people's attention, and some of them would join us and come to the conference.

Marty ■ I thought the work was real important and exciting too. I wanted to get more involved in it, but Mike was pulling back some. He was getting into his job heading up the Pediatrics Department at Lincoln Community Health Center, and he wanted to spend more time with our baby.

So we were having some problems that summer. I was gung ho and wanted to dig in more. I wasn't a key organizer, but I passed out leaflets. I really wanted to work in a factory. That fall, I got a job at Cabletronics. I was accepted for a job at Burlington Textile Mill; I was supposed to start working on November 5.

Sally ■ I agreed with Nelson Johnson's plan. It would be a demonstration like ones we had done many times before, with chanting, marching, shouting. We would get a permit and the police would be there, as they always were, to prevent any violence from Klan types. I was satisfied. It would be in Greensboro. It would be safe.

7

Countdown of a Death Squad

Death squads are secret, often paramilitary, organizations that carry out extralegal executions and other violent acts against clearly defined individuals or groups. Murder is their primary reason for being. They operate with the overt support, complicity, or acquiescence of government, or at least some parts of it. But death squads are clandestine groups, so that government officials can deny connection to them. One of the first death squads was the early Ku Klux Klan.[1]

How did armed Klansmen and Nazis converge in Greensboro on the corner where we were getting ready for an anti-Klan march? How did they take us by surprise, open fire on us, and kill five among us? Where were the police? Why weren't they protecting our demonstration? Because the death squad that attacked us was the result of Klan, Nazis, Greensboro police, and federal agent collusion.

The italicized text in this chapter and the next represents facts unknown to us at the time that we have reconstructed from later trial testimony, newspaper reports, and FBI files.

Organizing the Death Squad

July 26, 1979: The ATF and Local Nazis

Bernard Butkovich was an agent of the Bureau of Alcohol, Tobacco, and Firearms (ATF).[2] Less than three weeks after the China Grove confrontation, Butkovich—a short, dark, clean-shaven man with an eastern European, Jewish-sounding name—drove up to the home of Roland Wayne Wood, the local Nazi leader in Winston-Salem, thirty miles west of Greensboro. On July 26, he parked in front of Wood's small white house and walked over to the adjacent garage. Hardly more than a shed, Wood's garage was the office of the Forsyth County unit of the American Nazi Party.

Roland Wayne Wood, a hulking 6'4" man with scruffy reddish-brown hair and beard, wore a "White Power" T-shirt that stretched across his bulging belly. He was thirty-four years old, a sheet-metal worker whose arrest record dated to his early teens and included felony and misdemeanor convictions for forgery, larceny, and bad checks. In his twenties, Wood had joined the Federated Knights of the Ku Klux Klan and moved up to a North Carolina "klud" or group leader. Finding the Klan not extreme enough for his tastes, Wood gravitated toward the American Nazi Party and became head of the Forsyth County unit.

Roland Wood was "an effective worker," according to North Carolina Nazi leader Harold Covington. He moved "massive amounts of literature, distributing door to door. He held regular meetings, running training courses for ST men [Storm Troopers], getting on his CB radio, and rapping to all the people about Adolf Hitler." The courses took place at Nazi paramilitary training camps in two North Carolina counties.

On that July day, Bernard Butkovich shook Roland Wayne Wood's hand and told Wood he was a long-distance truck driver interested in joining Wood's unit of the Nazis. Over the following months, Butkovich hung out with Wood and his friends, encouraging them to acquire illegal weapons.

"Butkovich said he could train us in hand-to-hand combat if we wanted," Nazi Raeford Caudle later testified in court. ATF agent Butkovich offered to get them selector switches to convert legal semiautomatic weapons into illegal automatic guns.[3]

September 22: The United Racist Front

Butkovich joined his new friend Roland Wayne Wood and other Nazis and Klansmen to found the United Racist Front. They met over the weekend of September 22–23 on a farm outside Louisburg, thirty-five miles east of Durham.

On Saturday afternoon, the leaders held a press conference. Virgil Griffin, Grand Dragon of Invisible Knights of the KKK, pointed to a resurgence of racist sentiment in the South, claiming: "We're coming back strong. . . . People don't see it yet. It's underground. But we're coming back strong."

According to the September 25, 1979, Greensboro Daily News*: "Some of those at the meetings were heavily armed, and there were reminders of racial violence of the past. A rope noose, 'for purely inspirational purposes,' was strung from an old oak tree outside the lodge." North Carolina Nazi leader Harold Covington, holding high his AR-16 semiautomatic, shouted: "Piece by piece, bit by bit, we white people are going to take back this country."*

A reporter for the Greensboro News and Record *noted the "Niggers Beware" bumper stickers on cars.*

One hundred people attended the weekend event, including Wood, Gorrell Pierce, and Raeford Caudle, who had been at China Grove. Klansmen Jerry Paul Smith, David Matthews, Glenn Miller, Jack Fowler, and Chris Benson signed on to the United Racist Front over the weekend—all but Pierce would be in the caravan on November 3, six weeks later.

During the gathering, Bernard Butkovich wore a body mike that transmitted his conversations to other ATF agents scattered through the area. Three ATF operators who heard him urge Nazis Wood, Caudle, and Fowler to join forces with Klansmen in the United Racist Front did nothing.[4]

Paul ■ I read the newspaper account about the United Racist Front. This is why we need our anti-Klan campaign, I thought, to stop these guys before they grow. Fascists had killed my grandparents, aunts, uncles, and cousins—if only people had challenged the Nazis in Europe when their numbers were small.

Sally ■ Paul showed me the newspaper article on the formation of the United Racist Front. As I read it, a wave of fear hit me, renewing the dread that began in China Grove. The article quoted Klan leader Virgil Griffin and Nazi Harold Covington, but I noted to myself that they had not been in China Grove. The article mentioned Louisburg, which is ninety miles east of Greensboro, whereas China Grove is sixty miles southwest. Probably these are different groups of Klan and Nazis, I thought—there are a number of organizations with disagreements, just like left-wing groups. The article said nothing about China Grove.

I put the paper down and put the United Racist Front out of my mind. We had plans that day: Mike and Marty Nathan were coming over to help us paint our living room. We were developing a couples' friendship with them. We shared political involvement, and we both had baby daughters. It felt good to be friends with Mike; the pain of our divorce seemed far away. That Saturday, Mike, Marty, Paul, and I worked as an efficient team, painting our whole living room while we took turns to watch Leah, age four months, and Leola, almost two years. That evening, I cooked spaghetti and meat sauce and made a big tossed salad. The four of us had dinner with Mike's mother, Esther, and our two little ones. We talked about the joys and trials of parenthood. We discussed painting at Mike and Marty's house. It felt like a friendship that would last a long time.

I enjoyed that day, because for the two months since China Grove, I had felt disoriented and demoralized. I couldn't shake it. So I turned inward, focusing on my family, playing with Leola, and fixing up our apartment. I started prenatal care at my health clinic.

Nelson ■ We were moving ahead with our plans for November 3. I was particularly enthusiastic about the plans for the conference to deepen people's understanding of the Klan's secret supporters, their historical relationships with police and politicians. Signe Waller and I designed the poster to advertise the demonstration. We wanted it to stand out on the lampposts and bulletin boards. Across the top it said, "Death to the Klan!" which was the slogan that emerged out of the march in China Grove. Under that were photos from China Grove of determined-looking protesters, black and white. In clear letters it states: "Anti-Klan March and Conference, Saturday, November 3, 1979, Greensboro, N.C." In smaller letters in one corner of the poster it read: "March: Assemble 11:00 a.m. parking lot of Windsor Community Center." In the other corner it stated: "Conference: 1:00 p.m. All Nation Pentecostal Church."

On October 4, Signe finished the poster and ran off a bunch of copies. That day, our folks started putting the poster up.

Willena ■ We put the posters for the anti-Klan march and conference up all over the black community. Then, as fast as we put them up, the cops ripped them down! I saw the police taking them down in my neighborhood. I heard other people say they were taking them down around Morningside.

October 10: Greensboro Police Station

The Greensboro Police Department was already planning for the WVO's November 3 demonstration. At a staff meeting, Captain Larry Gibson was told to be on hand when Nelson Johnson applied for a parade permit for November 3. Police brass stipulated that the permit to be issued to Johnson's group should state that the demonstrators carry no weapons, open or concealed, and no sticks larger that two inches square. No police permit had ever before banned weapons. Greensboro police chief William Swing justified the unprecedented restrictions based on "inflammatory posters put up by the communists."

Chief Swing sent Detective Jerry "Rooster" Cooper an administrative memo to "get information on communist groups." Cooper and Gibson both had been officers in the GPD since the 1969s. They believed that Nelson Johnson was once again "stirring up trouble."[5]

October 11: GPD's Informant

Eddie Dawson had a reputation for instigating fights. A Klansman since the mid-1960s, he was repeatedly arrested for "cross burnings and violent night rides." In 1968 he served time in prison for "terrorizing the citizens" of Alamance County.

After his conviction, he got mad at the Klan for "not backing me up" during his court case. When the FBI approached him, he agreed to become an informant, although an FBI memo noted his tendency to "create a disturbance" at demonstrations and labeled him an "extremist informant." For the next eight years, the FBI paid Dawson to go to Klan meetings.[6] "They give you twenty five dollars for going to a local meeting," Dawson later explained. "Fifty dollars out of town, eight cents a mile, traveling."

In 1979, as Klan activity increased in North Carolina, the Greensboro Police Department recruited Dawson as an informant. On October 11, Detective Jerry "Rooster" Cooper, Dawson's control officer, told Dawson to go to a Ku Klux Klan rally in Lincolnton, North Carolina, on October 22 to "see if the Klan is going to Greensboro on November third."[7]

Nelson ■ We wanted our demonstration to have a militant posture and a high profile. We wanted to attract people to join our ranks. We did a vigorous mobilization in Greensboro, Durham, Chapel Hill, and other areas where we had ongoing work. And we also decided to put out the word in the China Grove/ Kannapolis area. So on Tuesday, October 11, we went to Kannapolis to hold a press conference.

Paul ■ I poured all my anger into the Kannapolis press statement. I thought about all my relatives who I had never met because they were killed by Nazis. I quickly drafted the press statement the morning we went to Kannapolis; it did not take me long to write. I drove with Marty Nathan to Nelson's house in Greensboro, and Nelson spent a few minutes going over the press release. "This is good," Nelson said. Then Nelson, Marty, Big Al, and I got in a car and headed for Kannapolis.

In front of textile-giant Cannon Mills, we set up a card table with copies of press releases and photos of China Grove. A handful of reporters huddled in front of the table. One TV cameraman taped the photos. Others listened as Nelson began: "The Ku Klux Klan is treacherous. They are scum produced by a dying system."

When Nelson stopped speaking, I addressed the Klan directly: "You are nothing but a bunch of racist cowards. We challenge you to attend our November 3 rally in Greensboro. Death to the Klan!"

Looking back, that was a stupid thing for me to say. But it certainly does not justify what they did to us.

Marty ■ I went to Kannapolis for the press conference with Nelson and Paul. I wasn't particularly scared. I was glad to see it happening.

Back in Durham, I remember sitting in Shoney's Restaurant with Mike. We had just gotten a copy of the letter Paul and Nelson wrote to Klan leader Joe Grady that had been made a leaflet. Mike looked at it and said bluntly: "This is crazy. This is really off the wall."

Once again my response was, "What's wrong with you?" This time I openly got angry at him. Why didn't I listen to him? Deep inside of me, it didn't make any sense to me either. That rhetoric was completely out of my line of living and being. It was because I wanted to see this group succeed.

"No Weapons"

Nelson ■ On October 19, I went to the Greensboro Police Department to apply for a police parade permit. I met with Captain Larry Gibson.

I gave him the required information: The march would start at noon; the gathering time was 11 a.m. The starting point was the corner of Carver Street and Everitt Street in the Morningside Homes housing project. There was no other time, no other location of the starting point, discussed with the police.

I gave Gibson the route of the march. From our starting point at Carver and Everitt Streets, we planned to march about a half mile to Windsor Community Center. Windsor was a second gathering point for our march. It was listed on our poster, because it was easy to get to, close to the highway, and therefore a good place to meet for people who did not know Greensboro well.

We also planned to march through several other housing projects, including Ray Warren Homes and Hampton Homes. People would be joining our march from these points as well.

"So, you gonna be armed?" Captain Gibson asked. I was surprised by the question and by the hostility in his voice. I was trying to be polite.

"Do you always ask people wanting a parade permit if they're gonna be armed?" I asked.

"Well, are you?" pushed Gibson.

"North Carolina state law allows people to carry unconcealed weapons," I said.

"But this permit states for you to be unarmed," Gibson replied.

"Why?"

"To avoid violence with the Klan," he said.

"Do you know something about the Klan planning to be there?" I asked. "Are you expecting trouble?"

"No, it's just a precaution," said Gibson.

I told him I totally disagreed with the position on weapons.

Gibson said, "In that case, no permit."

So I signed the application for a parade permit that said the demonstrators would carry no weapons.

October 20: Lincolnton KKK Rally

As the GPD had directed, Klansman/informant Eddie Dawson traveled to Lincolnton, a tiny town eighty miles west of Greensboro known for its Klan activity. On Saturday night, a few dozen Klansmen gathered for a rally. Jerry Paul Smith stood guard in his Klan security uniform as Virgil Griffin introduced the guest speaker. A slight man only five and a half feet tall, Griffin introduced Eddie Dawson as his friend of eighteen years.

The lanky, six-foot Dawson towered over Griffin. Never at a loss for words, he challenged the Klansmen come to Greensboro and "confront the communists and militant blacks."

It was a "pumped-up and mad speech," Chris Benson, a local Klan leader, later testified in court. "He got the crowd real emotional. He said, 'It's gonna be a fight. Take your shotguns and your long guns.'"[8]

October 21: Report of Klan Intent to the GPD

The next day, Dawson called his control officer at GPD, Detective Jerry Cooper. "Expect a fight" at the demonstration, he said. Rooster Cooper did not press him for details.

　　Detective Cooper reported to his superior officer, Lieutenant Robert Lee Talbott, that the Klan would attempt to disrupt the November 3 rally. Lieutenant Talbott passed this information up to the Greensboro police command.[9]

October 26: Report of Klan Intent to the FBI

Dawson was nervous. Were things getting out of his control? "We should stop the march," he later remembered telling Rooster Cooper and Cooper's supervisor, Robert Talbott, at the Greensboro Police Department.

　　"How're you going to do that?" asked Talbott dismissively.

　　"We'll get an injunction against the damn march," Dawson said.

　　"Who's going to get the injunction?" Talbott asked.

　　"Me! I'll go up to the city attorney and ask him for an injunction in the name of the Ku Klux Klan."

　　Lieutenant Talbott was unenthusiastic. "It's up to you. If you want to, do it."

　　Why were the cops so nonchalant? Dawson wondered. Well, he had other cards up his sleeve. He'd go see FBI agent Len Bogaty, his longtime employer in the Bureau. Dawson had worked for Bogaty both inside and outside the FBI. Over the years he had been at Bogaty's house many times, doing construction or painting.

　　Dawson went to Bogaty's office. "I want an injunction against the parade," he told the agent, "because of trouble with the Ku Klux Klan—"

　　Bogaty interrupted him. "If you think there's going to be trouble, don't go to the demonstration."

　　"I have to go!" Dawson hollered at him. "Otherwise, the Klan guys will think I'm an FBI informant!"

　　The FBI agent stood up, ending the meeting. "I can't get no injunction. I advise you to go down and talk to the police department."

　　"What?" Dawson blew up. He had just been talking to the police department. "Okay, you don't have to get up and throw me out of the damn door. I know where it's at. I tell you what, though, the next time I'll have to bring you a bucket of blood."[10]

October 27: More Details on the Klan's Plan

GPD Sergeant Tracy Burke stated approximately one week prior to November 3, 1979, he received a call to meet with GPD Detective Montgomery, who informed Burke that information had been received from an informer that some members of the Klan living in the Winston area had obtained a machine gun and possibly other weapons. The information further indicated these individuals planned to come to Greensboro on 11/3/79, and shoot up the place.

Sgt Burke stated that he took down the information and attempted to contact Agent Bud Hazelman with the Bureau of Alcohol Tobacco and Firearms. Sgt Burke stated his telephone call was not returned and within two days he passed the information on to Detective Jerry "Rooster" Cooper.[11]

Late October 1979: FBI Investigation

Daisy Crawford, an older African American, movement veteran, and organizer for the Southern Conference Educational Fund, had met Sandi Smith when Sandi moved to Kannapolis to join the organizing drive at Cannon Mills. In late October, two men flashing FBI badges knocked on the door of Daisy Crawford's modest home. Like many activists, Daisy was suspicious of the FBI. On her doorstep, the agents showed her a picture of a man and asked her if she recognized him. No, she said. A second, third, fourth, fifth picture. Nope, never saw those people either. At the sixth picture, Daisy sucked in her breath. In the FBI agent's hand was a picture of Sandi Smith.

Daisy Crawford years later issued a statement to the press: "I knew Sandi Smith well, and respected and liked her. I worked with her in the summer and fall of 1979, and together we planned ways to fight for the workers, and organize a union at Cannon Mills."

About a week before Sandi Smith was shot, I was visited at my home by two men who said they were FBI agents and showed me their badges. They showed me a picture of Sandi Smith, which I identified for them. They showed me other pictures of men which I did not identify at the time, but I believe they may have been members of the Workers Viewpoint Organization."[12]

The Communist Workers Party

Paul ■ The Workers Viewpoint Organization became the Communist Workers Party two weeks before the planned anti-Klan rally. Nelson Johnson, Jim Waller, Sandi Smith, Bill Sampson, César Cauce, Sally, and I all went to New York as delegates to the founding convention. In a rundown nightclub in a residential neighborhood somewhere in New York City, Jerry Tung articulated a vision of five years to prepare for socialist revolution in the U.S. We had to be prepared to make sacrifices, he said, and charge the bourgeoisie "wave upon wave." Our selfless actions in these years could prevent a larger bloodbath in the future. In retrospect, many called Tung's five-year framework a "hype line." It was a vague formulation that left many in the CWP believing that revolution was around the corner.

Sally ■   It seemed like everyone was enthusiastic at the founding congress but me. The five-year framework didn't make any sense to me. I felt sick the whole weekend and blamed it on morning sickness.

Jerry Tung demoted me from regional secretary and replaced me with Jim Waller. Jim was also selected for the CWP's Central Committee. I felt mixed about my demotion. Mainly I felt relieved, but it also made me feel like a failure. I was glad that Jim seemed so enthusiastic, even if I couldn't share the feeling.

Nelson ■   We changed our name to Communist Workers Party because we wanted to have integrity, to not be deceptive. Since we were communists, we should be open about it.

I was loyal to the change, although the party leadership thought I had what was called "right opportunist tendencies." I was concerned about having "communism" in our name, because it made it hard to use to build the popular movement. They criticized me for being more focused on the mass movement than party building. I was talking about communism to people; I was planning to talk about it in my speech on November 3. I was determined not to run abstract rhetoric, but to discuss communism only when I could connect it to something concrete, like the role of the Ku Klux Klan under capitalism and the need for an alternative political-economic system.

The massacre is not reducible to us changing our name. We did not use CWP on our literature until the day of the demonstration. But our name change and our language facilitated the attack against us and helped them to get away with it.

Willena ■   When WVO said we were going to change our name to CWP, I was scared it was going to mess things up. I agreed that we needed to be honest with people and open with them so they'll know what we're about. But I was afraid that we wouldn't get the chance to tell people, because they weren't going to listen.

While everyone was up in New York City changing from WVO to CWP, I was down in Birmingham, Alabama. I bought an old house there for $8,000. I was planning to move myself and my children there right after November 3. There were five or six of us moving down there. We were planning to do some union work in Birmingham. I had left my job with the Drug Action Council in Greensboro after training my replacement.

Final Plans

Sally ■ There were two weeks between the founding congress and November 3. On the weekend between, we met in Durham at César Cauce's house. A major agenda item was final plans for the November 3 march and conference. Nelson Johnson reported that the police still had not issued a parade permit and that the cops were taking down our posters. He suggested that we hold a press conference on the steps of the police station to expose the cops' tactics and pressure them to give us the permit.

Bill Sampson complained that the campaign was taking too much time away from the trade union work. He was running for president of his union local at Cone Mill's White Oak Plant, and he felt that the anti-Klan march was pulling him away from what he needed to do to win. Jim Waller countered that the Klan was quickly becoming the greatest danger to our union work. Sandi Smith pushed us to take the anti-Klan work seriously. "We're talking about the Klan here, the *Ku Klux Klan!*" She looked intensely from person to person around the room. "We've got to take a stand."

I avoided eye contact with Sandi. I felt dizzy. I couldn't even express my fears. Previously I had been so self-assured, always speaking my mind. But I had lost my confidence, lost my voice. Sandi, Jim, Nelson, and Paul spoke adamantly about the importance of our anti-Klan campaign, and there was nobody I respected more. Who was I to say, "Hey, wait a minute, this looks scary"? So I said nothing.

Willena ■ I missed that meeting. I was in the process of moving my furniture to Birmingham. I was thinking about where to apply for work, what union jobs would be the best to get. Then I came back to Greensboro to help with the November 3 demo and pack up my kids to move down to Alabama.

October 27–31: Trouble with the Parade Permit

Nelson ■ Police policy is that a group applying for a parade permit gets it within three days of applying for it. I applied on October 19, and we hadn't heard anything about our permit. November 3 was only a week away. So I started calling the Greensboro Police Department on the phone. I called three times on three different days, and each time they said I would get it the next day. Finally I went down to the police station. They said they didn't have it.

I said, "What is going on?"

They said the city manager had been sick and couldn't sign it, although they never said this on the phone. I thought about all the years of police lies and cover-ups. I remembered ten years back to 1969, when we had a Malcolm X memorial and the police opened tear gas on us. They said that a few tear-gas canisters "just happened to open up." So I figured that once again the police were lying and trying to complicate things for us.

The Wednesday before our demonstration, I went down to the police station again. We still didn't have the permit. The cops were tearing down our posters all over town. They said it was illegal to tape posters to the lampposts. But right next to our posters were the politicians' campaign posters; the cops weren't ripping those down.

We were planning to hold the conference after the march at the All Nation Pentecostal Church. I met with the minister that Wednesday, and he said we could *not* use his church. A church member who worked as a secretary in the police department heard gossip at the GPD that the church was going to be bombed and that many people would be killed. So she told the minister, and clearly he and the board had been intimidated and reneged on our earlier agreement.

So here it was Wednesday, October 31, and we had no church for the conference, no permit for the march, and our posters were being torn down. We decided to hold a press conference to expose all this the next day.

November 1: Press Conference

Paul ■ We were angry. It was two days before the demonstration, and the police still had not issued a parade permit! Nelson Johnson, Willena Cannon, and I went down to the police station with a big red banner that said, "Death to the Klan." Willena and I held the banner on the steps, while Nelson went inside the GPD.

Nelson ■ I ran around the police department that day, from this office to that office, and finally Captain Gibson gave me our parade permit. As I was coming down the hall, by chance I saw Captain Trevor Hampton, one of the few black police officers in the GPD. He said the police would be me at our November 3 meeting, planned for 11:30 a.m. at Morningside. The captain said, "See you there."

Then I joined Paul and Willena outside the police station on the steps. A few reporters stood around, anticipating our press statement.

A TV camera captured what I told the press: "The police hate us; we know it. They are out to do everything they can to disrupt us. And we are here to say that we are going ahead with the march. We just picked up the permit a few minutes ago, after running around the building two or three times this morning. The people in Greensboro are intent on smashing and driving out the KKK and their secret supporters."

I paused, thinking out loud, trying to anticipate what the police might do to undermine the march. "We fully expect the police to continue their slimy tactics," I said. "They will do anything to disrupt this march. They might harass us or send provocateurs into our ranks to try to disrupt the march. The Klan's nothing but a bunch of cowards, they're not coming here unless the police aid them."

But what I did not anticipate—none of us did—is that the police brass would bring the Klan in and keep the officers away.

November 1: Inside the GPD

While Nelson picked up the police permit from Captain Gibson, and Paul and Willena held up the "Death to the Klan" banner on the police station steps, Eddie Dawson was upstairs discussing "last-minute preparations" with Officer Rooster Cooper.

"Now, you know that the beginning of the march is at Morningside Homes?" Dawson later remembered Cooper asking him. "Do you know where Morningside Homes is at?"

"No," replied Dawson. "I never heard of Morningside Homes."

"Get downstairs and get a copy of the permit," directed Cooper.

So Dawson went downstairs and got a copy of the permit Gibson had just given to Nelson Johnson and headed outside.[13]

Paul ■ As Nelson was speaking, I noticed an older white man, lanky, maybe six feet tall, walk over to our group. He looked like he might be a reporter. After Nelson finished speaking, the man asked Nelson, "Do they have Klansmen in Greensboro here?"

"Oh, yeah," replied Nelson, "they have Klansmen everywhere."

The man said that he "couldn't believe there was still Klan in Greensboro in this day and age."

The reporters left, except for this tall, skinny man asking about the Klan. The man seemed relaxed, friendly, and I was glad he was interested. He spoke with a soft voice and a slight lisp. I thought it was strange that he hadn't noticed the KKK in the recent news articles and asked him about himself. He replied that he was a contractor, living in Greensboro. A small businessman has to be sharp to survive and probably would be aware of the highly publicized Klan. I invited him to the demonstration.

I didn't know that I was talking to Eddie Dawson, Klansman and police informant. I didn't know that the police had just given him a copy of our parade permit.

Later that afternoon in Captain Trevor Hampton's office at the GPD, field command personnel received "an up-to-date briefing on the intelligence concerning the WVO parade and the potential for Klan activities at the parade."[14]

In Winston-Salem, the Klan and the Nazis—Roland Wayne Wood, Jack Fowler, Raeford Caudle, Jerry Paul Smith, and ATF agent Bernard Butkovich—were meeting in Wood's garage to make final plans for their trip to Greensboro.

Butkovich encouraged them, not subtly, to arm themselves. "He wanted to know if I was going to take a gun," Wood later reported. "I said no."

Butkovich said, "Well, why aren't you?"

Wood told Butkovich he was afraid he might get in trouble if he took a weapon. The agent said, "You can conceal it, can't you?"

Nazi Gorrell Pierce remembered Butkovich saying, "If I were going on November 3, I'd want something backing me up."

Jerry Paul Smith told the men in Wood's garage that he had a pipe bomb he was thinking about "throwing into a crowd of niggers."

Butkovich later said that he reported to the ATF that there was "no talk of guns" at this meeting. Yes, he heard Smith talk about his pipe bomb, but he "didn't take him seriously." The Bureau of Alcohol and Tobacco did nothing to alert the demonstrators.[15]

November 2: More Warnings for the FBI

In New York City, Mordecai Levy, leader of the Jewish Defense Organization, received information from his organization's intelligence network that the Nazis planned to go to Greensboro to kill people. He immediately called the North Carolina office of the FBI and asked to speak to a Jewish agent. He told the FBI it was urgent.

"The Nazis are going to go to Greensboro with the Klan on November 3," Levy told an FBI agent named Goldberg, "to kill some people." Goldberg protested that he was not Jewish.[16]

Greensboro FBI agent Thomas Brereton told Micky Micheaux, the U.S. Attorney in Greensboro, that the Klan was coming to town the following day and that there were going to be "fireworks."[17]

On the Eve of the March

Late in the evening of November 2, Nazi/Klan informant Eddie Dawson called Jerry Paul Smith at his home in Mebane, North Carolina. Dawson told Smith to come immediately to Greensboro. Smith, Virgil Griffin, and Coleman Pridmore left for the city late that night with their guns. They met Dawson at 3:30 a.m. at an all-night restaurant. Guided by the parade permit the police gave Dawson, they drove in the rain along the planned march route.[18]

Nelson ■ On November 2, the evening before our demonstration, I was ready. Everything had finally fallen into place for our demonstration. We planned to have a lively program, marching through several neighborhoods with chants and a vibrant presence, and in that way to attract a large demonstration that would breathe and be alive.

I didn't expect an encounter with the Klan. If anything, I expected problems with the police. Big Man, who had confronted the Klan in the 1940s in Greenville, South Carolina, proposed a plan to protect the demonstrators. He and Dale Sampson went down to the housing project and got permission from some residents to have people with arms stand on their front porches to protect the demonstrators.

I argued with Big Man. He thought the main danger was the Klan, while I thought the main danger was the police. I told him: "No Klan is coming here with all these Greensboro police who will be at our march. I have discussions with Captain Gibson every time we do a demonstration, and there are always all these police around us."

I was worried that the cops would send someone that looked like a demonstrator to provoke us from inside our ranks. Some guy would be there with pistols and guns, and the police would know it. The cops would challenge that person, rush in to wrestle with them, and the demonstrators would rush in to defend the person. That sets up a context where they can have a police riot. That was what I was worried about.

Paul ■ We turned down Big Man's plan. After all, we were planning to march all the way through town. How could Big Man's proposal protect the marchers along the whole route? We did discuss the possibility of attack, perhaps by a sniper. Bill Sampson walked along the parade route looking for where we might be most vulnerable. No one ever thought we would be most vulnerable before the march even started.

Basically we relied on the police policy as specified on the permit. We knew nothing of the activities of Edward Dawson and Bernard Butkovich. We did not think the Klan would come at all.

Willena ■ There was some discussion about having people on porches with guns. I didn't think that was a good idea. The Klan was active in little places like China Grove; it wasn't active in Greensboro. This was our base.

I was really trying to figure out what the police was going to do. The police had never before prohibited guns. The weapons ban should have alerted me, but it didn't.

Kwame ■ I was looking forward to marching with my group, the Junior RYL. We had just gotten a box of red berets. We were planning to look sharp.

Sally ■ I wasn't thinking about the demonstration. More on my mind was changing our name to Communist Workers Party. The more I thought about it, the less I liked it, and I didn't know what to do about it.

As for the anti-Klan march and conference, it was just one more demonstration like hundreds I had participated in over the years.

Marty ■ I was not involved in any of the planning for November 3. I leafleted for the demonstration and talked to people, urging them to come with us. Several said they were afraid to come.

It is so easy in retrospect to lay a lot of things on what we did before November 3. But that day before, we were ready to go—that was it. The hard part of it is that we all did just expect to go to a rally. Who knew what would happen?

8

The Massacre:
November 3, 1979

Greensboro, before Dawn

In the rainy predawn darkness, Klansman/police informant Eddie Dawson, Imperial Wizard Virgil Griffin, and two other Klansmen finished driving the route of the anti-Klan march scheduled for that day.

7:30 a.m.

Eddie Dawson called Greensboro police detective Rooster Cooper at home to report that men and guns were already arriving in Greensboro. Cooper gave Dawson the phone number of his unmarked police car. Dawson headed toward the Klan's meeting place, Brent Fletcher's house on Randleman Road, just inside the Greensboro city limits.[1]

Sally ■ Paul woke me early on November 3. I could hear the rain splashing on the windows. I curled up, wanting to go back to sleep, my head heavy on the pillow. I was thirty-two years old and three months pregnant. I wanted to stay home, play with Leola, and do the laundry.

But we were activists, and today was a demonstration. I was obligated to be there. Tomorrow, I promised myself, I will spend the day with Leola and the washer-dryer. I got up and dressed. Leola was her smiley self as I dressed her. She was going to spend the day at our good friend Anne Finch's house.

Then Paul and I headed for Greensboro. As we drove westward, the sun peeked through the rain clouds. Maybe it would be a nice day.

Paul ■ I looked forward to the day. As we drove to Greensboro, Sally seemed withdrawn. I tried to cheer her up by giving her a pep talk about how boldness against the Klan is good, but she was so glum, I backed off.

Willena ■ I felt glad that morning and hoped a lot of people would show up for the protest. It was the first time we would call ourselves Communist Workers Party, and I was a little nervous about that. But I felt having this march was a good way to tell people about CWP. We were doing something important, and people could see that.

Nelson ■ I looked forward to the day. I hoped our numbers would grow as we marched through Greensboro's streets. My mind was on the speech I was going to give at the conference, after the march was over. I was planning to talk about the decay of capitalism and how the emergence of the Klan was the result of capitalism's weakness. I had my speech notes in my pocket.

Early in the morning I went to Jim and Signe Waller's house. We had breakfast and talked about the day. Jim was nervous, but he said he always felt nervous before a demonstration. As usual, he had spent a lot of time working on the speech he would give at the conference at the end of the march.

Marty ■ First thing that morning, Mike and I got into an argument. Mike said something about not wanting to go. I got mad at him. But then we got in our cars and picked up other Durham people who were going to the demonstration. We took Leah to Anne's house and headed for Greensboro.

9 a.m.

Klansmen and Nazis had arrived at Brent Fletcher's house on Randleman Road in the southwest outskirts of Greensboro. A yellow van pulled up from Lincolnton, a blue Fairlane from Winston-Salem, a car from Raleigh. Eddie Dawson was in charge, and he kept looking at his watch.[2]

9:30 a.m.

Across the street from Brent Fletcher's house, in an unmarked police car, GPD detective Rooster Cooper and GPD sergeant Tracy Burke watched the arriving Klansmen. Using binoculars, Cooper counted "about ten" cars in Fletcher's yard.

Eddie Dawson called Cooper's car phone and reported that "thirteen, fourteen, or fifteen" people had arrived, with "enough guns so it looked like the Klan and Nazis are prepared for war."

9:45 a.m.

Officers Cooper and Burke left Randleman Road and drove to the police station to attend a briefing.

10 a.m.

At the station, Cooper and Burke met with their commanding officer, Lieutenant P. W. Spoon, who was in charge of the march, Lieutenant S. Daughty, and others. Cooper reported that men with guns were gathering at a house on Randleman Road. Commanders told the cops responsible for protecting the march to "take a lunch break from 11:00 a.m. to 11:30 a.m." Cooper left for Randleman Road and brought along a police photographer.

Nelson ■ People gathered for our demonstration at Morningside Homes, where the march was going to begin at noon. Morningside is a public housing project in the middle of Greensboro's black community. It was the place listed on the police permit. We planned to start there with spirited chants and singing to attract others to march with us.

People from out of town were gathering at Windsor Community Center, about a half mile from Morningside, just off the highway. We were expecting people from Durham, Chapel Hill, Chatham County, Rocky Mount, and Kannapolis. Originally we planned to begin the march at Windsor Center and had put that location on our original poster advertising the march. Then we decided it would be better to start at Morningside and then march to Windsor to pick up people gathered there.

The starting point that we discussed with the police was always Morningside. They were supposed to protect our march. Our permit application said that people would begin gathering at 11 a.m., and the march would start at Morningside at noon.

Sally ■ Paul and I arrived at the Morningside site around 10:30 a.m. We parked on Everitt Street, which runs along the edge of the Morningside housing project. The rally starting point was at the point that Everitt Street makes a T with Carver Street. Carver is narrow, running through the single-story projects. On the side of Everitt Street opposite Morningside Homes, there was a row of single-story run-down shops. At this spot, a sleepy part of Greensboro, we gathered.

When we got there, the neighborhood looked peaceful. The first person we saw was Nelson Johnson, who greeted us as we drove up. Nelson's daughters, Ayo and Akua, ages six and seven, ran up and showed us the red berets that Willena Cannon had just given them. "Well, look at you fashion plates," said Nelson, hugging them hard. The girls put on their berets and ran to join the other kids, who were already wearing berets.

I noticed Willena's ten-year-old son, Kwame, who looked particularly handsome in his red beret. These kids made me smile.

Kwame ▪ Yes, I was at the Grove, which is what we kids call Morningside. The Junior RYL was there—me and Ayo, Akua, Ricky, Vaughn, about twelve of us. We all had on our red tams. We were out there on the corner where they had a Klan dummy. We were singing, "We shall not be moved."

Sally ▪ Durham activist Tom Clark strummed his guitar, singing civil rights songs. A bunch of kids, all in red berets, clustered around him, singing with sweet, cracking voices. Several TV crews arrived and took videotape of the lively children, who were clowning around for the cameras.

I saw Chekesha Powell arrive. She was eight months pregnant with her first child. Chekesha had become an activist a decade earlier, when she participated in a sit-in at her junior high school. She rarely missed a demonstration. We stood there on Carver and Everitt trading pregnancy stories. She teased me about my morning sickness, swearing that her baby wasn't going to slow her down at all. I told her, "Just you wait."

We watched the newlyweds, César and Floris Cauce, distributing the protest placards to people. I saw Jim Wrenn, who had just arrived from Rocky Mount, a city in eastern North Carolina. Allen and Dori Blitz, college friends of Paul's who lived in Virginia, prepared an open-backed pickup truck to be our sound truck. The truck would lead the march, carrying energetic speakers like Sandi Smith and Roz Pelles, who would lead the chanting. The energy of the marchers began to build. The sun was breaking through the clouds, and the air was fresh after the rain. The temperature was mild for November.

Willena ▪ That morning, I was mainly dealing with my children. Kwame, who was just about to turn eleven, was already at Morningside, running around with his new red hat on. But Imani, who was only six, and Kweli, only three, were too little to march through Greensboro. My sister Annette agreed to take care of them. I was at Windsor Community Center, waiting for Annette. Then she was going to drop me off at Morningside.

Paul ▪ At Morningside, Nelson Johnson and I stood at the corner of Carver and Everitt Streets, just a few feet away from the folksinging. We discussed the logistics of the march and the conference. We compared notes on our speeches. I planned to speak as a child of Holocaust survivors, focusing on the Nazis who had killed my relatives.

Marty ▪ Although Mike and I had fussed first thing in the morning, when we got to Greensboro we were friends again. We drove to Greensboro on Interstate 85, taking the Lee Street exit, which brought us to the Windsor Community Center, the meeting point for the people coming from out of town. We saw friends from around the state gathering in the parking lot. We parked and got out to talk to them.

There is a tendency to put déjà vu feelings on things. In fact, we were just there at Windsor Community Center. None of us had premonitions; none of us knew. In retrospect, we feel we should have known, but we didn't.

Jim Waller drove up in his old Saab and told me to send a first-aid car to the beginning of the march site. I was on the first-aid team, responsible for taking care of any accidents on the march. I asked Mike to go with Jim to drive our old station wagon, which had the first-aid supplies in it, over to Carver and Everitt, which was a half mile away.

That was my last conversation with my beloved Michael.

Sally ■ I watched Mike Nathan drive up Everitt Street in his old red station wagon. He parked, got out, and told me it was the designated first-aid vehicle. I laughed to myself as I watched Mike. He was still tall and lean, but his hair was thinning on top. Apparently as compensation, he grew a thick, dark beard. I knew Mike's little vanities well, but I couldn't get used to that beard. A fleeting memory of anger and arguments flashed through my mind. But those fights were years ago, and I was no longer angry. I smiled, and Mike winked back at me; we were both enjoying our friendship. I told him he should drive his first-aid car just behind the marchers.

10:55 a.m.

Eddie Dawson urged the Klansmen and Nazis to get started, reminding them that the demonstrators would begin assembling at eleven o'clock and marching at noon. The men grabbed their guns, got in their cars, and lined up in a caravan.

10:57 a.m.

Officer April Wise and her partner were investigating a domestic dispute in Morningside Homes, only a block away from Carver and Everitt. "Clear the area as soon as possible," Greensboro police radioed the team. Wise thought the directive to leave Morningside was "unusual because it was unexplained."[3]

11 a.m.

The two tactical squads of police responsible for protecting the rally went to lunch.

"KKK, everything okay?" Eddie Dawson radioed over his CB from the lead car of the Klan/Nazi caravan.

11:06 a.m.

Detective Rooster Cooper in the surveillance car on Randleman Road radioed the Greensboro Police Department about the Nazi/Klan activity: "Okay, you got eight vehicles parked and loaded on the ramp from down where we went this morning. They're on the ramp of [Interstate] 85 and [Route] 220. Looks like about 30 or 35 people, maybe not that many in the vehicles. So, we're gonna stand by here and kinda monitor them, see what they do."

Nazi Jack Fowler drove up in a blue Ford Fairlane whose trunk was a weapons arsenal. Eddie Dawson positioned the Fairlane at the rear of the caravan.

11:13 a.m.

Detective Cooper radioed to the GPD: "We're rolling now, headed that direction from this location. There's a total of nine vehicles."

11:16 a.m.

Detective Cooper: "On [Route] 29 now, approaching Florida Street."

Eddie Dawson led the caravan, Klan leader Virgil Griffin rode in the middle car, and Nazi leader Roland Wayne Wood sat in the last car with Jack Fowler.

11:19 a.m.

Detective Cooper: "Turning on Willow Road." One block from Carver and Everitt, Roland Wayne Wood announced into his CB radio, as the caravan turned down Everitt Street and entered Morningside Homes: "Heading into Niggertown."[4]

Paul ■ It must have been a few minutes after eleven o'clock. Sandi Smith arrived with a carload of people from Kannapolis. Sandi was a beautiful woman who even in old clothes always looked elegant. Sandi's high cheekbones and fierce gaze made her look like a warrior. She was smiling when she first arrived, but as she looked around, her face became stern.

"Where are the cops?" Sandi asked me. Sandi was savvy, an intuitive organizer who had a sixth sense for trouble.

We had a tense but consistent relationship with the police. They usually gathered in a swarm around us at least an hour before a march. They usually made no bones about what they thought of us. For this demonstration, they had grudgingly issued us a permit that specified that we were to carry no weapons. Most of us complied. After all, the police were there to protect us.

But where were they? There was no officer in sight.

Sally ■ Suddenly, a caravan of cars appeared, slowly driving toward us. Who were they? What were they doing? Why were they here? The cars were filled with whites, mostly men, some young, some middle-aged.

Then I saw the Confederate-flag license plate—it was the Ku Klux Klan! Fear swept over me. Where were the cops?

A big old Buick drew near me. A thin little teenaged girl wedged between four young white men stuck her head out the window. Our eyes locked, and she shrieked at me, "Dirty kike!" I heard other obscenities, "Nigger!" "Nigger lover!" Our group began chanting, "Death to the Klan! Death to the Klan!"

I prayed the cars would just pass us and keep moving away from us.

Paul ■ As the caravan drove up, people were yelling. I stared at the cars, trying to figure out what was going on. I saw a guy who I recognized, but I couldn't remember from where. Our eyes locked. He yelled, "You asked for the Klan, you got it, you commie son of a bitch!"

Weeks later, I realized it was Eddie Dawson, the guy I'd met two days earlier on the steps of the police station.

Nelson ■ I was standing across Everitt Street from the singing when the caravan approached. I didn't realize it was the Klan until they were right there at the intersection. I yelled and crossed the street to a group of about forty of our folks, bunched up in that area.

I saw a man in the front car of the caravan as he stuck the upper portion of his body out the window. He was holding a long-barreled handgun. He aimed it in the air at a forty-five-degree angle, not shooting at any person. He seemed to be trying to scare people or to send a signal. I yelled for people to move back. As I turned around, I heard more gunshots, but I was not clear where they were coming from. A lot of Klansmen jumped out of their cars. There was chaos, people hitting people. I saw Chekesha on her knees, bleeding from her head.

I was moving towards Chekesha when some black-haired guy charged towards me with a butcher knife. A friend threw me a stick. For a time I was sparring with this guy—knife against stick. I swung twice at him, but I missed. He stabbed me three times in the arm. I heard noise, but I had no sense of what was happening elsewhere. Abruptly, the guy turned and ran and jumped into a vehicle. Just that quick, he was gone.

I took cover behind a car. Then I ran across Everitt Street. I saw a sharpshooter, but he was not looking at me. I had a helpless feeling—all I had was a stick. I crouched behind a TV car for fifteen to twenty seconds. I saw the Klan put their guns back in a car and drive away.

Kwame ■ The caravan came down the street towards us. One of the front cars had a Confederate license plate on it. When I saw that Confederate sign, something inside me said: "There's going to be some mess. I feel it." Something like twenty seconds later I heard a sound like a cap gun, and I hollered, "They're shooting!" And I ran. I remember Ayo was close by me as we ran back into the Grove.

We were knocking on people's doors, trying to get someone to let us in. Some people were shutting the doors against us. A lady opened up her door, and me, Ayo, and a bunch of us Junior RYL all ran into her house. Ricky went back outside to get Vaughn. Vaughn was crying; he was scared. In the house, we just sat on the floor.

I was just so scared. I didn't know if they were going to start to go into people's houses, shooting them. I was just so scared.

Paul ▪ After the first shot, I ran back into the housing project with the crowd. Then I stopped and looked back. I saw César standing right on the corner of Carver and Everitt with a picket stick in his hand, trading blows with the Klansmen.

"Right on, César," I thought, "that's the way to fight."

Grabbing a picket stick, I ran to help César.

Suddenly something tore into me with a terrific force, throwing me to the ground. There was a strange tingling in my head and right arm.

Sally ▪ I was close to where the Klansman fired the first shot. I ducked between two cars. "Take cover!" I heard people shout behind me.

From where I crouched, I saw Mike Nathan loping along a brick building away from the shot. Should I follow him? I decided to stay put, a decision that may have saved my life.

Then, shot after shot rang out. I looked toward the truck where I had seen the first gun fired, but the truck wasn't there anymore. The shots were now coming from the opposite direction, from the back of the caravan. Later, I realized that the first shot had gotten people like Mike to run the wrong way—into the gunfire.

I saw a man carefully firing a rifle at demonstrators. I was in his range. With my eye on the gunman, I dashed across Everitt Street to a safer place. As I ran, I saw Nelson Johnson running three steps ahead of me. I huddled with the TV crews and other demonstrators using cars for cover.

From this new hiding place, I could see several Klansmen, their backs to us, firing weapons with careful aim.

Then I saw César on the corner, lying in an awkward position, his weight on his face and one shoulder. I couldn't take my eyes off him. What was wrong with him? Had he been shot? I wanted to go to him; he needed help. But the Klansmen were between him and me, still firing at people. The KKK gunmen were relaxed and took their time. It seemed like forever before they drove off.

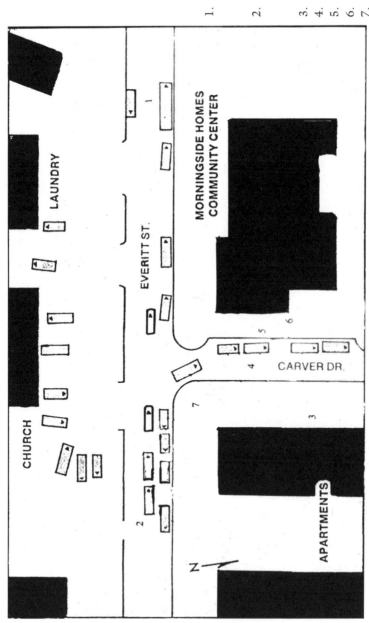

1. First shot fired by Klansman in truck at front of caravan.

2. Ford Fairlane with trunk full of shotguns and semi-automatic weapons.

3. Jim Waller shot in back.

4. Mike Nathan shot in head.

5. Bill Sampson shot in chest.

6. Sandi Smith shot in head.

7. César Cauce shot in chest.

Diagram of massacre scene, corner of Everitt Street and Carver Drive, Morningside Homes, Greensboro, drawn in 1980.

Finally, the gunmen left. I dashed across Everitt Street to César, still lying in that same position. I tried to turn him over, but he was so big. Allen Blitz was there, and together we turned César over. César was unconscious, and there was blood on his shirt. A gush of air came out of his lungs. I took that as a sign that he was alive. But the breath did not stop. It sounded like a tire deflating, not a man breathing.

"We need a doctor!" I shrieked. "Paul! Where is Paul?" I desperately looked around. Then I saw Paul's body. He was crumpled next to a brick wall. He looked like a pile of old clothing. I ran to him, crouched down, and rolled him over. His forehead was crushed, and his right eye swelling. He was mumbling—that meant he was alive! Blood oozed from his head and his arm. I pulled a handkerchief from his pocket and tied it around his bleeding arm, a temporary tourniquet. But his head—what do you do with a bleeding head? I dabbed at his forehead with my shirt. Was I helping him? Hurting him? I had no idea and wished I had medical skills. I kneeled over him, holding him, talking to him, trying to be calm. I looked around for help. Where were the police? Where were the doctors?

I saw Nelson and Signe Waller crouched over a body. Jim Waller.

Nelson ■ When those cars drove up and they started shooting, I knew immediately we had been set up. The police had known that the Klan was coming. They had stayed away on purpose.

After the last Klan car pulled away, I saw Jim Waller lying on the ground. Different people were squatting with the wounded, but nobody was with Jim, so that's where I went. He was breathing very heavy, laying face down. I could see shots in his lower back. I didn't know what to do. I tried to talk to him. He did not respond; he was not conscious. I turned him over because I thought maybe lying on his face was impairing his breathing. Then the breathing began to slow, and then it came to a stop. I pushed on his pulse and his eyelids went up. Then his eyes glazed over. Signe joined me then. I laid my coat over him, but I didn't cover his face.

A police paramedic ran over and said, "Is he still alive?"

"No," I said. "You all killed him."

I left Signe so she could be alone with Jim. I looked across Carver Street and saw Sandi Smith crouched on her knees with blood running down her face. I saw Paul Bermanzohn, his leg moving.

It was the most helpless feeling I've ever had.

Sally ■ Nelson came over to me and Paul.

"How's Jim?" I said, still holding Paul.

"He's gone," said Nelson, his eyes wide with shock and anger. Death was something I had never considered. I went numb.

I looked at Signe kneeling over Jim's body. God, I knew how much she loved that man. I watched Signe as her shock turned into a deep rage. She suddenly stood up yelling.

"The cops did this!" Signe shouted. She held her fist high in the air and started to rant: "Long live the Communist Workers Party! Long live the working class! And in spite of you goddam cops, we will have socialist revolution!"

She ran over and crouched down next to me. "Our march must go on," she whispered to me.

"No," I mumbled, clutching Paul. Shock affects us in unpredictable ways: Signe's grief had made her momentarily lose her mind. She ran off, sobbing.

Tom Clark, blood all over his shirt, came over. Suddenly, I remembered that Tom was an emergency medical technician for Durham County Hospital. But Tom was not usually part of our medical team because we were blessed with so many doctors.

"Sandi's dead," Tom told me almost mechanically. "Mike's still breathing. But part of his head's been shot off."

Suddenly, without warning, Paul rolled over, arms and legs flailing like a rag doll. He was trying to get up.

Paul ■ I heard people yelling: "Doctor! We need doctors!" I tried to respond but an unspeakable fatigue prevented me. I figured Mike Nathan or Jim Waller could handle it.

I saw blood on the grass around me and figured it was mine, but I wasn't sure. Then Sally was crouching over me. My vision was blurry, but I was relieved to hear her voice and to know she was okay. Things went hazy. I must have drifted into unconsciousness.

Then I heard Tom Clark say that Sandi was dead. Dead! That was a serious diagnosis! I knew I needed to help her, but I couldn't get up. I felt like a man centuries too old to stand up. It didn't occur to me that I too might be dying.

Sally ■ "Keep Paul quiet," Tom ordered me. "Ambulances are on their way."

I stopped looking around and just whispered quietly to Paul. My world grew small—just me and Paul. The growing chaos around us disappeared. I looked at the gaping wound in Paul's forehead. The area around his eyes was swelling up with blood. His arm was bleeding. Oh God, I thought, he can't die.

Nelson ■ We all knew immediately that the cops and the government were involved. Dori Blitz looked into a TV camera and said: "The Klan and the state did this. The state protects the Klan, and this makes it clear. The Klan opened fire on us. And we fired back in self-defense."

Dori and her husband Alan both had pistols on them. They lived in Virginia and may not have known about the cops' weapon ban against us. They were among the few who tried to protect us. The rest of us were helpless.

Willena ■ When the Klan opened fire, my sister Annette was driving me over to Morningside. Little Kweli and Imani were in the car, and Annette was going to take care of them while I marched. We got a block away, and suddenly I heard distant sirens and saw something going on. Oh, my God, there's been shooting! I jumped out of my sister's car and ran towards Carver and Everitt.

I got there just as the last Klan car drove off and before the cop cars got there. The first person I got to was a policeman in an unmarked car in front of the cleaners. "What the hell are you doing firing on people?" I yelled at him. An FBI agent behind the car said: "Look lady, I'm not shooting nobody. Somebody else is shooting. You better get down."

I saw the last Klan caravan car leave. The next car to pass through was an unmarked police car. Then police cars started flying in.

I saw César lying there on the corner. I ran towards him. Sirens all over, police all over. But no ambulances.

I was running everywhere, asking "What happened?"

Nelson Johnson told me, "People came in here shooting."

We saw Jim Waller laying face down and ran to him. Nelson turned him over, felt for his pulse. He was still alive. We could see life in his eyes, and then saw it go out.

I looked across the street and saw someone breathing into Bill Sampson's mouth and pushing on his heart. I spotted Paul Bermanzohn with his leg trembling and his eye all swollen—I thought he had been shot through the head. Sally was talking to him; he was mumbling.

I saw Rand Manzella next to César's body. A policeman was holding Rand down on the ground, handcuffing him. "What in the world are you doing with this man handcuffed?" I shouted at the police. "He's with us."

The police said, "I don't know who to arrest, just anyone with a gun."

Rand had a handgun. He said Bill gave it to him after Bill got shot.

So I said to the cop, "He's trying to fight the Klan, and you are handcuffing people trying to protect us from the Klan!"

Nelson and I stood Rand up. The cop was ready to let him loose when another policeman came up and yelled, "Take him!"

I saw the Klan's van down the street with people lying on the road handcuffed. They put Rand in the same van with the Klanners. I wanted to deal with that, to tell the cops that Rand was white, but he was not the Klan. He was the opposite of the Klan.

But then I saw the police giving a black man a hard time. It was Chekesha's husband, who was looking for her because Chekesha had been shot and she was eight months pregnant. I told him I would take him to Chekesha, because she needed medical attention. The police were trying to separate us, but then they backed off. They had to, because the people around them were really getting angry.

Then I heard Nelson telling the crowd what had happened. I ran to help him do that.

Nelson ■ People were pouring into the area, asking what happened. I started to tell people who was responsible. I said: "The police murdered us. It was a set-up. The police disarmed us. They wouldn't let us have guns. They let the Klan and Nazis come in and shoot us. This whole system is against the working class. We need a revolution. We declare war on them."[5]

People were responding, saying: "This is not over. We will not forget. There will be revolution. We must get ready now."

A police officer limply said, "You shouldn't say that."

Then a young guy said to me, "Come on, man, don't let them cops get you."

Willena ■ Nelson was talking to the crowd, and I was next to him. We were standing on the sidewalk facing the crowd, our backs to the street. I looked over my shoulder. There were eight riot-gear police moving in fast towards us. They got hold of Nelson.

Nelson ■ The tactical squad grabbed me. My arms were bleeding badly from the Klansman's knife. The cops said I was under arrest and wrestled me to the ground. I grabbed a chain-link fence. Several put their boots on my neck and kicked me loose from the chain. These scars on my neck are from those policemen's boots.

Willena ■ I hollered at the cops, "Let him go!" I didn't know what the police intended for Nelson, so I started pushing them away from him. But six of them had Nelson on the ground. His arms were bleeding. Police stuck their shoes on Nelson's neck and pulled his arm.

The police said, "Take her too." They handcuffed me.

I asked why I was arrested. They didn't know. They put me in a cop car and left me there.

Nelson ■ The cops put me in a police car and drove off. The policeman in back with me was frantic. "We're going to get blamed regardless," he said.

"Why did you let it happen?" I demanded.

"We didn't expect it to happen here, we expected you all would be attacked at the church," the cop said.

Willena ◼ Everything had all happened so fast. Sitting in the cop car was the first time I stopped for a breath. What about the kids? I thought. I didn't know what had happened to Kwame and the others. Were they okay? Had any of them been hurt?

The police finally came back to the car and said I was arrested for inciting to riot and interfering with an arrest.

The cop—a woman—took me to the police station. She was the most cruel person in the world. As she drove me to the police station, she talked over the radio, aware that I could hear her. She said three or four children had been shot. She was not sorrowful or nothing—she sounded like she was talking about chickens getting shot. I could feel hysteria rising up in me.

Kwame ◼ I was worried about my mama. We sat in that lady's house in the Grove for a long time, it seemed like forever. We were okay but scared. Really scared. I kept worrying that my mama was shot. Then someone came and said she got arrested. I was always scared when my mom got arrested. But this time I was glad—it meant she was alive!

Sally ◼ The ambulances finally arrived. They took Mike Nathan first, but I never saw him. I must have seen him; Paul and I were only about ten yards away. I guess my mind just couldn't let me see him.

Then they came to get Paul. As they put him in the ambulance, I started to climb in next to him. The ambulance worker, a young white woman, stopped me. "What are you doing?" she demanded.

"Going to the hospital. He's my husband," I said, pointing to Paul.

"You can't come," she barked, slamming the door in my face. She looked scared. She looked at me as if I were not human.

I went around to the front door.

"No room!" she yelled at me, slamming the side door. I stood there stunned, watching them take Paul away. Would I ever see him alive again?

My world had shattered. My friends had been killed in front of my eyes. My husband was dying, and I couldn't even be with him.

My emotions retreated to a remote part of myself that I never knew existed. I was in a trance; I could hear and see but could not feel. I lost a sense of time. If someone spoke to me, I could speak back, but I couldn't stay focused on the conversation. Everything seemed far away and in slow motion.

I saw growing numbers of people around me. The cops had arrived now, along with curious people from the neighborhood. Suddenly a feeling punctured my numbness: anger. "The cops did this!" I yelled. "The cops stayed away and let the Klan come in here and kill us!"

A cop pointed his shotgun in my direction. I ducked behind a car; I was afraid the shooting would start again.

Then Marty Nathan came up to me, sobbing.

Marty ■ I had been at the Windsor Community Center, the gathering spot just off the highway. We were just hanging around, waiting for the march to come over from Morningside. Suddenly, Joyce Johnson yelled at us to get in cars right away. I had no idea what had happened. We drove over to Signe and Jim Waller's house. Then Big Al came to the house and said some people had been shot. He drove Joyce and me over to Morningside. By the time we got to Morningside, the ambulance had taken Michael away. People told me about Mike.

"No! Not Michael!" I cried. Inside me was this scream, this unbelief, this abyss. I still feel that scream in my head.

I saw Sally Bermanzohn standing there on the curb in the middle of the crowd. I went over to her—and she told me not to cry!

Sally ■ I remember that. I said: "Don't cry, Marty. You can't cry!" I can't believe I said that to her. At the time, I was thinking, how can Marty cry at a time like this?

I was in a weird trance, and I couldn't deal with Marty crying. I had to give her something to do. "Call the hospitals," I said. "Find out where Mike and Paul are."

I was so out of it, it had never occurred to me that I should have found out what hospitals Mike and Paul were going to before the ambulances left. Just finding a pay phone and dialing Information seemed like an impossible task to me. Marty left to make the calls.

I stood there in a daze. The next thing I knew, Marty was back. "Paul is at Greensboro Hospital," she told me. "Go there right now. They want you there immediately. I am going to Cone Hospital where Michael is."

I didn't know where Greensboro Hospital was or how to get there. My car was surrounded by the crowd, and I felt totally incapable of driving. But Big Al was right there next to me. He drove me and a carload of other people to the hospital. One of them was Tom Clark, who told us he had birdshot wounds all over his legs. As the car pulled into the hospital parking lot, I jumped out and ran towards the emergency-room doors, mumbling to myself, "No, no, no, no . . ."

Inside the ER, a nurse pointed to a bed. Paul was lying there, unconscious but breathing, dressed in nothing but a hospital gown. A doctor approached me with a medical form, which I signed immediately, giving him permission to operate. He said there was a bullet wound in Paul's forehead and another in the back of his head, and he didn't yet know if one bullet went through his brain or if there were two separate wounds. Another bullet had pierced his right arm. The doctor poked Paul in the arm and leg and pointed out that there was no response on his left side. Paralysis seemed so unimportant. "Save his life!" I begged the doctor.

Medical personnel wheeled Paul into surgery, and I went into the waiting room. I sat there, numb, for five hours. I had blood all over my clothes, but I didn't think about that at all. There must have been other people in the waiting room, but I don't remember them. I vaguely remember Tom Clark and other friends checking on me. Several strange men said they were detectives, but I refused to talk to them.

Nelson ■ The police first took me to the hospital. I was in the ER for three hours. They stitched up my arm and put a splint on it. A policeman came in to interrogate me, but the nurse literally threw him out. "There will be no questions here," she said. "This is an emergency room and this is a patient being treated."

From there, the cops took me downtown to jail. There were lawyers down there, and they told me I was under a $500 bond but I couldn't be released for twelve hours. They situation was volatile, and the cops said I "represented a danger to the people." Then the guards took me to the jail cell. I had some discussion with the prisoners.

Around 10 p.m., they brought me down to the basement. Two civilian-dressed men were there—one FBI, the other a detective. The FBI threw his badge down. He started asking questions.

I told him, "I have nothing to say."

He had a tape recorder on the table. He said, "I'm Officer Somebody, and with me is . . ." He wanted me to say my name. The only thing I said was I wasn't going to talk. I leaned back against the wall and closed my eyes.

He said: "Are you tired? I'll kick this damn chair out from under you."

I didn't respond.

"How are your wounds doing?" he said. "I'll tear the bandages and reopen them damn wounds."

It was almost a television scene. He shifted his approach and said: "Whether you realize it or not, you are in a little trouble. There are three hundred to four hundred rednecks out there with your name on their lips. And they're not all Klan."

He was trying to make me think masses of white people were after me.

"You're a marked man, your name is on the lips of every Klansman in the state. Your days are numbered, and the best thing is for you to cooperate with me."

I said nothing. After fifteen minutes, he said to the guard, "Take him back up."

I asked for my medicine. My wounds were hurting, and they had given me pain medicine to take at the hospital. "Get the hell up there—we'll bring it," they said. Which they didn't. I got the medicine on the way out of jail the next day.

Willena ■   At the police station, they took me to a room downstairs. There was a big two-way mirror in it. At first I thought it was just a mirror, but then I saw it flicker when they opened and closed the door.

I was worried about the children. I tried not to think about them.

Then two men came in, an FBI agent and a Greensboro detective. They asked me a lot of questions—who I was, my address, telephone number. I wouldn't say anything.

"Willena, look, if you want us to find who did this to your friends, you have to cooperate. You may not believe this, but we want to help."

I snickered and looked down at my legs.

"Did you see it? Did you see who shot first?" I thought they meant which Klansman shot first.

"You're not cooperating."

"You sons of bitches did it—deal with yourself," I blurted out. This was against my plan, which was to say nothing.

They tried more stuff to get me to respond. "What did you see? Why do you think *we* did it?"

To keep from getting mad and saying something, I just focused on my childhood back on the farm, things that happened back then.

Then the two men left and closed the door, leaving me in the room. I had no one to talk to. I couldn't find out about anything. Everything went blank—I must have blacked out.

Then I drifted back to the room. I remembered where I was and what had happened. I wondered if Paul could be saved. I thought about Bill and hoped maybe Dale and the others had revived him. I thought about César and Jim. I had heard about Sandi, but I never saw her. I was still trying not to think about the children.

I got arrested at ten minutes to twelve, and I stayed in that little room until four o'clock in the afternoon. I could see a clock when they opened the door. The whole time, I worried about the children.

Finally they took me over to the magistrate. They dropped the "inciting to riot" charge, leaving "interfering with arrest." They told me that two people were trying to bail me out. This was a relief, because I was afraid no one knew where I was.

My sister Annette came and got me out. She told me that the kids were all okay. Then we went to a friend's house, where I found Kwame. He was crying, but all right.

Kwame ■ We stayed at that lady's house in the Grove a long, long time. Finally our friend Doris came, and she took us out the back door and through a section of the projects. We were all quiet. Then we came up on a little path that took us right beside a little store, and we crossed the street and went to Doris's house.

Finally, my mama came! It was dark. Mom took me to Signe and Jim Waller's house. All the fear came right back. I couldn't believe it. All the people who had gotten killed I knew. I had been at Bill and Dale Sampson's house. Here we were at Jim and Signe's house, where Jim helped me when my eyes hurt. And Sandi Smith—she lived with Nelson and Joyce Johnson, and we were over there all the time.

The grownups tried to put us kids to sleep. They put us in Signe and Jim's bedroom—where Jim had gotten up alive that morning! The grownups were trying to get me to go to sleep. I kept hearing people in the kitchen, which was the next room. They were having some kind of argument. I kept hearing loud noises and waking up. I was in a half-state of sleep. Finally I just woke up.

It was real late when I left with my mom from Signe's house. When they brought us outside, I saw one of our friends with a shotgun, guarding us. I saw that we had to be armed. It all had a big impact on me. I was young, and it really scared me. Shook me up real bad.

Sally ■ Paul was in surgery for hours. Through the waiting-room window, I saw the sky get dark. After a long time, I felt the need to pee. In the ladies' room, I remembered that I was pregnant—I had forgotten about it all day. I will miscarry this baby, I thought. I am not even three months pregnant. How can a fetus survive all this? Then I put it out of my mind.

For a moment, I remembered Leola, my two-year-old. I knew that my friends in Durham would take care of her. She was my flesh and blood, but I couldn't think about her.

A motherly nurse came up to me and asked in a soft southern accent if I wanted to call Paul's parents. I said, "No. God, no."

I sat there stunned, suspended in time. The nurse came back and again asked me about calling Paul's folks. Again I said no. The nurse persisted, stating, "Then they are going to find out on the news."

The news? I hadn't thought about the news. I could see Tema and Leib, Paul's parents, sitting in their little kitchen in the public housing project in the Bronx, watching TV: "The Ku Klux Klan kills demonstrators. Paul Bermanzohn shot in the head."

Okay, I had to call them. I followed the nurse to the phone booth. I dialed the number and Tema picked up. What was I going to say?

"Hullo," she said in her thick Eastern European accent. "Everything all right?"

"Paul's been shot," I said.

"What?" she screamed with alarm.

I paused. I couldn't tell her Paul's life was hanging by a thread.

"Shot in the arm," I said. "He's in surgery right now, and he will be okay. I'll call you later."

I paused, waiting for her response. But she had already hung up.

What a liar I was! It was true he was shot in the arm. I just left out the part about his head.

In the phone booth, it occurred to me that there were other calls I should make. I called my parents. I told them the truth. They were horrified and told me they would drive down the next morning to see me.

I also called Communist Workers Party office in New York. They couldn't believe it and said they would come down to North Carolina immediately.

Leaving the phone booth, I found a nurse outside the operating room and asked about how Paul was doing. The operation must have been going on for hours by now.

"It's touch and go," she said. "The main thing he has going for him is youth and vigor, and that can make the difference between life and death."

I sat and sat. Finally, the nurse told me that Paul had survived the surgery. She took me to a small room. Dr. Deaton, the surgeon, appeared and told me that Paul was in "very critical" condition. Deaton said that he had cracked open the entire top of Paul's skull to remove the bullet fragments from his brain. He had removed a third of the right frontal lobe of Paul's brain. He left some embedded bullet fragments in Paul's brain, figuring that it was safer to leave them in than destroy more brain tissue taking them out. Even though Paul had survived the surgery, all kinds of things could still go wrong. Brain swelling and infection were the greatest dangers—either one could kill him. The doctor ended our talk by saying that Paul had about a fifty-fifty chance of survival.

A nurse led me into the intensive care unit. Paul had bandages all over his head and arm. Tubes ran into his throat and nose and into his arm. The nurse told me that he was in and out of consciousness.

"Talk to him softly," she said. "And hold his right hand. Ask him to squeeze your hand if he hears you."

I did as told. Paul squeezed my hand. He was alive! A feeling suddenly washed over me, an overwhelming wave of love, of hope: Paul might live!

The nurse told me she would be watching him all night. I stumbled out of the ICU and lay down on a couch just outside the door. I slept, still wearing my bloody clothes.

Nelson ■ In jail that night, I managed to see the headlines of a newspaper. It said the Klan killed four people. I spent all night thinking about that. I didn't know who was dead, except Jim Waller, who took his last breath in my arms. I didn't know who was alive.

I remembered eating breakfast with Jim and Signe that morning, how excited Jim was, how nervous he was about the speech he was going to give at our anti-Klan conference.

I stayed awake all night, trying to figure out what had happened. I thought about the discussions I had had with the cops, Gibson and Hampton. I became more and more certain that the cops were involved in a planned, calculated murder.

Marty ■ Mike went into surgery at Cone Hospital. When he came out of surgery, he lay on a hospital bed, attached to machines. He was swathed in bandages. His head was swelling up like a balloon.

I stroked his hand softly. "I'm here, Michael," I whispered, "I'm here. Leah's fine. I love you. Please don't die."

But the doctors told me Mike had fragments of buckshot throughout his brain.

They told me he was brain-dead, and they showed me the X-ray. His heart was beating only because a respirator kept pumping air into his lungs.

I took a shower in the bathroom of Mike's hospital room. I had been breast-feeding Leah, and my breasts were swollen hard and caked with dried milk. I stood in the shower, trying to let the hot water take away the aching.

I lay on the floor of Mike's hospital room next to his bed and just bawled. Fitfully, I slept on that hard floor, crying, crying.

Gallery III.
Greensboro Massacre,
November 3, 1979

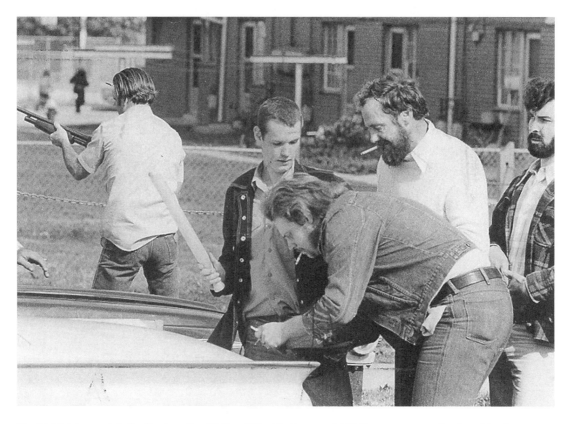

David Matthews, *left,* fatally shot Jim Waller, Mike Nathan, and Bill Sampson seconds after this photo was taken. "I got three," he told Harold Flowers just after the shootings. Other gunmen in photo, *from right,* Lawrence Gene Morgan, Roland Wayne Wood, Jack Fowler, and Claude McBride. In the background, people flee as Klansmen and Nazis unload weapons from the car trunk. (Courtesy of *News & Record,* Greensboro, N.C.)

Demonstrator Rand Manzella kneeling over César Cauce watches the Klan/Nazi caravan drive off. Jerry Paul Smith shot César point-blank in the chest; he died still holding a picket stick, defending demonstrators. Rand holds a handgun owned by Bill Sampson, also killed by the Klan and Nazis. (Courtesy of *News & Record*, Greensboro, N.C.)

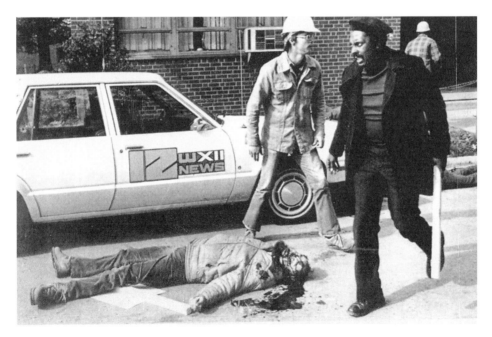

Michael Nathan lies in a pool of blood, dying from a shot in the head. March leader Nelson Johnson and other demonstrators look for victims and Klansmen. Next to building, out of sight, Sandi Smith died of a bullet shot between the eyes. WXII-TV was among the news media that caught the massacre on videotape. (Courtesy of *News & Record*, Greensboro, N.C.)

Nelson Johnson kneels over Jim Waller, dead of gunshot wounds to the back. (Courtesy of *News & Record*, Greensboro, N.C.)

Sally Bermanzohn crouches above Paul Bermanzohn, shot in the head and arm. Paul survived, permanently paralyzed on his left side. (Courtesy of *News & Record*, Greensboro, N.C.)

Kate White comforts Jim Wrenn, who survived gunshot wounds to the head and chest. (Courtesy of *News & Record*, Greensboro, N.C.)

Dale Sampson and Tom Clark try in vain to save Dale's husband, Bill Sampson, shot through the lungs. (Courtesy of *News & Record*, Greensboro, N.C.)

After the massacre, Greensboro police arrest occupants of the last car in the Klan/Nazi caravan. Police took no action to protect the demonstrators. Weeks earlier, the Greensboro Police Department gave a copy of the demonstrators' parade permit to Edward Dawson, a Klansman and police informant, who organized and led the caravan and told the police and FBI of the attackers' plans. On November 3, police followed the caravan to the Morningside neighborhood where the demonstrators gathered, as the police command center pulled other police officers out of the neighborhood. (Courtesy of *News & Record*, Greensboro, N.C.)

Greensboro police arrest Nelson Johnson, stabbed by a Klansman, and Willena Cannon, trying to prevent the police from beating Nelson.

Floris Cauce and police officer kneel over the body of César Cauce. (Courtesy of *News & Record*, Greensboro, N.C.)

PART IV

Keep on Walking Forward

9
Aftermath

On November 3, the Klan and Nazis had fired their guns for eighty-eight seconds. They killed four demonstrators at the corner of Everitt and Carver: Sandi Smith, Bill Sampson, César Cauce, and Jim Waller. Three others lay in the hospital in critical condition: Paul Bermanzohn, Mike Nathan, and Jim Wrenn. The police had arrested several demonstrators, including Willena Cannon, and kept Nelson Johnson in jail overnight.

The Morning After

Sally ■ At dawn on Sunday morning, I awoke with a jolt. Was Paul alive? In sock feet, I ran into the ICU. Paul was breathing. He still had an air tube down his throat, another up his nose, and an IV in his arm. His head was completely bandaged, including his eyes. It was hard to recognize him in the mound of gauze, but his upper lip looked familiar. A nurse told me that Paul's vital signs had been stable all night.

She took one look at the dried blood on my shirt and threw me out of the ICU. I was a germ hazard.

Nelson ■ In jail, I had been awake all night thinking about what happened. By morning, I was clear that we were the victims of a planned, calculated murder by police and FBI.

It was a military maneuver. The convoy was led by a vehicle which set a slow pace. At the back of the convoy was the arsenal car with the people who carried out the assassinations. Other vehicles were in the middle. The slow funeral-like pace of the caravan and the race curses of the Klansmen drew people to the convoy. There was a signal shot fired out of the window of one of the front cars. All vehicles stopped. This was designed to move people away from the signal shot and back towards the assassins' bullets.

Right after the signal shot, the Klan jumped out of the vehicles and picked fights with César, myself, and others. Some Klansmen fired birdshot at people. All this created chaos, designed to disperse the crowd.

The bunch of demonstrators unbunched, and this made it possible for the Klan to assassinate selected people. It is a classic tactic. You cannot assassinate in a crowd. The Klan acted in semi-military precision, jumping out of cars, attacking people, and then suddenly retreating. I believe it is called an "L maneuver" in military language. Push the crowd one way, then the other way. If people are not trained, they fall right into the trap. The police and FBI knew we were not trained. They knew what our spontaneous actions would be, that our folk would respond spontaneously with hatred for the Klan and do things like kick the Klan's car tires. They knew we would not leave our people staggering. So our leadership was the first to fall. The Klan opened fire, *not* in response to protesters kicking their cars: It was a carefully calculated plan.

In that jail cell that night of November 3, I couldn't sleep. I spent the whole night thinking.

The next morning, a lawyer named Bill Martin got me out of jail. He told the judge that I was not a danger to the community.

Willena ■ That morning, my sister Annette and I were at the jailhouse for Nelson's release. We were very worried about Nelson being in jail. Who knew what those cops would do to him? When Annette saw Nelson come out of the jail, she ran up to him and hugged him 'round the neck. She was so relieved to see he was all right. The TV cameras got a picture of her hugging him, and it was all over the TV that evening. The next day, Annette's boss called her into his office and threatened to fire her for hanging around with communists.

Nelson ■ There were a bunch of reporters asking me questions as I left the jailhouse. I told them that it was a setup, and that the police had participated in it. "I have a message for white youth," I said. "This was not the action of white people, but of a few racists. White and black must unite against this system."

Sally ■ The Greensboro newspapers ignored what Nelson said. The *Greensboro Daily News* had already pegged Nelson Johnson. On November 4, as Nelson got out of jail, the paper on the newsstand carried an article that blamed him for the massacre:

Violence Not New to Leader of Rally

Nelson Johnson, the leader of the protest rally in Greensboro Saturday, is no stranger to violence. His presence at the Saturday violence marked the second time in 10 years Johnson has been a leader in activity that brought death, destruction and injury.

Ten years ago in May, Johnson, a student government leader at A&T State University at the time, was a leader in racial riots at the university and at Dudley High School.

Like the violence Saturday in east Greensboro, the earlier turmoil ended in death.

The article contained outright lies. It blamed Nelson for the murder of Willie Grimes at North Carolina Agricultural and Technical State University a decade earlier. It stated that Nelson "was released from an Alabama prison last spring" (news to his family and friends) and concluded: "Saturday, Johnson was at the center of the action again and has been charged again with inciting a riot. This time four persons were killed and 10 were wounded."

It was the beginning of a press onslaught against us. We did everything we could to tell reporters our story, and then we watched helplessly as the press twisted and distorted what we said.

Marty ■ That Sunday, the doctors told me that Mike still had no signs of brain activity. I knew Mike would not want to be a vegetable. My friends Anne Slifkin and Kate White took care of me at the hospital. They stayed with me, hugged me, let me cry.

The doctors turned the machines off. As Mike lay there, I promised him that I would care for his mother, Esther, and that I would make sure our daughter, Leah, was strong.

Sally ■ That Sunday morning, the surgeon removed the tube from Paul's throat and the bandages covering his eyes. I was allowed back into the ICU because I had on clean clothes borrowed from friends. Paul's eyes were swollen shut, with two huge black rings around them, the largest black eyes I had ever seen. The nurse called it the raccoon effect. Paul's face was so puffy that his nose, normally long and prominent, looked tiny and pudgy, hardly protruding between his swollen cheeks. Paul responded to my voice, but the only word he could muster was "sore" as he pointed to his throat. Then he faded out of consciousness.

Paul ■ The first feeling I had was a terrible sore throat, caused by the respirator jammed down my air tube. I remember getting the bandages removed from my eyes, but I couldn't see because of the bleeding and swelling. The bullet to my brain had shattered my forehead into dozens of bone fragments, all under my skin. I touched my forehead and followed the fault lines of all those bone fragments, the channels and cavities in my head. The ridges had the consistency of Rice Krispies. I would push a ridge, and it would make a crunching sound like I had squashed a Rice Krispie.

Nelson ■ After I got out of jail and finished talking to reporters, I went to my old friend Lewis Brandon's house. Joyce was there, along with a bunch of friends. She told me our children were all right and with my brother, away from Greensboro. We went to Signe Waller's house, which had become our makeshift headquarters.

People from the CWP headquarters in New York arrived. Their guidance was greatly appreciated—our local leadership had basically been wiped out. After talking to them, I went from place to place in Greensboro, from one group to another. In discussions with a lot of folk, it became clear to me that the police and the media had placed me at the very center of these murders. I gave some thought on how to lead a response, but at that point, I didn't know what to do.

Sally ■ We were worried about the other wounded demonstrators. The Klan shot Jim Wrenn in the lung and head. Doctors operated and put a plate in his head, and Jim seemed to be recovering quickly. The Klan had sprayed Chekesha, eight months pregnant, with birdshot all over the back of her legs, and then she had fallen and cut her head. But she was okay, and the doctors thought her baby was going to be all right. Tom Clark, Don Pelles, Rand Manzella, and others were also hit with birdshot, but their wounds were not serious.

I stayed at the hospital with Paul, sleeping on the floor of his hospital room. Lots of people came to the hospital to check on how he was doing. Friends told me that Mike Nathan was not going to make it, but I still could not think about him; it hurt too much.

People told me how Bill Sampson had died. Almost all of us were unarmed, obeying the police permit, but Bill had brought his handgun, and when the Klansmen started targeting people, Bill shot back, trying to defend us. Then he was hit by gunfire in the chest, which killed him. To me, Bill was a hero. I wished we had all been armed.

Big Man came to see me and said that he was surprised by the daytime attack, because the KKK were nightriders who hid their identity under hoods.

Another visitor gave me the chills. He was a lanky white man in his twenties who said he and Paul were co-workers at the Burlington Emergency Room. I didn't recognize him until he reminded me that we had met once. "Listen," he said in a heavy southern drawl, "I got friends in the Klan. What happened yesterday was way beyond the Klan."

The Next Week

Marty ■ After Mike died, I went back home to Leah and Esther, Mike's mom. Esther's whole life revolved around Michael, and living with her was the hardest thing of all. I know that she blamed me for his death, and that she was angry at me for the rest of her days.

It was very hard, taking care of my daughter's six-month-old needs and my mother-in-law's overwhelming sorrow. I was constantly torn, because I knew that this was a political attack, and that I had to fight back.

Sally ■   For a few hours after the massacre, the newspaper coverage was straight-forward. The *Greensboro Record* headline on the afternoon of November 3 was, "Klan Ambush Kills 4 WVO People." The next morning, November 4, the *Greensboro Daily News* had a front-page article written by a reporter who had witnessed the murders, Winston Cavin. In "Without Warning, the Shooting Started," he provided a clear account of how the "ambush was quick, violent and deadly."

But that was the end of the fair-minded coverage. Greensboro's two newspapers, which were both published by the same company, consolidated around the Police Department/FBI viewpoint. The banner headline of the *Greensboro Daily News* on November 4 announced a "Klan-Leftist Shootout" and described it as a "shootout between extremist groups." We were labeled weird and dangerous, while the Klan and Nazis were poor guys who hated communists. The papers turned reality on its head, portraying the City of Greensboro as the victim, the police department as just doing its job, and us as the culprits.

The national media followed suit. The day after the massacre, Sunday, November 4, U.S. hostages were seized in Iran. Suddenly the hostages became the only in-depth national news story. The national media rarely covered events in Greensboro, and when they covered the massacre, they used the "shootout between extremist groups" soundbite.

The murders continued to appear in the headlines in the local media day after day. It was an ongoing hurt. On Monday, November 5, when Michael died, a *Greensboro Daily News* article, "Shooting Victim's Wife Says He'll Struggle Harder," included the following statement: "Two victims of Saturday's shootings in Southeast Greensboro were medical doctors who lived strikingly similar lives—and who even married the same woman. . . . When Nathan divorced his wife, Sally, . . . Bermanzohn married her." The three years between my separation from Mike and my marriage to Paul didn't matter; the article made me sound like a bigamist.

Two days later, on November 7, the *Greensboro Record* ran an article by Naomi Kaufman under the headline "Nathan, Bermanzohn Said on Extreme Left" that included these observations: "They'd been talking about 'the struggle' and 'when the revolution comes' for years. But even those who knew them and thought them crackpots were stunned by their deaths. . . . Paul Bermanzohn . . . is known as a firebrand, sometimes cocky and impatient with those who don't agree with his views. . . . 'I can't help but feeling they had a death wish,' said one woman. . . . 'You had to wonder what spaceship they stepped off of,' said another."

On November 6, one article in the *Daily News* ridiculed our organizing work: "WVO 'Targeted' Cone, Other Mills for Infiltration." Another made us sound like aliens for being fearful: "Anonymous Communist Tries to Explain Dedication."

On November 7, in an article buried on page 16, the *Daily News* for the first time mentioned Edward Dawson. The headline ran, "Mystery Man Got Parade Details in Advance, May Have Told Klan." Eddie Dawson was no "mystery man" to the police and FBI—he had worked for them for years. The paper quickly dropped its analysis of Dawson's role.

Paul ■ I spent days in darkness, most sleeping. I lost a sense of time. I felt so tired, like a ninety-year-old man. I wanted to know what had happened.

Sally ■ The first question Paul asked when he regained consciousness was, "Did anyone get hurt?"

I hesitated. He was still in the ICU; his eyes were still swollen shut. Aren't you supposed to shield the very sick from terrible things happening around them? But I had always been honest with Paul. I told him who had died.

Paul ■ I kept thinking about our five people and my own wrecked body. Gradually, I discovered that my left side was paralyzed. I had to sleep with my left arm on a pillow, arranged by a nurse. I had no use of my left leg or arm.

Sally told me that my parents were coming. That freaked me out. I was really afraid my mother was going to bawl me out, that I was in for the tongue-lashing of my life: "You went and got yourself shot. How could you do this to me? Don't you know you are killing your father?" (I had been killing my father for several decades by now.)

I was not looking forward to the visit.

I still couldn't see, but I could hear, and suddenly the ICU got real quiet. "Ma?' I squeaked.

She hugged me around my chest, the only place that wasn't all bandaged. She said, "Son, I'm proud of you." That still brings tears to my eyes. A really big moment. I had stood up to the Klan and Nazis, and my mother was proud of me. (I learned later that a friend told my mother in no uncertain terms that if she gave me a hard time, he was going to yank her out of the hospital and not let her see me.)

Sally ■ Later that day, Paul's mother told a Jewish friend of ours that she was sorry Paul hadn't married a Jew. I was a shiksa, and she was sure I would leave him.

Nelson ■ The week after the massacre, I got almost no sleep. Greensboro was really tense, and I was in the eye of the storm. We all felt threatened. There was intense confrontation on all levels.

On Monday night, I reported to work at Rockwell Industries. I had been working there for several months on the night shift driving a forklift. Suddenly several carloads of police arrived to tell me I had been fired and escort me off the property. Joyce and I got threatening phone calls to our house, so we moved out temporarily. We didn't know what would happen next.

I had not dealt with the Klan-government axis before November 3. It had not registered in me that these policemen were consciously, with forethought and with malice, setting up something to kill us. The press kept tying our confrontation in China Grove with November 3, saying that the massacre was revenge for us burning the Klan's Confederate flag. But the media never discussed the role of the police and FBI in plotting against us; they ignored what Marxists call the State. But the concept of the State is useful to analyze government, the elected officials, and institutions like the police, FBI, and prisons.

I believe that the State was able to use the Klan to carry out this massacre precisely because our anti-Klan campaign was not a part of a coalition. We were out there alone. Although we had a strong base among working-class and poor black people in Greensboro, our militancy led us to be increasingly detached from the middle-class institutions in the black community.

I was determined to rebuild our relationship with the upper strata of the black community to prevent the police and the media from reducing this to just a Communist Workers Party thing. I held a meeting with Reverend George Gaye, the pastor of St. Stevens Church; Dr. George Simkins, the president of the Greensboro NAACP; and John Kilimanjaro, editor of the *Carolina Peacemaker*. We all agreed to immediately join together to protest the massacre—we left that meeting agreeing on it. George Simkins agreed that the NAACP would call for a mass meeting cosponsored by several churches and the black press.

Then George Simkins got stopped by the national NAACP office in New York. Someone broke into Reverend Gaye's church and vandalized it, and people said the CWP did it. I went to see Reverend Gaye, who had been a friend and an ally for years. When I got to the church, the police were guarding him in his office. The cops were guarding my friend—from me! That's how crazy it was. *Peacemaker* editor Kilimanjaro couldn't strike out on his own, and he basically blocked us from having the kind of access to the main newspaper of Greensboro's black community, where for years I had published articles and gotten fair coverage of my press statements.

In the space of a few days, relationships I had built over decades broke down. If we could have held a mass meeting cosponsored by major black institutions, we could have organized a united response to the Klan and the cops. But the weight of anticommunist propaganda knocked out our initiative. The forces of isolation descended on us with such rapidity and weight that we quickly found ourselves out there all by ourselves.

We wanted to hold a funeral march. The Greensboro Police Department banned all marches. We said we would bury our dead. The central issue throughout that week was whether or not we would have guns at the funeral march. We were still reeling from the massacre. We said we would never again put ourselves in the position of being disarmed by the police and then gunned down. We would not rely on the police to defend us.

That got interpreted to mean that we would always be armed and dangerous. The media boxed us into that corner. There was a press conference every day for the whole week. No matter what else was said, they would get back to the issue of carrying guns. We never said, "Yes, we will be armed." Every day the press would say something like, "The CWP will not disavow that it will bring arms."

We talked to the reporters about what the police did and didn't do on November 3. We could stand there and talk for an hour, and they would reduce it down to "CWP Plans to Have Guns," "CWP Refuses to Go by the Greensboro Police Department Curfew." That was a week in which we were burned into the consciousness of the collective mind of Greensboro in a way that has endured. I think more than any other time, it was that week.

It was a tough week. We had meetings with Mayor Jim Melvin and the colonel in charge of the National Guard and a whole bunch of city officials and finally hammered out a plan for the funeral march, to be held Sunday, November 11.

Sally ■ I was scared and stuck in the hospital with Paul. I watched Nelson in those press conferences and cheered him on. I was so glad he was alive, healthy, and strong.

Marty ■ It was an emotional week. On Monday night, there was a memorial service for César Cauce. His friends from Duke University and his co-workers from Duke hospital were there. People talked about him—what a great guy he was, how much he had done, and what a loss his death was.

I was so impressed with Floris, César's widow. Floris Cauce is the most practical woman I've ever met in my life. Even in the face of César's death, she was able to talk at his memorial about the realities of César's life and death. And I remember thinking, I wish I could be as feet-on-the-ground as Floris is. I got closer to Floris. We shared these deepest wounds of our lives, exposed to the whole world. We talked to each other about our lives, and missing our lovers, and waking up to nobody in the bed beside us. Every day at 5:30 p.m., I would wait for Michael to walk in the door. Every day, I would re-experience it all over again, I would go through it again and again. I felt so very alone and hopeless. And it helped to talk to Floris, who knew exactly what I felt.

Sally ■ A funeral home in Greensboro held a wake for Jim Waller, Bill Sampson, and César Cauce. It was one of the few times I left Paul at the hospital. Lying there in the caskets, they looked so young. Jim had on his favorite red corduroy shirt, which looked so colorful next to his black hair and beard. Bill was wearing his familiar plaid flannel shirt, his hair blond and wavy. And César was dressed up in his beige wedding suit, looking uncharacteristically elegant with his bushy red hair. They looked relaxed, peaceful. Not dead. Any minute, they looked like they would get up and start talking to us.

Nelson ■ I did not go to memorial services or wakes. I was too busy running from meeting to meeting to press conference, dealing with the plans for the funeral march. But I grabbed some time to go see Sandi Smith before they put her in the ground. Her parents decided that Sandi would be buried at their home in South Carolina, but Joyce persuaded Mr. and Mrs. Neely to let Sandi be in the funeral march. So her body was at Hargett's Funeral Home awaiting the funeral march. I have been working with Hargett ever since I've been in Greensboro. (He's the undertaker who lent me a casket way back in 1968, when I organized a protest against the Orangeburg massacre.)

But Hargett's men stopped me at the funeral home door and said I could not see Sandi. I was astounded. "Say what? You tell me I can't go see her?"

Hargett appeared.

"No, I'm not even listening to this," I said to him. "I'm going to look in every casket until I find her. I'm going to see her before she gets put in the ground." I started moving towards the back of the funeral home, where the bodies were.

Hargett relented immediately and said, "I'll show you where she is, even though I'm not supposed to."

I said, "You're not supposed to? Says who?" This made no sense to me. This was how heavy this demonization, this propaganda against me, got. Trying to stop me from seeing my Sandi, my sister.

Marty ■ I put together a memorial service for Michael. I wanted the casket to be open, but Michael's face was so disfigured by the gunshot wound. So we had to close the casket. I remember thinking, How can I make these decisions?

Sally ■ Marty asked me to say something at Mike's service. At first I thought I could not possibly speak. I was having so much trouble accepting that Mike was dead. I grieved for all five of my friends, but Mike was the one who came into my dreams. In one dream, we were dancing to a waltz in a crumbling-down building; in another, Mike was lying on the ground, bandaged from head to foot. I decided to do whatever Marty asked me to.

Mike's memorial was at Scarborough Hargett Funeral Home, one of the oldest black businesses in Durham. It was in the downtown area on the black side of the railroad tracks, near Edgemont, where Mike and I had met twelve years earlier. The service was in a huge room, packed with people who had been touched by Mike's life. I saw Jim Wrenn for the first time since he had been wounded.

Sydney Nathans came to the service. He was a Duke professor whose class I had enjoyed, more than ten years earlier. He later gave me notes that he wrote just after the service:

> I went to the Scarborough Hargett Funeral Home. Greeted by two black women and Mike Nathan's wife, Marty. Marty was stoic, pleasant, greeting people who came to the service, taking their praise of Mike and their condolences with strength, warmth. She asked me how I knew Mike, and I said when he was a student at Duke in the late 60s.
>
> I saw Sally Avery Bermanzohn. (Sally was Mike's first wife, and through her I got to meet him at Edgemont Community Center.) I embraced her, she kept her arms at her side, looked at me. I identified myself, "under this beard . . ."
>
> "Sydney Nathans," she said. "So you still teach at Duke," she asked/ stated, as if trying to recall it herself.
>
> "Yes," I replied. "It's been a long time . . . about 200 years."
>
> She laughed, half nodded, half dissented, I thought. Then she turned to talk to someone else.
>
> Jim Wrenn came in and I was shaken to see him up walking, head wrapped in bandages, wearing camel-colored floor length coat. I went up to embrace Jim. We wept, heads on each other's shoulders, gripping tightly, for what seemed like a long time. His head bandaged, his front right teeth out. It was so good to see him alive, standing, the joy and wit and body and mind still intact. He told me that he had a plastic plate in his head. He still had pellets in his side and had to do lung exercises. But expectation was that his lung would not collapse, that pellets would work their way out. No bones broken.
>
> Jim told me about the encounter. Everything was happening fast, terribly fast. He saw that Mike was on the ground, bleeding. Jim went to help him, running at half crouch, with his right arm and shoulder dipping towards the ground. That's when he was shot.
>
> I asked how long Nelson Johnson had been with them. (I was pursuing theory or possibility of a set-up; that Nelson was an import to heat things up to exploding point.) Jim said Nelson had been with them for three years. A look in Jim's eyes: we weren't expecting what happened.
>
> I went inside and sat down. With the room nearly full, Mike's mother came in a wheelchair (stroke victim), and wailed as she came down the aisle toward the closed casket. First and strongest expression of emotion. Mike's baby came in last. Sally sat next to Marty.
>
> Marty spoke first. She said it may be unusual for wife to speak at memorial service for her husband. Addressed the alleged "inconsistencies" in his

life. A wonderful doctor, who served the poor and unattended, who gave long hours to his practice, who called his patients to see how they fared. A loving husband and father—emotion choked her voice. A loving son. And a communist. Communism was a consistent part of his life, she said. Born of a working-class family. Father died when Mike in his teens. Mother went to work, worked long and hard. Mike went to medical school. Before then got involved in anti-war movement, civil rights struggle, organizing medical students, at Edgemont Community Center. Saw disparities. In clinic, a child came in, got diagnosed, couldn't afford medicine to treat it. Realized you could not treat a gaping wound with a band-aid. Became a communist. The gaping wound was capitalism. Died in Greensboro trying to help. He took a stand.

Sally spoke next. Mike her oldest friend. Knew him twelve years. Like a brother to her. Why did they go to Greensboro? Capitalism—greedy, filthy, disgusting capitalism. Third world ripped off to keep American capitalism going. In U.S., inflation rampant, wages low. Capitalism may seem strong, but is crumbling. There is and will be resistance. Communist Workers Party is part of and will lead resistance. (Some softness, but mostly stridency in her voice.) Not just the Klan in Greensboro—the Klan, FBI, police in it together.

Floris, César's widow, spoke. Calm, apologized that she was not in shape to talk, yet she was articulate and calmed. Half smile fixed on her face. She went to help Mike after he had been shot. Could not help him or his head wounds. Said she was a medical secretary—they do not teach medical secretaries how to give medical aid.

A couple from Zimbabwe spoke. Mike had raised money for refugees—$50,000 worth of medicine. The man said Mike was a father to him, that his own parents were dead. He was formal, we express our condolences. He cannot be replaced. Loss to Africa, to world.

Sang song: "We are soldiers." "Hold up the blood stained banner." Many sang it. Many cried. Marty said, "thank you for coming."

I appreciate Syd Nathans for reaching out to us. It's funny that he was suspicious of Nelson, while people in Greensboro who knew Nelson were suspicious of us white folk from Durham.

Marty ■ Syd Nathans introduced himself to me as if he was one of Mike's cousins. "I'm another Nathan," he said, "but with an *s* on the end."

Some people were already blaming us for the murders. Mike's best friend from high school came to the funeral. He was real mad (and is still mad at me) because it was a political funeral—because we said that Mike died for what he believed in.

But other people were deeply understanding and supportive. Like Judy and Anthony Mushipe, the couple from Zimbabwe. They gave us personal solace and political understanding. They told us about friends of theirs in ZANU [the Zimbabwean African National Union] who had died fighting for Zimbabwe.

Everything seemed surreal to me. I felt like the end of the world was near, that fascism—hell—was on its way. I think that frequently happens to people who face such a shock. There was increasing repression, and for us it was magnified because it had happened *to us.* The whole world had changed.

Funeral March

Nelson ■ That week I totally focused on the funeral march. I felt like I was living between two worlds. I was loyal to the black community in Greensboro, but that pulled against my loyalty to CWP. I lived between two worlds, those of "my people" in the community and "my people" in the organization. The main thing that bothered me was that I couldn't bring people together. In 1969, after the murder of Willie Grimes at A&T, I was able to bring people together in spite of intense police pressure. But in 1979, there was an additional factor. People in the black community were suspicious of my communist friends. "Someone else is calling the shots," they said. They called on me to break ranks, but I did not break ranks. Not a single person broke ranks.

The main thing that consumed me that week was to project the image of being fearless. The Klan, cops, and FBI had killed our people. We were standing for right; we would not give ground. We would bury our people. We succeeded in doing that—and scared the death out of everybody.

Willena ■ It was miserable and cold for the funeral march. It was like the world was crying with us. I was scared as hell about going to the funeral march. For most of the week, it looked like the police were going to arrest anyone just for marching! They really tried to frighten people. And they sure scared me when I saw all those troops—National Guard, state guard, local police. They were in a shooting stance with their guns on us. I thought, They can't kill more of us. But I wasn't sure.

Then I got mad, I went from scared into anger. Why are they doing this? They were talking about being out there to protect us, but they acted like they wanted to shoot us.

Marty ■ Many people were afraid to come, but people who knew the five wanted to honor them. There was a good-sized contingent from Durham, and we traveled in a long line of cars on the highway. The police stopped us, searched every car, and arrested every person who had a handgun. The cops wrote down the license plates of every car, and at least one person lost a good job just for going to our funeral march.

In Greensboro, I walked next to Mike's casket. Next to me was this young National Guardsman. He wasn't mean, but he had a gun with a bayonet that he kept pointing at my head. I felt like that characterized what my life was—walking through the streets with this bayonet pointed at me, on and on and on, through freezing rain, not particularly caring, just knowing that I had to be there. I knew that there was a purpose to all this, that it was important to fight. But there was no joy left. Michael was gone.

Sally ■ At the funeral march, I met Anne Braden, who had traveled all the way from Kentucky. I had heard so much about her, organizing for people's rights for decades in Louisville. I was heartened that she had come to our funeral march.

Surprisingly, the newspaper coverage of the funeral march itself was not that bad. "Funeral March Peaceful," announced the *Greensboro Daily News* on November 12.

But the articles that demonized us continued. Two days before the funeral march, on Friday, November 9, there was a front-page *Greensboro Record* article headlined: "Slain CWP Man Talked of Martyrdom." It included an interview with a co-worker of Jim Waller—a man who was known to be an alcoholic. The unnamed man stated: "The CWP was looking for a martyr and national news coverage." Signe Waller vehemently argued with the reporter over printing the alcoholic's statements, to no avail. The newspaper included a picture of Signe, looking haggard.

Paul ■ It was so outrageous to imply Jim Waller wanted to be a martyr—no one loved life more than Jim. The Greensboro newspaper never portrayed the real Jim. People who knew him remembered the wonderful character he was. Twenty-three of Jim's co-workers from the Lincoln Collective at Lincoln Hospital in the Bronx sent a letter to his father:

Dear Mr. Waller,
We met together in grief and shock, those of us who worked with him, who loved him, who argued with him, who sang and drank with him, who organized, demonstrated, and leafleted with him, who studied with him, taught him, learned from him and were constantly challenged by him; who endured his poetry, his soup, and his constant belly-aching; who were inspired by this loving, hard-working, scientific, compassionate dedication to the care of children at Lincoln Hospital, and finally who felt his mixture of pain and excitement as he left pediatrics to sink roots among the working class, to work as a communist in a factory building for the revolution. While Jim's murder

brought us pain and anger that are almost impossible to bear, we take some comfort from the fact that he lived according to his beliefs, that he got a taste (how brief!) of the political work that he'd wanted for so long.[1]

Sally ■ The press continued its rampage against us. On Saturday, November 10, the *Greensboro Daily News* front-page headline declared: "Slain Man 'Was Firing' Gun at Klan Group, Witness Says."

Who was the witness? Me! There was my glum-looking picture, right on page 1.

I had talked to a reporter the day before. I was still at Greensboro Hospital, camping out in Paul's hospital room. I did not want to talk to the press. But Signe Waller and Nelson Johnson asked me to talk to a young black reporter from the *Cleveland Plain Dealer* who seemed sympathetic to us. I agreed to talk to him because I thought the *Plain Dealer* was a progressive newspaper, different from the Greensboro papers. I hoped that he would write an article that would explain what actually happened. So I talked to that reporter about the five who had died.

I told the reporter how each of the five had died protecting the rest of us. I told him that Bill Sampson had a handgun and had tried in vain to defend us. The reporter looked up at me with a funny look, a smirk. He quickly concluded the interview and left. The next day his interview with me was part of the *Greensboro Daily News* article.

Nothing I said to that reporter was news. Bill had a handgun, and after he was shot, he gave his gun to Rand Manzella, who was arrested for holding it. Rand's picture holding the gun had been in the papers all week. I told the reporter that I had not seen Bill or Rand with that handgun that day but only heard secondhand about Bill's valiant attempt to protect us. But the *Greensboro Daily News* and the *Greensboro Record* reflected the position of the city's elite: Blame us for the massacre. They sought anything to bolster their view, no matter how much they had to twist the truth.

That article made me feel like crawling in a hole and never coming out. I felt so manipulated. I no longer understood the world. Wasn't Bill a hero for trying to defend us against the Klan? But the press had used this story against us. Ever since then, I am so cautious about talking to the press. Every time I speak to a reporter, I imagine every phrase I say taken out of context, blazed across the headlines.

And the media used this and other distortions to build their case against us. On November 11, the *Greensboro Daily News* incorporated my statements about Bill Sampson with those of Jim Waller's unnamed alcoholic co-worker. The headline read, "Police Suspect WVO Fired First Shot."

The basis of this assertion? Jim wanted to be a martyr (Friday's lie), and Bill had a handgun (Saturday's distortion). By this time, the media seemed to have us all pegged: Nelson was a crazy black troublemaker. Paul, Jim, and Mike were loud-mouthed Jews. Signe, the other widows, and I were weird, heartless women.

It took the *Greensboro Record* a little longer—until November 20—to peg Bill Sampson. He had been a good-looking, blond-haired white man. How could this guy have been in such a group of renegades?

Sampson: Did Early Promise Go Wrong?

He had a beautiful face, lean and Nordic, and the kind of awesome intellect heaven grants to maybe one in a million. . . . He was Phi Beta Kappa . . . earned a master's degree at Harvard and was about to finish medical school at the University of Virginia when he went to work in a textile mill.

Somewhere, something went wrong.

Other people who actually knew Bill wrote good things about him, but they were not published in the Greensboro papers. Philip Zwerling, Bill's closest friend at both Augustana College and Harvard Divinity School, had become a minister of the First Unitarian Church of Los Angeles. Zwerling wrote to the *Los Angeles Times*: "It would not have taken many changes along the road, or many quirks of fate, to imagine Bill as a Unitarian minister today, as I am, or to imagine me in his place in Greensboro."

Meanwhile, the Greensboro papers wrote *no* article featuring Sandi Smith. She had resided in Greensboro for a decade and graduated from Greensboro's Bennett College, where she had been president of the Student Government Association. She had led a union drive at Cone Mill's Revolution Plant. She was a young, vibrant, beautiful African American woman shot down in Greensboro's streets. And the *Greensboro Daily News* and *Greensboro Record* totally ignored her.

Marty ■ The editors and owners of the newspapers were consolidated on blaming us for the Klan's massacre. But some newspeople who saw the attack expressed a different view. For example, Jim Waters, a cameraman from WFMY, Greensboro, who shot much of the video of the incident told me: "Some say it was a shootout, but to me it was a complete massacre."

In a statement distributed at the tenth anniversary of the massacre, Lee Mortimer, a resident of Greensboro and radio reporter in nearby High Point, wrote:

The Klansmen and Nazis came to Greensboro clearly intending to kill people. They methodically unloaded an arsenal of pistols, shotguns, and automatic rifles from their vehicles and opened fire on the demonstrators. A "shootout" never occurred. The "shootout" was a myth created and perpetuated by the *Greensboro News and Record*, leaving a perception that Nov 3 was a confrontation by two equally evil extremist groups, which average citizens need not be concerned about. . . . In the weeks and months following—the rest of the media followed the lead of the newspaper coverage. As a reporter for a radio station in High Point, I remember an incessant stream of stories and "the shootout" on the UPI news wire. I tried in vain to persuade a UPI editor to use a more appropriate description such as "shootings" or "killings." He said the "shootout" description would stand, until or unless the trial showed that it was not a shootout. I didn't think journalists needed a court opinion to define the news.

Coping with Living

Marty ■ I was suicidal. I felt responsible for Mike's death. He was right about our anti-Klan campaign. I thought to myself, Oh God, you fool. Why didn't you listen to Mike? Where was your thinking? Every day I faced that question. I would wake up to it, go to sleep to it. I was devastated. I can't even describe how I felt. I still have this image of walking down the road near my house—I don't even know what I was doing, just thinking. I thought of myself as a body that had lost half of its limbs, just a bloody pulp. I thought seriously of killing myself but decided I couldn't. I had promised Mike I would take care of his mother and our daughter.

It was really important for me to figure out whether Mike had decided for himself to be at the demonstration. I spent weeks talking to people about how Mike felt about being there. Was he there just because I had pushed him? Ultimately, I knew the answer, because I knew Mike. Mike was nobody's fool. He went on November 3 because he knew he belonged there; he believed in it. When the Klan came, he went into the fight rather than away from it. That wasn't because anybody told him to do that, but because that was the way he was. Finally, years later, I am resolved to that. It was important to me to figure it out.

Those years with Mike had been the happiest ones in my life. But I knew it couldn't last. We were as close as any two people could be. Those arguments we had just before his death pierced my heart.

Sally ■ I was talking to Mike right before he was shot. I know he was at that demonstration because he wanted to be there. After the Klan's signal shot, I saw Mike run back alongside the building, away from the man with the gun. I saw others running back, and I asked myself, "Should I run back, or should I stay here? Which is safer?" It was chance. People were running for cover, away from where the first shot came from. Mike was running to take cover. And I believe that he saw César or Jim fighting with the Klansmen. Mike went to help them; that was Mike's character. And that explains why the Klansmen shot Mike, and he fell right there on the street.

Mike, along with Jim, César, Sandi, and Bill, were all killed trying to protect the rest of us. They were heroes who prevented the Klan and Nazis from killing more of us.

Marty ■ And I now think Mike would be pissed off that I had my doubts.

Paul ■ I kept thinking about the five who had died. When I was able to communicate a little better, I asked questions to everyone who visited me, and I tried to piece together what happened. It was urgent for me to find out what each of the five were doing at the moment when they died. I had seen César in the moments before we both were shot. People told me that Sandi herded children to safety, that Jim and Mike had tried to fight off the Klan, and Bill had tried to defend us with his gun. Everybody had died trying to help other people. They deserved medals of honor, in my book.

People told me I was the lucky one. At that time, I didn't think so. I couldn't move my own body. A nurse's aide, this really strong, friendly young guy, picked me up and put me into a wheelchair for my first trip out of the hospital room. There was suddenly so much light, it was blinding. He took me to a room where a doctor removed the bandages on my right arm where a bullet had gone through the muscles. When we came back into the room, the nurse's aide had to pick me up again and put me back into bed. I had no connection to the left side of my body.

The bullet wound affected my brain like a stroke, paralyzing me on my left side. After twelve days, they moved me from the hospital to a rehabilitation center in Durham. I stayed at Duke rehab for two and a half months, relearning how to move, to dress myself, to walk. It was a funny experience, because I had been a medical student at Duke. The people who treated me the best were the folks I had met during the union drive—the LPNs, the ward staff—whereas people I had gone to medical school with acted like they didn't know me.

In the rehab, I began to realize that I was seriously disabled. They put me in physical therapy, but there was no "physical" to do therapy on. They would hook my left arm to an exercise apparatus and tell me to move it. There was no motion. The part of my brain that was supposed to give orders to my left side had been destroyed.

Sally ■ Meanwhile, I had to rebuild our family life. I was separated from Leola for twelve days after the massacre. She had been well cared for and loved by our dear friends Mae and Sheila Jones. When they moved Paul to rehab, I had a joyous reunion with Leola.

Leola and I went back to our little house. It looked just like it had twelve days earlier: a mess. Dirty dishes were still in the sink from our breakfast that morning. Laundry was still sitting in baskets waiting to be washed. It felt good to clean up; it got my mind off my problems. But that night, after I put Leola to sleep, I lay down in Paul's and my bed, and I felt afraid. I did not want to live in that house alone.

And we had no source of income to pay rent. I had left my job months earlier. Paul had been supporting us with two part-time jobs, which were enough to feed and shelter us, but he had no medical or disability benefits. We had seen ourselves as young, healthy, invincible—it never occurred to us that we might need savings or insurance. I was in no position to get a job, since I had Paul and Leola to care for and another baby on the way.

My friends Charles and Anne Finch invited me to move into the basement of their house. Leola and I moved in. There was a large empty room, a bathroom, and a laundry room that I transformed into a makeshift kitchen.

I applied for every type of social service I could get, and I learned firsthand about America's fragmented safety net. As a woman with no income, no savings, a child, and a totally disabled husband, I qualified for Aid to Families with Dependent Children, food stamps, the Women, Infants, and Children Supplemental Food Program, and Jimmy Carter's emergency fuel vouchers. Because Paul was gainfully employed when he was wounded, he qualified for Social Security Disability, but the application took eight months.

To get the benefits, I needed determination, persistence, and the ability to withstand humiliation. Each program operated out of a different building and involved its own qualifications and application process. At the Welfare Department, they were suspicious of me. Who was this college-educated white woman who says she needs welfare? If I didn't have mouths to feed, I would have given up.

Meanwhile, many friends around me were getting fired from their jobs and threatened in their homes. Many of us were so overwhelmed that all our energy went into sheer survival.

Every day, I visited Paul and he complained bitterly about the nurses. At first I thought they were mistreating him, but I talked to them, and they said that he resisted doing anything. I realized that Paul could end up sitting in a wheelchair doing nothing for the rest of his life.

Paul ■ I spent my days trying to dress myself. Every morning, I would sit on my bed in the rehab and debate with myself whether I should put a shoe or a sock on my foot. Which went first? I would sit there for hours contemplating this deep thought. And the nurses would be all over me. "Come on, you're missing your physical therapy session. Just put your shoes and socks on."

And I didn't know what to do. I was so confused. I thought the nurses were persecuting me. They sent me to a psychologist, who taught me that to bypass the damaged circuits in my brain, I should always talk to myself and tell myself what to do. Soon it took me only two hours to get dressed instead of four.

I didn't think I had much future. I couldn't even walk. They put me between these parallel bars at the rehab center. I thought they were insane, telling me to stand up on this left leg. I was sure it was going to cave in under me. So I was standing balanced on my one good leg, holding myself up with my one good arm. Suddenly Leola and Sally appeared. Leola yells, "Daddy!" and runs towards me, grabbing me around the legs. My two-year-old just about knocked me over.

Sally　■　Leola was sweet, affectionate—and traumatized. She was scared of loud noises, like dogs barking. They must have sounded to her like gunshots. She had seen the TV news, which over and over showed the videotapes of the massacre. She was afraid of white men in army haircuts.

Before November 3, she was toilet trained. But when Leola's secure little world disappeared, so too did the toilet training. It was back to diapers for six months. She never wanted me to leave her. She talked in a voice an octave higher than before, a piercing little squeak. I cringed every time I heard her and told her over and over, "Talk low, Leola, talk low." I tried to be calm and steady with her, but I was not in such great shape myself.

Kwame　■　November 3 was hard. Some people couldn't deal with it. You go through something like that and it just sticks; you never forget it. For me, it was scary just to see that Confederate flag, that Klan symbol, on the car. But then they started shooting, and I thought they were going to shoot everybody, and I didn't know where my mom was at. Man, that is one of those things I will never forget.

Afterwards, I couldn't digest it. I didn't want to do nothing, didn't want to go to school, didn't want to go to leave the house. I wanted to be gone from Greensboro. I remember a guy who stayed with us to protect us. He put his gun on a gun nail over the top of the front door. Man, I wanted him to get out of the house with them guns. I know he was trying to protect us, but to me that's like we were still expecting something to happen. Like the threat is ever present.

Willena　■　I didn't deal with my kids the way I should have. I should have explained things more, but I was busy. Kwame was very affected. He asked lots of questions. Imani, who was six, was really affected by it. She still talks about how scared she was, how she saw Kwame crying (big brothers aren't supposed to cry). She was scared to ask questions, and no one would tell her things. Kweli was only three, and he was the only one who did not seem traumatized.

We were always meeting at Signe Waller's house, talking about all that was happening. It was a period of intensity; we were trying to figure out what to do. I didn't know if the Klan might try to come kill the rest of us.

I almost shot our neighbor. We had a freezer outside the house. One night, I heard a sound outside and I saw this shadow, and I thought it was a Klan. I almost squeezed the trigger. The shadow moved, and I saw the fifteen-year-old boy who lives next door stealing ice cream out of our freezer.

Kwame ■ I woke up, and here's Mama creeping around the house with this gun. I'm like, "Oh Lord, they came back. They know where we live."

Mama said, "Tell all your friends we're going through tough times, and they don't need to be around the house late at night."

I thought, It ain't over.

At the time I had just turned eleven. I just wanted to get away. I really wanted to go to my dad's. I remember asking if I could go up to Dad's. Mama would just ignore it.

Willena ■ I wouldn't ignore it—Kwame and I were fighting.

Kwame ■ I just wanted to get away—to anywhere but Greensboro. I wanted us to move to Birmingham, Alabama. I was all for the move. I wouldn't have given a damn if we moved to Alaska. But we stayed in Greensboro.

November 3 disturbed my memory. And it didn't stop. It just kept going. I always had fear in me. I didn't want to be around the movement any more.

My mind goes back over and over to that night at Signe and Jim's house, that night after the murders. Us kids was in the back bedroom. We were hearing people holler. The grownups were arguing about something in the kitchen. We were crying cause we didn't know what was going on.

Sally ■ People were arguing over how to survive.

Kwame ■ But as a child, I didn't understand everything. If you see violence, especially against your parent, then all of a sudden whatever it is your parents are doing, you don't want to participate in that.

The November 3 shooting was the final straw. I didn't want to be no more part of this movement. I was wishing my mama wasn't in it.

I even had a small resentment with Nelson Johnson, because he brought my mama into this. But then when I talked to him, I loved him again. But when Mama was going out somewhere with him, I thought, Leave my Mama! Y'all quit being friends!

There was times when I tried to talk to my mama. I said, "Let it go. You don't need to be a part of that."

But she wasn't hearing me. She would try to explain to me, but it was one of those things when people are having a disagreement. Most of the time both of them are so intent on getting their point across that neither one hears the other. 'Cause for me, at that time, there was nothing that she could say that could make me see why she needed to be in that. So most of the time when she was explaining to me, I wasn't even listening.

After November 3, me, Ayo, and Akua [Nelson and Joyce Johnson's daughters] were targeted by the kids in school because everybody knew our parents. The newspapers were trying to label Nelson the scapegoat. To their thinking, Nelson was the one who led the lambs into the slaughter. And he was still out here, still doing this protesting. So people thought, Oh, there he go again.

I'm sure Ayo and Akua struggled with Nelson to let it go. But it was just like me and Mom, where neither could hear the other.

As far as employment, Mom had gotten cut off bad in Greensboro. Before it happened, Mom was working at Drug Action Council. Just before November 3, she gave her notice because we were going to move to Birmingham. But then Nelson decided that he needed more help here. Mom tried to get her job back, she couldn't get it back. Not only couldn't she get that job back, she couldn't get any job. Mama ended up working at Biff Burger, and from there to all kind of fast-food places and odd jobs. We got help from all kind of little churches. We were really, really struggling.

It was odd because before November 3, life was so comfortable financially. When Billy Sutherland and Mama were together, we had my mother's income and Billy's income. We had a huge house on Liberty Road. That was like a dream house. We had intercoms in every room. Mama would go downstairs every morning and cook breakfast. She would hit on the intercom, turn on a little music, and say, "Kwame, it's time to get up." The intercom was right beside my bed, and I would say, "Okay, I'm coming down." Everybody had their own bedroom. We had this huge living room and a den and a kitchen with isle cooking.

So imagine to have to adjust to living on Watson Street, where we kept the front door shut by a bent-down nail. The latch didn't work. There was no lock. And Mama was going to work at night, leaving me and Imani and Kweli in this area where there were winos and all walks of life hanging out. There were people singing out loud at night.

Times was really hard. We had a little wood stove to heat our house, and there were times the hot water didn't work. Mama would get up in the morning and get the stove going and put a pot of water on so we could wash up. We were on welfare, so they would give us those bags of pinto beans. Mama would always have a big pot of pinto beans on the stove cooking throughout the day. So we would have those beans and cheese sandwiches.

Sunday was like a treat for us, because there was a preacher who would come on the corner of Watson and Gorrell Street and play a saxophone and deliver messages. He would give out sausage biscuits, steak biscuits, and chicken biscuits to all the homeless people. So me and Imani and Kweli would go up there and raid that dude. He had all the sandwiches in a little barrel, and we would go up there and get them. We already got ours, and I told him, "My mama's back in the house, can I get one for her?" We got one for Mama, and she enjoyed it. I think she looked forward to Sunday too, because she would be so tired, she would be dragging. She would sleep the weekend through 'cause she was working some hectic hours at those fast-food joints, just trying to make it. She had three kids on her own.

Willena ■ I had never in my life had a problem getting a job. Suddenly I was blackballed all over Greensboro. I had worked at the Drug Action Council for over seven years, a good-paying, decent job. I could buy clothes for the kids and take them on vacation to the beach or the mountains. Then it all evaporated. I had quit the Drug Action Council right before November 3 in order to move to Birmingham. They wouldn't give me the job back—I had trained my replacement.

Nelson Johnson couldn't get a job either, but at least he had Joyce, who still had her job. I didn't have nobody to help me support the kids, to help me make decisions.

I had to move out of my house because I couldn't pay the rent. I had to move into the cheapest place I could find. It was a terrible street, where people hung out and got drunk. It was terrible that my children were exposed to all that—drunk people, people having sex. I begged public housing to let me into the projects, but they said there was a long waiting list. People were scared to help me.

Marty ■ I was so absorbed in my own problems, I didn't even know what other folks were going through. I didn't know what to do with Leah, my six-month-old baby. That's a complicated thing, raising a baby. I had relied on Michael; he was the pediatrician. And if he didn't know what to do, we came up with something between us. But now I had nobody to talk to and felt so very alone and hopeless.

At the same time, the FBI was swarming at my door. A friend of mine chased them away by telling them that I had a shotgun and knew how to use it. And that went into the FBI records, and the FBI brought it up six years later. In the first weeks after November 3, there were threatening phone calls and visits by strange men. An unmarked car tried to run my CWP friends off the road. Jim Wrenn's co-worker was found with a hand grenade, and it seemed like it was a setup. Some white man told me he was in the meatpackers' union and he was interested in the CWP. At one point, he wanted me to come over to his house and I said, "No way."

The Fight-back Campaign

Nelson ▪ Nationally, there were initiatives to respond to the massacre. Within a few days, I heard from Lucius Walker of the Inter-religious Foundation for Community Organization (IFCO), who suggested building a coalition to respond to the attack. Lucius Walker told me he would not talk to CWP, and I made it clear that I was a part of the CWP, that anything I did I would have to do in concert with them. I set up a meeting in New York that included CWP leader Jerry Tung, Owusu Sadaukai, long=time Greensboro activist Jim Lee, and Lucius Walker. We discussed Lucius Walker's proposal, and it was the beginning of an anti-Klan coalition, including labor, community, and church organizations.

People decided to hold a big march in Greensboro on February 2, 1980. It would be sponsored by a national coalition, including SCLC, IFCO, us, and a bunch of other organizations.

Marty ▪ I immediately got involved in protests and coalition efforts in Durham. I went with friends to a vigil just a few days after the murder, organized by the Triangle Vigil Committee. But they did not welcome us. There was tremendous fear—and anger at us, the victims. And we were in shock, angry and suspicious of everyone, and not capable of bridging that gulf. But we decided that we would speak at any opportunity we got. We would work with coalitions and also take our own initiative.

It meant I had to start making speeches. I hated it; I was incredibly shy when it came to public speaking. I developed this ritual. I would write the speech, and then I would imagine that Michael was holding my hand and making fun of me. Mike would laugh, saying, "What's wrong with you?" And I would say to myself, "It doesn't matter, nothing can be worse than what it is now."

Sally ▪ In December, there was a forum on the massacre in Greensboro at the Uhuru Bookstore. It took guts to host that forum, and it made me appreciate Lewis Brandon, who had spearheaded the Uhuru since the early 1970s, when it was one of the institutions that developed during the black liberation movement.

At the forum, on a cold rainy December night two months after the massacre, Nelson talked about our fight-back campaign, Signe Waller spoke about Jim, Dale Sampson about Bill, Joyce Johnson about Sandi. Kwame and Alex, two little eleven-year-olds, gave a lively presentation on their memories of Jim, Bill, and Sandi, and how they wanted to be sure justice was done. Alex was a sweet, awkward boy who idolized Jim Waller, his step-dad. Kwame was spunky, exuberant, and articulate, with a thick head of hair that needed a haircut [see photo in Gallery IV].

People presented a slide show about the five. I remember watching it in the dark during the forum, looking at the pictures of my friends looking so alive. Tears ran down my cheeks—the first time since the massacre I had cried. As I wiped away the tears, I became aware of my growing belly. I felt a twinge, like a frog kicking me from inside my stomach. It was my baby, whom we would name after Sandi Smith. My little Sandy was letting me know that all this trauma was not stopping her from growing into a person.

Nelson ■ Problems developed in the February 2 coalition because the CWP announced the February 2 march before SCLC and IFCO did. That sent IFCO leader Lucius Walker all the way up the wall. And it made it hard for the coalition to come together. From that point all the way through February 2, there was a difficult, contentious relationship with some of the coalition forces.

I can't defend everything CWP did, but it was clear to me that there was an attempt to bury us completely in this united front. I am thoroughly convinced that state machinery was at work to isolate us in Greensboro, and isolate us in any national coalition. In retrospect, I think that when people get in your face about this and that, you get back in theirs. Both sides probably had too much testosterone, and we didn't know how to work it out. We wouldn't back down; it wasn't our style.

People lobbied me pretty hard to break with the CWP. Nobody said that in exactly those terms, but they were saying, "Agree with us on this," "Don't tell that." I consistently conveyed that I couldn't do that, I was a part of CWP. I was not the main CWP representative in the coalition process, but I was the main person that many black activist leaders sought out, because I was the one they knew. There was a gradual acceptance that I was a part of the CWP, which meant that people perceived me as kind of being . . . "brainwashed" is too strong a term, but some lesser term along that line. After they realized I was locked in with this group and I wasn't going to budge, they lightened up and just included me as part of the CWP crowd.

So the coalition came together, and it was hostile to the CWP from the very beginning. The person who consistently stood with us was Anne Braden, a white longtime civil rights activist from Louisville, Kentucky. Even though she disagreed with some of our politics, she did it in a way that showed understanding and respect for us. She was almost a lone voice supporting us.

Marty ■ I was involved in the February 2 coalition in Durham. There was an increase in this trend to isolate us as victims, to try to maintain a "pure" antiracist movement not "contaminated" by communists who had been killed.

Paul ■ The main thing I wanted to do was fight back. It was not a time for fear or questioning. It was a time to close ranks against a very powerful enemy.

I finally got out of Duke rehab at the end of January. I could walk very slowly with a cane. I was so shaky, a breeze could knock me over.

The February 2 anti-Klan march was approaching. I went with Marty Nathan to a meeting about it in Durham at someone's house. It was in a middle-class neighborhood, and there was this lawn I had to get over. It was January, and slippery. It seemed like it took me a half-hour just to get across that lawn. So we finally made it into the house, and then people told us to leave. They threw Marty and me out of a meeting held to protest our being shot! These were people who didn't want to antagonize the local power structure. This put them in the position of being verbally upset about the murders, while they iced us out of the fight back.

Marty ■ When they asked us to leave that meeting, I was so angry, I wanted to cry. We hadn't done anything. We certainly were not disruptive. We were sitting on the floor. I remember Paul trying to get up off the floor with his one leg and no arms because his right arm had still not fully healed. We tried to help him get up. I can't even remember what kind of arguments they used to justify kicking us out. What could you use against the people who had been shot?

A day or two later, I was asked to speak at a church meeting to build up for February 2. Ben Chavis, of Wilmington Ten fame, was the featured speaker. This was a big deal for me because of my phobia about speaking. The organizer (who will remain nameless) was willing to give us one five-minute slot to speak—no more than five minutes. Paul had just gotten out of rehab, and I wanted to bring him to the front of the church because he was near mortally wounded and a community leader. It seemed more than appropriate to recognize him. I gave my speech, and I kept getting these messages that I had gone over the time limit. I spoke for a whole ten minutes, and then I introduced Paul. Ben Chavis, the featured speaker, was really happy about that. Ben and I went down the aisle and pulled Paul up onto the stage. Everybody was clapping and screaming and standing up. Paul spoke for a few moments.

Everybody thought it was fine—except the nameless organizer, who twenty years later still talks about how I spoke too long at the church! To me, it shows how frightened people were and how that fear turned itself into a blind self-protection. Then came the opportunism: they would get more funding if they continued to trash the communists.

Paul ■ At another meeting to build for the anti-Klan march, there was a professor who claimed to be a good friend of César Cauce's. He said things about César that were total lies, and he went on and on. None of us were allowed to speak. I was so frustrated, and my whole left side started shaking. I couldn't control it. Nelson Johnson was standing behind me. He grabbed both my shoulders and squeezed hard, and the shaking went out of my left side.

Nelson ■ We took the same position on the February 2 march that we had taken on the funeral march about upholding the right of armed self-defense. That led, eventually, to the February 2 coalition taking a vote and putting us out. And we said we did not accept being put out.

On the day of the march, ten thousand marched through Greensboro, led by the widows [see photo in Gallery IV]. (Jack Scism's article in the *Greensboro Daily News* on February 3, "Rights Parade, Rally Peaceful," said there were 7,500.) Until the very hour of the rally at the Greensboro Coliseum, the coalition leadership's position was that we would not speak. Our position was that we *would* speak. Ben Chavis brokered the negotiations while the march was going on. We were all behind the stadium, and Ben was trying to put restrictions on the time, what we would say.

Paul ■ The February 2 rally was phenomenal. Thousands of people filled the Greensboro Coliseum. It was my first time back to Greensboro since I had been in the hospital. Sally and I didn't march, we drove. Our march was just getting from the parking lot into the coliseum. That took a very long time.

Ben Chavis introduced me during his speech. Sally and I stood up, and I waved my cane. Phil Thompson spoke for the CWP. He called the four widows to join him on the stage, and they stood there with their fists in the air. Very powerful.

Feelings

Marty ■ During the fight-back campaign, we didn't talk about how we were feeling. We just did the work. I don't think I talked to anyone about anything, except one time, when Sally and I talked about Mike.

Sally ■ I remember that talk with Marty. It was Thanksgiving. How do you deal with holidays when your life has fallen apart? You have a potluck at Marty's house with friends who love you. Floris Cauce, Tom and Liz Clark, Charles and Anne Finch, Kate White, Jim Wrenn, Roz and Don Pelles, and I'm sure there were others. Floris played with little Leah and told us she wished she was pregnant with César's baby.

After dinner, we cleaned up, and most people left. I found Marty in her bedroom, weeping. We talked about Mike. She showed me pictures of her and Mike at their wedding, on vacation, hiking, laughing, playing with Leah. We cried and hugged and bonded over Mike's memory. It was strange to feel so close to my ex-husband's wife.

Marty ■ The kinds of standards and ethics we had set for each other were that personal things don't matter, that it was not "proletarian" to talk about your feelings. In fact, I thought that if I talked about how I felt, I would fall apart into one blubbering mess. And if I fell apart, a whole bunch of others would get discouraged. So I didn't talk about feelings.

We just fought back. We did it with each other and for each other. I just remember going out day after day and knocking on doors and giving speeches and knowing that I was not a full, living human being. I had to go out and do what I could. That was all there was to it.

There was no safe place. Every night I would go back to Leah. For many years, I would go to bed not knowing if someone would shoot into our windows or break into our house. I got Bruno, this enormous German shepherd, who became incredibly mean to everybody else. But he was my savior because when Bruno was there, I was less afraid. I knew he would growl and probably scare the bejesus out of anybody who came into our house.

Paul ■ When I was at Duke rehab, I was afraid the Nazis and Klan would come into the hospital to finish me off. After I got home, I would sit out in the yard with a handgun, sure that someone was going to come down the driveway to hurt us.

But our fight-back campaign was exhilarating to me, a dizzy excitement. I became a spokesperson. People would listen to me who wouldn't listen before. Suddenly, I was endowed with the ability to get people to listen, just because I had gotten shot.

Sally ■ I pulled away from the political work. It was partly because Paul was so sick; every day I took him to outpatient physical therapy. I had to take care of Leola. So I was not out in public; I didn't go to meetings. In awe, I watched Marty, Dale Sampson, Floris Cauce, and Signe Waller carry on our fight back. I didn't think I could do what they did. I was so disoriented, I didn't think I could handle it.

Marty ■ Sally and I were in different situations. For me, Michael was dead. That makes a big difference. I felt that I could do something, that people would listen to us widows. And I'm glad CWP was helping us, because I could not have done that myself. I didn't have the strength, the courage, the know-how, or the will to do that. The Party gave me a sense that my work was important, and by helping me to interface with the world, it gave me a sense of reality.

I was terribly depressed. I spent hours in my kitchen scrubbing the floor, thinking about the big Nazi, Roland Wood. I spent a lot of time thinking about how I wanted to kill the Klansmen. The lack of justice was so frustrating.

It was important for me to work for justice. I came in contact with people and helped plan our fight back. I came to understand what it meant to fit my own personal loss into a larger movement. I learned that "single drops make a mighty stream." I understood how my life fit into the social context, and that whatever the circumstances, I could do something to make things better.

Sally ■ I did do one political project. I went around and interviewed all of the protesters who had been at the anti-Klan rally, everyone who had witnessed the massacre. I also interviewed everyone who knew the five people who died. I carefully typed up the interviews. I wanted to write a book about our experiences.

Nelson ■ I recall an awful lot of fear in the movement at that time. In one meeting just before the February 2 march, a leader of a national group who will remain nameless said to me, "You aren't going to get me killed like you got your own people killed." He said it in a meeting in my presence. That was actually the view some people were operating on.

It made me feel like a pariah in the movement. I always had my own individual peace, in the sense that I wasn't going home worrying about who I am and what I'm doing. People can say that we wanted to get people killed; people can say anything. But I was there when it happened. I'm the point man on this. I know what I did. I know who I talked to, and I know what happened. The problem was, I couldn't get some people to see it. But it's not like I'm agonizing internally. I was very clear on that point.

Sally ■ We, the victims, were clear on what happened. And we were clear on the way Nelson and the widows were fighting back. It was the basis of our unity, which grew stronger through all that happened. We knew we only had each other. Only together could we have any chance . . .

Nelson ■ To come through this. And I would add that we did create a more authentic coalition. It took time. We built it around the Greensboro Justice Fund, which we began during the trials.

10
Trials

*People who commit violent crimes are usually tried in state criminal courts, pros-
ecuted under state statutes. If their victims are not satisfied with the results, they
can petition the federal government to examine the crime under the lens of a federal statute, as in the case of constitutional violations of civil rights law. The U.S.
Attorney General's office handles these cases. Victims can also bring a civil action
for damages; the remedy for damages is money, not a prison sentence.*

*Three trials dealt with the Greensboro massacre: a state criminal trial for mur-
der in 1980, a federal civil rights trial in 1984, and a civil trial brought by the
victims in federal court in 1985.*

Marty ■ Believe it or not, the Klan and Nazi killers walked away free from all
three trials. They were never punished, never spent one day in prison. How can
the justice system acquit murderers who four TV videotapes show firing into a
crowd and killing five people?

Those three trials were all we did for five years. Despite the travesty of justice, we gained a lot, because the third, civil trial found the Greensboro Police
Department jointly liable with the Klan and Nazis for wrongful death.

The First Trial:
North Carolina State v. Jack Fowler et al.

Paul ■ The first trial was a setup from the beginning. As Lindsey Gruson
reported in the December 9, 1979, *Greensboro Daily News* in "District Attorney
Says He's 'Caught in the Middle of a No-Win Situation,'" Greensboro district
attorney Michael Schlosser announced on December 8 that he would try the
Klansmen and Nazis for murder, but the DA stressed at his press conference that
he saw *us*—not the Klan and Nazis—as his enemy. "I fought in Vietnam and you
know who my adversaries were then," Schlosser said. Then he added [referring
to a recent letter in the *Daily News*] that most people in Greensboro "feel the
communists got what one recent letter to the editor called 'about what they
deserved.'"

Aghast, I read Schlosser's statements in the newspaper. He was the one responsible for prosecuting the Klan. We, the victims, had no choice of lawyer in the state criminal trial. I was still in the hospital with bullet fragments in my brain, trying to relearn how to walk. Schlosser could not have demarcated himself more from us. Clearly, "our" lawyer was working hand-in-glove with those who were trying to get the Klan and Nazis off the hook. He was going to try to kill us a second time, this time in the courtroom by the so-called justice system.

Marty ■ We tried to get a private prosecutor who would represent us and assist the DA in the prosecution. William Kunstler, a well-known civil rights lawyer in New York, offered to help us, but the DA rejected our proposal, stating [in the same article by Gruson] that a private prosecutor could lead to a "vindictive prosecution" that could "provide a forum through which the CWP could turn the trial into a political showcase." One of the very few people who spoke out for our proposal was Duke history professor Syd Nathans, whose letter appeared in the December 12 *Greensboro Daily News* explaining why there should be a private prosecutor.

> Editor of the *Daily News*:
> I support the appointment of a private prosecutor to assist the DA's office in the case of the Greensboro shootings. . . .
>
> Watergate appeared at first to be a minor burglary. Not until the right people were asked the right questions did it become clear that the break-in was part of a pattern of wide-ranging White House repression. The CWP view of a "conspiracy" against it may indeed be wide of the mark. Yet one can see why they might be suspicious: the police withdrew at the moment of confrontation; four of the five victims were labor organizers, the killings themselves were achieved with military precision. . . .
>
> That the prosecution should be vigorous is also important. It will have to contend against the notion that the "Death to the Klan" rhetoric got the CWP what it deserved. The provocation theory misses essential facts about the KKK . . . .
>
> Wherever the Klan has existed, . . . violence has been its companion and its instrument. Intimidation is its essence. There is a more disturbing fact. The Klan has rarely risen and has never existed for long without the tacit permission of the community to carry out its work.
>
> Sydney Nathans

Nelson ■ Officials closed ranks against us, trying to hide the police/government involvement in November 3. They spun out cover stories to protect themselves from the truth. Hiding their involvement was more important to them than convicting the Klan and Nazis.

Three weeks after the massacre, Greensboro police chief William Swing issued a report that concluded that everything the police did was "adequate and proper," even though five people were killed in a demonstration under their protection. The chief's excuse was that the police were "confused." He claimed that (1) the march organizers were not clear to the police on the demonstration's starting point, and (2) the police didn't know where the Klan caravan was.[1] Both are bold-faced lies.

First, there was no confusion about the starting point. I was the main march organizer, and on the police-permit application form, I wrote that we would begin the demonstration at the corner of Carver and Everitt Streets. I submitted that application on October 19, 1979. No police officer called me about any "confusion." Officers were supposed to have a meeting with me at that corner on the morning of November 3. Instead, the Klan/Nazi caravan drove in.

Second, there was no confusion for the GPD about where the Klan caravan was. The details in the police report completely undermine the report's conclusions. For hours preceding the murders, according to their own report, the police knew where the Klan was assembling, that they were armed, and that they intended to disrupt the anti-Klan march. Police officers observed the Klan cars in a caravan eighteen minutes before the murders and followed them as the caravan proceeded towards the demonstration starting point. These officers reported to headquarters repeatedly, so that the GPD was aware of the caravan's location and direction at all points. So many wrong decisions were made by so many people—like sending the police to lunch at 11 a.m., even as the Klan caravan was assembling. It goes beyond mere police incompetence and strongly suggests criminal intent on the part of some people within the Police Department.[2]

But Greensboro officials closed ranks behind the police. The mayor praised Police Chief Swing, and several days after that, the city council voted to accept the police report and rejected public demands to fire Police Chief Swing.[3]

I resolved to take every opportunity to explain that November 3 had been a planned daylight assassination in which the GPD and FBI participated. I testified at every hearing, spoke everywhere possible, talked to the press every chance I could. And it fell on deaf ears.

On January 18, 1980, the state court arraigned thirteen Klan and Nazi gunmen, but the DA ignored other people who played key roles in the massacre. There was no indictment of Edward Dawson, who organized the Klan and led the caravan, and who was a link between the Klan, Greensboro PD, and FBI. There was no indictment of the police who gave the Klan and Nazis free rein to murder us.

We went to court to observe the arraignment, and then we held a press conference to point out how the court was covering up reality. "This is upside-down justice," I told the press. "It is the same old slavery-time scapegoat justice. . . . The police should be indicted because they should have warned us that the Klan was coming. The cops should have stopped the caravan. They did nothing."

Then a lawyer friend and I went to the county magistrate's office to get arrest warrants against Police Chief William Swing and Edward Dawson. We knew we wouldn't get the warrants, but we wanted to point to who was responsible for these murders.

Sally ■ State and federal officials backed the Greensboro police lies against us. North Carolina governor Jim Hunt campaigned for reelection in January 1980 as the trial preparations began. He effusively praised Greensboro mayor Jim Melvin, as the *Greensboro Daily News*'s Charles Babington reported January 10 in "Superlatives Abound at Breakfast": "I don't think there's any city that has better race relations than Greensboro." This is two months after Klan and Nazis murdered people.

Anyone who raised questions risked public chastisement. For example, Bobby Doctor, regional director of the U.S. Commission on Civil Rights, responded to the governor's praise: "I don't think five people can be shot down in the street in this city, and all of us go away with the idea there are no problems existing in Greensboro. . . . Black residents here are angry that the police were not at the scene when the shooting erupted." Doctor got roundly criticized for straying from the official line. Mayor Melvin declared Doctor was "irresponsible," and the *Greensboro Daily News* devoted a full editorial on January 10, "What Really Matters," to criticizing him as "someone who really hasn't examined the circumstances in which the shootings of the five demonstrators occurred."

Creative Resistance

Willena ■ The whole thing made me sick. The mayor, the police, the media were trying to revert back to the old days when people were too afraid to even talk. We were locked out of fair coverage by the press.

So we developed our own methods of communication with the public— posters and spray paint! For a year, I was on this campaign to get our side of the story out, and we spray painted "Avenge the CWP 5!" all over Greensboro. Oh, God, that was something; it felt good to do something. A CWP person from New York trained me in spray painting and postering and taught me a lot about how not to get caught by the cops. The next thing I knew, I was in charge of postering in Greensboro.

Marty ■ When we started spray painting, people thought we were crazy, that we had become vandals. But we had lost everything, and the injustice went on and on. We had been marginalized, the press portraying us as terrorists. We kept trying to talk to people, but we were so isolated. Even people on the left avoided us.

Backed into similar situations, other groups had taken up violent actions. We didn't. We just took spray-paint cans, posters, and glue. I think that's much more effective. We didn't hurt anybody. I think if I ever got in a situation like that again, I would do the same thing.

Kwame ▪ I didn't know what was going on. All I knew is that I was scared, and kids were blaming my mama and Nelson Johnson for killing people.

Willena ▪ We first started postering and spray painting in December 1979. Bill's widow, Dale Sampson, and three others got arrested on one of our first attempts. We learned from our mistakes and got good at outwitting the police in all kinds of ways. When we saw a cop car, we turned off our car lights and calmly left.

Kwame ▪ Mama would be cooking stuff in the house, and I'm thinking, Oh good, something to eat. And then she says she's cooking glue so that they can stick up posters!

One time she sat me down and said: "I might not come back tonight. I just might get caught and be going to jail. Don't worry, I'll be back in a couple of days. Somebody will be here to take care of you."

I was standing in the bathroom while she's packing up. She's putting her toothbrush and toothpaste in her pocketbook. I'm thinking, This don't make no sense. People done killed all our people. Haven't we had enough?

Marty ▪ My heart goes out to Kwame that he had to go through it. It was hard on Leah, too. She was only a baby and couldn't understand what was going on at all. But we had to do what we did. There was nothing else to do. It was a way of fighting back against crushing injustice.

Kwame ▪ So Mama would come home early in the morning, five or six in the morning, with glue in her hair. There would be about seven or eight of them— two teams she took out. They're sitting up here in our house, high fiving and talking about what they did and how they got away. And I'm thinking, Why does my mama got to be a part of this? Send me to my daddy.

Marty ▪ I spray painted in Durham. Our teams were bold. My favorite spray painting was the headquarters building of the phone company in Durham. After the first time we painted it, General Telephone and Electric put up a new set of lights to discourage us. So we painted it again—under their new bright lights. We were very proud of that.

Our friends Liz Wilderman and Roz Pelles got caught by the Durham police, and they were arrested, tried, and sentenced to the county jail. Liz was pregnant, and by the time they were put in jail, she was in her ninth month of pregnancy. We were worried that Liz would go into labor in jail. Thankfully, she got out in time. She and Tom Clark named their baby César, after our fallen hero.

Our friend Jean Chapman was also pregnant and a great spray painter in Chatham County, North Carolina. She and Yonni named their baby Sandi. All these little people whose names carry on the memory of our loved ones.

I think our folks were really amazing. We could have fallen apart—a lesser crowd of folks would have fallen apart. Instead, we resisted creatively. Our postering got attention—the Durham paper published an editorial cartoon about us.

Nelson ■ The government continued to absolve itself of responsibility. In April 1980, the Carter Justice Department cleared the Greensboro Police Department of any criminal wrongdoing on November 3.

I held a press conference and stated: "Yesterday the civil rights division of the U.S. Justice Department put its stamp of approval on the assassination by saying the police were 'not guilty' of conspiracy and denial of civil rights. For those who had illusions about the Justice Department, this makes it clear that the government on the highest level is covering up the Greensboro massacre."[4]

Less than a week later, the government brought charges against *us*. The state grand jury indicted six anti-Klan demonstrators, including me, for felony riot on November 3. Two protesters, Lacie Russell and Percy Simms, had yelled at the Klan as the caravan drove up. After the Klan and Nazis shot people, Allen Blitz, Dori Blitz, and Rand Manzella had tried to protect the demonstrators with their small pistols. When the Klan and Nazis drove off, I tried to explain to bystanders what had happened. For these "crimes," we were indicted, arrested, and jailed. Those indictments hung over us until the first trial was over.

The CWP held a demonstration on May 3, 1980, exactly six months after the murders. Right before the rally, I got out of jail on $15,000 bond. I told the crowd that we would fight the trumped-up charges against us, and that any trial against us would make Greensboro even more notorious as a symbol of oppression.

Some of our boldest friends spoke out at the rally. They included Reverend James Barnett of Charlotte, who had been a friend of Sandi Smith; Winston-Salem alderman Larry Little, former Black Panther and longtime friend of mine; and Reverend Leon White of the Commission on Racial Justice, who we had worked with on the Wilmington Ten campaign.

We had another surprise speaker—Paul's mother, Tema Bermanzohn.

Paul ■ My mom represented the Bermanzohns at that rally. Sally and I wanted to go to that demonstration. But Sally was in the hospital having our baby, who we named Sandra Michele after Sandi Smith and Mike Nathan. And I couldn't go, because Sally was my wheels, my left arm, and my left leg.

My mother had just come down from New York City to help us with our new baby, so we sent her to the rally. She told us she would go only if we promised not to tell my father, who was on his way to North Carolina. We promised to keep her secret. My mother went with our friends—and she ended up giving a speech at the demonstration. The next morning, May 4, we had to hide the paper from my father because the front page of the *Greensboro Daily News* had three pictures of Tema giving her speech!

> Tema Bermanzohn, the sole member of her family to escape the Nazis during World War II and the mother of Paul Bermanzohn, compared the shooting of her son, who suffered a critical head wound on Nov. 3, to the initial stages of Germany's attempt to eradicate the Jews.
>
> "If they get away with this, they'll do it again and again," she said with a breaking voice. "Don't say it can't happen here, because it already has." Bermanzohn said the government is trying to make the CWP a "scapegoat" to hide the government's guilt.
>
> "The country should be proud of people like this," she said, recalling her son's decision to dedicate his life to working with poor people in the heart of Durham's black community instead of pursuing a lucrative private medical practice. "They're doing something for people."

I was so proud of my mother. For me it was a thrill to work with her to fight for justice against the Nazis and Klan. During the trials, I feel like my mother came to terms with me as an adult.

Jury Selection

Paul ■ The trials were slated to begin with jury selection. We wanted to be in court to protest the continuing cover-up. We met on the steps of the courthouse, and I was supposed to lead our procession to the courtroom. I couldn't walk without falling on my face, so I was in a wheelchair. Willena Cannon was on one side of me, and Tom Clark was on the other. They were looking after me, because people didn't want me to get hurt. There were several dozen protesters behind us. We went single file to the room where the jury selection was underway [see photo in Gallery IV].

An officer at a security checkpoint stopped us and said that only members of the family of the deceased would be allowed in. I took strong exception to being prevented from going into the courtroom—the people on trial had almost killed me, and I needed to be in that courtroom. I raised my voice, got very angry, and argued with him. Quickly, it became a standoff. The courthouse corridor was filled with people yelling, cops and protesters everywhere. Somebody pushed me, and my wheelchair ran over the foot of the security guard. There was arguing, pushing, shoving, yelling; more than a few fists were swung and people were hit.

Some police officers grabbed Tom Clark and had him in a chokehold. At the same time, they grabbed my wheelchair. I pulled hard to get away, and Tom Clark and Willena Cannon tried to protect me. Over my objections, the officers wheeled me into a corridor on the side. I was afraid the cops would try to hurt me, and I didn't want to miss the action, so I wheeled my chair back to the protest. People were still yelling; reporters were busily scribbling notes. Cops were pulling people, hitting people, and demonstrators were fighting with cops. They arrested Tom and Willena for protecting me.

I felt really good about the whole thing. I thought I wouldn't be able to ever do anything physical again. I had been hospitalized for months and then holed up in a basement. It felt great to be in the middle of a serious struggle, a physical struggle, even though I was incapacitated. It made me feel energized and alive.

This is how the June 16 *Greensboro Record* covered the incident:

CWP Stirs Up Battle Outside Courtroom

A melee between CWP members and police and sheriff's deputies broke out at the courtroom door when deputies tried to limit CWP entry to the trial. The pushing, shoving, fighting and shouting ended after 20 minutes when four CWP members were carried kicking and screaming into custody. . . .

The confrontation started when 20 to 25 CWP members ended a news conference . . . and started toward the courtroom door where deputies were positioned. The CWP procession was led by wheelchair-bound Paul Bermanzohn. . . . When deputies announced that only two people representing each of the five CWP members who were killed would be allowed in the courtroom, the CWP delegation began protesting loudly. . . . Many began pointing to Bermanzohn and demanding that he be admitted.

"I have a bullet in my head and you are not telling me you are going to keep me out of the courtroom," declared Bermanzohn, who is reportedly paralyzed on his left side.

When party leader Nelson Johnson taunted an officer and was told to "hush," Johnson roared, "Don't you tell me to hush."

While shouting continued two CWP members—the widows of César Cauce and Michael Nathan . . . were given permission to enter the courtroom. Mrs. Cauce brushed past deputies, declaring, "You killed my husband. Out of my way."

Marty ■ Jury selection is contentious, because lawyers for the prosecution and the defense try to seat jurors they believe are sympathetic to their opposing sides. Each side is allowed to eliminate a certain number of jurors during the questioning period. It made sense for the Klan defense lawyers to try to eliminate black and white liberal jurors. But we expected the government prosecutors to eliminate jurors who were racist or anticommunist. Instead, they did the opposite and helped choose the most pro-Klan jury possible.

Schlosser's prosecution team asked prospective jurors if they could be fair, given that "the victims were communists, who stood for everything we despise in this country." They allowed jurors with startling bias: a woman who said that she did not think the six Klan/Nazi defendants were guilty, and that she did not like communists because they didn't believe in God; a man who grew up next door to Klan leader Joe Grady; a man who said that he believed that it was less of a crime to kill a communist than anyone else (he was allowed by the prosecution but not seated on the jury for other reasons); and a Cuban American who said during the questioning that the Ku Klux Klan was patriotic and the Nazis were very patriotic. (He was the only jury member with a high school education, and he became the jury foreman).[5]

The resulting jury was not just all white but extremely racist, much more reactionary than the overall white population of North Carolina. It was a jury that was capable of hearing the pitch of the excellent Klan lawyers that the gunmen had killed five of us in self-defense.

Exposure of Federal ATF Agent

Sally ■   In the middle of jury selection, an investigative reporter revealed the involvement of a federal agent from the Bureau of Alcohol, Tobacco, and Firearms in planning November 3—Bernard Butkovich! *Greensboro Record* reporter Martha Woodall wrote a dramatic exposé, published July 15:

'Shortly after Shootings' Undercover Agent Gave Report to District Attorney

One or two days after the Nov 3 shootings the district attorney's office here learned that a federal undercover agent had observed a planning meeting for the Greensboro motorcade, but the information was never shared. . . .

District Attorney Michael Schlosser today confirmed that his office learned "shortly after the shootings" that undercover agent Bernard Butkovich had infiltrated the Forsyth County unit of the National Socialist Party of America and had attended a key caravan planning meeting in Winston-Salem on November 1.

Schlosser declined to comment on whether his office deliberately kept Butkovich's involvement secret.

Agent Butkovich had been involved with the North Carolina Nazis since the summer before the massacre, and DA Michael Schlosser knew it and covered it up from the day of the murders. The article went on to state that the police captain in charge of the November 3 murder investigation had found out on the afternoon of November 3 that the ATF had "someone" involved with the Nazis in Winston-Salem. The captain stated that he shared the information with the assistant DA. The day after the massacre, prison guards allowed ATF agent Butkovich into the Greensboro County Jail to talk to Nazi gunman Roland Wayne Wood. For the same article, Martha Woodall interviewed the police captain, who "confirmed that the [jail] interview took place, [and] . . . said he did not believe a transcript of the Butkovich-Wood session was made. . . . The meeting was not recorded on a detailed summary of Wood's interviews on Nov. 4. And Butkovich's name appears in none of the transcripts of Wood's interrogations even though Wood . . . identified Butkovich in a photograph for police."

So the district attorney's office, the police, and prison officials all knew about the involvement of ATF agent Butkovich, gave him access to the Nazi gunmen, and kept it secret. In the days that followed Woodall's exposé, these officials exercised damage control by contradicting themselves. A *Greensboro Daily News* article, also on July 15, was headlined, "Police, FBI Said Unaware Nazis Infiltrated by Feds." In it, Police Chief Swing said he "knew nothing until several weeks ago." He "did not recall how the officer came upon the information . . . [and] was unaware of reports that Butkovich and Wood were allowed to confer alone at the police department on Nov 4." The Treasury Department, which oversees the ATF, said that an investigation of Butkovich's activities "found nothing inappropriate in his role as an undercover agent." An ATF spokesman stated: "Just assume he was there for a good reason, that's what he is paid to do." He declined to elaborate because "it might jeopardize a future case."

Paul ■ Trial preparations were under way when the ATF's involvement was exposed. On the same day as Woodall's article, the court released a list of 273 possible witnesses to testify in the trial. The list did *not* include ATF agent Butkovich, *nor* police informant Eddie Dawson, *nor* FBI agents. Reporters asked the DA if Butkovich's name would be added to the witness list, and, as Martha Woodall reported in "Undercover Agent Gave Report to District Attorney" in the July 15, 1980, *Greensboro Record*, "Schlosser reaffirmed that the state did not plan to call Butkovich to testify."

Instead, the witness list included the names of the CWP national leadership, who had not even been in North Carolina on November 3! It looked less and less like a murder trial, and more and more like an anticommunist witch-hunt.

Marty ■ All we could do was protest. A few days later, we demonstrated at the Bureau of Alcohol, Tobacco, and Firearms offices in Charlotte. It was a coordinated action with CWP people in New York City, Chicago, Los Angeles, San Francisco, Denver, Baltimore, Washington, D.C., and other cities. While people picketed outside the Charlotte ATF office, several of us went inside, up the elevator, and asked to speak to John Westra, the head agent in North Carolina. He was a huge man with a thick neck, green tie, and an ugly checked suit. I stood in his face and just ranted at him about Michael being killed and the ATF's responsibility. Then we turned around and went back to our friends in the picket line outside.

Our demonstrations led to reporters asking officials about ATF involvement in the murders. But officials continued to stonewall. U.S. Attorney Mickey Michaux in North Carolina said his office planned *no* investigation. "My understanding is that Butkovich was here investigating gun-running activities tied to individual Nazis and that was his sole purpose," he told the *Greensboro Record,* as reporter Rice Stewart reported July 24 in "CWP Staging Protests to Expose Agent's Role."

So we kept up our creative disruptions. President Jimmy Carter was running for reelection, and Rosalyn Carter spoke at a fund-raiser at Wake Forest University in North Carolina. I got all dressed up, and they allowed me into the fund-raiser. When Rosalyn started talking, I interrupted her, yelling, "Your husband is responsible for murdering my husband." Secret Service grabbed me, removed me from the room, and drove me away and dumped me out somewhere in the middle of nowhere. I had no idea where I was but found a pay phone and called friends, who came to get me.

Out of context, it looks stupid to attack the Democratic Party during the 1980 campaign that ultimately elected Ronald Reagan. But the press and the public seemed completely uninterested in the government involvement in the atrocity against us. Our people had been killed; survivors had been kicked out of jobs and threatened. The state was planning to try six of our folks for felony riot charges with possible prison sentences of twenty years apiece. We were angry and in deepest grief.

Nelson ■ Despite the investigative reporting by a few good reporters like Martha Woodall, officials and newspaper editors tried to quickly bury the story without looking at its implications, without probing for more information. So we continued with our own means to tell the public about the new evidence.

A week after the Butkovich revelations, I confronted Governor Jim Hunt at a press conference in Raleigh. I walked right up onto the stage where Hunt was and charged him with being part of the cover-up. Our eyes locked; I saw his lips tremble. The Secret Service came towards me, and I said to them, "Don't touch me!" Then I walked off the stage and out through the door and into the store next door, completely evading the police.

A few days later, Dale Sampson, Signe Waller, and I spoke at the Greensboro

City Council to raise the issue of Greensboro mayor Jim Melvin's complicity. Dale spoke directly to Melvin: "You have the blood of my husband on your hands." The police arrived just as Signe and Dale were speaking and arrested them for disorderly conduct.

Nelson in Jail

Marty ■ A day before the state murder trial was scheduled to open, we held a little rally in front of the courthouse. Nelson climbed up on this platform on the plaza in front of the courthouse and said what we had been saying all along, that it was a conspiracy and the police were in on it. Suddenly, two columns of police marched up and grabbed him.

Nelson ■ As eight or ten cops charged me, I was saved by a big, black cop who bear-hugged me from behind. He just threw his big arms around me and jerked me back and forth. He was talking in my ear, saying: "I got you little brother. I got you. I got you." He was actually keeping the other cops from beating me.

I felt his spirit; I knew he was protecting me. He didn't want it to be known, and I didn't either (I've never seen him before or since). He had me tight, and he was right on my ear calling me "little brother." He was telegraphing me that he was going to keep them from beating me, but I had to let him take charge. And that's how I came out of that scuffle with my legs.

This is how Steve Berry and William March at the *Greensboro Daily News* covered it on August 2 in "Higher Bond Sought for CWP Leader": "Johnson climbed on top of a monument on the plaza and shouted obscenities. When police Captain Larry Gibson asked him to stop, Johnson refused and then assaulted Gibson when Gibson tried to arrest Johnson."

I did not assault Gibson; he assaulted me. And I had not cursed, because I do not curse. Cursing is not part of my upbringing.

Marty ■ I cursed. Cursing *is* part of my family's tradition. I was standing fairly close to Nelson when the cops attacked him. I saw Gibson—the same cop who gave a copy of our police permit to the Klan—punch Nelson in the stomach. I started cursing at the cops, telling them to get their hands off Nelson. So the cops arrested me too.

I'm proud to be arrested for trying to help Nelson. It was the first time I had ever been arrested for anything. It was scary, but important. The system was laid bare to me. It had killed the person I loved most in the world. It was important for me to personally face down the murderers.

Nelson ■ They threw me in jail for speaking the truth. They were trying to silence me. DA Schlosser requested raising my bond by $100,000. It was already at $15,000 from the federal indictments.

Marty ■ The audacity of the courts to raise Nelson's bond to $115,000! The highest bond for the Klan murderers was $52,000. Nelson was on bond for twice the amount of murderers—for the crime of speaking the truth.

Nelson ■ The cops wrote me up as a danger to myself and to the community. That is the closest thing to being declared insane. Once you are declared as a danger to yourself, it is like, "We got a crazy man here." They wanted to keep me in jail under that huge bond that was more money than any of us had. At the bond hearing, the assistant DA pointed at me and stated that I was "morally responsible" for the murder of the five! He said that I precipitated events and left others to be killed or injured. It was too much. I tried to speak; the judge ordered me to be quiet. My supporters in the courtroom expressed outrage. So did I. The judge ordered the deputies to remove me from the court.

Willena ■ I was at Nelson's bond hearing. When the assistant DA started calling Nelson the devil, Nelson turned to the people sitting in the court and tried to say what really happened on November 3. Then the guards grab Nelson, hit him, and dragged him back to jail.

Our Dilemma: Refuse to Testify?

Marty ■ While Nelson was in jail, the trial of the Klan and Nazis began. The jury had been selected and was set to be impaneled on August 4, 1980. All our names were on the witness list. We had to decide whether or not to testify, whether or not to participate in this trial. It was a big decision, because refusing to testify is contempt of court, punishable by jail time. And the sentence for contempt of court is indefinite—they can hold you 'til hell freezes over.

Paul ■ We had to assess both sides. The argument to testify was that we could add information to help convict the killers. But what evidence could I add? I had gotten shot in the head, but I had not seen who shot me. I had not seen any of the killers. The DA meanwhile had lots of evidence against the Klan and Nazis: the TV videotapes, the police photographs. As Rick Stewart reported in "Nazi Quotes 2 Comrades' Saying They 'Got' Some," in the *Greensboro Record*, September 10, the Klansmen and Nazis had bragged to each other about killing people as they were leaving Carver and Everitt Streets. Roland Wayne Wood told police after his arrest that he had heard David Matthews say, "I got three of them," and Jack Fowler say, "I got my few." The police, the FBI, and ATF agents knew what had happened. I had told the FBI what I had seen. What more could I add?

The argument against any of us testifying included (1) the DA's statements that we were like his enemies in Vietnam; (2) the DA and his assistants' role in the jury selection, producing the most pro-Klan, anticommunist jury possible; (3) the witness list, which left off government officials who were involved in the murders and included CWP leaders who were not even in North Carolina that day; and (4) the indictments against six of our people, including Nelson, who were facing felony riot charges and twenty-year prison terms.

On balance, we decided that none of us should testify. It was obvious to us that the trial was designed to continue the attack on the CWP. What had killed five people in Morningside Homes was going to continue in the courtroom. So we decided that rather than getting hit by the oncoming truck, we would get out of the way. We said: "We will not dignify this proceeding with our participation. We will not legitimate this kangaroo court by testifying."

Willena ■ I held a press conference and stated that I was not going to testify in court because it would not do any good. I told the reporters that the DA Mike Schlosser was a sham; he was not trying to get at the truth. While I was speaking, I saw the FBI watching me.

Nelson ■ What we decided was related to our understanding of the whole situation. No matter how it looks to somebody else, we had to assess our real options at that point. From November 3 to the opening of the trial the following August, the powers that be made their intent clear: They were not after justice.

As the trial opened in August 1980, I was still in jail under $115,000 bond, facing felony riot charges. The whole system—cops, courts, political leaders— were setting me up to take the blame and punishment for November 3. If our people had testified at the trial, it could have been much worse for us than refusing to testify. Our people could be manipulated into a position to testify against each other. I think our refusal to testify was a responsible position under the conditions we faced. We did the right thing.

Opening Day, August 4, 1980

Marty ■ On August 4, the trial began, and I went into the courtroom. When the proceedings started, I stood up and denounced the trial as a sham. They court officers grabbed me, but I kept yelling. Then they put white tape three inches wide over my mouth. The judge charged me with contempt of court, and the cops took the tape off my mouth so I could answer the judge's questions about my defense. I denounced the court again. The cops put the tape back over my mouth and hauled me away.

After they took me away, Floris Cauce stood up and denounced them. They hauled her away. We were thrown in jail for thirty days.

The *Greensboro Record* reported:

[the widows] rose from their seats in the court's spectator section and began shouting insults and communist propaganda. Nathan had to be gagged with tape while the judge ruled her in contempt of court and imposed a 30 day jail term. Cauce began her disruption a few minutes later and also was held in contempt of court and sentenced to 30 days.[6]

Later, the court hauled in their first demonstration witness, Tom Clark, our red-haired guitar player, whom the Klan and Nazis had shot with bird pellet. The officers brought Tom in against his will. He did not want to testify in this kangaroo court. The judge asked him a question, and Tom refused to speak. The judge said that he would be ruled in contempt of court and jailed for thirty days if he did not answer questions.

Tom responded, "I have nothing but contempt for this court."

The judge threw Tom in jail for thirty days. We wondered how many other people they would jail. But the prosecution stopped calling our people to testify. And Tom, Floris, and I sat in jail for a month. We got more jail punishment than the Klan and Nazis ever did.

Thirty days in jail was hell, especially being separated from my daughter, who was only fourteen months old. It was horrible; I worried about Leah all the time. But I needed to stand up in court and say my piece, even if it led to jail. The system had no legitimacy for me at all. I was willing to be its enemy, even if I died doing so.

Willena ■ Marty Nathan, Floris Cauce, Tom Clark, and Nelson Johnson were in jail. What was going to happen next? We were especially worried about Nelson, because we knew how much some of those cops hated him. We had to do something—something bold.

We were spray painting "Free Nelson Johnson!" all over downtown Greensboro. We decided to paint the jail, which was in the Guilford County Sheriff's Department in the middle of downtown Greensboro. That was my best job—spray painting "Free Nelson Johnson!" on the jail.

I carefully planned the jailhouse spray painting. I went to the courthouse and saw all the guards looking at the surveillance cameras. I learned that they did not put the cameras to video places that were wide open, like the front of the courthouse on Market Street. The cameras didn't show the side of the building exposed to the public. I carried that concept to the jail and decided to spray paint where the cameras couldn't see.

But I thought we might get caught, 'cause it was the jail and there are always a lot of guards around. We went after five o'clock in the morning, just before the shift change at six.

Big Al was one of our team members. I told him to stand at this pay phone right near the jailhouse and act like he was not with us. I told him: "You're talking to us on the phone, but don't look like you are. If we get caught, act like you don't know us."

We drove up to the Sheriff's Department, and two of us got out of the car. We sprayed "Free Nelson Johnson!" three times on that big jailhouse wall. Then we walked down the street, got in our car, drove out to the highway. We stopped at a pay phone, and I called Channel 2 News and said: "Some nut is spray painting the jail. You ought to go see it."

At nine o'clock that morning, we were standing up there at the jailhouse in a crowd, watching the Sheriff's Department sandblast the paint off. It took them three hours to get "Free Nelson Johnson!" off. Every one was stopping to look.

Nelson ■ I heard about that "Free Nelson Johnson!" spray painting because the deputies in the jail were talking about it. I was in my jail cell, and in my presence, the deputies talked about how outraged the sheriff was that people had gotten up to his jail and painted this stuff. The sheriff thought it was an inside job, and the guards were suspicious of each other. Some of the white guards thought black guards had done it.

Willena ■ It was my best spray-painting job. Nobody knew who did it; nobody had seen us. I thought we might get caught that time—Kwame had seen me packing my toothbrush. But they didn't catch us.

Kwame ■ I'll never forget seeing Mama put that toothbrush in her pocket. I thought, She really is planning to be gone. And then a while later, she did go to jail.

Willena ■ They caught me a few weeks later spray painting on Lee Street. It was not long after we spray painted the jail, and I was tired, overconfident, and getting arrogant with the police. I broke my own rules: I taught my teams that you only have so much time before the cops find you, so if you leave where you are spray painting, don't go back. That night, we spray painted on Lee Street and left because we saw a cop coming. Later, I went back to finish the job, and that's when they got me.

Nelson ▪ Meanwhile, I'm still in jail under $115,000 bond. They brought me to a second bond hearing. This time the judge was Elreta Alexander-Ralston, and what a difference a fair judge makes! She said she was not going to have her court turned into a kangaroo court, and she let me represent myself. Then she heard the assistant DA's statement and my statement. She was one of the first black women judges in Greensboro, and I knew her from back in the sixties. She stated that she had known me since I was a student at A&T, and that she was confident that I would show up for trial on the plaza incident the following month. She dropped the bond from $115,000 to $15,000 where it had been, and I walked out of the court and went home.

During my trial a few weeks later, Judge Alexander-Ralston questioned Officer Gibson. This is the *Greensboro Daily News* article for September 6, titled "CWP Leader Seeks Debate Privileges":

> Greensboro police Captain LS Gibson, a 15-year department veteran who assisted in Johnson's arrest, testified Friday that police approached Johnson after he waved his fist at the courthouse and used vulgar language. Gibson said he thought the curse and speech were about to provoke violence.
>
> But Gibson, who alternately cradled his head in the palm of his hand and laughed nervously, admitted during his hour-long testimony that he strongly disliked Johnson because of his political views and because the police officer had several friends killed fighting communists in Vietnam.
>
> "But do you like the Constitution?" Alexander-Ralston asked, clearly disturbed at Gibson's testimony. She proceeded to give the officer a civics lecture and concluded with the advice that he read the preamble to the Declaration of Independence, which explains why the colonies revolted against the British.

It was so unusual for a judge to question an officer. Judge Alexander-Ralston ruled that I had not assaulted an officer, although I might be guilty of resisting arrest. The local politicians criticized Judge Alexander-Ralston and tried to establish that she had some kind of improper relationship with me.

Judge Ralston also ruled that I had to serve twenty days in jail for contempt of court for disrupting the bond hearing. That sentence hung over my head for the next year, as I appealed it to the higher courts.

Sally ▪ As the first trial got underway, Paul and I moved from North Carolina to New York City. We left our friends in jail.

Leaving North Carolina was a big decision for us. I had lived in Durham for fifteen years, my entire adult life. Paul had been there for eleven years. But I wanted to move because I felt so vulnerable. We were living in a fishbowl. Everywhere Paul and I went in Durham, people recognized us. Most who spoke to us were African Americans, and friendly. But I also felt that many whites recognized us, and some of them did not wish us well. I had a newborn baby, a toddler, and a husband who could hardly walk. If somebody wanted to hurt us, we were an easy mark.

After November 3, living in North Carolina scared me. Every time I saw a pickup truck, my heart started beating faster. I checked to see if white men were at the wheel (they usually were) and if they had shotguns in the windows (too often). I worried they were following me. Even at home in the basement, lying in bed a night, I felt afraid. I would hear cars driving down our unpaved street. They would drive slowly—like the Klan/Nazi caravan. The sound of the tires on the gravel would trigger a flashback. Suddenly I would be back on Everitt and Carver Streets, the Klan and Nazis shooting at us. Over and over, I saw that big Nazi firing at us, the cigarette dangling from his lips.

Paul ■ Moving away was hard for me. A big part of me did not want to leave North Carolina, because I didn't want to appear to run away. But we had to move. Living there was just too hard. I was constantly afraid. I would take a gun just to sit and soak up some sun in the yard behind our basement apartment, and I would think about Nazis coming into the yard to finish us off.

I needed to walk a lot to build up strength in my paralyzed leg. In those days, every step was a conscious step. I had to think and look at my feet the whole time. (It was years later before I could walk without thinking about it.) I was so slow, it would take me a half an hour just to walk up to the corner. And whenever a car drove by, I thought, This is it, they're going to get me.

Sally ■ We needed to live someplace where people on the street did not know us, someplace where we could rebuild our lives. So we put everything we had in a U-Haul truck and headed up to New York City. We moved in with CWP people in New York City and depended on them for help and support.

During the months before and after our move, I was trying to write a book about November 3. I had interviewed many of the surviving demonstrators, and the friends of the five people who had died. I had typed up all the interviews and written a draft of our experience on November 3 and rough biographies of the five. But I had never written a book before and struggled with how to go about it.

When we got to New York, Jerry Tung told me to finish the book right away, because he wanted it to come out during the trial. I tried to write it quickly, but the writing just didn't happen as fast as he wanted. (Among other problems, I had two babies, a sick husband, and no money.) So he took it out of my hands and gave it to a committee. A book came out in late 1980 with Paul and me listed as the authors. But Paul was too sick to do any of it. My interviews and some of my writing were in the book, but mainly it was the CWP national leadership's view of things.[7]

Four Months

Marty ■ The trial dragged on. The Klansmen claimed self-defense, and the government essentially supported them. The FBI analyzed audio tapes of November 3, which they said showed that the third, fourth, and fifth gunshots could have come from the demonstrators. The Klan claimed that the first two gunshots were nonoffensive, that the next three shots came from us, and therefore the barrage of gunfire after that was self-defense.

A few demonstrators with us had small pistols, but they had not fired them until after the Klan and Nazis were shooting people with their big guns. But, of course, we had no way of proving this.

The FBI, on the other hand, had all these sophisticated instruments. In this first trial, they concluded that they didn't know where shots three, four, and five came from. (But in the next trial, the government would reverse this position and show that the third, fourth, and fifth shots came from the Klan and Nazis.) Basically, in the first trial, the government lied about not knowing where the third, fourth, and fifth shots came from.

And the prosecution made sure it covered up the role of government agents, despite the evidence. Klan and Nazis testified about the active role of the police informant and ATF agent in the murders. Klan defendants stated on the witness stand that Eddie Dawson played the principal role in organizing the ambush; one stated: "We'd never have come to Greensboro if it wasn't for Ed Dawson berating us." Nazi members said that [ATF agent] Butkovich told them to buy equipment to convert firearms into automatic weapons and offered to buy them illegal weapons, including grenades and explosives. After November 3, Butkovich offered to hide fugitives at a farm in Ohio. Nazi Roland Wayne Wood testified that when Butkovich visited him in jail on November 4, Butkovich offered to burn down a house and blame it on the CWP.[8]

Yet the DA called neither Dawson nor Butkovich to testify in the trial. The government continued to cover up their role as major conspirators in the murder, and the press let them get away with this. One of the few articles that raised these questions was by Michael Parenti and Carolyn Kazdin in *Monthly Review*, who asked:

> Why did the police insist the CWP be unarmed? Why did the police inform Dawson, a known Klansman, of the location on the permit? Why didn't they tell the CWP organizers that the Klan was so informed? And why did they

allow the heavily armed Nazi-Klan caravan to go to a rally of ostensibly un-armed people?

Four elements were necessary to carry out the massacre: (1) gunmen, (2) weapons, (3) information about the rally, and (4) effective organization and ambush tactics. Government agents helped provide all four. Indeed, had it not been for their efforts, the ambush could not have occurred.[9]

Verdict: Klan and Nazis Not Guilty

Marty ■ On November 17, 1980, the jury announced the verdict: The Klan and Nazis were not guilty. The white right-wing jury stated that the Klan and Nazis acted in "self-defense" as they shot and killed us.

The public was shocked. Jim Schlosser in "Calm Holds after Verdict—But Disbelief Is Vocal" for the November 18 *Greensboro Record* wrote that outside the Greensboro courthouse, a large, bearded black man ranted: "Your jury was hand picked by the KKK. Your people wearing guns and badges kill our people. Those people who got murdered were human beings. Are we gonna permit this to happen? I don't believe in communism. I believe in God. I'm just outraged with the law. I blame it on the cops." Schlosser and other reporters interviewed people on the street on their way to work the next day. Most expressed disbelief:

"I thought those guys should have gotten something."

"I was really surprised. Someone killed somebody down there, didn't they? These people didn't kill themselves."

"I thought they would at least get them for manslaughter."

"What went wrong? I saw a man with two pistols shoot someone. Why isn't he in jail?"

"On the videotape you could see one of them running down the sidewalk firing a gun. How can that be self-defense?"

Longtime civil rights leader Floyd McKissick said that it reminded him of trials held in the Deep South years earlier, where the Klansmen always went free after committing violence, Schlosser wrote. The head of the Greensboro NAACP, Dr. George Simkins, said that the verdict revealed that "Greensboro is a racist city." Mayor Jim Melvin jumped on that remark, saying: "Dr. Simkins is out of touch with the community. He keeps on talking that same tired old rhetoric of the 1960s."

Sally ■ The Klan and Nazis were thrilled with the verdict, calling it in the *White Patriot* for December 1980 "a victory for America and white people everywhere." Far-Right activity and violence spread through North Carolina and the South.

The Klan labeled Virgil Griffin the "hero of Greensboro," and at rallies Griffin "delighted in displaying autopsy photos of the African American killed by his group," the *Raleigh News and Observer* reported on March 30, 1997. Virgil Griffin kept marching and publicly advocating violence into the mid-1990s, leading as many as seventy-five marches a year. His Klan organization was sued and convicted of involvement in the 1996 burning of an African American church.[10]

The Klan made a videotape of Jerry Paul Smith, who is clearly visible on film shooting César Cauce at short range. Dubbing him the "John Wayne" of Greensboro, the Knights advertised their video in the April 1984 *White Patriot*. In 1981, Smith opened up his farm as a paramilitary training camp, telling people: "What happened in Greensboro is nothing compared to what's to come."[11]

Concerned southerners founded the National Anti-Klan Network in 1979, determined to expose and defeat the Klan resurgence. For the three years following the not-guilty verdict, the NAKN documented more than 130 incidents of racist or other hate-oriented activity, including the 1982 murder of a black man in Durham County for the "crime" of walking on the road with his white girlfriend. Other incidents included stabbing, harassing interracial and homosexual couples, burning crosses, and burning black churches. There were few arrests and no convictions related to these incidents.[12] Law enforcement was letting the Klan get away with terrorism.

Nazi activity also picked up after the not-guilty verdict. North Carolina Nazi leader Harold Covington told the press that the verdict was "fantastic; . . . it shows we can beat the system on their own ground." The Nazi newspaper, *New Order*, for December 1979 had a banner headline: "Reds Ripped in Carolina!" The paper portrayed November 3 as the "Lexington and Concord of the Second American Revolution . . . the first time Klansmen and Nazis actually faced the enemy together." They bragged about killing "a Jew abortionist from New York" and a "nigger female."

The day after the not-guilty verdict, November 18, Covington announced that Nazis planned to establish a whites-only nation in North and South Carolina called the "Carolina Free State," flying the Confederate flag. The "Free State" would set up a "bureau of race and resettlement" and offer African Americans, Jews, Hispanics, and others living in the Carolinas a cash settlement for their property before they were deported. The Nazis would recruit "white racialists from all over the world into the Carolinas."[13]

Four months after the verdicts, six Nazis were arrested for conspiring to blow up four targets in Greensboro with homemade bombs if the trial had found the Klan and Nazis guilty.[14]

Paul ■ When I heard the news of the not-guilty verdict, I was shocked, stunned, infuriated. In New York, we were removed from the scene of the crime. It was a cold, rainy day when the verdicts came down. It was mid-November 1980, and Ronald Reagan had just been elected president. The future looked gloomy.

Willena ■ I felt angry, hurt, but not surprised. The way Schossler ran the trial, I knew that not-guilty verdict was coming. That evening, I went out in the community to see what people were saying about the verdict. People were angry. They said, "We knew the police and the Klan were the same—some wear sheets and some wear uniforms." Some was saying, "All white people are Klan." Others said, "There are some good white people, but most are Klan." And all kinds of other things, but mostly it was "the police and the Klan are the same."

We didn't know it then, but a police informant named Mary Miller was among us. She got involved with us right after we went to China Grove in July 1979. Mary was facing drug charges, and the cops got her to inform on us. The night of the not-guilty verdict, Mary tried to set me up. I had been out in the community talking to people until late at night. Then I fell asleep on Mary's couch. The next thing I know, she was waking me up, telling me she had been arrested when she was in my car. Mary had talked this guy into driving my car, leaving me asleep on her couch. Mary brought a Molotov cocktail in the car and threw it into a grocery store, and then the police stopped them. Meanwhile, I'm asleep.

When I found out, I was so angry with her. "What were you doing?" I yelled at her. The grocery store was closed, but there were people cleaning in there. It was right in a working-class neighborhood, and it was lucky no one got hurt.

I found out later that when the cops took Mary down to the police station, Mary said that I was the mastermind, the commander, that I had given instructions. She left out that I had given instructions *not* to do stuff like she did. So they arrested me and put me in jail, charging me with conspiring to firebomb a grocery store. But it didn't stand up in court. And that is how we found out that Mary was an informant, and the police were trying to get us any way they could.

Marty ■ How could the North Carolina court acquit the Klan and Nazis with all the evidence—including TV videotape—of the murders being committed? The prosecution blamed us—even two decades later, Schlosser still pins the loss on our refusal to testify.

Should we have testified? I think there is a legitimate argument both ways. Maybe we should have sacrificed ourselves in the hope of a very shaky possibility of justice. But how could we have any hope after the DA described us as his enemy? After he made felony indictments of Nelson and five others? Schlosser dropped the felony indictments right after the first trial was over. It was Schlosser's prosecution that blew the trial. They chose the most racist, anticommunist jury they could. They organized the bogus analysis of the third, fourth, and fifth gunshots. They were outrageous.

I never expected Schlosser to imprison the Klan and Nazis. The whole world was topsy-turvy; the government was behind the whole thing.

But the not-guilty verdict woke up the public. Around North Carolina, there were spontaneous demonstrations in every college town as young people protested the not-guilty verdict. In Durham, I spoke at two protests. North Carolina Central University students led a march of hundreds to downtown Durham, demanding federal prosecution of the Klan and Nazis, and Duke students left their classes to rally on campus. And we began the mass organizing needed to bring two more trials.

The Second Trial:
United States v. Virgil Griffin et al.

The Greensboro Justice Fund

Nelson ▪ Pushing for federal intervention is a longtime tradition in the black community, dating back to Reconstruction. It is a way people respond to the outrages like the complicity of cops and Klan. In the face of entrenched racism of local and state government, people hope that federal intervention will bring justice. But sometimes, federal law enforcement is in on the conspiracy to deprive people of their rights. Nevertheless the tradition is to demand federal intervention, even if it doesn't bring justice but only national attention.[15]

When the North Carolina court freed the Klan, many realized that the federal government needed to get involved, and that only massive public pressure would get the feds to do anything. Progressive people who had shied away from us after the murders realized that we needed to work together to galvanize public opinion in Greensboro.

A coalition in Greensboro came together around the demand for federal prosecution. The Quakers were among the first to take up the cause. Joe Grove, a white Guilford College professor, and Charlie Davis, a black Quaker who had respect from the older local black leadership, pushed hard for the Quakers to play a positive role. Longtime friends joined in, like Lewis Brandon, director of the Uhuru Bookstore; A. S. Well, a director of American Federal Savings and Loan Bank; B. J. Battle, who was a leader in the NAACP and a senior officer of the American Federal Savings and Loan; and Sarah Herpin, an African American active in the American Friends Service Committee.

This coalition was the beginning of the Greensboro Justice Fund. The victims of November 3 had great initiative. The widows were active from the beginning. Signe Waller, a movement activist in Greensboro since the Vietnam War days, focused on working with the media. She was the CWP's press contact and probably has the world's biggest newspaper-clipping file on the massacre. Dale Sampson, who had become an articulate spokesperson the day after her husband was killed, moved to New York and provided leadership to our cause, traveling all over the country. I hardly knew Floris Cauce or Marty Nathan before the murders, but I watched them become effective speakers. Floris moved to Washington, D.C., after the first trial. Marty stayed in North Carolina and became more and more involved in building the movement for justice.

Our fledgling coalition met every week, issued statements, and hosted people coming in from out of town. One of our first visitors was Tyrone Pitts of the National Council of Churches, who would eventually get the endorsement of that organization for our efforts.

To get a federal prosecution requires demonstrating broad-based public support. We spent a lot of time in early 1981 getting signatures for our petition for that suit. In my office at the church, I have this big book with those signatures. Many people worked on that effort. My wife, Joyce, played a big role, keeping that book, getting those signatures.

In the spring of 1981, a delegation went up to Washington, D.C., to present the Justice Department with that book of signatures. I met with Justice Department officials and provided them with written and verbal information about the November 3 murders and the miscarriage of justice in the trial.

Marty ■ To pursue justice in the courts, we needed help, needed lawyers and organizers, a strong core of people at the center of coalition pushing for federal intervention. So we put out a call across the nation. And these hippies from South Carolina, Lewis Pitts and Katie Green, came to town. Lewis had a thick southern drawl, long hair, and he never wore shoes, only sandals. He was a dynamic lawyer who had done Herculean work as a public defender in South Carolina and with the Christic Institute defending anti-nuke demonstrators. Katie Green was a gifted community organizer. Lewis and Katie joined with our hardworking lawyers, Gayle Korotkin and Earle Tockman. So we had a full-scale, completely unpaid legal department in the Greensboro Justice Fund! We attracted a fine group of people who were willing to work for little or nothing. Shelly Wong came all the way from California to fundraise. Eventually we began to raise money, but always far less than our expenses. Although our main effort focused on getting the Reagan Justice Department to prosecute in a civil rights lawsuit, our lawyers also spent a lot of time dealing with the harassment our folks were facing and trying to keep us out of jail.

I focused on building the Greensboro Justice Fund through local organizing, raising money, and building public support. People were still very scared, but some courageous people stepped out. I went to a lot of churches back then, black and white, though mainly black. Leah, who was then a toddler, always came with me.

One minister, Reverend Percy High, allowed me to speak to his Durham congregation. After I finished my little talk about the trials, he made me laugh, saying: "Now, I'm going to pass the plate for the Greensboro Justice Fund. And I don't want to hear any clinking. I want to hear the swish and the shuffle of bills."

Things began to look up when Mickey Michaux, the U.S. Attorney for our section of North Carolina, concluded in June 1981 that a "firm basis" existed for a federal civil rights prosecution of Klan and Nazis and "others." Michaux was the first black U.S. Attorney in North Carolina, and he reversed his position of a year earlier, when right before the first trial he said there was no reason to investigate the ATF's connection to November 3. He was retiring, and he pushed for the federal trial as his final recommendation before he left office.

In the summer of 1981, I went up to Washington, D.C., and went all over Capitol Hill talking to congressmen and their staff members about supporting a federal civil rights suit. On July 17, 1981, I read the following press statement at the Guilford County Courthouse in Greensboro:

Support Grows for Greensboro Civil Rights Suit

This week six US Congressmen, members of the Congressional Black Caucus, endorsed the Greensboro Civil Rights Suit as an important and necessary means of exposing the truth about the Greensboro Massacre. The endorsing Congressmen are Hon. Parren Mitchell of Maryland, Hon. Mickey Leland of Texas, Hon. Ronald Dellums and Hon. Mervyn Dymally of California, Hon. Gus Savage of Illinois, and Hon. George Crockett of Michigan.

These endorsers join celebrities such as Harry Belafonte, Pete Seeger, actor Ed Asner, and Michael Douglas; civil libertarians such as Frank Wilkinson, Michael Meeropol, and Michael Parenti; leaders of the Black community and women's movement; professors, doctors, lawyers, poets, and priests. All share in supporting the full hearing of the suit.

Implicit in these endorsements are disgust with the Klan/Nazi acquittal and the demands that all the glaring questions about federal and local government involvement in murder and coverup be fully answered and that the guilty be punished. . . .

We invite all justice-loving people, especially North Carolinians, to join us in support of the Greensboro Civil Rights Suit.

Jail Hunger Strike

Nelson ■ While public support for the federal lawsuit picked up, I faced a jail term for contempt coming out of my courtroom protest a year earlier. In July 1981, my appeal to the higher court was rejected. During the same week, an Asheville [North Carolina] court freed six Nazis who planned to bomb downtown Greensboro if they didn't get the verdict they wanted in the November 3 trial.

The day before I went to jail, I held a press conference. Bob Hiles quoted it in "Johnson Lambastes Feds, but Promises Help in Klan Probe" in the *Daily News* on July 29. I said:

> The Klan and Nazis killed five people—my friends and co-workers, yet they have been convicted of nothing. The Nazis who conspired to blow up Greensboro if the Klansmen had been convicted also have been set free. Yet I have been hauled into court in order to silence me. Am I contemptuous of this court? Yes, I am as contemptuous as can be.

I was sick of going to jail. I had hurt no one. I had committed no crime. As I entered jail, I issued a statement saying that I would be on a hunger strike to protest being held as a political prisoner, and to demand full punishment for all government conspirators and the Klan and the Nazis for their crimes on November 3, 1979.

Willena ■ Nelson in jail again! We passed out flyers all over Greensboro telling people how crazy it was for Nelson to be in jail while the Klan and Nazis were walking free in the streets. The flyer said that Nelson was on a hunger strike to protest.

So then the newspapers pick up the story, not about the issues, but about whether or not Nelson is eating. "Johnson Is Said Eating Despite CWP Reports," said the *Greensboro Record* headline on Monday, August 3. The reporter quoted the Sheriff's Department saying that Nelson's eating trays were empty. So the article basically said we were lying.

We had a press conference the next day, and Joyce Johnson told the reporters that Nelson was not eating, he was only drinking water. His eating trays were empty because he was letting the other prisoners eat his food. The press still didn't believe us. The next day the *Daily News* headline was "Johnson on Jail Hunger Strike?" But when the twenty-day jail term was over, the newspaper had to admit that Nelson hadn't eaten, because he was twenty-six pounds lighter. You could see the change in him; jail had taken a toll.

Marty ■ During the fall of 1981, Greensboro Justice Fund hosted Father Daniel Berrigan, who went on a speaking tour that included Raleigh, Durham, Chapel Hill, and Guilford College in Greensboro. Daniel Berrigan identified himself with us, saying, "Once one aligns himself with anything decent or human, one is in the gun sights." He said that Greensboro was a place where "official lawlessness and disorder is wearing still the impermeable masks of law and order, even while it is refusing justice to the dead and the living." Daniel

Berrigan's visit was food for my soul. Every place he spoke, he complimented us for our disruptive tactics, for our "uncivil" behavior. He said that "civility often masks madness."[16]

That fall, the Institute for Southern Studies issued *Third of November,* a report that condemned the Greensboro Police Department and criticized the media's biased coverage. Our list of supportive groups continued to grow. I issued a press statement with a list of one hundred groups and individuals, including the National Council of Churches, that were behind our suit.

Sally ■ In November 1981, Paul and I came down from New York to the Greensboro Justice Fund's commemoration for the second anniversary of the massacre. There were a series of programs to honor Sandi Smith, Michael Nathan, Jim Waller, Bill Sampson, and César Cauce.

The most meaningful was a gathering on November 3 in Greenwood Cemetery. It was my first time back there since the funeral march two years earlier, and beforehand I dreaded it. The gloomy weather and cold gray skies matched my mood. When we drove in, I noticed two police cars stationed near the entrance of the cemetery. "They are trying to make amends," Nelson whispered to me. We stood in a circle of survivors around the graves of our loved ones. Signe Waller, Floris Cauce, Dale Sampson, and Marty Nathan dedicated a joint tombstone monument to the five. There was no program; instead, people just talked as the spirit moved them about the pain and grief we were all going through, but also the strength we got from all those who joined with us to get justice. It was wonderful to be with our dear friends again. They were so strong, still fighting the good fight. The commemoration felt like a reunion of a big extended family. In the years since, our cemetery gatherings on November 3 have become a healing tradition.

Greensboro officials continued to deny involvement. In "80 Gather in Greensboro Cemetery to Mourn Leftists," the *New York Times* on November 2, 1981, quoted mayor Jim Melvin: "The locale of the shootings was an accident of fate provoked by outside extremists, and . . . it was ironic in light of the city's exemplary record in race relations."

The Federal Grand Jury Investigation

Marty ■ By 1982, the Reagan Justice Department was getting heat for not doing anything about the increasing racist violence in the country, and for its support of segregated schools. The Reagan administration needed to take some action to maintain their credibility on civil rights. Assistant Attorney General for Civil Rights William Bradford Reynolds said on national TV that there was a Justice Department investigation pending on the November 3 murders.

Soon after that, on March 22, 1982, the Justice Department convened a grand jury in Winston-Salem, North Carolina, to investigate the shootings. For the first time, we had a sense that the federal officials really wanted to prosecute the Klan. But they still did not want to probe the involvement of the police or federal agents.

We fully cooperated with the federal grand-jury investigation. We hoped to get convictions against the Klan and Nazis.

Sally ■ All of us who had witnessed the massacre testified before the grand jury. Paul and I came from New York, and I remember testifying at the court-house on a beautiful spring day. During the 1960s and 1970s, I had read about grand juries being used to abuse people's rights when they protested against government policies. So I was nervous as I entered the room to testify—a large room full of people. Michael Johnson, the Justice Department attorney, asked me questions. He was friendly, and I answered all his questions, describing what I saw on November 3.

Nelson ■ I also gave my grand-jury testimony in a relatively friendly atmosphere. Attorney Michael Johnson guided the questions. He asked about what I saw, and about the handguns carried by some demonstrators. I told him that I was not armed and had no knowledge of other demonstrators being armed at the time, and that we did not think there would be Klan violence because we expected the police to be there. When his questions were done, I challenged the grand jury to come up with an hour-by-hour account of ATF agent Bernard Butkovich's activities, starting with November 1, when we knew he had been in a planning meeting for the massacre. I told the grand jury that nothing short of that would bring out the truth. They needed to probe, not just settle for the cover stories of the federal agents and police.

Our high hopes for the federal prosecution quickly dimmed when the Justice Department appointed Thomas Brereton to head the FBI's investigation team for the trial. Brereton had a serious conflict of interest. He was the FBI special agent in Greensboro who had known about November 3 *before it happened.* He had a longtime personal relationship with Klan/cop informant Edward Dawson. After November 3, Brereton had conducted a pseudoinvestigation that was a cover-up. It made no sense for Thomas Brereton to be involved in this case. He was out to protect himself much more than he wanted to uncover the conspiracy that he was part of.

The federal Ethics in Government Law states that if there is an indication of conflict of interest, or a "taint," then the attorney general needs to ask for the appointment of a special prosecutor. Brereton had a clear conflict of interest in this case.

The Greensboro NAACP spearheaded a call for a special prosecutor, and we fully supported that push. We worked with groups across the state and across the country to get a special prosecutor. We lost. We never got it. The government said there was not enough evidence to justify appointment of a special prosecutor to investigate the shootings.

Marty ■ The federal grand-jury investigation went on for more than a year. During this time, we got more evidence of FBI knowledge and complicity in the massacre. It came mainly from individuals who knew a piece of the conspiracy and who were brave enough to tell the public. Daisy Crawford held a press conference about the FBI visiting her a few days before November 3 and showing her photographs of individuals who were then killed or wounded. Mordecai Levy of the Jewish Defense Organization made public his experience of warning the FBI in North Carolina of the impending attack on November 2, and how the FBI brushed him off. The Justice Department released some FBI interviews of Nazi defendants, where the Nazis accused ATF agent Butkovich of actively encouraging and helping to plan the violence.[17]

The Public Broadcasting System aired a documentary in January 1983 called "88 Seconds in Greensboro." It included a long interview with Edward Dawson, who talked about how he worked with the police every step of the way in the planning and carrying out of the attack. And he talked to the FBI agent, Len Bogaty, in Greensboro, trying to get Bogaty to call off the march. The FBI agent refused to do anything. The documentary reached a nationwide audience.

Nelson ■ All this information about FBI involvement was coming out in the newspapers, but the Justice Department refused to present it to the grand jury. I wrote a letter to the grand jury that I wanted to appear again to give them all this new information. It was refused. I wanted to talk directly to the jury but was threatened with arrest. I told the press: "The Justice Department is attempting to obstruct my efforts to provide the grand jury with information which shows FBI preknowledge and planning with respect to the assassination of Nov. 3, 1979."[18]

On April 20, 1983, I presented to the press the FBI documents obtained by Mordecai Levy that demonstrated that the FBI knew that the Nazis were coming to Greensboro to blow up the place. The FBI knew through Dawson that the Klan planned to come. The ATF knew through Butkovich that both groups were working together. Why is the grand jury not allowed to look at this information? Because the FBI is involved in these assassinations up to their necks. And they threatened to punish me and our lawyer, Lewis Pitts, for trying to bring this information to the grand jury.

Marty ■ On July 21, 1983, a day after Nelson's press conference, the federal grand jury indicted nine Klansmen and Nazis for conspiring to violate the civil rights of those who died. Klan police informant Edward Dawson was one of the nine. No police or federal agents were indicted.

Meanwhile, the ATF was trying to influence the Klan and Nazi testimony.

Through the Freedom of Information Act, we obtained FBI memos from 1982 that the ATF had tried to influence Nazi Roland Wood's testimony. The FBI memo, dated August 20, 1982, stated that ATF special agent Fulton Dukes "informed Wood that if they 'stuck together' everything would be all right." However, if they "lied about Bernard Butkovich, they would go to jail." It also stated that "Dukes may have made serious disclosures of the Grand Jury's inquiries, as well as from ATF investigative files to a potential defendant in the Grand Jury's proceedings."

A second FBI memo dated three days later describes another meeting between ATF agent Dukes and Roland Wood:

> Dukes became angry and told Wood that if he, and [Nazi Raeford] Caudle, and other members of the Nazis would stop telling so many godamn lies about the ATF, this matter would all be straightened out and no one would be in trouble. [Klansman Joe] Grady in further conversation with Dukes, said that Dukes felt that the grand jury was comprised of "good ole country folks" and that they would not hurt anybody; however, if the Klan and Nazis were to go in and lie about ATF and law enforcement officials, the Klan and Nazis would be indicted and go to jail.

Nelson ■ We took every opportunity to speak out on the Greensboro massacre. In August 1983, Marty and I went to Geneva, Switzerland, to attend the United Nations Second World Conference on Racism and Genocide. On August 10, I addressed the plenary session and said that one example of U.S. racism was the Greensboro massacre and the cover-up since then.[19]

Marty ■ Traveling was good for me. The other widows and I traveled, giving speeches across the country. I spoke in New York City, L.A., Chicago, Detroit, Denver, and other places. It is a big world, and there is lots of injustice, but also a lot of love and support for the fight for what is right.

Opening Day, January 9, 1984

Marty ■ The federal criminal trial opened in Winston-Salem in the U.S. Middle District court. It began with secret jury selection, and once again they seated an *all-white* jury. But because the process was done in secret, we know almost nothing about their selection process. They put a gag rule on the case, which meant we were not allowed to go into the courtroom, or to speak to the press outside the court. The press challenged the judge's gag rule, but it was not lifted.

Most serious, the Justice Department chose an inappropriate law to prosecute the Klan and Nazis. They chose a statute that made it necessary to prove racial animus on the part of the Klan in shooting people down.

They could have chosen another statute that involved proving civil rights violation "under color of state law." However, the government didn't want to use this statute, because they wanted to protect the role of the police and other government officials in the Klan/Nazi attack. The Justice Department wasn't going to touch the police. They had indicted Dawson, the police informer, presenting him as a rogue element. They continued to deflect any finger-pointing at the GPD, the FBI, and ATF.

In the trial, the Klan defense was first: "We didn't do it." When that didn't work, they said: "We did it in self-defense." When that didn't work, the Klan said: "Okay, we did it, it wasn't self-defense. But we were not motivated by racism. It was anticommunism that made us do it."

Believe it or not, this Klan/Nazi defense strategy worked, because the law the feds chose to prosecute under had to prove racial motivation. To anybody who knows anything about the Klan and its one-hundred-year history, racial animus should have been easy to prove. But the Klan said: "If we wanted to attack an integrated march, we could have just attacked a high school homecoming parade."

The federal prosecution had a losing strategy because they had a conflict of interest. They picked the wrong statute to prosecute under because they were trying to protect the role of their own agents. That was more important to them that prosecuting the Klan and Nazis.

Paul ■ The federal trial was an odd experience. In the first trial, the lines were clear—us against the Klan and Nazis and their secret supporters in the Police Department and federal agencies. In this second trial, the lines were much fuzzier. We were in the strange position of being in a coalition with the FBI, who we believed had participated in the planning and execution of the murders. Here we are working side by side, seeking a prosecution of the Klan and Nazis, working with the very people who helped set up the kill.

For me the most bizarre moment was when FBI agent Thomas Brereton rehearsed me for my testimony. In a way, that is probably illegal, because you are not supposed to rehearse witnesses. But Brereton, the head of the Greensboro FBI office, said he did not want me to get rattled by the cross-examination of the Klan and Nazi lawyers. So we did a role-play, with Brereton as a Klan/Nazi lawyer. He asked me a bunch of increasingly hostile questions. He got totally into it, and his questions became more and more emotional. He was clearly a partisan of the Klan and Nazis—it was grotesque. I sat there trying to answer his questions and thinking, My God, what a psychodrama this is.

Kwame ■ For me the trial was extremely boring. I only caught one of the days in court. I was fifteen at the time, and I went to Winston-Salem with my mother to see the trial. We sat there, and I asked Mama, "Which one of them shot them? Who shot who?"

Mama said, "It's them, right there," and she pointed to the little Klansmen.

After I knew who they were, I was waiting to hear the judge say, "I now pronounce a life sentence"—or some punishment for doing those murders. But they had to go through this and that, all these witnesses. They go through so many different steps before an actual verdict is handed down. To me at the time, it was just boring. I didn't even get to hear any of the Klan talk. I wanted to hear one of them, hear what they had to say. But when that didn't happen, I was ready to go.

Verdict: Klan and Nazis Not Guilty

Marty ■ On April 15, 1984, the all-white jury pronounced the nine defendants not guilty. They all got off scot-free. Again.

It hurt. We had worked hard on this trial, and I really hoped the Klan and Nazis would go to jail. It was like being in two worlds: the world of the court, and the entirely different world of Carver and Everitt Streets on November 3, 1979.

Paul ■ Each not-guilty verdict made me more outraged. The prosecutors had as much evidence as you could possibly ask for, including TV videotape, four hundred police photographs, as well as all of our testimonies. And these guys kept getting acquitted.

They were acquitted because the powers that be were trying to protect their behind-the-scenes murder preparations. If they got convicted, the Klan and Nazis would have no reason to keep quiet. I think they were trying to keep the Klan and Nazis silent with not-guilty verdicts.

Sally ■ Glenn Miller had ridden in the Klan/Nazi caravan but had never been arrested or even questioned by law enforcement. He stood outside the federal courthouse and boasted to reporters: "I was more proud to have been in Greensboro for 88 seconds in 1979, than 20 years in the US Army. . . . It was the only armed victory over communism in this country."[20]

Glenn Miller is a good example of what happens when the courts do not punish violent racists: They commit more terror. Before and after November 3,

1979, Miller used his Johnston County farm as a paramilitary training camp. In the months after the murders, Glenn Miller organized his own new group called the Carolina Knights of the Ku Klux Klan. Miller's KKK marched not in traditional white sheets but in army fatigues. They marched and rallied throughout North Carolina, openly displaying high-powered rifles and semiautomatic weapons.[21]

After the first not-guilty verdict in 1981, Miller openly defied a law that had just passed the North Carolina legislature that banned paramilitary training. Leading a heavily armed rally in Chatham County, Miller threatened to burn crosses in front of the state legislature. In 1983, Miller decided to run for governor because, he stated, "the situation of white people is critical and intolerable. We no longer control our own government nor our own destinies."[22]

In January 1984, Miller announced his electoral bid surrounded by men in military camouflage with Carolina Knights of the KKK insignia. He called the other candidates "Reconstruction scalawag race traitors who have turned their back on the South," according to the January 27 *Greensboro Daily News* article "Klansman Files as Candidate for Governor." As governor, Miller planned to fly the Confederate flag on state-owned buildings and to establish a 100,000-member "citizens militia to assist law enforcement officers," since he believed the federal and state governments could no longer be trusted to enforce white supremacy.

The focus of Miller's campaign was to attack public school integration. One day he walked into the North Carolina attorney general's office and demanded that the state establish a militia "to protect white school children from violent assaults" from black school children. Klansmen appeared outside integrated public schools in several counties, including Durham.[23]

On Primary Election Day, May 8, 1984, only 1 percent of the electorate voted for Glenn Miller. Law enforcement played little role in stopping Miller, while the public strongly indicated their opposition to the violent racists. In Durham County, twelve hundred people signed petitions against Miller's group that were published in three newspapers. Similar petitions were signed and published in other counties. Bobby Person, a black prison guard, applied for a promotion and then faced death threats from Glenn Miller's group. Person bravely filed a civil lawsuit against Miller that several years later helped to stop Miller's terror campaign. But Miller's group continued its violent rampages, including one that allegedly murdered three men suspected to be gay in an adult bookstore in Shelby, North Carolina. It wasn't until 1987 that the federal government finally cracked down and caught Miller.[24]

Marty ▪ The day that the federal trial acquitted the Klan and Nazis, I had to go on national TV, on a show called *Firing Line*. I had never seen *Firing Line* before and didn't know anything about it. They put me on that show along with Bill Wilkinson, the imperial wizard of the Invisible Knights of the KKK, which at the time was one of the biggest Klan groups in the country. There I am on TV juxtaposed to this audacious racist, after I had just gone through the second court acquittals of my husband's murderers. I was blown away, but I managed to say that Wilkinson demonstrated the issues of the Greensboro trials, because he was not only a Klan leader but also had been exposed as an FBI informant.

The experience that night, sitting alone in a TV station debating a Klansman on a TV screen, was symbolic of what we were up against. Suddenly I realized how exhausted I was, the insanity of the whole thing. But there wasn't any time to stop. I had to fly to New York and do a speech. I did a lousy job on the speech. I felt broken, couldn't keep going.

Before those acquittals, I felt like I was beginning to heal. Having a life seemed possible to me again. But part of my healing process was the belief that the Klan and Nazis would be put in prison, that there would be some sort of justice. And then the verdict completely dashed that hope. It was one of the most depressing times of all. I felt alone.

Then I realized I was not alone. I had wonderful friends, and the only way we survivors had brought about the federal trial was through friendship and support—everyone in Greensboro Justice Fund, our lawyers, and wonderful folks in the American Civil Liberties Union, the People's Law Office, the National Council of Churches Commission for Racial Justice, and many others. We had the help of people around the CWP in North Carolina and around the country who were so kind, generous, supportive. Leah was taken care of by more mothers and fathers than I could count. I had the support of neighbors that got me through that depressing time, local folks who were very, very brave. You could be a national person and not so brave, but to be a North Carolinian and support us meant you were under fire.

Our North Carolina friends were outraged by the acquittals. A few days after the verdict, several hundred people marched through downtown Greensboro in protest.

The Third Trial:
Waller et al. v. Butkovich et al.

Marty ■ The third trial was our last chance for justice. The first two trials had exhausted all the criminal-court remedies without any convictions, and that meant we had only a civil lawsuit. We—the widowed, injured, and jailed demonstrators—used federal civil rights and state wrongful-death and assault laws to sue for damages in U.S. district court. We named as defendants the Klansmen; Nazis; and Greensboro city, ATF, and FBI officials with prior knowledge of the attack. These defendants included Klan/police informer Edward Dawson, ATF agent Bernard Butkovich, GPD officer Jerry Cooper, and FBI agent Thomas Brereton.

The Greensboro Justice Fund, especially the widows, gave leadership to the whole trial. Dale Sampson and I had become best friends; she became the sister I had lost when my own sister had died. We worked side by side, shared our sorrow, and poured our energy into making this trial work. The civil trial was a time when we began to shine as women putting this thing together. We worked as equals with the lawyers, men and women. Dale, Shelly Wong, and I spent five years building the Greensboro Justice Fund. We showed to the world our development as women, our being able to size up situations, make plans, and just go ahead and do things that we never believed that we would be able to do.

The civil trial was the first time we could have *our* lawyers try the case. It was the first time we the victims were able to bring a legal action. We gathered outstanding lawyers: Flynt Taylor and Dan Sheehan were seasoned movement lawyers who had won major legal victories in other parts of the country. Flynt Taylor was part of the People's Law Office of Chicago, which had successfully litigated the Fred Hampton/Mark Clark Black Panther suit against the Chicago police. Dan Sheehan was part of the Christic Institute, which had waged Karen Silkwood's family's successful suit against Kerr-McGee. They, along with local counselor Carolyn McAllaster, joined our existing team of Lewis Pitts and Gayle Korotkin.

The legal team spent a lot of time deciding our goals for the trial. We wanted to expose the whole conspiracy against us, from the top levels of government down to the Greensboro officials. We wanted to prove that it was a planned assassination and, if possible, uncover any involvement of individuals, like the owners of textile mills where we had organized.

But we were very limited. We still faced public officials determined to protect each other. We had very little money to carry out an investigation. Lewis Pitts argued that we should prove the case that we had hard evidence on, and after lots of discussion, his view won out. We decided our goals were to (1) convict the Klan and Nazi gunmen; (2) convict the Greensboro police who helped carry out the attack; and (3) convict federal agents, like Bernard Butkovich and others, who at the very least knew about the plans of the attack and refused to protect us.

Trial preparations were difficult. We had to figure out how to convince a North Carolina jury that the bad guys did it, and we needed to convince the jurors that we were worthy of getting a settlement. We had to be able to explain our motivations to the jury, and to do that, we had to deal with our own mistakes. We had spent years defending ourselves from the media's propaganda barrage against us. For the first time, we began to talk about our own shortcomings, because we had to be able to explain our errors to ourselves before we could explain them to a jury. We knew that if we didn't talk in court about our mistakes, the defense would present them in the worst ways. That was painful.

Sally ■ We did make mistakes. A big mistake was calling our rally "Death to the Klan." Why did we say that? What did we mean by that?

By our slogan "Death to the Klan," we did not mean to hurt any individual, any Klansman. We wanted to tell the Klan, "We are not afraid of you." KKK history goes back more than a hundred years and includes thousands of murders of men, women, and children. The Klan had this aura that they could terrorize and kill people and nothing would ever happen to them.

In 1979, when we planned our Death to the Klan march, there were all kinds of Klan public meetings and open recruitment drives. We wanted our November 3 rally to be militant, to break that aura of invincibility that surrounds the Klan. We wanted to let people know that we were black and white and united, that racists would not prevent us from building unions and from working together on all kinds of issues. For a hundred years, the Klan had meant death, but we said, "Death to the Klan."

Then the Klan used our words as an excuse to open fire and kill us. In retrospect, our slogan was a mistake. We made mistakes, not crimes. The Klan and Nazis committed crimes. They murdered five people.

This was the conversation that went on in my head. I was five hundred miles away from Greensboro, not involved in the trial. I didn't talk to anyone much in those days.

Nelson ■ It made such a difference to have our own lawyers try the case, people we trusted. This time, we survivors worked with our lawyers to gather the evidence before the trial. We deposed all those officials involved in November 3 and their superior officers.

Of course, the defense got to depose us as well. This time, the defense included lawyers for the police and government as well as the Klan and Nazis. I vividly remember the defense's deposition of me—it lasted five days! There wasn't five days of information to get, but they asked me questions over and over, every little nuance of anything.

The defense lawyer asked me about a newspaper article in the *Peacemaker*, in which this group called the National Labor Committee, headed by Lyndon LaRouche, said I was a highly paid FBI functionary, part of some $18-million thing. The person from the Justice Department was questioning me intensely about that. I said: "If I'm an FBI agent, why the heck don't you depose the FBI and get the records? And you come tell me."

It was a psychological game they put me through, all kinds of nonsense. The FBI had my briefcase, which I left sitting somewhere, and they took it. It meant they had all of my papers, documents, notes. They put all that in front of me and kept badgering me with questions about what this note meant, what that document meant.

Marty ■   All our trial preparations, all the depositions, took money. We had to pay living expenses for our legal team. I don't know how we did it. It took personal sacrifice on the part of the lawyers and the rest of us. Dale Sampson, Shelly Wong, and I just dug in and raised every last penny that we could. We developed a direct-mail campaign, helped by Elizabeth Broder, a professional fund-raiser in New York, to solicit donations by individuals. Andrea Bernstein, a journalist, helped us with the press.

We had a series of national visitors come to Greensboro to focus attention on the trials. Jesse Jackson came with us to Morningside Homes, where he stated, as the April 14, 1985, *Winston-Salem Journal* reported in "Jackson Speaks at Rally Site with a 'Mission of Justice'":

> Greensboro is a city that in 1960 became a beacon for the world when, in peace and with dignity, four students sat down at the lunch counter at Woolworth's. Now, 25 years later, we return. We come back because there has been manifest here an attempt to turn back to the mean times. And we have come to say we will not go back.
>
> We assert non-violent direct action and the full use of the judicial process. Equal protection under the law is a non-negotiable right. Justice must be swift and sure to be effective.
>
> Death squads must not be allowed in Central America, in North Carolina, in South Africa or anywhere.

Many people and organizations supported us, including Tyrone Pitts and National Council of Churches, Lyn Wells (head of the National Anti-Klan Network), the ACLU, and others. We got endorsements from the Congressional Black Caucus, National Council of Churches, American Civil Liberties Union, Operation PUSH, the Presbyterian Church, and many more.

The trial was to take place in Winston-Salem, thirty miles west of Greensboro. Our legal and Greensboro Justice Fund team basically moved there and rented two houses, a men's house and a women's house. We shared the cooking, bought groceries, all of us pitching in. We were doing amazing things, but at great personal cost. I couldn't move to Winston-Salem, because Leah needed to be in Durham and I needed to be there with her. She had just turned five and started kindergarten. Mike's mother, Esther Nathan, had died not long before. So three or four times a week, I drove ninety miles from Durham to Winston-Salem, and then ninety miles home.

To top it all off, I broke my leg. In February 1985, just before the trial opened, I absent-mindedly walked across the street on a red light. A VW hit me, and through the trial I hobbled along on crutches.

Opening Day, March 11, 1985

Marty ■ On March 11, 1985, the civil trial opened in Winston-Salem. In a civil trial, there are six jurors. Perhaps the most important thing in the whole trial was the selection of the jury. For the first time, our lawyers were involved in questioning jurors. For the first time, one of the six jurors was African American, and another was a white woman, originally from New England, who seemed open-minded. They made a huge difference.

Paul ■ U.S. district judge Robert R. Merhige Jr. had been appointed to the case. He seemed like he might be fair.

Nelson ■ The trial exposed details about the role of ATF agent Bernard Butkovich. He had managed to avoid testifying at the first two trials, but in our civil trial, he was forced to testify. On the witness stand, Butkovich denied everything. Butkovich's back-up agents testified about the formation of the United Racist Front in September 1979. This agent said that Butkovich was wired for eight to ten hours at the United Racist Front meeting, and the agent said he heard Butkovich throughout that time period. But Butkovich claimed that his batteries had gone dead. However, his ATF partners remembered Butkovich urging Nazis Wood, Caudle, and Fowler to join with the Klan. That missing tape was never recovered. On the witness stand, Butkovich avoided admitting anything to the point that Judge Mehrige became furious and indicated that he thought Butkovich was lying.

Several Nazis testified that Butkovich pushed them to form the United Racist Front with the KKK and to plan the November 3 attack, and that Butkovich taught them how to make explosives and automatic weapons. TV footage showed Nazis gathered in Winston-Salem two nights before the murders, and Butkovich can be seen in Nazi regalia. At that meeting, one Klansman bragged that he had manufactured a pipe bomb for "throwing into a crowd of niggers."

The ATF revealed that there were two agents working with the Nazis in Winston-Salem. The other was a pilot, and though Butkovich was not present in the Klan/Nazi caravan on November 3, this agent testified that he was flying with Butkovich "in the vicinity of Greensboro" that morning. Why had Butkovich's operation ended on November 3, and why didn't he go with Nazis to Greensboro to pursue the use of illegal automatic weapons? He testified that he had found no illegal weapons and there was no further need to investigate.

ATF officials testified that they were aware of Butkovich's activities at the time. However, they had no guidelines restricting the provocation of illegal violence or mandating the protection of potential victims of violence.

Marty ■ The trial also revealed that the FBI knew about the impending attack before November 3 from several sources. Records and testimony revealed that the ATF had communicated and coordinated with the FBI and police since the start of Butkovich's operation in August 1979. Klansman/police informant Eddie Dawson testified that he told his old FBI control agent Len Bogaty that he was worried about impending violence. Agent Bogaty advised Dawson not to go to Greensboro but failed to warn the demonstrators.

FBI agent Goldberg took the stand concerning a phone call on November 2 from Jewish Defense Organization leader Mordecai Levi. (Levi had informed Goldberg that the Nazis were going to attack and kill people at an anti-Klan demonstration in Greensboro the next day.) Under oath, Goldberg first denied the call and then testified that he did receive the call, but he did not report it because he did not think it was important.[25]

U.S. Attorney H. M. Michaux testified that on the evening of November 2, FBI agent Brereton had told him that the next day there would be "fireworks" in Greensboro. Michaux's testimony verified our charges that the FBI agent, Brereton, had a fundamental conflict of interest in being the chief investigator for the federal trial.

Lots of evidence about the complicity of the Greensboro police came out in the trial. The GPD had conducted an investigation of the Communist Workers Party in the month before November 3 at the request of Cone Mills managers. They watched our houses and examined Jim Waller's trash. The report of this investigation has never been released.

Police documents revealed that officials met several times to discuss November 3. Chief Swing himself knew that up to one hundred Klansmen were coming to Greensboro, bringing an arsenal that might include a machine gun to "shoot the place up." In the days before the attack, Dawson went to police officials and the police attorney, and they told him nothing could be done. On the morning of the murders, as we were gathering at the corner of Carver and Everett, the police tactical squad designated to protect us met at police headquarters. They knew from Dawson and from GPD officer Jerry "Rooster" Cooper that Klansmen were gathering in Greensboro with guns to attack the march.

Most dramatic was the testimony of former police officer April Wise, who stated that on the morning of November 3 she had been sent to the vicinity of the anti-Klan demonstration to settle a domestic dispute. In the minutes before 11 a.m., she received a call from the dispatcher instructing her to "clear the area." Wise remembered the incident because it was unusual and incomprehensible, unless the police wanted no officers near the anti-Klan demonstrators. The order came from the police dispatcher, but it cannot be found on police tapes of radio communications for the day. The city denies it was ever given. But we brought into court Martha Shelton, a Greensboro resident, who testified she was listening to the police band that morning and heard the order to Wise to leave the area.[26]

Nelson ■ The Klan/Nazi/government defense lawyers once again centered their arguments on anticommunism. They played up our rhetoric. When I was on the witness stand, the Klan defense lawyer showed the jury the TV video of me on November 3, 1979, shouting, "This is war!" as the cops grabbed me and my arms bled from the Klansman's knife wound. This is the transcript of Klan lawyer Chapman cross-examining me:

Chapman: Mr. Johnson, when the officer placed you under arrest, you did not willingly go, did you?

Nelson: I believe I resisted because I believe I was improperly arrested.

Chapman: You were kicking and holding on to the chain there at the corner, weren't you?

Nelson: And I was being stomped as I was bleeding from a knife wound inflicted on me by a Klansman.

Chapman: And you had said, "we declare war against them, war" didn't you?

Nelson: Yes sir. And it expressed the intensity of my feeling about what had happened, sir . . . .

[Later]

Nelson: No, it's not my view that people who have the name Nazi and Klan don't have the right to exist. What that document is talking about is that I think we need to try to reduce and minimize racism and racist violence. . . .

Chapman: You think that views which you perceive to be racist should not even exist?

Nelson: It would be very good if racist views didn't exist, yes.

Chapman: And to that extent, the first amendment should not protect those ideas.

Nelson: I didn't say that. But again, I don't think that that makes them wholesome views that we necessarily want.

Chapman: Well, what you're saying now is that you would like to oppose those ideas whereas a minute ago, I thought you said you didn't think those ideas should even exist?

Nelson: Well, the reason to oppose them is to minimize them, and I would hope that at some point there isn't racism in this society. I really would hope that.

Chapman: Mr. Johnson, all your materials say, "Smash the Klan," "Death to the Klan." Words have meaning. You wanted violence at China

Grove and you wanted violence on November third, Mr. Johnson, didn't you?

Nelson: No, that is not true![27]

Marty ■ KKK grand dragon Virgil Griffin testified, and portrayed himself as patriotic. This is the transcript of our lawyer Lewis Pitts questioning him:

Pitts: You are the Grand Dragon of the Invisible Empire of the Knights of the KKK?

Griffin: Yes, sir, I am.

Pitts: Aren't you a convicted felon, Mr. Griffin?

Griffin: Yes, sir, I am.

Pitts: Do you deny advocating violence at your rallies, sir?

Griffin: No sir, I do not.

Pitts: Can you see this Mr. Griffin? (He holds up the Klan poster to go to Greensboro. There is a picture of a black man being lynched, the caption calls for old-fashioned justice against "race-mixers, Jews, communists, niggers, beware, the cross-hairs are on your neck. . . .")

Griffin: I recognize it.

Pitts: All right sir, don't you talk at your rallies about having a hundred dead people in the street, using a word other than "black" in those speeches.

Griffin: In my phrases I use a "hundred dead niggers in the street."

Pitts: You have said that?

Griffin: I have said if a white woman was raped and killed, they should find a hundred dead niggers in the street the next day. Yes, sir.

Pitts: And didn't you make a statement to the effect that all of the communists in the US should be executed?

Griffin: I think I said they should be charged for treason against the US, put in front of a firing squad and shot. I believe that's the words I said.

Pitts: And I believe you were at a church near Dallas, NC, the Whispering Pines Baptist Church, where the Baptist Minister is a member of the Klan. And at that church you got up and railed against communism and race-mixing, did you not?

Griffin: I don't remember. I think I mostly talked about communism.

Pitts: But there's no doubt that you're opposed to race mixing?

Griffin: No doubt. . . .

[Later]

Pitts: Sir, did you see any guns at the house that morning before you departed on November third for the rally in Greensboro?

> Griffin: I believe I saw two shotguns, and a rifle, two long guns or three long guns, I'm not sure, a pistol and the pistol I had at the house.
>
> Pitts: Didn't you hear Roland Wayne Wood ask you if he ought to take his tear gas grenade with him?
>
> Griffin: Yes, sir, he did.
>
> Pitts: And Eddie Dawson reiterated that if fights and an arrest situation occurred "we'd all go to jail together" and he had arrangements for bond?
>
> Griffin: Yes, sir.
>
> Pitts: And you still deny there were plans for violence on November third in Greensboro?
>
> Griffin: Like I said before, we just wanted to stand on the sidewalk and fly the American flag and the Christian Confederate flag and watch the communists march.
>
> Pitts: Isn't it true that after the shootings, you and another Klansman hid out in the swamp for about a week?
>
> Griffin: We stayed on a creek for about a week, yes, sir.
>
> Pitts: Isn't it true you were concerned that somebody would be turning state's evidence against you.
>
> Griffin: No sir. I wasn't worried. I didn't do anything.
>
> Pitts: Mr. Griffin, didn't you co-lead with Edward Dawson the armed caravan that went to Carver and Everitt Streets which resulted in the deaths of five people?
>
> Griffin: Yes, sir. [*Testimonies*, 219–21]

Paul ■ I was a wreck during the civil trial, very tearful, thinking about all the things that had happened to us. A few weeks earlier, I had broken my left foot, a stress fracture. Before that fracture, I was walking fairly well. But after I broke my foot, the doctors wouldn't put me in a cast because they were afraid I would lose all movement in that foot. And I couldn't use crutches because I didn't have a left hand to hold a crutch. So I was in a wheelchair during the trial.

Before the day I had to testify, our lawyer Carolyn McAllaster calmed me down and advised me on the types of questions the Klan/Nazi/government lawyers might ask me. When I took the witness stand, the questioning went all right at first—until Virgil Griffin cross-examined me.

Virgil Griffin, the rabid Klansman, began by examining me about my revolutionary views, engaging me in a political discussion. He asked nasty questions, very aggressively, one after another.

Carolyn McAllaster had told me to keep calm, regardless. I answered Griffin with an almost exaggerated politeness. I politely explained my views about what it would take to make fundamental change in this country. Griffin kept on and on, his politics obvious in his aggressive manner and questions. He was browbeating me for maybe ten or fifteen minutes. It seemed like forever, but I kept my cool.

Afterwards, Carolyn McAllaster apologized to me for not intervening during Griffin's cross-examination. She said she wanted the jury to see the contrast between the two of us. She thought the whole thing was useful for our side, even though it was an ordeal for me.

I had a strange experience at the trial—in the bathroom. One day in court, I needed to go to the men's room. I wheeled to the back of the courtroom, and there was a few of the Klan and Nazi guys standing around the door. Several of them made an effort to hold the door open for me so I could get my wheelchair through. They were downright friendly. It was weird, Raeford Caudle holding the door for me, saying, "Paul, you need some help?" The murderer, Raeford Caudle, calling me by my first name as if we were old friends. The whole thing made me feel very mixed up, because my first impulse was to feel warmly towards them, while at the same time I hated their guts. These were the guys who had shot us and who we were trying to get punished. It was confusing. And I never talked about it to anyone, not even Sally.

Sally ■   Paul did not talk much about the trials, before or after he went to North Carolina to testify. And I didn't ask. Paul seemed removed, preoccupied. And I was just trying to take care of our daughters, go to work, put food on the table—just the basics for survival. I didn't know Virgil Griffin cross-examined him or anything about the Klansmen in the bathroom.

I was not asked to testify at the civil trial and never went down to North Carolina. The trial, like the two before it, just hung over us. I had given up hope for any justice in the courts. I just wanted it to be over.

Paul ■   For me, the most dramatic moment of the trial was the testimony of Roland Wayne Wood, the big Nazi who shot at us with a cigarette dangling from his lips. When he got into the witness stand, he gave a Heil Hitler salute as he swore in.

Our lawyer, Flint Taylor, questioned Wood. Wood had these five pins on the lapel of his suit—they were skulls! This is a trial transcript of Wood's testimony:

> Taylor: Do these five skulls stand for the five people that were killed on the streets of Greensboro?
>
> Wood: No, it stands for the five attacks being committed against me by communists when I tried to express my freedom of speech.
>
> Taylor: You are proud that you're a racist, aren't you?
>
> Wood: Yes sir. I believe in the sovereign rights of the sovereign people of the sovereign states of the Confederacy that has never surrendered. Lee, the traitor, surrendered, but not my Confederate government. I

believe that my country is occupied. And I will fight as my forefathers fought to give me a free Christian republic. [*Testimonies*, 284]

I was sitting in the courtroom, listening intently, and I couldn't understand what Wood was talking about. He was becoming agitated. Then our lawyer asked him about some song Wood had mentioned about killing Jews. To everyone's amazement, Wood started singing this song to the tune of "Jingle Bells."

> Riding through the town
> In a Mercedes Benz
> having lots of fun
> shooting the Jews down
> Rat a tat tat tat
> Rat a tat tat tat
> Shot the kikes down
> Oh what fun it is
> to have the Nazis back in town. [*Testimonies*, 285–86]

It was surreal. The jury's jaws dropped. Judge Mehrige, who was a very proper and very controlled guy, looked shocked. It was the only time I saw any emotion displayed by the judge. Without any explanation, the judge tapped his gavel and said, "The court will recess for thirty minutes." It was a stunning moment. People had to collect themselves.

Marty ■ It was amazing to watch our lawyers question these Nazi and Klan guys on the witness stand, and to compare that to how they were portrayed in the media, as good old boys who just bumbled into shooting people.

Their testimony made it clear that they were reactionary, right-wing rednecks who were ideologically devoted to extermination of Jews and blacks and communists. They weren't just bumbleheads. They carried off a military operation. These guys knew how to shoot and knew who they were shooting at. And the government had failed to prove it in the first two trials.

In our trial, we proved it. They were ugly, ugly, ugly men. We proved that they were ugly men, and that the government knew that these ugly men were bent on killing us. Our side took eight weeks of testimony to present our case. The defense surprised everybody when their attorneys rested their case after less than four days of testimony. They had been expected to take up to four weeks to present evidence.

The Verdict: Joint Liability

Marty ■ On the second day of deliberations, the jury came to its verdict. They found liable for wrongful death: Greensboro Lieutenant P. W. Spoon, the commanding officer in charge of the November 3, 1979, march; Greensboro Police Detective Jerry Cooper, who had followed the Klan-Nazi caravan to Carver and Everitt Streets; police informant Edward Dawson; and seven Klansmen and Nazis. They were all found liable for the wrongful death of Michael Nathan.

A guilty verdict—that was the good news. But why only Michael? The only explanation seemed to be that he was the only one who was not a member of CWP.

And the jury announced that there would be a judgment for only three people: me, Paul Bermanzohn, and Tom Clark. What about Bill Sampson, Jim Waller, César Cauce, Sandi Smith? Didn't their widows and families count?

It was horrible. I was suddenly separated from my best friend and co-worker, Dale Sampson, who had just as much difficulty dealing with Bill's death as I had with Mike's. She and Signe Waller and Floris Cauce got no consolation from that trial. It was a terrible blow.

Dale, Signe, Nelson, and I were in court with our lawyers and friends when the jury announced the verdict. We left the courtroom stunned but quickly regrouped. Lewis Pitts argued that it was a victory—a southern jury finding the cops complicit with the Klan is a huge victory—only the second time ever that the cops had been found jointly liable with the Klan, despite their long history of complicity. So Nelson, Signe, Dale, and I went out to talk to the press, holding each other's arms high for victory.

Later, we learned that the dynamics in the jury room were intense. The African American man and a northern white woman fought for conviction of Butkovich, Dawson, and the cops. Flint Taylor, one of our lawyers, wrote an article on the case:

> Subsequent interviews with jurors revealed that the verdict reflected deep differences between them. The black foreman and the white woman originally from New England strongly supported a verdict on the civil rights conspiracy in favor of most of the plaintiffs and against the ATF provocateur and several of the police and federal defendants. They also favored substantial damage awards.
>
> The southern white faction, however, wanted a narrow verdict or none at all. They were unable to put their anti-communism and racism aside. They feared the reaction in their communities to a verdict for the plaintiffs and focused on the plaintiffs' rhetoric and the alleged possession of a gun or the firing of one in self-defense as reasons to deny liability.[28]

The Settlements

Marty ■ In civil cases, the remedy is money. Even if defendants are found guilty, they cannot be imprisoned. In our case, the settlement amount was small: The jury awarded $350,000 to Mike's estate, $35,000 to Paul, and $1,500 to Tom Clark. On November 6, 1985, the City of Greensboro paid a $351,500 settlement to the estate of Michael Nathan, that is, to me and Leah. They paid it for their cops, and for the Klan and Nazis. The Klan and Nazis never paid a dime; they never spent a day in jail. So the irony continued, as the government paid the judgment for the gunmen and their complicity.

What should we do with the settlement money? It wasn't that much, and there were so many victims—four widows, ten wounded, two unjust arrests—and so many lawyers and other people who had worked for years for near nothing.

Dale and I got together for the bizarre task of deciding how to divide the money. Dale pushed to organize the Greensboro Justice Fund as a foundation to raise money for grass-roots groups fighting against injustice in the South. I thought it was a wonderful idea—it would continue the legacy of Sandi, Jim, César, Bill, and Mike. So we divided the money. Fifty thousand dollars went to the lawyers and GJF staff. The rest by law had to be split between me and Leah. Leah's portion went into a trust. We divided up my half, $150,000, among the sixteen plaintiffs, according to a formula based on loss. The widows got the biggest share, then the wounded, and those unjustly jailed got almost nothing. We told people they could keep the money or donate it back to the Greensboro Justice Fund, and $75,000 came back to the GJF for us to continue a legacy of fighting for justice.

Willena ■ The outcome of the trial was such a letdown. That trial could have been used to stop the Klan, but instead they just pointed to a few bad policemen. No FBI or ATF found guilty, no prison. People still ask me about it.

But it was a victory, because it exposed all kinds of evidence about the Klan, the FBI, and cops. And I was glad all that came out.

Kwame ■ Those Klan and Nazis never went to jail! Nothing! I couldn't believe it.

11
Tribulations

Ronald Reagan became president in 1980, accelerating the U.S. political shift to the right. From 1980 to 1985, the Greensboro massacre survivors not only contended with the three trials but also worked at rebuilding their shattered lives.

Nelson ▪ After November 3, my life hit rock bottom.

Kwame ▪ I became a teenager, and there were all kinds of influences around me—the drug crowd, the gang crowd, the crowd labeled "mama's boys." I was young, but I made my own decisions. I made the decision to commit crimes, to break into houses.

Willena ▪ I thought things couldn't get worse, and then they did.

Sally ▪ We were each on our own painful journey. I was far away from North Carolina, not aware of what my friends there were going through. I was on my own lonely path towards breaking with the Communist Workers Party.

Paul ▪ I was trying to recover physically, trying to lead a normal life.

Marty ▪ The murders and the trials left me a broken person. I think we all were broken people. Healing was a long, slow process.

Rock Bottom

Nelson ▪ The trials were the low point of my life. I had dedicated myself to activism, to bringing people together to make social change. But after November 3, people who I had worked with for years shied away from me. I would be sitting in a meeting, and someone would stand up and say, "Why did you get those people killed?"—like an indictment. The media inundated people with this false, cover-up stuff. The papers printed every quack who wanted to take a shot at us, just making up stuff. We didn't have the strength or capacity to stop it.

I couldn't get a job in Greensboro, couldn't do organizing. Nobody wanted me around. For a decade, the massacre basically took me out of employment in Greensboro. The only thing I could do was defend us; I was out here every day denouncing some official about what had happened to us.

I was getting a dollar or two now and then from friends through the CWP, but it really wasn't adequate. Joyce was working full time at A&T. Our children were growing up, and their daddy couldn't get work. My marriage suffered. I was so tense, I wasn't much of a husband.

Mississippi is where I finally found some use for my skills. I had some friends there and met people in Greenville and Jackson. It was quite refreshing to organize in Mississippi. We were trying to build a third party, an alternative to the Democrats and the Republicans, and to run people for public office. It was a good strategy for developing political power in the black community. This was in the early 1980s, before Jesse Jackson began his first presidential campaign.

I was spending more and more time in Mississippi, and it became an issue in my marriage. I would leave Greensboro about four o'clock in the morning to be in Jackson by 8 or 9 a.m. Joyce asked me to stay in Greensboro, not to go to Mississippi. I told her I had to go, there was nothing for me to do in Greensboro except to hassle over this massacre. We discussed whether or not our marriage would survive. It brought me to tears. But I needed to do work in Mississippi; I really needed to get out of Greensboro. I needed to recover.

We made a good run in Mississippi. Jesse Jackson got a lot out of using our work for his 1984 presidential campaign. Our goal was to build a third party, and for a while, it looked like Jesse Jackson might run as a third-party candidate. But then Jackson met with Walter Mondale and some other folk and cut the deal to stay in the Democratic Party. That ended our work in Mississippi. The day Jesse Jackson cut that deal, I drove back to Greensboro. Joyce and I sat down and prayed over our relationship.

Kwame ■   I was searching for somebody to be close to, a father figure, a big brother, someone. Nelson, he was somebody you could easily cling to, but he wasn't there much, not even for Ayo and Akua. They wished that he was around more, and I wished my mom was around more.

Before November 3, there was Jim Waller and Bill Sampson, Nelson, Big Al—all those folks. They would play ball with me, do things with me. And we had RYL [Revolutionary Youth League] for the teenagers, Junior RYL for the preteens. My mama did a lot to put those groups together. It was like a big family; we were always in and out of each other's houses. But November 3 took it all away.

During the trials, we were very poor. We lived in the cheapest place my mother could find, where only a bent nail held the front door closed. I didn't get to hang out with friends because the environment was so downtrodden. I had to guard my sister and brother while my mother worked.

Willena ■ No one in Greensboro would give me a job. For a while, I lived on welfare. Then I worked cleaning townhouses after they were constructed. Later, I got jobs at fast-food places that were owned by big companies out of state. I had a tough time. I had to find the cheapest place to live, even though it exposed my kids to all kinds of bad influences.

I begged the housing authority to get me a place in public housing. Finally, in 1983 we moved to St. James Homes project. It was better, I thought.

Kwame ■ It *was* better; it had a lock on the front door. I liked it better, because I could get out of the house. Mama got a job where she was working a regular nine to five. She would be home shortly after Imani, Kweli, and I got home. I was fifteen, and I had time to meet friends and hang out. Life changed for me.

But during this time, the gang situation in Greensboro had gotten bad. And St. James Homes was one of the most heavily crack-infested areas here in Greensboro. You could get just about anything you wanted, right in that area. So there were all kinds of influences around me—the drug crowd, the gang crowd. The crowd labeled "mama's boys" was the crowd that I started hanging with.

We would go to this little club called the Depot, a club for high school and junior high school kids. A couple of times, guys from gangs would jump on us because they was from the Grove, and we were from another neighborhood. So you get forced into a position to where you are damned if you don't join the gang, 'cause they're going to jump on you.

I hung around a gang named the Q Dogs, because I knew if I was by myself, I would get jumped on. But the more I hung with them, the more involved I got with them. I started doing things that they were doing, like drinking. I had my first drink with my little gang crew. They were doing breaking and entering, or B & E's. We would go to UNCG and break into the students' apartments. I feel bad about that now; we were taking the bare essentials that the students had.

I was one of the youngest in our gang. The other guys were in senior high. Me and this other dude named Kenny would always try to do things to show we were worth something in the gang. The gang made me feel like I belonged to something—I finally got a group that I could call my friends, my buddies. They liked me and they were willing to go to bat for me. So looking back, it was easy to get caught up in that thought pattern.

Willena ■ When I saw Kwame's gang shirt, I cried, "Oh, my Lord, he's in a gang." I made him get rid of that shirt. I told him to stay away from gangs.

Kwame ■ Mama saw my little gang shirts with the panther on the back, and she blew up. I told her I was getting rid of the shirt.

Actually, I took the shirt to my friend Sean's house. So when I went to the Depot, I left my house in my regular clothes and went up to Sean's house to get into my thug gear.

Willena ■ I worked with the youth in St. James Homes and was successful at getting them to stop fighting each other. But I had some trouble with some of the adults in that housing project. They knew about November 3 and the FBI and police and my involvement in all that. They were afraid if they got involved, the FBI and cops would come after them. They were afraid that any good things we did would bring the whole oppressive apparatus down on them.

Marty ■ Around then, in the early eighties, Willena and I did some organizing together. Reagan was president and he was cutting taxes to give the rich more money, spending more on the military, and cutting programs for poor and working people. There were all kinds of cutbacks to social programs like the emergency food program, food stamps, daycare, and youth recreation. People were marching in the streets, beating pots and pans. Willena was there leading people, chanting, banging on her pan.

I went over to her house a few times and we would talk. I learned a lot about race and class from her. She was the way she has always been in the twenty-five years that I have known her: smart, hard fighting, get to the point, and fun to be with. She was poor as could be, yet with incredible pride.

She was living at St. James projects with her kids, Kwame, Kweli, and Imani. I didn't see Kwame much; he didn't hang around the house. Her kids were cute, funny little kids. They were smart as the dickens and very effective at getting attention. They were incredibly lovable at the same time they were bratty.

Sally ■ Five hundred miles north, we were in New York City, a tough town if you are poor. Our only income was Social Security Disability. At first we lived for free with CWP people in an old industrial building, four families sharing one kitchen and one bathroom. We all pitched in, and it worked fine until the heat broke down in the coldest part of the winter. Without heat, we couldn't bathe. We just layered on more and more clothing. I remember seeing the ice caked up inside and outside our windows.

We mothers went on an expedition to buy electric heaters. When we got home, we all plugged them in and blew a fuse that knocked the electricity out in the whole building. That night we had no light, as well as no heat. The next day, they fixed the fuse, and for more than a month those little heaters were our only source of heat. I was scared the heater would catch on fire, so I slept on the floor next to Sandy's and Leola's cribs. Paul slept alone in another, unheated room. I had nightmares of running away from the flames with babies in each arm. Somehow, Leola and Sandy stayed healthy, although several other children in our building had to go to the ER because they got pneumonia.

On the subways, I saw immigrant women in old clothes, clutching their bags of food. Their faces were grim but determined. That is what I felt like. It took determination just to survive.

Paul ■ Living in New York was a shock to my system. I was used to the slow-moving South. I was barely walking, using a cane and going very slowly. But going slow is not allowed in New York. I could not make it across a wide street before the light changed. Drivers would honk at me as I hobbled along. One time, I was trying to cross Atlantic Avenue, a six-lane-wide city street, and the light changed. This woman pulled up, almost hitting me, and honked at me. I wildly waved my cane and cursed at her: "Fuck you lady! I'm going as fast as I can!"

Sally ■ That spring, Paul and I moved to a two-room apartment. It was tiny and filthy, on the second floor of a four-story walkup on a corner in the middle of a rough neighborhood. Outside our window, we could see graffiti that said, "Turf of the Savage Homicides." I guess that was the name of a local gang. Needless to say, we didn't spend much time outside. At night, we heard drunken street brawls outside our window. I cleaned and painted the place as best I could.

Then we discovered another problem: rats. Mice were there when we moved in. I put out traps. But then a rat started coming up through the broken wall behind the sink. The rat ate the mice, leaving their remains for me to find in the morning. One night I saw that rat on my kitchen floor. It freaked me out. I got rat traps. One morning I found the rat's tail and hind foot in the trap—that rat must have chewed its own foot to escape. Every morning I woke up sick to my stomach, wondering what would be in the traps that day.

I wanted to get a job so we could move away from that apartment, which we called the Rat Hotel. But I couldn't just go out and grab a job. I had two babies who needed care, and Paul was still incapacitated.

Paul ■ It was a total drag to sit around in the Rat Hotel and do nothing. It was hard for me to do childcare, especially for Sandy, who was still a baby. We celebrated Sandy's first birthday there. I had never been able to diaper Sandy, and I needed help even to hold her. That made it hard for me to develop a close bond with her. When Leola was a baby, I diapered her and held her and played with her all the time—that is how you bond with your child. After I got shot, I could still talk to Leola. When Sandy was born, I spent hours playing with Leola, which freed Sally up to take care of Sandy. But it made it real hard for Sandy and me to connect up. That was something she and I had to work on years later.

Sally ■ We were lucky that our children were babies. They didn't notice the poverty, the rats, and the old clothes they always wore. I don't know what we would have done if they were older and needed to play outside. As it was, we could keep them inside, away from the street. But even that wasn't safe. Our neighbor upstairs was a crack addict and broke into another neighbor's apartment.

Those experiences of grinding poverty taught me a lesson I will never forget. Much of the world lives in poverty their entire lives.

Paul ■ Sally bore the brunt of all that. I was traveling a lot in those days. I became the official party hero, shipped around the country to limp and show off my scars. I loved the traveling and speaking.

Sally ■ Jerry Tung wanted Paul to keep traveling and speaking for the CWP. Jerry asked me to be Paul's secretary, to arrange trips and speaking engagements for him.

I refused. I told Jerry I could not, would not, do it. I was already mother, wife, and nurse, shouldering by myself the family's survival. But be Paul's secretary? No way. He was so unorganized, and I knew I would just get mad at him. I felt cold-hearted, but I decided that Paul was on his own in terms of rebuilding his career. I would feed and shelter him and take care of our kids as best I could, but otherwise he was on his own.

Paul ■ Traveling around the country for CWP was fun, but I wanted a real job. My physical recovery continued, and by spring 1981, I began to use public transportation. Buses and trains stop and start suddenly, and to ride them you need some balance. Balance is something I had lost when I got shot, and it took me a long time to get back some of it. As soon as I could walk up and down steps in subway stations, get on and off buses, and manage to hang on while they were moving, I started looking for work.

I decided I wanted to go back to psychiatry, which I had quit back in the mid-seventies to do political work. For most types of medicine, you need two hands. But to be a psychiatrist, all you need are eyes, ears, a mouth, and one hand to write notes. I applied to several psychiatry residency programs. I had a good medical-school record, good recommendations—the only problem was that I was a communist who had been shot in the head. In spite of that, several places wanted me. I chose to go to Maimonides in Brooklyn.

Sally ■ I didn't think Paul would be able to handle the residency program. He was so slow getting himself dressed and out of the house, so unsteady walking. I didn't think he could manage the subway. I didn't think he could do all those things necessary to get to work by nine o'clock every morning.

Paul ■ Going back to work was so important to me. It took me a lot of time and effort just to get to Maimonides Hospital, hobbling along on my cane. But going back to work helped me recover. After two weeks, I left my cane at work one day and didn't miss it until I was out on the street. At first I felt lost without it; then I thought, I can do this. And that was true for the residency, too.

My experience recovering has formed my philosophy for rehabilitation of all kinds. People need to normalize, to strive for a normal life. Doctors and rehab workers too often focus on trying to solve this or that little problem. Rehabilitation should focus on the big picture—helping people lead a normal life. Work is a big part of that.

Sally ■ I was surprised when Paul did so well. And residents' pay, about $20,000 a year, made our income almost triple. When Paul got his first paycheck, I immediately went out and found us another apartment. It was in a poor drug-infested neighborhood, but it was clean. No rats.

Paul ■ I was a resident at Maimonides for three years and then worked there for another three years as a staff psychiatrist. I still have a strong and fond connection to Maimonides Medical Center.

I continued to work with the CWP, but it was difficult. I did not find the same level of camaraderie, the deep shared experience that we had in North Carolina. The CWP in New York was more centralized. There was not the back-and-forth discussion and debates that we had in North Carolina.

1984

Sally ■ The murders, the aftermath, the trials, unraveled the tight community we had built in North Carolina. I didn't even know what my friends down south were going through. I was focused on my little ones. I put them in daycare and went back to work as a clerical worker on Wall Street, then a bookkeeper for a brokerage, and then a teacher in a public daycare center. Thankfully, the girls flourished.

I felt very alone. I was deeply committed to my marriage with Paul, but we stopped talking to each other except about the most superficial things. I didn't know where his mind was at, and I didn't talk to him about what I was going through.

In 1984, I decided to leave the CWP. I had been a member for eight years, and my best friends were still in the Party. There was a big need for all of us to remain united, because the third trial was scheduled to begin in early 1985. I was in charge of running the Party's Brooklyn district, but I just couldn't do it anymore. My body would no longer let my mind tell it what to do. I just stopped.

Leaving the CWP was the culmination of many things. Mainly, I no longer believed in it; I no longer had faith in the Party leadership or trusted their judgment. In my experience, democratic centralism, the organizational principle of Marxism-Leninism, was just centralism. CWP leader Jerry Tung made too many unilateral decisions, and I was no longer able to follow them. I wanted to have my own thoughts, come to my own conclusions.

My last work in the Party was in November 1984. We organized a commemoration of the fifth anniversary of the Greensboro massacre in New York City. Judy Brussell, a playwright and childhood friend of Marty's, wrote a wonderful play about Greensboro. We filled a huge theater for the opening. I felt better about mobilizing for that play than I had about doing Party work for a long time. I was still committed to justice in Greensboro, but no longer to the CWP

As far as I knew, most all my friends were still into CWP. I was quiet about quitting because I didn't want to hurt our effort during the civil trial. My break was individual; I consulted no one and didn't talk to Paul about it, except to inform him what I was doing. I told him he should do what he decided was right for him.

Nelson ■ We all went through our lonely journeys in the early eighties. When I had no job and was shunned by many, it compelled me to think. In my isolation, I recovered some memories of my childhood. I had grown up in a religious setting; the church was central to my family. I remembered my great-uncle Dee, and the stories he would tell—all the stuff he and his people went through, just on the other side of slavery. How they prayed, how they went through all those hard times as a community. I thought about the deep need we humans have for community. As alienated as we can become, we are ultimately social creatures. I was searching for meaning, for connection.

In the sixties in the movement, I had become critical of preachers, didn't respect their behavior and therefore their beliefs. I had tied God and preachers and the church too closely together. I credited my religious upbringing with teaching me morals. In the sixties, I dedicated my life to organizing for social change, a commitment I have maintained. For several decades, I was a moral person but not a spiritual one.

In the seventies, as an activist, I became a communist. Marxism-Leninism is based on materialism, which sees the material world as what we have to work with. Marxists criticize preachers who focus on the afterlife rather than pushing people to fight for better things in this world. Hence the Marxist line that "religion is the opiate of the masses."

In the eighties, I decided that materialism was too limited if it is seen as an ultimate. I still wanted to organize for social change, but I needed a spiritual side. I longed for connection, for meaning. So I started to go to church and talked to ministers I respected and asked them if they really believe in God. I joined the church to be part of my people, part of my community. It was a faith venture. I had not drawn any conclusions, only rejected some of my past beliefs.

Joyce and I went together to many different churches. Joyce was fully into it, and it felt like we had gotten married again. We discussed what we heard and what we felt, about what made sense and what didn't. Joyce and I were received in the church. When I went to the courthouse, people in the courtroom would get up and move away from me. But in church, people welcomed us as part of their community.

I learned a lot from Reverend Otis Hairston, who was a preacher that many considered dry and dull. But I wasn't looking for a lot of noise (I could listen to James Brown for that). One of the scriptures Reverend Hairston talked about was Michael, chapter 6, verse 8: "And what does the Lord require of you, except do justice, love mercy, and walk humbly with your God." There was a package in there: mercy that was open and kind and embraced people, sometimes in spite of what they do; life that was an intense fight for justice and was sustained by a connection within the laws of the cosmos, in harmony with some power greater than us. I wanted to get ahold of all of it, so I started to read the Bible, to read the ancient stories for myself.

Before my spiritual journey, I didn't have a clue who Jesus was. He seemed like just a nice guy. But I began to hear what happened to Jesus. I actually identified with him. He was doing good things, challenging the establishment, reaching out to the exploited. He spoke against the structures of power of Roman imperialism, which were enshrined in the established religion of that time. And ultimately, those powers got together and conspired against Jesus, put him in prison, put him on death row, and killed him. I came to an understanding of Jesus that helped me understand the world. He had the most thoroughgoing concern about the betterment of others. I wanted to be that kind of person.

As my philosophical view changed, I developed a critique of some parts of Marxism. I disagreed with the concept of the dictatorship of the proletariat. Marxism-Leninism holds that in the course of working-class revolution, there is the need to create a dictatorship of the working class over the bourgeoisie, to lock up some capitalists, and in some cases, even kill those who opposed the working-class revolution. Some Marxists held out little possibility for the transformation of the rich capitalists.

Today, I continue to have a class view of society, of profit motive driving the system. But I changed in how I see moving towards the good society. I think that all people have the potential for good and bad, that there is potential for transformation within all human beings. I think we have to view each other as individuals as well as part of social classes. My worldview is to seek the good in everyone.

In 1984, I decided to finish college so I could go to divinity school. I went back to A&T to get my undergraduate degree.

Kwame ■ By 1984, I had lost interest in school. I just wanted to be there because my friends was there, but as far as school itself, studying subjects, I was losing it. One day I was wearing a spiked belt. It was a new fad that had came out, and most of our gang members would wear it. But most of them wouldn't wear it to school because we had a really bad assistant principal at Grimsley. I was wearing this spiked belt and I was in the cafeteria. The assistant principal came up to me and told me to take the belt off and give it to him. And I said, "No, I'm not giving it to you."

He said, "You can't wear that, it's gang stuff."

And I said, "Show it to me in the dress code."

And he said, "Come in my office." And so I went to his office.

He said, "Give me the belt." And so I took the belt off and threw it at him. He called my mama to come to the school. Before she got there, I called him a bald-headed punk. My mama got there and the assistant principal said, "He called me a bald-headed punk."

And I told him, "Because you are a bald-headed punk." I said that right there in front of my mama. So I got smacked in the mouth, and he kicked me out of that school for that. I was sent to what was called an optional school.

The optional school was different; the hours were from four to eight. Most kids didn't really even attend that school. I went to that school maybe four times out of the entire rest of the year. When I was in school, everybody else is out, so if I went to school, I couldn't hang with my friends. I decided that my friends come first, so I stopped going to school.

Mama sensed that I was still hanging with the wrong crew, and she decided we needed to get out of St. James Homes. So we moved again.

Willena ■ I wanted to get my kids out of St. James. Kweli, my youngest, told me something about a roach, and it was not the bug kind. He was only eight years old but already learning the language of drugs. I moved to a solid working-class neighborhood that I hoped it would be a safe place for the kids to grow up.

But Kwame was still rebellious.

Kwame ■ By then I was in too deep. Our new place was in another gang territory, and that gang knew that I was part of the Q Dogs. When we first moved over there, I thought, I'm neutral now. But it don't work like that. Guys you been in stuff with, they know you.

It was summertime. A few days after we moved, I went to the swimming pool near there. I got up on the diving board, and I saw a guy we called Cheater standing at the fence. Cheater saw me. I dived off and got back up on the diving board. When I looked over there at the fence, Cheater had got all of his dudes. I was on the high diving board, and my sister, Imani, was on the low diving board. I told Imani, "Oh, my God, look at the fence." And she looked over there and she seen all them dudes.

I didn't even dive off. I felt sick, didn't want to swim no more. I walked back down the ladder and told Imani, "Go call Mama." At the time, Mama was working close by as the manager at Church's Chicken.

Well, Imani called Mama, and Mama come up there quick. She got her pocketbook with her, and I didn't know if she got a gun or not. She came to the fence—all of them dudes right there—and she said, "Come on out here."

I'm like, "Yes." So I started going through the locker room, but there was gang guys in there. I come back out and I said, "Mama, there's people in the locker room, I can't even go through there." So she came through the women's locker room and took me right back out through the women's locker room.

But that gang still thought they were going to get me. A few months later, I turned sixteen, and Mama gave me a secondhand Volkswagen for my birthday, November 23, 1984. I drove up to the Church's Chicken where my mama worked. Cheater was in the project right across the street, and he saw my car and see me drive up to Church's. He and his gang figured, "Oh, we got him trapped in there now." They didn't know my mama was the manager. So they came up there, and as soon as I seen them come, I went around back in the business part where my mom was. I told my mom, "That's them guys again."

Willena ■ There were eight of them, coming after Kwame. I sat them all down and talked to them. I told Cheater, the oldest one in the gang, the leader: "Look, my son is being trapped into this mess. He was getting beat up when he was not in a gang, so he joined a gang so he would not get beat. I moved him out them projects over there to this area so he wouldn't have to bother with that. Y'all need to cut that out."

Cheater started coming by Church's Fried Chicken late at night and helped me clean up. I fed him and his guys leftover chicken.

Nelson Johnson and I met with Cheater's gang. We talked to them about how the gangs were hurting the communities and hurting each other. We got leaders of several gangs together to talk. We said, "Talk, don't fight." They agreed and stuck to it.

Kwame ■ Cheater developed a lot of respect for my mom. He left me alone. In fact, we became friends. And I was finished with gangs.

Marty ■ When anyone says 1984, I think about George Orwell's book of that name, which is about living under fascism. I felt like I was living under fascism in the 1980s, after the massacre and during the trials. I thought fascism was coming, because it was all I could see in North Carolina, all those years, people coming at me. I thought I would probably be killed.

For a long time, I was so angry, I would yell at Leah, and a couple of times I smacked her. To this day, Leah and I still talk about it. She remembers me acting like a witch one night, and it was scaring the living daylights out of her. I had so much anger, and I couldn't control it. I was alone; there was nobody to take it out on. I thought, Oh God! Stop me! The only person I had to talk to was my good friend Roz Pelles, and she didn't know what to say to me, and she tried to "give me concrete advice, comrade." We both knew that wasn't working, and we said to each other: "We need counseling! We need therapy!" But at that point in North Carolina, poor, isolated, and in the spotlight, I couldn't do therapy. It had to wait.

At some point in those years, I realized that I was going to survive. And I began to want some happiness. I don't know what made me come to feel like a whole person again. Part of it was time, part was going through the recovery process, part was dreaming about the future.

For Dale, Signe, Floris, and me, these were our men who got killed. Putting our lives back together involved finding love and romance. I found love in a couple of relationships, but there were problems. Even though those relationships fell apart, they did make me feel like a whole person.

Then I met Elliot Fratkin, right after we lost the second trial. I was exhausted, and my life was a mess. He was the one person who really allowed me to heal. He got me to do things I never imagined doing, getting me into the woods, into nature. We went on a trip to Florida and went bird watching in the Loxahatchee Swamp and saw a beautiful anhinga.

Elliot was an anthropologist who studied people in Kenya, Africa, and had a professor job in Baltimore. During the third trial, he traveled back and forth between Baltimore and North Carolina. He was wonderful, helped me in so many ways, taking care of Leah, taking care of me.

1985 and 1986

Marty ■ Our civil trial started and ended in 1985—we got our partial victory in June 1985. A month later, Elliot and I got married. We went far away, to the end of the earth, to British Columbia, Canada, to get married. Me and Elliot and Leah and friends of Elliot's from Africa were there. Then we came back to Durham and had a party.

Elliot, Leah, and I planned to go to Africa. Elliot went first, at the end of October, to do research in Kenya. I stayed in North Carolina because I had to organize another November 3 commemoration for the sixth anniversary of the massacre.

Every year, I had to organize these commemorations. It was god-awful. You cannot imagine what it was like to organize in North Carolina. Some people would say things to me they wouldn't say to a dog; they would tell me what a pathetic character I was and slam doors in my face, over and over again. Every year, November 3 would come around, the hardest time of the year for me, and every year, I had to organize a big celebration to support the case. It always had to be me, because I was the one responsible for the Greensboro Justice Fund in North Carolina. I would always organize it. I would never let November 3 pass without it being in the limelight. I never had been allowed a November 3 without huge amounts of responsibility on my head.

That November 3, 1985, I put together the commemoration, and it was okay, a nice event. I came home afterwards and Dale Sampson Levin was staying with us, with her husband, Eliot. Dale's Eliot and my Elliot were cousins—so now Dale and I were family-in-law, as well as close friends. Dale's Eliot had been tremendously supportive to Dale during the trial, and they also got married right after the trial. Meanwhile, during the trial, Dale got pregnant! She was thrilled, because she had always wanted to have children. So on that November 3, Dale was pregnant, and it was a nice little family scene—except that all my pent-up emotions burst out. I just started screaming: "I never want to be responsible for a fucking thing ever again! I want to have my own personal private grief without having some reporter there to write down my responses, to twist them in print. I want to grieve without having the responsibility of teaching someone about the massacre."

It was one of the first times I ever let go. And then I felt real bad about it. Dale had been through as much shit as I had. I was just too mired in the pain and the disappointment. I couldn't do anything more and just wanted to leave. So it was very good that Elliot was in Africa, and that Leah and I could follow him there.

We traveled in Africa and then in Europe. I was trying to figure out whether life was worth living. It was important to see the world was big, that North Carolina and all that pressure was not the only place on earth. I learned that time will continue and got a sense of my very small place in history. I needed to know that people were herding their cattle in eastern Kenya, and there were people selling their wares at the London market—that it had been going on and would still be going on. Life has scope physically and temporally. I thought life had stopped on November 3.

I remember lying in this featherbed in Switzerland. Elliot had fallen asleep. I started thinking about the trial. For the first time, I just cried and cried.

Demise of the CWP

Paul ▪ In the mid 1980s, the Communist Workers Party tried to reorganize itself as the New Democratic Movement. It was a failure. The CWP leadership had realized that in the U.S. a revolutionary party could not be successful and call itself communist. We had all these superb grassroots leaders in the CWP who would say, "I can't lead because I'm known as a communist." Communism, rather than being a guide to action, had become an obstacle; it had become an excuse for failing to lead.

So in 1985–86, the CWP tried to transform itself into the New Democratic Movement. It failed because the NDM was never democratic. There is an expression, "Old habits die hard"; the CWP leadership could not let up their control, their old habits of centralism and secrecy. The NDM elected leaders, but then everything those leaders did had to be cleared by the CWP. NDM never had a life of its own.

I found working with New Democratic Movement frustrating. I asked lots of questions and was told by CWP leaders to stop asking them. I had always gotten along well with CWP leader Jerry Tung, before and after the massacre. But I am the kind of person who has trouble shutting up, and when he said not to ask questions, I wrote a letter of resignation. I still think a revolutionary party is needed, but it must develop ways to be democratic.

Quitting the Party was tremendously difficult for me, a big struggle inside me. My whole self-conception rested on building a communist party to lead the working class. Leaving the Party was like losing a close relative or dear friend. I was very disoriented. I talked to close friends who also left CWP about what we could do outside the Party. The only thing we came up with was "just survive on our own as best we can." It was years later that I realized that without a party, people can continue to fight for justice. But in the mid-1980s, the demise of CWP was the beginning of a long period of demoralization for me.

Marty ▪ In 1986, I had a big argument with Jerry Tung over the money from the third trial settlement. The City of Greensboro paid us the $350,000 settlement, and Dale and I worked out how to divide up the money between all the victims. There was one big problem: Jerry Tung wanted the money for the New Democratic Movement. I had heard that there were struggles within NDM over openness and democracy and leadership. Dale and I decided that the money belonged to no organization; it belonged to the victims of the attack.

I had to go up to New York to tell Jerry. Gayle Korotkin, our lawyer since the beginning of the trials, came with me. We hoped that Jerry would like our plan, because we thought it was a good one. We met with Jerry and a few other people, and they did not like the plan. Jerry looked upset, but he didn't speak much. The others attacked us for being disloyal and selfish, and guilt-tripped us about all the CWP members who had sacrificed.

It was very upsetting. The CWP had been the backbone of our struggle, especially at the beginning. It was heartbreaking. But the bottom line was that the money belonged to the victims. They could donate it to CWP or NDM if they chose, but it was their choice.

Nelson ■ I always felt that Jerry Tung was an extraordinarily gifted person, deeply analytical. But he (and others, including myself) had a problem dating back to before the massacre. Jerry emphasized the power of will to break through objective factors and make something happen. But that has to be balanced with reality. You can't will yourself to run into that tree out there. You can run into it, but it will knock you down. I think our organization began to operate outside the laws of consequence, and we live in a universe governed by laws within which we are ultimately constrained to operate. I can't breathe out all the time: There's a law that recognizes you've got to breathe in. It doesn't matter how strong your will is.

In 1979, in the months before November 3, we were out of balance. I wasn't aware of it because I was part of the leadership and part of promoting what we were doing. I think a healthy dose of humility would have served me and some of the rest of us. We were doing some good things, but we were losing some balance.

Right after the massacre, I felt that Jerry and all of the CWP national leadership were very helpful in helping us fight back. But somewhere through the years, I don't really know what happened. He seemed to be saying a lot of things that were not valid, that were a reflection of fear and insecurity.

Sally ■ CWP leadership did help us greatly right after the murders. I also credit them with helping us to come together in North Carolina in the first place, back in 1976. But all along, I never felt like Jerry respected me or other women, and I believe that he had a deep bias against women. Jerry had a weakness in listening, and I don't think he had the capacity to lead a truly democratic organization.

I did not know about Marty's argument with Jerry about the settlement money until years after it happened. I do remember that Paul got a check, his portion of the settlement, and that we decided immediately to give it all back to Greensboro Justice Fund. The continuation of the Greensboro Justice Fund was a ray of light coming out of long-stormy skies.

Willena ■ The Party just seemed to disappear. For a long time, I had had questions about communism in this country. Could people come to see it as a good thing? The injustice, knowing how the capitalist system is, all that was clear—is still clear—to me. The question is, What is the way out of this? But NDM never appealed to me. It seemed flaky.

After the trials, nothing much was happening politically in Greensboro. People focused on their own problems, and I sure had enough of those. Kwame was so rebellious, getting in trouble.

Breaking and Entering

Kwame ■ By 1985, I was finished with gangs, but tricks had been instilled in me, like breaking and entering. It was like I had learned a trade that got me money. I was sixteen, then seventeen, and I had been rebelling since I was thirteen. My mom was having a lot of problems with me. I kept telling her I wanted to go see my dad. Then when I would get with my dad, I would want to go home to mom. I really didn't know what I wanted. Something was always missing.

It was like my thinking pattern had gotten off track. I became a very selfish person. I thought, If Kwame wants something, then Kwame is going to get it. If I wanted a radio, I was going to get it, even if I had to break into somebody's house. It wasn't drugs; I've never been on drugs.

I can't or won't sit here and try to justify myself by saying, "November 3 is what caused me to get into crime," because that would be totally wrong. I'm the one who decided to commit breaking and entering. But the massacre may have had some effect on my thinking pattern. At the time I was doing my crimes, I was ignorant of the law. But I was thinking, Hey, I'm fifteen/sixteen years old, I've never been in trouble. If they catch me, they can't do but so much to me. I got that part from November 3, because those Klan and Nazis killed people and they never served time.

It is still hard for me to understand why I got into crime. There were times when our family was really struggling to make it, especially after the murders when my mom couldn't get a job and she was alone with us three. It would seem like I would have done the burglary then. When I was doing the burglary in 1985–86, Mom was getting herself established. I had a regular fast-food job myself. I don't really understand what went wrong with me.

There were bad influences around me. I was still looking for a father figure, a big brother, to pay attention to me. My cousin was about ten years older than me. He would sometimes come by on his motorcycle. Then I was afraid he was shying away from me. One day, I says: "I don't need your motorcycles. I don't need you." Then my cousin started getting more interested, hanging around me as if we were peers. He started going out with me when I did my crimes, but he would never do the breaking and entering. He would never go into the houses. He would look over the houses during the day while I was at school and come pick me up from school in his BMW, which he had just painted Carolina blue. That was a big thing, to have this dude stop out in front of school to pick me up. He was older than me, but he was cool with me. He was hanging out with me at a little drive-in where older people like him hung. They sold weed and drank, and he offered me beers and bought them for me. To me that was a huge thing, my older cousin digging me like that.

Then it got to a point where he was wanting me to do the B and E's more frequent than I wanted. There would be times he needed something for the car, something for this, something for that. "I staked this neighborhood out," he would say. And I looked up to him so much, I preferred to get in trouble rather than to disappoint him or to fail him.

Then I got caught. The police scared me into confessing six burglaries. I'm in this room in the police station, and this big guy comes in and he is threatening me. I just wanted to call my mom, but they wouldn't let me call home. I was so scared that I told him, "Just take me to the jailhouse." I thought over there I could at least call my mom. But they said, "We want to get this straight now." So that is how they scared me to confess.

Willena ■ Kwame was held under a half-million-dollar bond. It was all over the news, on the TV. He was charged with first-degree burglary, which is the same as breaking and entering but more serious because it was committed after midnight.

Kwame ■ They put me in jail. Mom tried to implicate my cousin on the crime—a mother trying to save her son.

Willena ■ Without my knowing, Kwame's cousin had come into my house in the middle of the night, when we were all asleep. He had waken Kwame up and taken him out to do these crimes. This guy was twenty-seven years old, college degree. I told his lawyer, "Kwame had an adult with him when he did the breaking and entering." I wanted the lawyer to cut a deal if it would mean Kwame would serve less time.

I told my family that Kwame should tell on his cousin if it could cut his time. Usually, when an adult is involved with a juvenile in committing crimes, the authorities try to punish the adult and go lighter on the younger child. But Greensboro officials were not interested in this adult, only in getting Kwame. It was a way they could punish me.

Kwame ■ Then the DA asked me if my cousin was involved, and I said, "He had nothing to do with it."

And I went back and called my cousin, and it just made me feel like this huge hero when I told him: "Cuz, they asked about you. But don't worry about nothing. 'Cause I ain't saying nothing on you. They can't do nothing. Don't worry about nothing." That just made me feel so big.

He said: "I appreciate it, cuz. Be strong." One of the reasons why I had really took that stance was because my cousin was twenty-seven, and if he went to prison, he would go to Central Prison, one of the roughest prisons in North Carolina. I was going to a youth camp. So I was thinking, I can handle a youth camp better than him handling Central Prison. 'Cause my cuz was little, a pretty boy. I was little, too, but I was going to a prison where everybody was little.

I felt like it was a way of showing everyone that I wasn't a little tattletale no more, because all my male cousins had me labeled tattletale. When I turned sixteen, I had started challenging them to wrestling, and I wanted to just show them that I wasn't the same little tattletale. I wanted them to know I was carrying the weight.

It was my responsibility. I made the decision to break into homes. I was young, but I made that decision. So it wasn't like something that I could really hold my cousin accountable for.

But my cousin was so influential over me. Years later, when I was in prison, I thought back about my crimes. This was when I was in my late twenties, and I was processing what had happened. I used to wonder, What if my cousin had given me that same attention but focused it on my school and other constructive things. Came to pick me up from school and say: "How was your day? What's going on today? Let's go to the park."

I was in the Guilford County Jail for a month. Then they sent me to the mental hospital to see if I was competent to stand trial. After twenty-seven days there, they brought me back to the jail. Then one day, not my court day, my lawyer says to me: "We're having court today. I'm putting your case on."

Willena ■ When I hired that lawyer, I thought he was a good lawyer. Later I found out he was an alcoholic. After he became an alcoholic, he became incompetent.

Kwame ■ I asked my lawyer why we were going to court ahead of schedule. He said, "We're going to try to avoid the press." The papers had been making a big deal about my arrest, about catching the cat burglar. So they put me in a little holding cell.

In the trial, my lawyer says, "This is the best I can do," and shows me a paper saying two life sentences. It was a plea bargain.

The judge kept asking me . . . It was almost as if the judge didn't want to give me that sentence. He asked me if my mother was present. I said no. The judge said, "I will grant him a new trial date when his mother can be present."

I said, "No, I just want to get it over with."

The judge said, "Are you sure you know what you are doing?"

I said yeah, but I didn't have any idea.

Then they gave me the sentence—two life sentences.

Willena ■ My sixteen-year-old child. They gave him two life sentences, a harsher sentence than they give to murderers. He had committed crimes, but he never had been physically violent. Then the news media was coming to me, showing my house on TV, trying to get a comment from me. People kill people around here, and they don't get that amount of media coverage.

I felt that they gave Kwame such a big sentence to punish me. Detective Thomas made sure that Kwame got that maximum sentence. He was the director of investigation of the Greensboro Police Department. During the first trial, he was the man who tried to grab Paul when he was in the wheelchair. I didn't know he was a police officer because he had on civilian clothes, so I thought he was a white citizen with racist views. I hit him in the back of the head, and I got arrested. Later, I found out that Thomas was one of the police who tried to hide evidence about the massacre—he was a defendant in our civil suit. Then a year and a half after the civil suit, Kwame got caught. Detective Thomas made sure that I got punished by putting Kwame in prison for life.

Nelson ■ I have known Kwame since he was three or four. He was a pretty little boy. He grew up in the movement, along with my children. They were movement children, and in and out of each other's homes. I watched him grow up. When he was a teenager, I struggled with him over some of the things he was doing. I was deeply concerned for him. I sensed him being rebellious and his mother not being able to bring him in. It was mostly normal for a young teenager, and within the context of his history and circumstances.

Then I heard about him being caught as a cat burglar. I had a couple of emotions. First, I just felt bad for him and for Willena. Secondly, I felt that what he did was not good for who we were trying to be. People tried to paint us as hoodlums and thugs and criminals, and here's this kid who was so closely identified with us. But I put that out of my mind. I was not involved in his trial. I left Greensboro to go to seminary shortly after Kwame got convicted.

Nothing was going on in Greensboro. All our organization had been focused on the trials. After the third trial was over in 1985 until the early 1990s, there wasn't any organizing going on anything. It left Willena in a terrible lurch. She retreated to her family, for the most part. I visited her when I could, and she would talk about these different things she was trying to do. I supported her in going through all that, but I did very little.

Sally ■ I did not see Willena Cannon for a long time, because it was years before I went back to Greensboro—in 1989, during the tenth anniversary, and I sought Willena out at the nursing home where she worked as a housekeeping supervisor. I was taken aback seeing Willena; she looked like a broken person. I remembered her in the 1970s as a woman of tremendous spirit. Afraid of nothing, she was always at the head of the march, chanting loudly. But a decade later, that spirit was broken. Willena was glad to see me, but our talk seemed hard for her, and she often trailed off. The greatest thing weighing her down was Kwame, who had been in prison for two years at that time with a sentence far too severe for the crimes he had committed.

Kwame ■ Mom told me, "They're punishing you so hard because they're trying to get back at me." She told me about the policeman she hit because he was trying to dump Paul out of the wheelchair. I didn't quite understand. It was a mess. After my trial, they sent me to the prison called Morgantown High Rise. I got called down to my custody review, and the counselor says, "Your parole date is 2006."

I said: "What? My lawyer said I could get out in seven to ten years if I'm good." I was scared; I was praying that he didn't know what he was talking about.

He said: "You are serving two life sentences. You're not eligible to get out of prison for twenty years."

12
Healing

Healing from the massacre was a long journey that stretched through the 1980s and 1990s into the millennium. During these decades, the plight of the poor grew worse in the United States, even as the country's economy boomed. Inequality increased as most of the economic gains went to the small fraction of the nation's wealthiest people. At the same time, there was a prison construction boom and a big rise in incarceration, especially among people of color. By the year 2000, there were more young black men in prisons and jails than there were in colleges and universities.[1] One of them was Kwame Cannon.

Sally ■ I interviewed Kwame in the North Carolina Penitentiary in Reidsville on March 9, 1992. To tape an interview with an inmate, I had to get permission from the sergeant in charge for a special appointment. I was escorted into an administrative building within the prison compound. Two armed guards brought Kwame, in handcuffs, into the room. During the entire interview, Kwame had to sit awkwardly with his wrists cuffed behind his back, while an armed guard stood just outside the open door.

I felt like telling the guard: "Kwame's not dangerous. He is a sweet kid I have known since he was little." But I said nothing, and Kwame ignored the handcuffs. We talked for the one hour allotted us.

The Prison Interview

Kwame ■ I've been in prison for six years, and it's good to look back to where I was and see where I am now. When I first got locked up, I had an angry frame of mind. Any little thing that someone said would set me off. When I first was sent to prison in 1986, and my counselor told me I couldn't come up for parole until 2006, my attitude was "Whomp it!" I used to walk around muttering, "I got two life sentences, and I don't care!" I got infractions [write-ups] because I would blow up at whoever I was talking to, officer or inmate. I was assigned to work in the kitchen. I'd be doing my work, cleaning, and then the supervisor would try to tell me a way to get it cleaner or a way to do it better. And I'd just start yelling. People shied away, left me alone. I was pretty much isolated, along with the other thugs, the crazy ones, the crowd that had the life sentences. I didn't care. I wasn't coming home. I wasn't going to listen to nobody.

My counselor called me down to talk, probably after an officer had told him that I was on the wrong road. I was at Morgantown High Rise, a youth prison, because I was seventeen. My counselor told me, "When you're eighteen, you gotta leave, because this is a youth camp." He said they were planning to send me to Polk Youth Center, a tougher prison. At the time, there were rumors running around that at Polk the bigger ones molest the little ones. Those kind of rumors frightened me.

I said, "What if I'm good?"

He said, "Well, sometimes, if you're not causing the officers any trouble, if you're working and your bossman throws in a good recommendation for you, they'll hold you here."

I said, "I'm going to try to be good."

But it seemed like just as soon as I left my counselor, I was right back to the same bag of trying to throw my weight around. And by then, I had some weight to throw around. I gained a lot and was pretty close to 200 pounds. I had been lifting weights, so I was strong. Now I'm back down to 165.

Me and a few guys got into horse playing. The guards kept catching us. One time, I'm down in the kitchen, horse playing, and one of the guys I'm playing with burns me on the arm with this steam faucet that shoots hot water and steam. He was a little white kid. Me and him were good friends, and I wouldn't have done nothing in the world to hurt him. I looked out for him. I liked him because he was small and stood his ground. He didn't let people push him around. But he burned my arm, and I had to go up to the hospital floor. They bandaged me up, and when I came back down, I told him, "Boy I'm gonna get you tomorrow, I'm gonna get you tomorrow." I was teasing.

The next morning, I'm waiting on them to open my door, and they don't open it. The man says, "You're on floor restriction; you got written up."

I said, "For what?"

He said, "For communicating threats."

I said, "Oh, man." The little white kid thought I was threatening him.

My counselor came up that same day, while I was on restriction. He said, "I told you, you got to stay out of trouble, and you're dissing that." It was right around Christmastime, and I had just turned eighteen. He told me that the sarge was going to process the write-up, and I had a choice. He said: "We'll send you to Polk and forget the write-up. Or you can stay here, with the write-up, and try to redeem yourself and be good again."

I said, "Well, I don't want the write-up, 'cause I'm going to try to keep my record as clean as I can." So I left High Rise and went to Polk, where I did three years.

Polk wasn't as bad as everybody had made it out to be. I was big by then, and soon I was right up in the ranks of the ones that was pushing their weight around. I was in medium custody, and I had eighteen points because of my write-ups for infractions. If my points went up any higher, I would be moved to an adult prison, a tough one like Central Prison or Caledonia or Erwin Farms. At Polk I had a lady counselor, Miss Daley. She sat me down and had a good talk with me about getting back on my college course, about straightening up. She told me about the living conditions at the adult prisons and the type of inmates they had. And she instilled a little faith in me that I could be good. I thought, Well, hey, I'm not such a bad guy no way.

Miss Daley was a good lady; she helped me out. She got me a good job at Polk in the boiler room. It was a pretty prestigious job; people would try to get the job. That's when I really started straightening up. She started calling me up all times of the month. Usually the counselors call you once every three months, but Miss Daley started taking time with me and helping me straighten me out.

Mom came to visit me. But those were some terrible visits. Mom at that time had gotten saved; she had found God. She was coming to see me, trying to preach the word to me. I didn't want to hear it. Those visitings were really sour. Sometimes I even wanted to say to her, "You probably are the reason I'm in here with all this time now!" I would never say it, but it came to my mind a lot. Because sometime when she was leaving, and we'd both be in ill moods, it would come to my mind. I never said that I blamed her for my long sentence, but I know my mom was thinking that, because she would cry. We both ended up crying sometimes in the visiting room. It was just some terrible visits.

Then my aunt came to see me. My aunt is an evangelist. I put my defense up; I was prepared to blast her out as soon as she said anything about God. I guess she sensed it, so she didn't say too much about God. She just started writing me letters, and I started writing back. Then she came to visit again, and this time, I didn't have my defense up. She brought out God that time. I was touched. It's funny, she just stayed behind me a lot, writing, talking. I started reading the Word every now and then. And I quit all the craziness that I had.

Over the years, I got moved to other camps. Now I'm at this camp at Reidsville, which is closer to Greensboro, so my mom and other people can visit me easier. About seven months ago, I got into the word of God and started practicing his word, walking in faith. It's changed me; its changed my life a lot. It's changed the way I think about things. It took a lot of anger, a lot of hate, out of my heart.

Before, I would be quick to jump into a fight. If someone said something, I would be quick to say something back, which would eventually bring about a fight. I had a terrible temper, and so I worked on controlling my temper. Now, if someone says something, I either ignore it, just let it go, or I say, "I'm gonna pray for you." That's one of the first things I holler to them, "I'll pray for you!"

Just today, a guy wanted to show me conflict in the Bible. I said, "We can talk about it, but as far as you trying to show me a contradiction in the Bible, I'm not even gonna deal with you on that level." He's a Muslim. The Muslims and the Christians don't usually have that many problems here, it's just this one guy. That's been about my only temptation today, because I've been in my course all day long. I haven't had any room; my mind's been busy all day.

That's another way that God has shown me—keep myself occupied, always doing something constructive. 'Cause anything you do that is good is of God. That's what the Bible tells you, and that's what I believe. 'Cause your mind gets idle and then you start doing a lot of little stuff that I was doing before.

Sally ■ Can you imagine people saying something or doing something to you that would get you angry?

Kwame ■ Hmmm . . . no, not anything thing they could *say*. Before, the smallest, littlest thing someone said would jump-start me. And now talk wouldn't bother me the least. If somebody says something to me, I strike back with the word of God. Usually, if they're an unbeliever, they don't want to hear scriptures. So they will either stay away from me, or if they persecute me more, I just ignore it. It doesn't make me upset.

If somebody *does* something . . . if they hit me, I ain't strong enough . . . I ain't that strong yet! I try to avoid a lot of mess, stay out of trouble. Because I want to be home with my mama and my brother and sister. I feel like I have less time in a day to do things. Before, it was like, "Dog, I can't wait 'til this day get over with." And now, up until late at night, I'm writing scriptures. I'm always busy; I always have something to do. It seems like I don't have enough time. I stay pretty busy.

But in my daily walk, I do get upset. It's hard. Sometimes I feel like I am so really drained, that's when I either hit the basketball court or maybe go play a game of Ping-Pong, or a game of chess.

Sally ■ Willena has been talking about an investigation of your case, to make the court look into the unfairness of your long sentence and reduce it. What are your hopes? What are your fears?

Kwame ■ Well, my biggest fear is if they investigate and let me out, and that I walk astray from God and get in trouble again. That's my biggest fear.

Okay, as far as my hopes—sure, I'm hoping to get out. The hopes . . . oh, I've got so many. It's seems like I wouldn't have enough time in the day out there. I want to talk to young kids; I want to be able to guide my younger sister and brother. I would like to just go to a community center where I could get a bunch of kids together and talk to them, with them, and tell them to slow down, leave that mess alone. I would go into Morningside and grab a handful of kids and just sit down and talk with them. Not just one time, but a weekly-type thing so they wouldn't feel like it was someone talking to them and now that's gone. I want them to feel that I would be someone that would be behind them. Sometime when you feel that someone cares, you don't stray out there with the worst of them. I would try to give them a sense of love, a sense of hope that they can make it.

I'm hoping to get back in school. I was studying a course here in prison, but it got me so frustrated. It's hard when there isn't a teacher to explain it to me. I want to grab me a job when I get out, where I could be earning a few dollars, putting them away, or giving them to Mom. A lot of my money would have to go to my mom.

My mom's been my backbone. Without her . . . I don't know. She's just been a strong woman, like she always has. She has really stuck behind me through all my bad times. Now it seems like it is really starting to get good between the two of us. We've really gotten tight over the past two years. When my mom comes up here to visit by herself, that's when we have so much fun. My mom is crazy. We are mother and son—and best friends.

Sometimes seeing the people from the old days, from the Party, I feel ashamed of being here. I feel I let people down. The whole time I've been in, I haven't seen Nelson or Joyce or Akua. Ayo is the only one who comes to see me. It's hard for me to even call them. The whole time, I've probably written them twice. I want to see Nelson so bad, but I feel shame, I feel like I let him down. I just wish I'd been put in here for something like a struggle for what my mom stands for. Then it wouldn't bother me to be in prison, it wouldn't be a burden on me.

But then I think, I was even worse off out there than in here. I'm a better person now; the last two years have helped me. That's one way I try to keep a little of the shameness off me. I feel more peace with myself now than I ever did when I was outside at home. A guy was just asking me about it today. He really is an excellent person—Mike, from right here in Reidsville. We were just sitting out in the sun right after lunch and talking. He said, "Kwame, have you heard anything?"

I said: "I haven't heard nothing, not yet. But the Lord is with me, and I will hear something soon." Then I asked him, "Mike, how much time you got?"

He said, "Life, class A, twenty years mandatory."

I asked him what it was about.

He said: "The only reason I got so much time is 'cause I killed a white guy. I was going with a white girl right here in Reidsville."

So he got a lot of time, but I got more than him. And I didn't threaten no one, didn't carry no weapons, didn't assault nobody, rape nobody, none of that. There are so many people who's been run in and out of here that have done worse crime than I have. Sometimes it bothers me. It gets depressing.

All I know is that in here, it isn't easy. But it's even harder out there. 'Cause in here, everything is done for you. It is easy to become institutionalized in here, because the same things you do today, you do tomorrow. Get up, lay down, go eat—you fall into a cycle. I fell into it. I stopped writing everybody. One time on visiting day, I told my daddy that it didn't bother me no more to be locked up, that I had gotten used to it. He reached over to me and smacked me. Then he started crying, my mama started crying, and I started crying. Here are all three of us in the visiting room crying!

When I got moved to my first adult facility, I got in a fight my first week. I lost a basketball game, got mad, and kicked the basketball over the fence. People were looking at me like, "What is wrong with this fool?" And I ended up in the hole.

After that, this guy Lamont Woods, another prisoner, said, "Man, you are institutionalized."

I got defensive, 'cause I didn't understand what he was saying. He said: "As long as you can gamble, as long as you got some money and can buy you something out of the canteen, you happy. When is the last time you wrote somebody a letter?"

He was the first person I started talking to. And the only reason I could take it from him was that he was funny, he was short, and he had never been aggressive towards me. He helped me figure out what I really wanted. I started writing poems, and the more I wrote the better I got at it.

Now, it does bother me to be in prison. I won't be satisfied until I'm home. All I want is another chance. I have so much I wa—

[Guard]: Time's up. Visit's over.

Ups and Downs

Sally ■ It was wonderful to see Kwame. I had not seen him for a decade, since he was a little twelve-year-old kid. When I first visited him in prison in 1992, he was twenty-two years old, a young man wise beyond his years. Yet he was energetic, animated, happy to see me. In the worst conditions—prison— Kwame was growing, learning, beginning to heal. If only he could get out of prison.

For the rest of us, healing was easier, but still a process of ups and downs. For me, a big part of my process has been interviewing the other survivors, hearing their stories. Like many who experience violence, I had posttraumatic stress disorder. For years, I had flashbacks, caught in the memory of the massacre. No matter where I was, my mind would go back to the corner of Carver and Everitt, my heart pounding: the Klan/Nazi caravan driving up, the big Nazi shooting calmly, deliberately, at people. At night I had nightmares of white men trying to break into our house trying to kill us. I would wake up sweating. It was all I could do to focus on daily routines, taking care of the kids, going to work.

I had a series of jobs, low paid and boring. I wanted to go to graduate school so I could get an interesting job. When Paul finished his psychiatric residency and got a doctor job, we decided it was my turn to go to school. I discovered the City University of New York, a high-quality public university with low tuition. I began the master's in urban planning program at Hunter College and loved it—the studying, the books, the students, writing papers, getting graded, the whole thing.

But I could not talk about the massacre to any of my graduate school friends. I studied urban planning for five semesters and got my master's degree without talking to anyone about November 3. I was like a homosexual who was in the closet, hiding a major part of my life. I had no visible wounds from November 3. No one could see my flashbacks or the long stretches of time every day when I thought about my dead friends. I felt like my heart had been slashed, then superficially healed over and covered by clothing. Underneath, I felt deep pain, even if nobody could see it. Paul's wounds, in contrast, were highly visible, and he could not choose to keep the massacre secret. At every job interview, doctors asked him why he limped, why his arm didn't work.

I decided to go for a Ph.D. in political science at the CUNY Graduate Center. I saw it as a career opportunity, and also as a chance to work out my own political understanding of what had happened to us. I wanted to understand how and why powerful people could fail to see the powerless as human. I wanted to study government, its responsibilities, why it sometimes does the opposite of its principles. And I wanted to study social movements and evaluate strategies for change.

I also vowed that I would come out of the closet. In 1988, during my first semester in the Ph.D. program, I continued to hide my Greensboro connection. But I knew that I had to talk to someone, so I got up my nerve and made an appointment with my advisor and favorite professor, Stanley Renshon. He is a professor of political psychology and a therapist as well, so I figured he was a good person to talk to. My palms sweating, I tried to keep my voice calm as I told him about the massacre, my five dead friends, and Paul's wounds. Stanley remembered the incident, but he quickly changed the subject to give me advice about what courses I should take. I couldn't believe it! Here I had bared my wounds, and he acted like it was no big deal. I quickly left, and as I rode the subway home, I berated myself for opening up.

As I walked through my front door, the phone was ringing. It was Stanley Renshon. He apologized for not responding to me during our appointment. He said he thought the massacre had been horrible, and he was proud to have me in the doctoral program. And I sighed with relief.

At the time, I thought I needed to "come out" just for my own psychological stability. But that discussion opened the door to interviewing survivors. Less than a year later, I started a research project, under Stanley Renshon, to conduct in-depth interviews with massacre survivors. In October 1989, I drove down to Greensboro with Dale Sampson Levin, Bill's widow, who was director of the Greensboro Justice Fund. The tenth anniversary of the massacre approached, and Dale was organizing commemoration programs. I interviewed her in the car as we drove around and found out that she too had posttraumatic stress syndrome. Dale had not been to Greensboro for four years, since the end of the trials. I had not been there for eight years, since I testified before the grand jury. When we got to the city limits of Greensboro, we both had flashbacks of November 3. We got lost and panicked when we saw pickup trucks with white men in them. Finally, we made it to Joyce and Nelson Johnson's house and felt better in their warm kitchen.

Over the next three years, I interviewed fifty-three people who had been demonstrating against the KKK on November 3, 1979. I was still close friends with some of them, others I didn't know at all, and most I had not seen for years. It was emotional, because in every interview, I relived the massacre through the eyes of another survivor. I was fascinated with people's life stories, their parents and childhoods, how they joined the social movements, why many of them became communists, how the massacre had affected them, and how they were recovering from it. Willena Cannon was a tremendous help, getting me in touch with many survivors whom I had not seen for a decade. She told me, "I want you to write a book for everybody, but especially for our own children, so they will know what really happened on November 3." I was an emotional wreck just doing interviews. I couldn't imagine writing a book.

But Willena was right. I got great feedback on my interview project from professors and students, and eventually I decided to expand it into a dissertation. Over the next five years I wrote *Survivors of the 1979 Greensboro Massacre: A Study of the Long-Term Impact of Protest Movements on the Political Socialization of Radical Activists*. I got a Ph.D. from CUNY in 1994, and a job teaching political science at Brooklyn College. It has been a gratifying healing process.

Nelson ■ Healing for me involved having time to gather my thoughts and think through what I believed. I pondered humanity, including those humans who were the Ku Klux Klan. I went to Virginia Union School of Theology in Richmond for three years, 1986–89, and it was a most enjoyable period. I stayed with Joyce's parents, who loved me and fed me well. It was good to get out of Greensboro and to come back only on the weekends to see Joyce and my daughters. For those years, I was no longer a community organizer, had none of those demands on me; no one expected anything of me.

In seminary, I reevaluated my view of communism. Our experiences as the

Workers Viewpoint Organization and the Communist Workers Party, as a group of people, were wonderful; a deep, eternal communion grew out of it. The WVO/CWP critique of capitalism and the economic forces, how they shape social consciousness, was helpful, and I'll be forever grateful for the insights. Yet at the end of the day, I disagreed with writing off whole groups of human beings, like the ruling class and like the KKK.

Yet I didn't know what to hold with. I debated Marxism with my professors and friends throughout the whole time I was in seminary. It was a time when I felt somewhat defeated, because as WVO/CWP, we actually thought we had the answer: It was just a question of working hard, getting people to see it, and we'd all get there. I no longer thought we had the answer, only some good insights. And I began to come to my own views.

I studied the history of theology. Sitting in dark libraries with dusty old books, I felt unnerved by all the terrible things that have happened under the banner of religion, both long ago and now. Bishops were killing each other on the way to the conference at Nicaea to decide what the Bible was. I was sitting there thinking, Do I have to follow this? One can fall into a deeper well of cynicism. Yet through it all, I drew closer to an understanding that we are all on a very long journey, that we are all human beings constructed similar to each other.

Humans have this ease with which we can dismiss one another, blame one another. I realized that I didn't have the capacity to understand how everybody was going to change—indeed, whether everybody was going to change. But I needed to be open to the possibility that people can change for the better. I now hold that as essential to the vocation of being human. I tried to apply the philosophy to the questions I faced. I thought, Who is this Klan? What are these people about? We fought these folks, and we bear the marks of the encounter with them. But putting them on a permanent dismissal list was something that I was increasingly uncomfortable with.

The summer after my first year in divinity school, I gave my first sermon in Greensboro, and the *News and Record* published an article on it on July 14, 1986:

Johnson Turning to Christ

With oratorical passion he once used to damn capitalists, Nelson Johnson exhorted Christians to a mission of mercy, justice and peace Sunday night in the first sermon of his ministerial career.

Johnson, 43, was one of several Communist Worker Party members wounded in a violent confrontation on Nov. 3, 1979, in Greenboro between party members and Klansmen and Nazis. His rhetoric was calmer, but equally critical as he preached at Shiloh Baptist Church on Sunday.

He chided TV preachers for scaring people to seek Jesus out of fear, not love. He blamed President Reagan for using visions of Armageddon to spur America to military might. He denounced Christians who use Scripture for their own aims, not the betterment of all.

"Some people treat religion as a rationale for selfishness," Johnson said. "I'm not interested in being an acceptable, don't-rock-the-boat preacher. The Jesus I know and love rocked the world!"

Cries of "Amen" and "Yes, Yes" echoed in Shiloh's rounded red-brick and oak sanctuary. Johnson's fiery, 45-minute message earned him a standing ovation. Shiloh's pastor, the Rev. Otis Hairston, moved to the pulpit, and Johnson's brother, the Rev. James M. Johnson of Littleton, grabbed his brother in a bear hug. . . .

Several hundred sat in Shiloh to hear Johnson. . . . Martha Nathan and Signe Waller, both widows of Communist Workers Party members slain in the 1979 confrontation heard him preach . . . [and] Johnson's wife, Joyce, who sang with the Shiloh choir; his two teenage daughters, Ayodele, 14, and Akua, 15; two of his four sisters, three of his four brothers, . . . and his father in law.

In an interview at his home last week, Johnson said reflection on his faith and life brought him to the ministry. His voice was soft, almost somber, in a room decorated with family photographs and athletic trophies won by his two teenage daughters. . . .

"I developed as a social activist," Johnson said. "And I've always felt I was doing what was right . . . I don't see myself as having made a lot of radical shifts."

He believes in liberation theology, a philosophy that preaches Christ as liberator of the oppressed. But Johnson says he's also read the works of John C. Calhoun and men like him to understand what motivates white Southerners and white-supremacy advocates like the Ku Klux Klan.

"I've been part of the civil rights movement, the black liberation movement, the socialist movement. . . . I'm less inclined right now to put whole people into categories. I'm no less inclined to be critical of certain ideas, of ideas I believe to be wrong. But I think there's a way to do that that's not condemning other persons."

Could he have helped to avert the violence on Nov. 3, 1979?

"In looking back, I can see errors and weaknesses in my thinking."

The *Greensboro News and Record* did *not* publish my answer to that last question. I told the reporter that this city had organized a North American death squad against us, and my becoming a preacher did not change that.

In the 1980s, the Klan was very active in North Carolina, marching in many cities and towns in the state. But 1987 was the first time since 1979 that the

KKK said they would march in Greensboro. When I came back home to Greensboro the weekend after the Klan announcement, I got numerous calls with people asking, "What is the CWP going to do?" I would not be part of the anti-Klan protest, I decided, because I was in Richmond five days a week and only came home on the weekends. I knew that if I got involved in the anti-Klan protest, I would end up just running my mouth and not have time to do the necessary organizing work.

But the more I heard about the Klan coming to Greensboro again, the more I thought it was a disaster. These Klan people were coming as mockery, spitting on the graves of our five people. I discussed it with a few professors around the seminary who knew my connection to the massacre. I told one professor, Dr. Robertson, that I was agonizing over what to do, and that I was inclined to find a way to get to these Klan members and have a discussion with them. He was a professor of Christian ethics, and he told me: "There are some people you can't have a discussion with. I think it would be quite unwise for you to go down there messing with those folk."

I talked to another professor, Dr. Kiney, professor of systemic theology, the best teacher I've ever had. I told him that I was inclined to try to find a way to talk to the Klan. Dr. Kiney was not encouraging. He said, "It has its pros and it has its cons, but in the end, you have to be led by what you think."

I talked to my two best friends in the seminary, and they said they thought talking to the Klan was a great idea, and that they would pray for me.

Back in Greensboro over the weekend, I came to my pastor in Greensboro, Reverend Hairston, and he helped me grapple with it. I told Joyce, and it frightened her. She wanted to know what Reverend Hairston thought. I told her he supported me, and so she didn't oppose me, although she was worried. She prayed with me.

I reached a spiritual, faith decision that I was going to find these Klan guys and ask them not to march in Greensboro. And whatever else the Klan wanted to talk about, I would talk about. I asked around to find their leader, and the name that came up most was Gorrell Pierce. I read in a newspaper that he lived in Mount Eula, about forty miles west of Salisbury headed towards the mountains. I picked a weekday and drove down from Richmond. I came by Greensboro and had a prayer with Reverend Hairston.

Then I drove on towards Salisbury. I had my map and I found Mount Eula, which was a village, a crossroads. I asked some people if they knew Gorrell Pierce. With very little work, they gave me the directions to where he lived. I had typed up a statement, where I quoted from the gospel of Matthew, from Jesus' teaching that "we love our enemies, pray for those who despitefully use us." I wrote in there about the terrible thing that happened in '79: "I have tried in my spirit to forgive you for what you did. My desire now is to be reconciled with you. And to discuss with you why you are coming to Greensboro to stir this up again. And to ask you not to do it. We have a common claim, whether we understand it the same way, our common claim is to be Christians."

I went out there to where Gorrell Pierce lived, and there was a sign that said, "No niggers allowed." There was his trailer sitting down from that field. I drove down there and knocked on the door. I was nervous but not that scared; I had made up my mind, and once you've made up your mind, you get some peace. My deepest conviction was that, to the best of my ability, I was doing what was right. That was my peace.

Nobody answered. I called out Gorrell's name, and nobody came. So I folded the note up and pushed it under the door. And I drove back to Greensboro to my house and called Gorrell. (I had his phone number now, because I had found it in the local phone book.) He answered the phone. I said, "Gorrell Pierce?"

He said, "Yes."

I said, "This is Nelson Johnson in Greensboro."

Gorrell said something like, "Not that goddammed communist!" He started cursing right away, attacking me for calling him.

I told him, "I'm calling you because I want to talk to you." I was trying to calm Gorrell down. I said: "I'm serious, it's not a hoax. I want to talk with you."

He said, "What in the hell are you talking about?"

I said, "I've been down there to visit you, but you wasn't there."

He said he didn't believe me.

I said, "Go and look under your front door."

He said, "You've been to my goddammed house?"

I said, "Yes, and I left a word for you."

He started to listen. I said: "Go get it and read it. I'll call you back in fifteen minutes." And we both hung up.

I waited about thirty minutes and called back. He asked me, "What the hell are you up to?"

I said: "I'm up to what I said. I want to talk to you about y'all's plan to come and march in Greensboro. But I want to talk about more than that."

He said, "You are a fool if you think I am coming to Greensboro to talk to you."

I said: "I didn't ask you to come to Greensboro. I'll come to anywhere that you say." At this point we were talking.

He said, "If we talk, it's because you come to where I say."

I said, "You give me a day and a time, and I'll be there."

And he did. He gave me a service station off of Interstate 85, about five miles past Salisbury. And he described it clearly and told me he would be wearing a baseball hat with some team name on it. He asked me if I was going to be by myself. I told him yes.

I went back to Richmond and I told folk, and my professors got more upset.

But I had decided to go. A couple of days later, I drove to Salisbury. Along the way, I got nervous, so I stopped and prayed. I was afraid the Klan was going to lead me way out onto a farm somewhere, to meet in a barn. I was just going to chance that. Once I prayed, I felt okay.

I came up to the service station, and this guy with a baseball cap walked out. I walked over to him and said, "Are you Gorrell Pierce?"

And he said, "Yeah."

I said, "I'm Nelson Johnson."

And he said, "Follow me."

He got in a truck that had two or three other people in it, and two more trucks followed. To my surprise, we went towards Salisbury instead of away from it. He pulled into a Holiday Inn, and I got out. I recognized another guy, Virgil Griffin, because I had seen him at the trials and in newspapers. He was dressed in overalls. Gorrell Pierce, Virgil Griffin, and I walked to the counter at the Holiday Inn, and they said they had reservations for a room and picked up a key. I didn't see the other two trucks any more. It was the three of us. I walked between them. We went into the motel room on the first floor. There was a round table with chairs in front of a big window. They opened the curtain to the window, and the three of us sat around the table.

I asked, "Could we pray together before we start the conversation?"

They said, "Pray as much as you want."

I tried to pray sincerely for our own understanding and a sense of the right thing to do. Then I started the conversation by laying out to them that I had two goals for being here. One was just talking to them generally, and second was to ask them about their planned march in Greensboro.

Gorrell Pierce started with a string of cursing—black folk had taken advantage of white folks. I listened very attentively. He talked about black men raping white women, and black people taking white folks' jobs. I told them I wanted to talk straight at what he raised. I asked them were they aware of the range of colors in the black race. I said, "Gorrell, where do you think the range of colors in the black race came from?"

He hemmed and hawed. I said: "I'm going to tell you plain where it came from. It came from white folks raping black folks."

We talked some about the economy, about black people "taking" their jobs. I said: "First, black folk weren't allowed in most workplaces before the 1960s. Second, who gets hired in these places is actually a decision that white people make. And third, a lot of these businesses are leaving the country, and black people didn't make that decision either. So in truth, there are fewer jobs for both you and for black folks. What really makes sense is coming to an understanding of why we don't have jobs. And if we got to the truth of that, good sense would require that we struggle together."

Gorrell said he didn't know about all that. And Virgil started talking about other things. But I felt that I had rebutted him in a language that they understood. Then I pointedly asked them: "Will y'all *not* march in Greensboro? That's what I want to leave here with."

By this time, it was actually a conversation I was having with two human beings.

They said: "Actually we don't really want to march in Greensboro. We did, but this conversation . . ." They were telling me they had been influenced by our conversation. But they went on to say that they couldn't go back and tell the rest of the Klan they weren't coming because Nelson Johnson persuaded them not to, Gorrell said. "So we can't make that commitment."

We talked about that for a while. They gave their word that even if they marched in Greensboro, they wouldn't start anything violent.

Then they asked me if I knew why I was sitting in front of the window that faced onto a quad inside the motel. I said no, I didn't know. They said, "Because we got men inside several rooms, on the second floor, and they have a bead on you." They were confessing that they thought I might be armed. They assumed that I had set up a trap for them. I think they didn't lead me into the country because they thought that I had five or six carloads of people already down there who could possibly get them. So they wanted to be in the city, in a place where they had me under the gun.

I told them I appreciated them telling me. I asked them if they saw any potential in any kind of relationship based on things we could agree on. They said they were open to talk. We shook hands and I left. I came back and shared it with Reverend Hairston. My two buddies in seminary thought it was a great victory. I shared it with my professors, who didn't seem very excited about it.

We had a second meeting, this time in Greensboro at the Ramada Inn off Interstate 85. Ten Klansmen met with me, my two seminary friends, and two ministers from Greensboro. We bought food and we had a table big enough for all. It was us and ten poor white men, some of them chewing snuff. For me, the discussion was far less meaningful. We recapped the first meeting, discussed the issues. It didn't take long, we shook hands, and that was that.

A few weeks later, Virgil Griffin and Gorrell Pierce came to Greensboro and led their KKK march. There was a counter-demonstration of people denouncing the Klan, and there were lots of police, lots of noise, but no violence. I had done what I thought I could do to engage the Klan. I had a sense that Gorrell and Virgil had done what they told me they would do, but that they never were in control of their Klan group.

I sent a letter to several white ministers, and I told them about my meetings with the Klan. I told them I'd opened a door, taken a first step, but I couldn't be the main person trying to reach the Klan. I never heard from any of those ministers, not a word.

Over the following years, Virgil Griffin kept marching with his Klan all over the state of North Carolina. In 1993, Klansmen from his group were caught burning down a rural African American church in South Carolina. The Klansmen were tried, found guilty, and Virgil's group was put out of business. Other Klansmen kept living in Greensboro, including Eddie Dawson [the Klansman and police informant], who continued to pick fights with people over racial issues. David Wayne Mathews, the man who killed four of our people on November 3, still lives in Greensboro.

I graduated from seminary in 1989 and was offered a job at a church in Richmond. But Greensboro is my home, and I returned to work in Greensboro as a minister and an activist. My vision was to work along two axes—one was churches and the other was poor folk, and I wanted to bring them together. What poor folk bring into the church is their person, their reality, which is an indictment of the powers of our imperial social order. If the church is not indicting these social powers, then it is co-conspiring with them. Church folk can only know poor folk when they face them in the flesh. It is very simple: Are you capable of standing with a person in the belief that they do deserve a good and decent life?

After several years of working as an assistant pastor in Greensboro, I realized the best way to practice my vision was to found a new church. By then, Joyce and I had built a small community of faith around us, so we founded the Faith Community Church. We bought an old building in the poor side of Greensboro, which we transformed into our church. Next door, we converted an old house into the Beloved Community Center as a service center for the homeless and other community groups. Beloved Community Center hired Willena Cannon as a staff person.

We worked on many issues over the years. When workers at Greensboro K-Mart distribution center went on strike in the early 1990s, I built a community/labor coalition to support their struggle for union recognition, which culminated in a victory.[2] The movement for quality public education continues, as well as other issues, including homelessness and drug treatment programs. One major issue was the fight to free Kwame Cannon.

Marty ■ Healing involved time, and so did putting my fragmented life back together. First, I had to rebuild my relationship to my daughter and build a new marriage. Second, I needed to find meaningful work.

During the Klan/Nazi trials, I had become such an outcast. Leah started kindergarten in Durham public school 1984, and her teacher was horrible—one time, this woman slapped Leah's hands because she "squirmed." During the trial in 1985, I was constantly on TV and in the newspapers, and because of my notoriety, I worried about putting Leah back in public school. I went to the Friends School and asked them, "Do you know who I am? Do you know that Leah's father was killed by the Klan and Nazis? Will you still take her?"

The Friends School said, "We would love to." It was so nice to hear that. So Leah went to the Friends School, where she was loved. And I ended up speaking to the Friends School children about what it was like to be a communist, what it was like for Leah to lose her father. It was the beginning of us rejoining the Durham community as human beings. The next year when we were all in Africa, Elliot did his anthropology research, and I home-schooled Leah. Leah and I spent all our time together, and I felt like I began to know her again.

Building my new marriage with Elliot was a challenge. My biggest problem was dealing with Mike, who had been dead seven years by then, but who still lived in my mind, who still talked to me. I wanted to have happiness with Elliot, love and joy. I didn't want to feel guilty about Mike. But Mike was bugging me, and it pissed me off. So I thought, Okay, time to go to counseling to work this one out. I found a counselor and told her I wanted to put my life together out of all these fractured parts. I needed to just be able to figure out all these pieces— the murders, our mistakes, the trials, Leah, Elliot, Mike. I needed to chew these things up until I could swallow and digest them.

I began to talk it through with Mike, to talk to him about my new relationship with Elliot. I was pissed at Mike for trying to get Elliot out of the bedroom. I told Elliot about these talks, and he said, "Okay, I can understand that," and he would make a joke about it, and he was loving. This was not an easy family to enter, and I think only Elliott could have done it. We were a triangle. No, we were actually a quadrangle: me, Mike, Elliot, and Leah. Leah was not about to let anybody else into our house without her stamp of approval.

Elliot loved me through all that; he was on my side, no matter what. He was interested, excited, he wanted to participate in it. I got to the point where I would giggle when I would want to argue with Mike about getting out of my life. Mike is still in my mind, usually right there over my right shoulder; he is my friend, somebody special who has no other parallel in my life.

Then there was medicine. Since 1979, I thought I could never go back into medicine, never take responsibility for treating people, never make crucial decisions about people's lives. But after the trials were over, I decided to try medicine again. In '86, I went back to the University of North Carolina and made it through three hard years of residency. I tried to organize a union of residents, but I found it too hard, because residents are too tired and they don't have the time. And then as soon as we had something going, our three years were up and we were no longer residents.

Elliot and I moved out into the country to Efland in Durham County in 1987, which was wonderful. We bought horses, and I began to love the North Carolina spring and fall. Our community of November 3 survivors began to talk to each other about our personal feelings, rather than just about political analysis. The trials were finally over, and we could say what it all meant to us. It was real helpful.

Elliot, Leah, and I, in 1989, moved away from North Carolina, where I had lived for sixteen long, painful years. Elliot got a job teaching anthropology at Penn State University, so we moved to Pennsylvania. In 1995, we moved again because Elliot got a job at Smith College in Massachusetts. I have continued to work as a public health physician. Family life has also been wonderful. Elliot and I always wanted to have children, and we decided to adopt. Mulu and Masaye came into our lives from Ethiopia. They have their own stories, which they will tell. For Elliot and me, bringing them into our lives was our proclamation about living. Meanwhile Leah, after surviving her rebellious teens, has grown into a wonderful young adult. She is carving out her own path, and she is happy with who she is, with a lot of compassion for other people, intellectual curiosity, and anger over injustice.

My main work has been building the Greensboro Justice Fund. After the trials were over, we redirected the GJF. Dale was director from 1985 through 1992, when I took over. In 1986, using the $75,000 that plaintiffs donated back to us from the settlement as seed money, we continued raising money from our mailing list for groups fighting against racism, bigotry, and economic injustice in the South. At first, the grants we gave were very small—one $300 grant in 1986, several grants totaling $800 in 1987, $1,200 in 1988, a little more each year.

In 1991, there was a fire at the Imperial Chicken Farm in Hamlet, North Carolina, and twenty-five people died because management illegally kept the doors of the factory locked. I heard the news about the fire on the radio, including an interview with Ashaki Binta. I knew Ashaki and her group, the Black Workers for Justice, which was one of the groups that GJF was funding. So I called Ashaki and said, "Tell me what the Greensboro Justice Fund can do."

She said: "Raise money. This is a big fight, and these folks are poor."

We immediately wrote up an emergency letter about the fire and the oppression of the poultry factory workers and sent it out to all of our list. We raised $5,000 and sent 75 percent of it straight down to Hamlet (the other 25 percent covered the cost of the mailing).

The fund-raising for the Hamlet fire was a breakthrough for how we organized GJF. Since then we have focused on immediate struggles, funding groups fighting environmental racism, families who lost loved ones to police brutality, lesbians under homophobic attack, and the Committee to Free Kwame Cannon. These are grassroots groups who often find it hard or impossible to obtain funding from mainstream foundations for their vital work, for what is going on right now. We send out mailings to our growing mailing list that say that giving to the Greensboro Justice Fund means you are part of a national movement of support for these small but important struggles in the South. Over the last decade, we have distributed over $300,000. It is a fitting tribute to the memories of our five brave people who died on that Saturday morning in Greensboro.

Many survivors are active on our board of directors, including Nelson Johnson, Paul Bermanzohn, and Willena Cannon.

Greensboro Justice Fund also organizes commemorations of November 3, which have become important vehicles for the massacre to become remembered history. For example, at the tenth anniversary, the women of Bennett College, Sandi Smith's alma mater, held a beautiful program for her that challenged Greensboro to remember Sandi. Bill Sampson's brother, David, is a musician who composed a piece dedicated to Bill and got the Aspen Woodwind Quintet to play it for our commemoration. Those were just two of a series of wonderful programs a decade after the murders.

The fifteenth anniversary, in 1994, was also important. The high point for me was our tradition at Greenwood Cemetery. We stood in a circle around the graves of our loved ones, and people just spoke as they felt moved to do so. But this time, our children spoke up. Ayo Johnson talked about how so many of us had been mothers to her. Alex Goldstein, Jim Waller's stepson, read a poem he wrote. Sandy Bermanzohn talked about being honored to be named after Sandi Smith. Roz Pelles's son, Hugh, talked about turning twenty-five and realizing he was the same age as César Cauce was when he died. Leah stood next to me, crying and holding my hand.

And the playwright Emily Mann participated in the fifteenth anniversary with us. She was writing a play called *Greensboro (A Requiem)*, which was performed in Princeton in 1996.[3] Emily's play was a huge success for us. It put the facts out there on the table again, which was what we needed, and it put heart into the story.

In 1999, at the twentieth anniversary, UNCG professor Marsha Paludan produced Emily Mann's play *Greensboro (A Requiem)* in Greensboro for the week of the anniversary. That was a wonderful opportunity to educate people about what happened. There were so many programs during the twentieth-anniversary commemoration—at colleges, churches, synagogues, and community centers—that no one could go to all of them.

Paul ■   My physical recovery is not complete and never will be. I still walk with a limp and always will. I have no use of my left hand. I can't open it, which means my left arm is basically useless, because your hand is the main reason you have an arm. So basically, my whole left side is incapacitated.

But I was very lucky to have survived. And things being what they are, life has been pretty good for me. I function well; I'm a productive physician and researcher. I am the medical director of a day center, and my mission has been for the center to increasingly focus on rehabilitation. It was a way of translating what I had learned about rehabilitation in my own skin and to help other people's recovery. I figured out a few useful things in trying to understand schizophrenia more deeply. I've taken care of a lot of patients over those years, and some of them have done well and gotten out of the mental-patient rut and become functioning people.

I feel satisfied with my work and life. I have enjoyed married life. Sally and I have a routine of going out on Saturday night (there are lots of things to do in New York). We also take an annual vacation for just the two of us. I enjoyed raising our daughters as they grew to be such interesting people. And I enjoy living close to my parents. My father died in 1993, and my mother moved into our neighborhood, so now I see her several times a week.

But for a long time, my life, politically, was nowhere. For me, it was a big blow when the CWP essentially collapsed. I was disoriented for years. I still had revolutionary views that capitalism has got to go, and that we have to replace it with a more just, equitable, and human system. I still believed we have to have socialism in some way, shape, or form. But I wasn't doing anything about it. Over the years, I kind of marinated in that disgust with myself at my apathy.

Sally was running around to all these meetings for all these causes, and she would tell me who to vote for. I would hear about Nelson Johnson, Willena Cannon, and other friends of ours organizing on all these issues. Marty Nathan was building the Greensboro Justice Fund, and she yelled at me to become involved. So I did get involved. GJF supported all these grassroots groups, and many of the struggles reminded me of Whitakers in eastern North Carolina, where we avenged the murder of Charlie Lee. It truly has been a good legacy of our five people.

In the early 1990s, we were in Greensboro visiting Nelson and Joyce when we met Emily Mann, who was writing a play on the massacre. She interviewed Sally and me, and some of what we said made it into her play, including me saying that I saw myself as a "vaguely progressive guy." In the play, that line always got laughs.

But I wasn't making a joke. When I told Emily that, I was depressed, demoralized, and referring to the fact that I wasn't doing anything politically. Progressive views don't do anything to change the world unless you're engaged in carrying out a fight based on those views. I was inactive and hence ineligible to call myself much more than a vaguely progressive guy. I was disgusted with myself.

At the twentieth-anniversary commemoration in 1999, I realized, Hey, man, you got to get off your butt and do something. It was great to see Nelson and others in the middle of this ongoing fight to bring out the truth about the massacre. That really got my old juices bubbling again. I came back to New York and returned to activism. I became engaged in a campaign against genetically engineered foods and got the Park Slope Food Coop active in the effort. There is a growing coalition of people around the world fighting against these biotech corporations taking over the world's food supply.

I feel much more energetic, much more alive. It makes for a more complicated life because I have things to do all the time and there's not as much time to just hang out and relax. I have hardly watched TV in a year. I have returned to my calling as a fighter for justice. That's my life.

Willena ■ For me, healing took a long time because things kept happening that ripped open my wounds. Kwame went to prison, and I would wake up at three o'clock in the morning thinking about my seventeen-year-old child in prison with two life sentences. Kwame called me all the time. I went to see him almost every Sunday. He was defiant, so angry—at me, at everybody and everything. Sometimes I felt like I was going to lose my mind.

Once while I was driving, I started talking to God about my problems. I actually felt some spirit and cried with joy. I had me a little sermon right on the side of the road, and my spirituality took root from that.

It was a big thing for me to become religious again, because I had rejected the church as a college student. When I was growing up, the church was the heart of the black community. The minister was the highest, the most respected person. The church became a social place for me as a little child. My father was very strict, so the only courting I could do was at the church. I wink at somebody, they wink at me, I might get to sit beside them. But that was it. So I would go to church to socialize. Spirituality was good, but as a teenager, I didn't see it applying to my life. I thought maybe I would get religious when I got old and needed to straighten out my life so I could go to heaven.

Once I got to college, I didn't have any use for church. At A&T, I had more freedom, 'cause my father wasn't there. I got into socializing. During the movement, I became very critical of the church. I went back home and had my standoff that desegregated the Dairy Queen. My mother had this black minister come out to the house to talk to me against Martin Luther King. This preacher tells me that we were cursed as a race of people. I wasn't buying none of that malarkey, but I could not say that to him, because I had been taught to respect him. So I was sitting there, steaming, listening to this crap, while my friends are eating at the Dairy Queen 'cause I had desegregated it! I thought, I don't need to hear no more black preachers—they ain't nothing but Uncle Toms, talking about pie in the sky and being cursed and there was nothing we can do. I saw no hope in that, no change, no nothing. So I rejected the church and the preachers. I came back to religion almost thirty years later, when Kwame went to prison. I started talking to God again. I began to try to read the Bible and to better understand it. I saw that there are some good preachers pushing for change. So I studied a lot, prayed a lot, and it gave me relief. Sometimes I felt like I was going to lose my mind. When I turned to God, I found peace.

My politics basically stayed the same. I see the injustice; I know how the capitalist system works in this country. The question is, What is the way out of this? I doubt that communism would ever work in this country; I doubt people would ever come to accept it. I still want justice for people. The question is which road to take, and how can an advanced capitalist system be changed. To me there is need for grassroots groups and progressive socialists to make short-term changes. Overall, the long-term strategy, I don't know. Sometime, people say let's get together and talk, but that hasn't happened. I'm not sure if people are burned out or disillusioned.

The main thing is to organize people for change. There are lots of issues. The drug problem is one huge issue that affects many people. Drugs are really killing people, and the media and political leaders like Nancy Reagan say, "Just say no." But it is harder than that. The politicians don't say anything about the big dealers who own the banks and work on Wall Street making millions. They just point to poor people, to small-time dealers who never had nothing. Homelessness is another big issue. So is poverty and youth. With all the cut-backs, there is nothing out there for a lot of kids.

As far as my jobs, I finally got out of the fast-food business in 1990, when I got hired as a lab technician. It was a better job, but not something I was that interested in. It wasn't until 1994 that I got a job in the work I love—community organizing. I was hired as a housing counselor for Habitat for Humanity, and as a staff person at Nelson's Beloved Community Center working with poor people.

Free Kwame Cannon!

Willena ■ The most healing thing for me was organizing a campaign to get Kwame out of prison. When Kwame was arrested in 1986, people who committed crimes like Kwame's went to prison only for a few years. In North Carolina at that time, the longest time served for multiple burglaries was under six years. But Kwame at age seventeen had been sentenced to a minimum of twenty years in prison before he had a chance at parole.

Kwame's lawyer, Pinkney Moses, was an incompetent alcoholic when he was representing Kwame in 1986. When we found this out, I got a lawyer to file a motion for appropriate relief in 1989 stating that Moses was under the influence on several occasions while counseling Kwame. But the North Carolina justice system denied this motion. Then Moses himself turned in his law license, stating that he was incompetent due to alcohol abuse, so clearly we were right. But the court system ignored it, because the system was not after justice, it was after punishing us again for November 3.

We focused on Kwame's sentence being way out of proportion to his crime. In 1993, I petitioned the governor to grant Kwame executive clemency. Jim Hunt denied the request. But that setback made us step up the campaign. Kwame began writing a column for the *Carolina Peacemaker* called "From the Inside." I built the Committee to Free Kwame Cannon that began circulating a petition to release Kwame. Nelson Johnson became very active in Kwame's case, and he and seven other ministers wrote to Governor Hunt urging him to grant Kwame clemency.

Many people got involved in the Free Kwame campaign. The most unusual was Myra Anne Dean, whose house Kwame broke into the night he was caught. This is an article from the *Carolina Peacemaker* from April 11, 1996, that explains how Myra Anne got involved:

What Price Redemption?
Man Serving Two Life Sentences for Non-Violent Crime

One of the individuals petitioning for Cannon's freedom is Myra Anne Dean, his last burglary victim, a single mother with a teenage daughter. . . .

"I expected that there would be a trial and I would be contacted," said Dean. After several months passed, she noticed a small article in the daily newspaper reporting Cannon's double life sentence. Dean assumed that he had been violent during the crimes or there were other aggravating circumstances, such as drug use.

Eight years later, Dean saw an announcement for a play by North Carolina A&T graduate Lei Ferguson, called "Reaching towards Nevermore: Kwame Cannon Speaks." Dean said, "If the name hadn't been so unusual, I might not have recognized who the play was about." After watching the performance, Dean began to delve into the details of Cannon's case, trying to decide if the consecutive life sentences were too severe. . . .

One of Dean's stipulations for involvement in Kwame's case was that he had never been violent or used a weapon. "I didn't make up my mind until I met him," said Dean of the first time she visited Cannon in prison.

I took Myra Anne Dean to prison to visit Kwame. Kwame felt so bad about burglarizing her house, he wouldn't even look at her at first. Then they started talking. Myra Anne saw that Kwame had changed his life around. She decided his sentence was too harsh, and she joined our work to free him. She wrote to Governor Hunt, heard nothing, and then wrote him again.

Meanwhile, hundreds of people were writing to Governor Hunt, including the president of Guilford College, college professors, and prominent Greensboro businessmen. In the summer of 1995, Greensboro mayor Carolyn Allen and three city council members petitioned for Kwame's release. Nelson Johnson and the Pulpit Forum kept up steady pressure, sending letter after letter asking the governor for clemency for Kwame. In June 1996, Nelson organized a meeting that discussed launching a statewide campaign to withhold votes from Governor Hunt, running for reelection. By that time, Hunt had received over one thousand letters calling for Kwame's release.

Kwame ■ I was on a roller coaster of emotions. From prison, there was so much I couldn't see of the Free Kwame Cannon campaign. I saw some of it on TV and newspaper, so I knew people were working on it. Things would build for six months, and then there would be nothing for six months. I hated those dry periods; I would feel like people tried, but the fight was over. Then all of a sudden, people would say, "You're about to get out." And my hopes would be back up. Then I don't hear nothing else for another year. For about six years, my feelings went up and down, up and down.

Mama told me that they were about to let me out, that the District Attorney was doing checks in Greensboro to see if anybody had problems with me moving back home. But my release got turned down because the man who turned me in to the cops said he was afraid of me. Mama didn't tell me the release got turned down for a year! She was just giving me little false hopes, these little hope lines. She was borrowing time. "Give me nine months," she said. Then after nine months passed, she would say, "Give me six months" or "three months." She would sense how I felt. If I was in a good mood she would be, "Give me nine months." But if I was in a "I can't take it no more mood," she would say, "Three months." I think that's how she did it. Because after each visit, I would feel renewed, I would feel like I got this hope that I can hold onto.

Sally ■ In 1996, Kwame had been in prison for ten years; it was the end of Kwame's first life sentence. We were all hoping the state would put the two sentences together and make them concurrent rather than consecutive and let Kwame out.

I was in Greensboro with Nelson and Joyce Johnson at the Faith Community Church. It was a warm, beautiful, summer Saturday night, and the church was having a community picnic. Little children ran around, teenagers played basketball, grownups talked. A lovely scene. Willena arrived and quietly showed Nelson and me a letter that stated that Kwame's first sentence was over, and the second life sentence had begun. This meant that there was no concurrent sentence, that Kwame had to be in prison for ten more years. A feeling of gloom descended. I felt bile churning in my stomach. And there seemed to be nothing we could do.

Kwame ■ Actually, when I got that letter, I felt relief. I had finished one life term. A lot of people that have life terms don't complete them after ten years. They could have kept me on that first life sentence for twenty years and then start the second life sentence. I know that sounds crazy, but I've seen too many guys do too much time on one life sentence.

Sally ■ Every couple of years, I would go visit Kwame, and we'd always talk about what he would do when he got out. We would talk like he was getting out the next month. And then years would go by, and he would still be in prison. It was awful.

One time, I was at home in New York. It was November 3. The phone rings, and this voice says, "Hi, Sally."

I said, "Who's this?"

"Oh, it's Kwame."

"Kwame, you're out!"

And then there's this long silence and Kwame says, "No."

And I just couldn't think of what to say.

Then Kwame said, "There is a long line of people here trying to make a phone call, so I better go." I remember feeling like a fool. Rather than talking to Kwame about what was actually going on in his life, I'm thinking that he's out of prison.

Kwame ■ There were times when I could call people, and they would ask me if I was out. Believe it or not, it never made me feel bad. It made me feel loved, that people wanted me to be home. But also it made me feel disappointed somehow.

Then the students from Guilford College and other colleges got involved and stayed involved. They would write me letters, come down to see me, set up interviews with newspapers. I saw there was something moving out there. Then it made me feel really good, gave me a lot of hope, knowing that somebody was keeping it going.

The visiting policy was one hour for visiting every week on Sunday morning. I could only see three visitors at a time. When the students got involved, I had forty students on my visitor list. They would come in droves of three, each week a different three. There were two students coordinating it, an African girl and a white girl. The students coming weekly had cut my family visits out of the picture. Mom would have to sneak a visit. She would have to get to the prison before the students got there and then leave when they came. The movement to Free Kwame had overran her; it was bigger than Willena. And that made me feel good to know that she wasn't the only engine trying to push that movement.

It became exciting, just seeing the energy that the students had. I could expound these ideas to them, and they would fly with them. It was—oh, man, all my conceptualizing came to light. One of my ideas was to start a group for youth called DREAM—Development of Rational Educated Ambitious Minds. I also got the students to visit other inmates that I knew who had problems with their sentences.

Nelson Johnson visited me and gave me lots of hope. He came when I was on the downside of the roller coaster and beginning not to trust the movement. I thought it was great that people were putting their energy into this but was afraid it still wouldn't get me out. Nelson told me the movement was like boiling water. It's steam before water begins to boil and you don't see it, and then all of a sudden there's this pot of boiling water. He said: "Right now we're just in the steam phase. We're heating up."

Nelson ■ I knew that we could get Kwame out if we could line up support from the black politicians and clergy. A movement had grown up around Kwame because he symbolized the plight of thousands of black youth on dead-end streets, locked in cages of poverty. We had to reach out all over the state and box Governor Jim Hunt in so that he had no choice but to release Kwame.

I went to see Kwame several times. We decided to organize a march to free Kwame Cannon, from Greensboro through other cities to Raleigh, over one hundred miles. The march would be in April 1998, on the thirtieth anniversary of the assassination of Reverend Martin Luther King, Jr. We would invoke Martin King's vision of redemption, of beloved community, and how this meant freeing Kwame.

On March 25, 1998, one week before our march, Jim Hunt finally met with a delegation to discuss Kwame's clemency. We brought an impressive delegation. Among the twelve were four women, four whites, eight blacks, six clergy persons, a person whose home had been broken into by Kwame, the North Carolina State NAACP president, the Greensboro Pulpit Forum president, Greensboro mayor Carolyn Allen, state senator William Martin, and Guilford County commissioner Melvin Alston.

We told Hunt that Kwame as a teenager had committed nonviolent burglary, a crime for which one can get no more than nine years. Research showed that Kwame's sentence was the harshest for a comparable crime in the history of the state. Many people believe Kwame received such a harsh sentence because he was black, poor, and the son of a political activist. As the meeting with Hunt was breaking up, I made sure I was the last person out of the room. I stopped at the door and said, "Mr. Governor, thank you for the meeting." He was nervous, but he shook my hand. I wanted to look him in the eye, to be present to him.

A week later, from April 1 to April 4, we marched from Greensboro to Raleigh, over a hundred miles in four days. It was a fine movement, all these people from all over the state, from Charlotte in the west to Rocky Mount in the east. The students from Guilford College and other schools weighed in powerfully. We marched through Durham and Chapel Hill and other communities, where friends had built support for Kwame's release. We spoke out against Hunt and said that we were not going to support him unless he released Kwame.

Kwame ■ When they had the march to Raleigh, my biggest fear was that everybody was going to march, then go home, mission accomplished—and I'm still in prison.

Nelson ■ We had to bring all the political power into play, everybody contributing in their own way. We had to get that energy to focus at a point and hone in on Hunt like a laser beam, to threaten to actually split the Democratic Party. It was headed that way. Then the best thing to do was for the governor to let him out. I knew when we had that meeting with Hunt that he had to release Kwame. It was just a matter of when.

Willena ■   A year went by after our meeting with Governor Hunt and the march to Raleigh. Pressure continued to mount on Jim Hunt, a Democrat. Republican congressman Howard Coble supported Kwame's release; Republicans were trying to change their image and win black votes. Guilford County sheriff B. J. Barnes wrote a letter stating that he did not oppose Kwame's release, and his next election he got over 80 percent of the black vote. The Democrats started telling Hunt if they didn't release Kwame, there were going to be a bunch of black people voting for Republicans, and it could overturn the North Carolina majority in the state legislature.

Free at Last!

On April 1, 1999, the *Greensboro News and Record* reported:

Cannon Is Released from Prison

His face crumbling with emotion, Kwame Cannon walked out of prison Wednesday, freed after serving almost 13 years of a double life sentence for burglary.

His friends and former fellow inmates at Randolph Correctional Center gathered at the prison fence. . . . "You can do it, Kwame!" one of them shouted as Cannon approached the gate. "You'll make it!" another yelled. "Hold your head up, brother!"

As Cannon began the 30-mile drive . . . friends and supporters in Greensboro prepared to welcome him home with a celebration at Faith Community Church.

At that celebration, called the "Jubilee 2000 Kwame Cannon Homecoming," the Rev. Nelson Johnson, with Cannon at his side, announced the establishment of a Kwame Cannon Prison Justice Fund that would be used to identify and work for the release of "thousands of other Kwame Cannons" who may be serving unjust sentences.[4]

Kwame ■   I was finally out of prison, after almost thirteen years. I felt like a time traveler, thrust into the future into an unfamiliar society. CDs, VCRs, cordless phones, personal computers, fax machines—they were all unfamiliar to me.

I tried to withdraw twenty dollars from my checking account through an ATM machine. I was struggling to get the machine to accept my card. Willena comes over and says, "Here, let me see your ATM card." I handed her my card. She smiled and said, "Kwame, this is your driver's license!"

One day I was driving around, going to the Four Seasons Mall, not to get anything particular, just to be out. And this car pulls up beside me, and this cute girl gives me a thumbs up and a big smile. And I gave her a "right on" fist. A few months later, I got a message on my message machine from someone named Angie. She had looked up all the Cannons in the phone book. She started at the end, planning to go up from backwards. And she hits "Willena." So she called my mama and said, "Does Kwame Cannon live here?" And she left me a message to call her back. And so I called her back, 'cause she sounded really nice. She said she just wanted to meet me and congratulate me, 'cause she had signed a petition for me to get out of prison.

I was on restricted probation and had to be in the house from 6 p.m. to 6 a.m. every night for the first six months out of prison. So I was always looking for things to do at the house. I said: "Do you know how to play a little bit of cards? Do you know how to play spades?"

Angie said, "Yeah, a little bit."

I said: "That's all I needed, just a player who could play just a little bit. I'll carry you the rest."

So she came over, and me and Angie played spades against my mama and another friend. And they beat us to death. We had a really good time.

We were both in school at the time. Angie was working to get her certification for dental assistant. She had her boards coming up. I'm going to A&T, with some tests coming up. We both had a lot of studying to do. I had a term paper due, but my printer was down. So Angie says, "I got a printer." So then I start coming over to her place, using her computer and hanging out with her. At that time, I was trying to carry out the plans I made in prison. I was doing a lot with the kids in my neighborhood. When Angie came along, it helped me a lot because it gave me another car to haul more kids. So we was taking kids to karate tournaments, and hanging out with them at parks, and all kinds of stuff with them children.

One day Angie said, "You know what, you just want me hanging around you 'cause you're on curfew." That was not true. Because just as soon as I got off curfew, we was still hanging out. And not long after that, I proposed marriage to her. I started spending the night at her house and going to school from there. Then I was bringing clothes to her apartment, piece by piece. Then all of a sudden, I didn't have nothing else left at my mama's house.

Willena ◼ On September 9, 2000, Kwame and Angie got married. Nelson Johnson married them in a big fancy church wedding. Loads of family and friends came. At the party afterwards, I was dancing with Kwame, and we were both saying, "Can you believe this?"

My children are finding themselves. Imani has her cosmetology license and is studying sociology at Shaw University. Kweli is studying computers. Each of my children had to endure so much just because I was their mother. So many people were afraid of me because the FBI and the cops had come down on us.

I am blessed with grandchildren: Imani's Tendai, and Kweli's Taj, Choneci, and Laura. I look forward to more grandchildren when Angie and Kwame decide to become parents.

I turned sixty on March 1, 2000. Maybe I'll retire. Probably not. As long as I am healthy, I will fight for justice. There is so much to do. I am currently the director of Jubilee 2000, a statewide prison reform project. I work with inmates, ex-inmates, and the families of inmates on many issues related to the state prison system.

Kwame ■ It's so much easier to conceptualize an idea or a dream while you are in prison. Once you're released, bringing those ideas to life is a lot different, and a lot harder, than you thought. In prison, I had so many thoughts, and they helped me keep myself together. One was DREAM (Development of Rational Educated Ambitious Minds), a program for at-risk youth. That is still a goal of mine. But now that I am out, I see that things just don't work the way I thought they would.

When you are in prison, you have one thing on your mind: freedom. You are just so focused on that, that you make plans for what you'll do when you get out. But they are not really solid because all you can think about is surviving in prison and getting out of there.

But when you get out, you have this whole new different set of problems. And you have no clue of how to deal with them. You need a lot of people helping you, supporting you, who can help you deal with these new problems. Otherwise it's easy to end up back in prison.

For me, it's been a difficult transition. I freak out when we get bills, 'cause I'm not used to dealing with them. My family and my wife, especially my wife, have helped me. I got in trouble for speeding, and I said to Angie: "Damn, life was a lot easier when you're in prison, because you had no responsibilities, no work, no bills. If you want to lay down, you lay down." Angie helps me see things from a different angle. When I get upset, she stops me from thinking that it's easier to go back.

I was out of prison a year and a half when Angie and I got married. People say the first year of marriage is hard. It is another new adjustment period; it's learning about another person. I'm a nightowl; she's a morning person. She had to learn to leave me alone in the morning. She would be trying to kiss me in the morning, and, well, I don't like to be bothered in the morning, but I didn't want to offend my wife, so I didn't say nothing. Then she's trying to kiss me again the next day, and the next day. Months go by like this, and all of a sudden I was like: "Get gone now! I can't take it no more!"

Angie is big into celebrations. I mean, she doesn't have a birth*day*, she has a birth *week*. It takes me some getting used to. In prison, I stopped celebrating anything. I just got numb, let those days go by, it's just another day.

In prison, I had all these big plans. But now, they are blurry. I have a good job at Music Garden that I have held over a year. I am so comfortable with my position that I sometimes think that maybe that's where my future is. I like my boss, and I've learned a lot in that company. I can talk to people who are interested in our program, and it makes me feel good to be able to explain what it is about. And then there are times when I have to deal with the database in the computer, and that's fun. It's a good working environment, not stressful.

Sometimes I think about wanting to complete school, about pushing on further and attaining my maximum potential. For me, it's not really clear right now. At one time, it was a panicky kind of thing where I kept wondering, Where do I belong? But now I'm getting to a place where I feel comfortable with not exactly knowing what I'll be doing.

Sally: It felt so good to go to Kwame and Angie's wedding. They were both glowing, and Willena was radiant. Healing means living, both coping with problems and seeking joy.

The weight on my shoulders is this book. I have been working on it, off and on, for twenty years. For so long, I could not figure out how to tell this story. Now I feel good about it but will feel even better when it is all done.

I love teaching at Brooklyn College, where I plan to be for the rest of my working life. I look forward to growing old with Paul. I am proud of our daughters, who have become caring and dedicated young adults. Leola is an artist, and Sandy is an organizer who loves working with children.

Paul ■   These survivors are wonderful people that I've been working with for just about my whole adult life. They are my dearest friends, like family. I love them. We see them every chance we get. They have strengthened me and permitted me to go on and continue to wage a good fight for justice. I think we are getting better at it as we get older. We get more tired, but we also get a little bit smarter.

Marty ■   My family is rooted firmly here in Massachusetts. We have lots of friends, who see me as Mike Nathan's widow, Professor Elliott Fratkin's wife, a doctor at a community health center, the director of the Greensboro Justice Fund, and the mother of Mulu, Masaye, and Leah. Elliott and I are very happy together and have continued doing political organizing around the Justice Fund and whatever else comes our way.

Back in those hard times, I don't think I could have imagined being so full of life as I am now. There is still a lot of bad things in the world, especially Bush being president. But I personally am very happy, which has come from the support and love of friends. And from the movement. Some people believe in heaven; I just believe in the movement, helping each other—to survive, to get out of jail, to find justice. I think that's where we are at our best. I am happy seeing our children take up the struggle. I feel sometimes I could die tomorrow and that would be okay. 'Cause it's been a wonderful life.

Nelson ■ I want to acknowledge the power of the meaningful relationship I share with my wife, Joyce Hobson Johnson. She and I have worked as a team throughout our careers. I have never made any money. Joyce worked as the director of A&T's Transportation Institute for almost two decades, supporting our family. Now she is director of the Jubilee Institute, which means we are working together today more closely than ever.

I want to acknowledge my wonderful children. They grew up as their father was portrayed in such negative ways. I remember one reporter describing me as a low-life, manipulative, who brought down curtains of death upon the community for narrow ideological goals. My daughters have endured tremendous pressure, and it left marks. But it has not destroyed our love. I am tremendously proud of both of them. Akua is the assistant budget director at A&T. Ayo is a nurse. I appreciate the quality of our relationship. And I am tickled to high heaven with Akua's daughter, my granddaughter, Alise Jamil Brown.

In terms of healing, Greensboro has a long way to go. The new century represents the beginning of another level of struggle. The city still needs to publicly repent for November 3. Greensboro took the low-life approach of organizing a North American death squad that took the lives of five people, and it must confess to that in some way. It cannot be the great city that it ought to be with this massive lie buried just beneath the surface. The lies about the massacre are a cancer in the body of the city. It infects its people, its institutions. Every time November 3 comes up, people tell more lies. It is in the interest of Greensboro to find a way to give expression to the reality that it was deeply involved in this massacre, and that this incident is linked to a whole way of being that suppresses, enslaves, and beats people down.

Unearned suffering is redemptive, and there is a great measure of unearned suffering that we went through and that others have gone through. I want to gather it all up and own it and focus it so that its redeeming possibilities come alive in this place. Blood was shed here. Those lives were taken here. Widows were humiliated here. In some sense, the whole national movement suffered because of what this city chose to do.

We will all continue to work to bring justice.

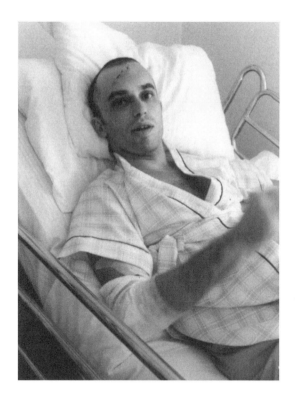

Paul Bermanzohn in a rehabilitation center, December 1979, recovers from gunshot wounds to the head and right arm. After five hours of brain surgery on November 3 put Paul on the critical list for more than a week, he spent over two months in rehab. (Photo by Sally Bermanzohn)

Jim Waller's stepson Alex Goldstein, *left*, and Kwame Cannon speak at commemoration at Uhuru Bookstore, Greensboro, December 1979. At table, *from left:* Joyce Johnson, Signe Waller, Dale Sampson; *on right:* and Nelson Johnson. (Photo by Sally Bermanzohn)

March Against Klan Murder, Greensboro, February 2, 1980. Front row, *from left,* widows Floris Cauce, Marty Nathan, and Dale Sampson; Phil Thompson, Nelson Johnson, and Ben Chavis. (Courtesy of Greensboro Justice Fund)

Protest at first Klan/Nazi trial, June 1980: *from left,* Nelson Johnson, Roz Pellas, Earl Tockman, Dale Sampson, Dory Blitz, and Rand Manzella; *from right,* Signe Waller, Marty Nathan, Tom Clark with hands on hips, Willena Cannon behind Paul Bermanzohn in wheelchair. (Courtesy of *News & Record,* Greensboro, NC)

Greensboro Justice Fund supporters at 1983 Washington, D.C., demonstration include, *left*, Marty Nathan; *center*, Dale Sampson; *next on right*, Willena Cannon. (Courtesy of Greensboro Justice Fund)

Nelson speaks on Greens-
boro massacre. (Courtesy of
Greensboro Justice Fund)

Jesse Jackson at site of the
November 3 massacre
during third, civil trial,
1985. Nelson Johnson
stands behind Marty
Nathan, on crutches; Leah
Nathan on right. (Photo by
Elliot Fratkin)

Marty, Nelson, Dale, and Signe celebrate after winning settlement in civil court, June 1985. (Courtesy of *News & Record*, Greensboro, NC)

Kwame Cannon, Easter Sunday 1999, three days after his release from thirteen years in prison. (Photo by Sally Bermanzohn)

Kwame Cannon and Angie Allen marry, September 2000. (Courtesy of Kwame Cannon)

Kwame and Willena Cannon on Kwame's wedding day. (Courtesy of Willena Cannon)

Angela Dawn Allen
and
Kwame Kambon Cannon

September 9, 2000
St. Stephen United Church of Christ
Greensboro, North Carolina

Marty Nathan with her family, 1998. *Clockwise from left*: Elliot Fratkin, Marty, daughters Leah and Masaye, son Mulu. (Courtesy of Marty Nathan)

The Bermanzohns, summer 1998. *From left,* Leola, Sally, Paul, and Sandy. (Photo by Bev Grant)

Nelson and Joyce Johnson with grand-daughter Alise Jamil Brown, 2001. (Photo by Lewis Brandon)

Sally Bermanzohn and Willena Cannon, summer 2000. (Photo by Paul Bermanzohn)

EPILOGUE

Greensboro Truth and Community Reconciliation Project

What does it mean for a community when five people are killed at a well publicized, legally planned march and no one is held criminally accountable? More than two decades after November 3, 1979, profound questions remain unanswered: What was the role of the Greensboro Police Department? Of federal law enforcement officers? Of other government officials? Did other groups, such as business or textile interests, contribute to the unfolding of these events? Can we ever expect official acknowledgment of killings and injuries that violate basic civil liberties—the rights to peaceable assembly, to free speech, to organize, and ultimately the right to live?

For survivors, family members, and friends, the massacre anniversaries have become opportunities to push for answers to these questions. In 1999, for the twentieth-anniversary commemoration, the Greensboro Justice Fund and the Beloved Community Center organized "A Night of a Thousand Conversations"; discussions about the massacre took place in living rooms, dormitories, churches, and community centers across the city. Several thousand people viewed Emily Mann's play *Greensboro (A Requiem)*, produced by the Theatre Department of University of North Carolina at Greensboro. Survivors, including Nelson Johnson, Paul Bermanzohn, Marty Nathan, Willena Cannon, Kwame Cannon, and me, spoke in programs at many colleges in Greensboro and Durham. The commemoration culminated in a forum at Bennett College that featured Harvard Law professor Lani Guinier, Columbia University professor Manning Marable, Rosenberg Fund director Robert Meeropol, and veteran civil rights activist Anne Braden.

The commemoration led to several significant achievements. The *Greensboro News and Record* stopped referring to November 3 as a "shootout," and two cable production companies decided to produce documentaries on the massacre that in time reached a national audience. But, as Marty noted: "The city government, the police, and the federal law enforcement continued to deny culpability for the violence. And they continued the falsehood that we were to blame for the failures of the police and justice system." And Nelson added, "I firmly believe that this city cannot be whole, cannot reach its potential, unless it faces its history."

People discussed how to pull national leaders and Greensboro community leaders together to thoroughly reassess the facts of November 3 during the twenty-fifth-anniversary commemoration. "The question," said Nelson, "was how to do a meaningful reassessment. We knew that we needed help." A student intern searched the internet and found the Andrus Foundation, which suggested contacting the International Center for Transitional Justice (ICTJ), an organization that assists societies around the world that are pursuing accountability for human rights abuses.

"Many countries are holding truth commissions organized by governments or nongovernmental organizations," Priscilla Hayner, research program director for the ICTJ, explained in our phone interview on January 31, 2003. The ICTJ has facilitated projects on five continents—in Bosnia-Herzegovina, Afghanistan, Sierra Leone, Mexico, Peru, and East Timor, among other countries. "The many truth-seeking projects reflect a global realization that something is missing in the process of addressing human rights abuses, even when the victims have successes in courts. A nation, or a community within a nation, needs to reflect, to come to terms with specific incidents or patterns of injustice."[1]

ICTJ president Alex Boraine was the deputy chair of the South African Truth and Reconciliation Commission, which pioneered the model that deconstructed apartheid. "Using the model developed in South Africa is very significant for us," Nelson Johnson believes. The South African liberation movement defeated apartheid using creative, nonviolent means. The experience of people like those in ICTJ who have carried out a truth and reconciliation process benefits Greensboro in immediate, practical ways. "We learn from the strengths and weaknesses of their work, from what had worked and what had not," Nelson said.

The ICTJ stresses that because every project is based on unique circumstances, the truth and reconciliation process cannot be transmitted whole from one country to another. Most projects take place in countries moving from authoritarian to democratic rule, and the truth seeking becomes an arena for addressing human rights abuses and promoting justice and peace. "Greensboro is the first serious, formal truth-seeking initiative in the United States," Priscilla Hayner told me. "It is the first time an American community has asked us to facilitate a truth and reconciliation project."

There are important differences between Greensboro and the South African Truth and Reconciliation project; for example, in South Africa, the liberation movement leaders are now heads of government. "But their model is still helpful for us," Nelson Johnson says. "Ours is a hard path. But we have the collective voice of the people who understand and demand the truth."

Organizing the GTCRP

Politically isolated for many years, the Greensboro survivors knew that a wide, strong community base must be in place before a public call goes out. The result was a local community task force cochaired by Carolyn Allen, mayor of Greensboro from 1993 to 1999, and Reverend Zeb Holler, the retired pastor of Greensboro's Presbyterian Church of the Covenant. The task force sought support for a Greensboro Truth and Community Reconciliation Project and won the endorsement of one-third of the city council, two county commissioners, many African American churches, and ministers of some of the large white churches in the community. Representatives of the Greensboro Police Department attended planning meetings.

The task force also created a national advisory board, cochaired by Dr. Vincent Harding, director of the Martin Luther King Jr. Center at the Iliff School of Theology in Denver; Professor Cynthia Nance of the University of Arkansas Law School; and Dr. Peter Storey, former chairperson of the South African Council of Churches and now a visiting professor at Duke Divinity School.

On January 16, 2003, the project was launched at a press conference. Former mayor Allen and Reverends Zeb Holler and Nelson Johnson released the Declaration of Intent, signed by thirty-two community leaders, which begins: "It is the declared intent of the signers of this document to work with all sectors of Greensboro and with a cross section of national and international leaders to forge a broad and effective GTCRP. . . . Our overall purpose is to lead Greensboro into becoming a more just, understanding and compassionate community. We believe this project can have positive implications for cities and communities throughout the United States."

The purpose of the Greensboro project is not to find scapegoats or to absolve anyone from criticism or blame, but to "name the truth, to examine the whole community's role, to look it in the face, to forgive, and to find room for healing." The press statement continued: "We believe that by helping to clear up lingering confusion, division and ill feelings and by promoting reconciliation among individuals, sectors and institutions within our community, the project will transcend the hurtful legacy of events of November 3, 1979. It is our conviction that this undertaking will go a long way in both healing long-standing wounds and opening new possibilities for Greensboro to become a better, more just and compassionate city."

The project intends to create a commission composed of people with "integrity and a variety of gifts, who are willing to commit themselves to seeking through amidst all the data and perspectives surrounding this complex situation." The commission will hold its first hearing in the fall of 2003, followed by community discussions of its findings.[2]

According to the Associated Press on January 17, 2003, Melvin Alston, chair of the Guilford County Board of Commissioners, stated that "the project will be useful for the community." The AP also reported the opposition voiced by Greensboro's current mayor, Keith Holliday: "I regret the decision of this group to revisit an event that happened 23 years ago. It is the wrong time and the wrong focal point. Many of our residents were not even here when this tragic event happened."

Resistance to a truth-seeking project comes with the territory, Priscilla Hayner told me: "Before an initiative gets started, there is often a sector of the community who may feel culpable, and who argue that such a project will be conflict producing or embarrassing. But often during the course of the inquiry, the same people come around and ultimately support the project."

Under the headline "A Wound Unhealed: Nov. 3 Re-examined," the *Greensboro News and Record* on January 17 issued a strongly supportive editorial: "We can run from Nov. 3 but we can't hide. As painful as its memory may be, never has there been a true reckoning of what that day means to us. Aside from a collective community reflex to blame it on warring 'outsiders,' earnest reflection on the shootings has been rare." And tellingly: "Over the years, this community has relived permutations of the same racial and class tensions that shaped that day. Time and again they surface, from the Kmart labor dispute in 1996 to the police's fatal shooting of a young black man, Daryl Howerton, in 1994. . . . The events of Nov. 3 also were about jobs—about labor unrest in local textile plants and attempts to unionize mill workers. They also were about race and class, issues that still color community discussions."

Model for Other U.S. Communities

"The Greensboro TCRP is the first time a project has been city-based, while other truth-seeking projects have been nationally based," the ICTJ's Priscilla Hayner told me in our interview. "It could become a model for other communities." Tragic episodes haunt many U.S. communities, including the massacre of hundreds of African American in Wilmington, North Carolina in 1898, in Atlanta in 1906, in Tulsa in 1921, and in Rosewood, Florida in 1923. Between the 1880s and 1960s, lynch mobs killed more than three thousand people. More recently, hate crimes and police brutality have torn communities apart. The Greensboro survivors hope the Greensboro Truth and Community Reconciliation Project can become a model for such communities who, like us, want to address human rights abuses.

NOTES

Introduction

1. On U.S. political repression of blacks, labor, and leftists, see Herbert Shapiro, *White Violence, Black Response* (Amherst: University of Massachusetts Press, 1988); Kenneth O'Reilly, *"Racial Matters": The FBI's Secret File on Black America* (New York: Free Press, 1989); Philip Foner, ed., *Black Panthers Speak* (New York: DeCapo Press, 1995); Richard Boyer and Herbert Morais, *Labor's Untold Story* (New York: United Electrical Workers, 1976); and Mari Jo Buhle, Paul Buhle, and Dan Georgakis, eds, *Encyclopedia of the American Left* (Chicago: University of Illinois Press, 1992).
2. Sally Avery Bermanzohn, *Survivors of the 1979 Greensboro Massacre: A Study of the Long Term Impact of Protest Movements on the Political Socialization of Radical Activists* (New York: CUNY, 1994).
3. William Chafe, *Civilities and Civil Rights: Greensboro, NC, and the Black Struggle for Freedom* (Oxford: Oxford University Press, 1981), pp. 178–248, discusses Nelson Johnson's leadership role in Greensboro in the late 1960s.
4. Signe Waller, *Love and Revolution: A Political Memoir* (Lanham, Md.: Rowman and Littlefield, 2002).

1. Growing Up

1. For a history of racial violence in the United States, see Shapiro, *White Violence and Black Response*. For an analysis of racial violence in the South, 1940s–1960s, see Sally A. Bermanzohn, "Violence, Nonviolence, and the Civil Rights Movement," in Kent Worcester, Sally Bermanzohn, and Mark Ungar, eds., *Violence and Politics: Globalization's Paradox* (New York: Routlege, 2002).

2. The Sixties

1. On the Woolworth's sit-in, see Chafe, *Civilities and Civil Rights,* pp. 71–101. North Carolina A&T was founded in 1891 as a coeducational liberal arts land-grant college for black students and became part of the North Carolina university system in 1972.
2. See Michael Krenn, ed., *The African American Voice in U.S. Foreign Policy since World War II* (New York: Garland, 1998).
3. The Supreme Court in 1954 found in *Brown v. Board of Education* that segregated

schools violated the U.S. Constitution. The decision overturned the Supreme Court doctrine of "separate but equal" (*Plessy v. Ferguson,* 1898) and spurred the development of the civil rights movement and the push for integration. But many African Americans, like Nelson's cousin, questioned whether integration should be the goal of the movement. On the debate over tactics, see Bermanzohn, "Violence, Nonviolence," pp. 146–64.

4.   See James Forman, *The Making of Black Revolutionaries* (New York: Macmillan, 1972); Stokely Carmichael and Charles Hamilton, *Black Power* (New York: Vintage, 1967).

5.   Chafe, *Civilities and Civil Rights,* p. 181.

6.   On the Weathermen's Days of Rage, see Sale, *SDS,* pp. 600–615. Jesse Jackson directed Operation Breadbasket, which was part of Martin Luther King Jr.'s Southern Christian Leadership Conference. For Jackson's views, see his *Straight from the Heart* (Philadelphia: Fortress Press, 1987).

7.   During Reconstruction, African Americans were elected to all southern state legislatures, and fourteen were elected to Congress and two to the Senate. After Reconstruction was overthrown and white racist rule was reestablished in the South, no blacks were elected to state or federal office until the 1960s. See Edward G. Carmines and James A. Stimson, *Issue Evolution: Race and the Transformation of American Politics* (Princeton: Princeton University Press, 1989), pp. 28–29.

8.   For an account of the 1968 Duke vigil, see "Remembering the Silent Vigil," *Duke Magazine,* March 1998, p. 1.

9.   See George Katsiaficas, *The Imagination of the New Left: A Global Analysis of 1968* (Boston: South End Press, 1987).

3. Movement Peak

1.   Nelson's letter is reprinted in Chafe, *Civilities and Civil Rights,* p. 202.

2.   For an account of the City College battle for open admission, see Karen W. Arenson, "Returning to City College to Revisit a 1969 Struggle," *New York Times,* October 29, 1999.

3.   For the roots of SOBU/YOBU in the black-nationalist movement, see Rod Bush, *We Are Not What We Seem: Black Nationalism and Class Struggle in the American Century* (New York: NYU Press, 1999). SOBU is mentioned on p. 192. On the black liberation movement in the late 1960s and 1970s, see Manning Marable, *Race, Reform, and Rebellion: The Second Reconstruction in Black America* (Jackson: University Press of Mississippi, 1991).

4.   It is unconstitutional to apply a law retroactively. This is the doctrine of ex post facto, one of the checks and balances between the judicial and legislative branches of government.

5.   Paul Bermanzohn and Tim McGloin wrote an article, "Cool Hand Duke," for a left-wing journal, *HealthPac,* Bulletin of the Health Policy Advisory Center, 1973, p. 1.

6.   On the New American Movement, see Buhle et al., *Encyclopedia of the American Left,* pp. 515–16.

7. On the FBI repression of the black liberation movement, see O'Reilly, *"Racial Matters."*

4. The Seventies

1. For a description of the appeal of Leninism to U.S. movement activists in the 1970s, and the origin and development of the new communist movement, see Max Elbaum, *Revolution in the Air* (New York: Verso, 2002), pp. 55–58.

5. Party Life

1. Paul Luebke wrote in *Tar Heel Politics:* "The Wilmington 10 prosecution appears to be a prime example of racial traditionalism. The three major witnesses for the prosecution, two of them convicted felons, recanted their testimony in 1976 and early 1977 after a five year campaign by defense attorneys and political support groups. Nevertheless, the Wilmington 10's state and federal appeals were exhausted before the witnesses' recantations became public" (Chapel Hill: University of North Carolina Press, 1990), p. 113.
2. Bennett College was founded during Reconstruction as a private school for African American women. It originally held classes in the basement of a church and later established a residential campus in Greensboro.
3. For descriptions of the siege of Wounded Knee in the 1970s, see Mary Crow Dog, *Lakota Woman* (New York: Harper Perennial, 1991). On the Attica rebellion, see http://deepdish.igc.org/lockdown/, part of the Lockdown USA series. Descriptions of antiwar demonstrations in the nation's capital and at the 1968 Democratic National Convention in Chicago appear in a number of books, including Sale, *SDS.* See also Buhle et al., *Encyclopedia of the American Left.*
4. On the political difficulties faced by unions in North Carolina, see Luebke, *Tar Heel Politics*, pp. 85–101.
5. Signe Waller wrote a book on her relationship with Jim; see Waller, *Love and Revolution.*

6. We Back Down the KKK

1. On the history of the KKK, see Wyn Craig Wade, *The Fiery Cross: The Ku Klux Klan in America* (Oxford: Oxford University Press, 1987). On the Decatur Klan attack, see Bill Stanton, *Klanwatch: Bringing the Ku Klux Klan to Justice* (New York: Weidenfeld, 1991).
2. For more on Jean Sharpe Chapman, see Sally A. Bermanzohn, "The Greensboro Massacre: Political Biographies of Four Surviving Demonstrators," *New Political Science* 20, 1 (1998): pp. 69–89.
3. On armed self-defense, see James Forman, *The Making of Black Revolutionaries* (Seattle: Open Hand, 1990); Robert F. Williams, *Negroes with Guns* (Detroit: Wayne State University Press, 1998); and Bermanzohn, "Violence, Nonviolence."
4. On *Birth of a Nation* and the high-level political support it received, see John Hope

Franklin, *Race and History* (Baton Rouge: Louisiana State University Press, 1989), pp. 10–23.

5. Jack Betts, "Brook Raps Union, Wage Rate Lures," *Greensboro Daily News,* September 5, 1981.

6. *Basic Understanding of the Communist Party of China* (Toronto: Norman Bethune Institute, 1976), pp. 57–70.

7. Countdown of a Death Squad

1. See Bruce B. Campbell and Arthur D. Brenner, eds., *Death Squads in Global Perspective: Murder with Deniability* (New York: Palgrave/Macmillan, 2002), pp. 1–26.

2. The Bureau of Alcohol, Tobacco, and Firearms (ATF) is a federal agency created in 1972 to combat violations of federal firearm, alcohol, and tobacco laws. In the 1970s, ATF's southern region developed a reputation as a white male bastion, sometimes blatantly racist. See William J. Vizzard, *In the Cross Fire: A Political History of the Bureau of Alcohol, Tobacco, and Firearms* (Boulder, Colo.: Lynne Rienner, 1997), pp. 8, 203–4.

3. Meredith Barkley, "Klansman, Nazi Say Agent Urged Guns for Rally," *Greensboro News and Record*, May 7–14, 1985; Roland Wood, Raeford Caudle, and Bernard Butkovich, testimony, *Waller v. Butkovich*, North Carolina, 1985.

4. *Greensboro Daily News,* September 25, 1979; Meredith Barkley, "Agents' Testimony about Microphone Conflicts," *Greensboro News and Record*, 10 May 1985; Wood, Caudle, Butkovich, Gorrell Pierce, Jack Fowler, testimony, *Waller v. Butkovich*.

5. William E. Swing, "Administrative Report of the Anti-Klan Rally, Greensboro, NC, November 3, 1979," Greensboro Police Department, November 19, 1979; *Greensboro Record,* November 5, 1979; John Healey, "Ex Police Chief Expected Fights at Klan Rally," *Winston-Salem Journal,* May 2, 1985.

6. Edward Dawson, interview by Emily Mann, in *Greensboro (A Requiem)*, in Mann, *Testimonies: Four Plays* (New York: Theatre Communications Group, 1997); when the FBI's COINTELPRO operation ended in 1974, the formal relationship with informants like Dawson was terminated, but in Dawson's case, the financial relationship continued in various forms. For example, Dawson did work on FBI agent Len Bogaty's house.

7. "88 Seconds in Greensboro," *Frontline*, Public Broadcasting System, January 24, 1983; Dawson, interview; Edward Dawson, Jerry Cooper, and Chris Benson, testimony, *Waller v. Butkovich*.

8. Dawson, Benson, and Virgil Griffin, testimony, *Waller v. Butkovich*.

9. Lt. R. L. Talbott, interview by FBI, November 28, 1979; Dawson, testimony, *Waller v. Butkovich*.

10. Dawson, interview; and see "88 Seconds in Greensboro"; Liz Wheaton, *Operation Greenkill* (Athens: University of Georgia Press, 1987).

11. Sgt. T. L. Burke, interview by FBI, June 3, 1980 (report obtained by the Greensboro Justice Fund through the Freedom of Information Act).

12. Daisy Crawford, press statement, 1983; Bruce Siceloff, "Woman Says FBI Tracked CWO Activist before Death," *Greensboro Daily News,* July 1, 1982. Many activists

wondered whose side the FBI was on. During the 1960s, the Bureau seemed to spend more time tapping Martin Luther King's phone than stopping the terror of the Ku Klux Klan. When it finally took on the Klan, the Bureau infiltrated it so extensively that one-fifth of all Klan members nationwide were informants. In North Carolina, the FBI organized forty-one Klan chapters (see "88 Seconds in Greensboro"). One of the four Klansmen who murdered activist Viola Liuzzo in 1965 was an FBI agent (see O'Reilly, *"Racial Matters,"* pp. 195–98).

13. "88 Seconds in Greensboro"; Dawson, interview; Dawson and Cooper, testimony, *Waller v. Butkovich.*
14. FBI interview of Talbott.
15. Butkovich, Wood, and Pierce, testimony, *Waller v. Butkovich;* Meredith Barkley, "Ex Nazi Says Agent Urged Him to Take a Gun," *Greensboro News and Record,* May 6, 1985; Meredith Barkley, "Klansman/Nazi Says Agent Urged Guns for Rally," *Greensboro News and Record,* May 7, 1985.
16. FBI record of Levy's call; FBI agent Goldberg, deposition, *Waller v. Butkovich.*
17. Micky Micheaux, testimony, *Waller v. Butkovich.*
18. Dawson and Griffin, testimony, *Waller v. Butkovich.*

8. The Massacre

1. Dawson, testimony, *Waller v. Butkovich.*
2. Testimony, *Waller v. Butkovich.* Unless otherwise noted, the source for the timeline and the information in italics in this chapter is Swing, "Administrative Report."
3. "Ex-Police Officer Backs Victim in Her Testimony at Klan Trial," *New York Times,* April 22, 1985; April Wise and Martha Shelton, testimony, *Waller v. Butkovich.*
4. Wheaton, *Codename Greenkill.*
5. Nelson can be seen saying these words on the videotape taken by local TV camera operators Ed Boyd, WTVD-TV, and Jim Waters, WFMY-TV.

9. Aftermath

1. This letter appears in Paul Bermanzohn and Sally Bermanzohn, *True Story of the Greensboro Massacre* (New York: César Cauce, 1980).

10. Trials

1. Swing, *"Administrative Report."*
2. Nelson Johnson wrote a letter dated February 1, 1983, containing these points to Mayor John Forbis, city council members, and the city manager entitled, "Why Police Chief William Swing Should Be Fired."
3. *Greensboro Daily News* and *Greensboro Record,* November 20–29, 1979.
4. Martha Woodall, "Report Pleasing to City," *Greensboro Record,* April 30, 1980.
5. For more on jury selection, see Institute for Southern Studies, *Third of November,* Special Report, Durham, N.C., October 1981.

6. Jim Wicker and Greta Tilley, "Tolling of 'Not Guilty' Ends Longest State Trial," *Greensboro Record,* November 18, 1980.

7. Bermanzohn and Bermanzohn, *The True Story.*

8. See Wood, testimony, *Waller v. Butkovich.*

9. Michael Parenti and Carolyn Kazdin, "The Untold Story of the Greensboro Massacre," *Monthly Review,* November 1981, p. 42.

10. Ronald Smothers, "Church Sues Extremist Group over Fire," *New York Times,* June 6, 1996.

11. National Anti-Klan Network, "Incidents of KKK Activity and Racially Motivated Violence," Special Report, Atlanta, 1984.

12. National Anti-Klan Network, "North Carolina: A State of Siege," newsletter, spring–summer 1983, pp. 1–14.

13. Martha Woodall, "Nazis to Attempt Establishment of Segregated Nation," *Greensboro Record,* November 18, 1980.

14. National Anti-Klan Network, "Incidents."

15. Although most cases of police complicity with the Klan never come to light, a few are documented. For example, in 1964, the Mississippi Klan murdered three civil rights workers, James Chaney, Andrew Goodman, and Michael Schwerner. A deputy sheriff drove the carload of Klansmen and allowed them to commit the murders (see O'Reilly, *"Racial Matters,"* pp. 163–93). A documented case of federal complicity with the Klan and local police occurred in 1961. Alabama cops told the Klan they would "give them 15 minutes" to attack Freedom Riders who were integrating the interstate bus system. Through an informant, the FBI knew about the Klan's plan for a "baseball bat welcome" but did nothing to protect the Freedom Riders. Two decades later, the severely injured Freedom Riders won a lawsuit against the FBI (see O'Reilly, *"Racial Matters,"* pp. 83–96).

16. Larry King, "Berrigan Says Civility Masks Madness," *Greensboro Daily News,* October 1, 1981.

17. Larry King and Flontina Miller, "Grand Jury Apparently Not Near End of Investigation," *Greensboro Record,* April 13, 1983.

18. Flontina Miller and Larry King, "CWP Spokesman Mails Letter to Grand Jury," *Greensboro Daily News,* April 14, 1983.

19. "Two Greensboro Residents to Attend UN Conference," *Greensboro Daily News,* July 29, 1983.

20. Kevin Flynn and Gary Gerhardt, *The Silent Brotherhood* (New York: Penguin, 1995), p. 202.

21. Institute for Research, Education, and Human Rights, "Carolina Knights Continue to Terrorize, Do Poorly in Elections," *Hammer,* no. 7, summer 1984; and see James Ridgeway, *Blood in the Face,* pp. 100–102.

22. On cross-burning, National Anti-Klan Network, "Incidents." "KKK Leader Miller Runs for Governor," *Greensboro Daily News,* October 13, 1983.

23. Mab Segrest, "The Klan Attack on the Schools," *Southern Exposure,* July–August 1984.

24. Morris Dees, *Gathering Storm* (New York: Harper Perennial, 1997), pp. 92–102; Mab Segrest, *Memoirs of a Race Traitor* (Boston: South End Press, 1994), pp. 67–86, 139–64.

25. See "Deposition of Agent Goldberg," in Mann, *Testimonies,* pp. 312–14.

26. See "Ex-Police Officer Backs Victims in Her Testimony at Klan Trial," *New York Times,* April 22, 1985.

27. Mann, *Testimonies,* pp. 215–17. The quotes that follow, also from *Testimonies,* are cited by page number in the text.

28. G. Flint Taylor, "Waller v. Butkovich: Lessons in Strategy and Tenacity for Civil Rights Litigators," *Police Misconduct and Civil Rights Law Report* 1, 13 (January–February 1986), pp. 151–52.

12. Healing

1. On the economy, see *New York Times,* June 17, 2002; on black men in prison, see *New York Times,* August 29, 2002.

2. See Barry Yeoman, "No Ways Tired," *Southern Exposure* 14, 2 (summer 1996).

3. Mann, *Testimonies.*

4. Kwame wrote an article on his experiences: "Keeping a Door Open," *Greensboro News and Record,* May 23, 1999.

Epilogue

1. See *www.ictj.org* for more information.

2. See *www.gjf.org* and *www.belovedcommunitycenter.org* for more information.

INDEX

*Page numbers in **bold italic** refer to illustrations*

ABBREVIATIONS